The Countryside in Colonial Latin America

Diálogos

A series of course adoption books on Latin America:

Independence in Spanish America: Civil Wars, Revolutions, and Underdevelopment—Jay Kinsbruner, Queens College

Heroes on Horseback: A Life and Times of the Last Gaucho Caudillos—John Chasteen, University of North Carolina at Chapel Hill

The Life and Death of Carolina Maria de Jesus—Robert M. Levine, University of Miami, and José Carlos Sebe Bom Meihy, University of São Paulo

The Countryside in Colonial Latin America—Edited by Louisa Schell Hoberman, University of Texas at Austin, and Susan Migden Socolow, Emory University

The Countryside in Colonial Latin America

Edited by

Louisa Schell Hoberman

and

Susan Migden Socolow

UNIVERSITY OF NEW MEXICO PRESS
Albuquerque

Library of Congress Cataloging-in-Publication Data

The countryside in colonial Latin America / edited by Louisa Schell
Hoberman and Susan Migden Socolow.—1st ed.
p. cm.—(Dialogos)
Includes bibliographical references.
ISBN 0–8263–1710–3.—ISBN 0–8263–1711–1 (pbk.)
1. Latin America—Rural conditions.
2. Latin America—History—To 1830.
I. Hoberman, Louisa Schell, 1942–   .
II. Socolow, Susan Migden, 1941–   .
III. Series: Dialogos (Albuquerque, New Mexico)
HN110.5.Z9C62318   1996
306´.098—dc20   95–41737
                                                 CIP

For those who have gone before us:
May Magriel
and
the memory of
Edith Ginsberg Migden, Sigmund Migden,
and Irving Schell

and those who will continue after:
Ari and Joshua Socolow
Steve and Rick Hoberman

Contents

Illustrations

Maps

Preface

Our success with *Cities and Society in Colonial Latin America* emboldened us to approach a group of distinguished scholars to do a book on the rural world. In undertaking what we envision as a companion volume, we requested that these historians write original essays synthesizing their specific research and the rapidly growing number of other works on the Latin American countryside.

Those acquainted with our earlier work will notice one change in the format we have adopted: we have included two types of essays, those that focus on rural structures and others that deal with social groups. Once again, this book is intended primarily for upper division undergraduates and beginning graduate students.

Because we are committed to keeping these essays as accessible as possible, we have omitted much of the scholarly apparatus that is usually found in historical studies. For those students whose appetites are whetted by these essays, we offer a comprehensive Suggestions for Further Reading section. Foreign terms are defined in the glossary.

We would like to take this opportunity to thank the scholars involved in this project for the quality of their essays and their almost endless patience. Lyman Johnson's suggestions and those of the anonymous readers were invaluable in strengthening this volume. Thanks also to the staffs of Woodruff Library of Emory University and the Benson Latin American Collection of the University of Texas at Austin. The students in the Emory graduate seminar on rural colonial society willingly served as guinea pigs and editorial consultants for this manuscript. Steve Flinchpaugh and Larissa Smith proved admirable aides in preparing all illustrations. As always, the respective men in our lives—John Hoberman and Dan Socolow—have been invaluable in making this book a reality.

Economic Geography of Colonial Spanish North America

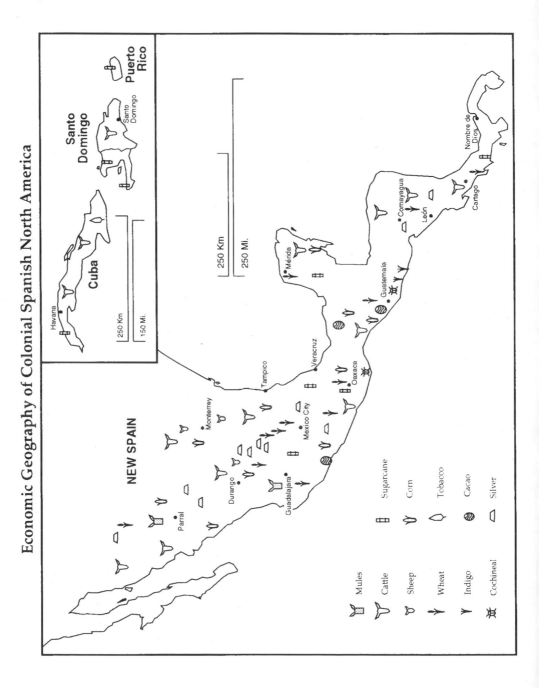

NEW SPAIN

Parral
Durango
Monterrey
Guadalajara
Mexico City
Tampico
Veracruz
Oaxaca
Mérida
Guatemala
Comayagua
León
Cartago
Nombre de Dios

Cuba
Havana

Santo Domingo
Santo Domingo

Puerto Rico

250 Km
150 Mi.

250 Km
250 Mi.

Mules
Cattle
Sheep
Wheat
Indigo
Cochineal

Sugarcane
Corn
Tobacco
Cacao
Silver

Economic Geography of Colonial South America

The Countryside
in Colonial
Latin America

Introduction to the Rural Past

Susan Migden Socolow

To observers of present-day Latin America, just as to conquerors, settlers, and travelers who have been coming to the region for the last five hundred years, it is obvious that rural life and values are central to the region. Throughout the colonial period, between 75 and 90 percent of the total population of Spanish and Portuguese America lived in the countryside. Rural Latin America served as a major source of wealth and social prestige for some, and the basis of a precarious survival for others.

By *rural* we are referring to those zones outside of the immediate perimeter of urban centers, places where the majority of residents supported themselves completely or in part by agriculture or stockraising, contributing food, raw materials, and migrants to the towns and cities. In these regions, living in villages of less than five thousand people, hamlets, or scattered throughout the countryside, people were closely linked to the land. Although rural inhabitants traveled to markets and mines, on the whole, they were more isolated than their urban counterparts.

Rural life must be viewed within the larger context of the social, economic, and physical landscape as well as in relationship with the population patterns that shaped rural reality. But the countryside was more than just a place where things happened to country people. Ruralness, isolation, and economies dependent on agriculture and pastoral pursuits affected people's behavior, choices, and very culture. The seasons of agricultural production, for example, tied people to the land in ways that conditioned their ability to act. Put another way, a peasant was highly unlikely to leave his plot of land, to travel to the city, or perhaps to join a revolt when his crop was due to be harvested.

Sixteenth-century conquistadors and early Iberian settlers were in awe of the dimensions and grandeur of the New World. The Portuguese would eventually come to control a colony more than fifty times larger than their European homeland while Spanish possessions in America covered approximately twenty times more territory than the Iberian motherland. Both groups of Europeans were acutely conscious of the strange new physical and human landscape. Time and time again they reflected the physical world in their choice of rural place names, such as Arroyo Seco, Aguascalientes, Rio de Janeiro, or Bahia. Nonetheless, this awareness produced little desire to protect or preserve what had existed before the conquest. Portuguese traders along the Atlantic Coast, for example, destroyed entire forests of Brazilwood trees within the first fifty years of discovery. (See Figs. 1–3.)

Indigenous peoples had perfected a complex agricultural system, based on the cultivation of such crops as corn, squash, and potato, and in certain regions, the use of irrigation and terracing, well before the arrival of the Europeans. Although Iberian conquerors and settlers continued pre-Columbian agricultural production, they modified and adapted the social and economic organization of agricultural production, as well as technology and the crops themselves to new mercantilist ends. New crops, new animals, and new relationships to the land were also introduced. Agricultural and pastoral products consumed locally or exported to transatlantic markets became, along with the mining of precious metals, the economic backbone of the Iberian colonies in America. In the words of one eighteenth-century observer, "The produce of the earth is in fact the sole basis of permanent opulence."[1]

Although the primary activity of the rural zones was agriculture, some regions also produced nonagricultural goods. The Jesuits in their remote jungle missions of Moxos and Chiquitos established a small cottage furniture industry specializing in the manufacture of chests of drawers (bargueños). Textile manufacture took place both in rural obrajes located on haciendas and in individual households. In South America, such obrajes could be found in Peru, Bolivia, Ecuador, and Chile. Jesuit obrajes in Chile produced quantities of ponchos for local consumption and export to neighboring regions. In the production of textiles Indian technology was complemented by European methods and materials. For example, while the indigenous backstrap loom continued to be used, the European frame loom was also introduced into rural America. Rural Latin America produced both cotton and wool garments, including those made of native vicuña and alpaca wools as well as the wool of European-introduced sheep. The quality of these fabrics varied from coarsely woven woolen bayetas to luxurious vicuña ponchos.

Just as rural Latin America produced much of the wealth and foodstuffs that allowed the colonies to survive, rural life reinforced the social model brought by the Spaniards and Portuguese to the New World. This model, heavily influenced by the medieval ideal of the seigneurial manor, gave special social power to those fortunate enough to own large tracts of rural property and control numbers of Indian laborers on this land. In addition, Iberian settlers believed that landownership in and of itself brought economic advantage and social prestige. Elites invested in land and took pride in its ownership. Owning landed property was also a preferred form of protecting one's inheritance.

These large tracts of land, so-called "haciendas," are often considered to be the hallmark of Latin American rural society. Nonetheless there has been an ongoing debate in the historical literature as to how the hacienda emerged and how ubiquitous it was during the colonial period. Some historians believe that the Spaniards were initially more concerned with access to Indian labor than Indian land, while others stress that these two processes were not as distinct as originally believed. The relationship between a variety of legal systems devised to tap Indian labor and land ownership continues to be explored.

The rural history of colonial Latin America was greatly influenced by pre-Columbian population patterns. At the time of the conquest, the native population was distributed unevenly across the North and South American continents. The highlands of central Mexico and those of Peru, home of sophisticated empires based on intensive agriculture, were far more densely populated than the lowland home of hunting and gathering tribes. A conservative analysis of the pre-Columbian population of the entire American hemisphere, including the islands of the Caribbean, puts the total at slightly over 50 million inhabitants, although other scholars speculate that total population was as high as 200 million. The population of central Mexico alone has been estimated as between 5 and 25 million.

Regardless of widely varying assessments of pre-Columbian population, the arrival of Europeans in the New World produced a demographic disaster for the native peoples of America. In the Caribbean the indigenous population was almost totally obliterated by 1570. This was an extreme case, but even the most optimistic estimates suggest that throughout Latin America within a century of contact with European settlers at least half of the Indian population was lost to epidemics of smallpox, measles, dysentery, typhoid fever, typhus, diphtheria, influenza, and bubonic plague, as well as overwork and famine. In central Mexico the Indian population fell to one million by 1605. Depending on the base estimate used, this decline reflected a loss of between 80 percent and 95 percent of the original numbers inhabiting the region approximately ninety years earlier. In other areas, the extent and chronology of the decline varied somewhat—in the northern Andes, for example, the Indian population was reduced to one-fifth of its original size within one hundred years—but in all cases the Amerindian population suffered greatly from the consequences of European conquest.

Because of the continual ravages of disease coupled with falling birth rates, the numerical low point of the indigenous population probably did not occur until the middle of the seventeenth century in the case of Mexico and somewhat later in Peru and other parts of South America. Nonetheless, Indian populations in central Mexico and the Andean highlands retained sufficient numbers to sustain, albeit at times just barely, agricultural and mineral production. By the middle of the seventeenth century the rural Indian population of America began to stabilize; after approximately 150 years of exposure, Indians had developed a degree of natural immunity to European diseases.

Population decline produced multiple effects on the economy and society. Within twenty years of the conquest Spanish bureaucrats were frantically trying to understand and control depopulation, calling for head counts of the Indian population and eventually issuing the New Laws (1542), an attempt to end the most blatant abuses of the Indian population by Spanish conquerors and settlers. This legislation, lamentably, was frequently honored only in the breach. In Mexico as in Peru, the Spaniards also repeatedly reorganized the shrinking Indian population into fewer and fewer communities. This process of *congregación* eventually reduced the number of Indian villages in some districts from fifty to two.

As Indian population declined and people were shifted into new communities, Spaniards seized newly vacant land. In developing haciendas, landowners sought to be close enough to Indian communities to enjoy a steady labor force. In the Andean region, members of the Indian community inadvertently aided the *hacendados* in their search for an adequate labor supply. Here Indians fled their communities to avoid paying tribute and serving in the forced labor drafts for the mines (*mitas*), relocating in neighboring communities as *forasteros* or settling on haciendas as free mestizo (mixed-race) peons.

Nevertheless, in large regions of Mexico and the Andes, landowning Indian communities survived the colonial period. These Indian towns and villages were, of course, greatly affected by Spanish society, which systematically extracted land, labor and tribute. Depending on their proximity to Spanish settlers, on geographical location and historical circumstances, traditions including communal ownership of land and a social fabric based on kinship and reciprocity persisted more or less intact. Gradually Indian leadership was replaced by new caciques co-opted by Spanish administrators or by their own greed who violated the traditional norms of Indian society. Indeed, many Indian communities were eventually divided between an economically prosperous elite and a mass of peasants.

Where the Indian population had disappeared completely, if a lucrative crop could be found, a new source of labor, African slaves, was introduced into the countryside. The African and African-American population was overwhelmingly employed as unskilled and semi-skilled laborers on rural plantations, although in some haciendas and ranches in Spanish America, slaves could be found working in supervisory positions. The total number of Africans brought to Latin America from the time of the conquest to 1810 was approximately 3.5 million people; 72 percent of these slaves were brought to Latin America in the eighteenth century.[2]

The eighteenth century began a period of demographic growth for all racial groups. For Spanish America in general, by the middle of the century the rural population was approximately 9.4 million people, increasing to about 14 million by the end of the colonial period. Indians still comprised the rural majority, accounting for approximately 55 percent of the rural population by the end of the eighteenth century. Those who were considered to be Spaniards were next (23 percent), followed by peoples of mixed race (15 percent) and blacks (6 percent).[3] In Portuguese America, the population grew from about 1.8 million to 2.4 million by the end of the century; blacks were in the plurality (45 percent), followed by whites (30 percent), peoples of mixed race (20 percent), and Indians (5 percent).[4]

Population growth resulted from patterns of birth and death marked by high mortality and even higher fertility. In Sacasa and Acasio, two rural communities of Alto Peru, for example, the crude death rate for the period 1775–99 averaged 23.7 while the crude birth rate was 34.6. In spite of birth rates outstripping death rates and a gradual population increase by the eighteenth century, Latin America continued to experience recurrent demographic crises caused by famine and disease.[5] In Mexico, for example, smallpox epidemics devastated the population in 1779-80, 1798, and again in 1804. Approximately one out of every four years produced at least a minor demographic crisis in some rural districts throughout the eighteenth century. During these periods the crude death rate soared, while the birth rate fell. In the crisis year of 1805, for example, Sacasa and Acasio had a crude death rate of 111.3 and a crude birth rate of 28.0. Although rural isolation tended to slow down the spread of communicable diseases, the lack of education, low levels of sanitation, abysmal medical attention, and malnutrition produced by famine guaranteed high mortality.

As the rural population of Latin America continued to increase, the relative percentage of people of mixed race within the population slowly grew larger. In general in those areas where the Indian community maintained a balanced ratio of men to women there was little race mixture. Where, because of mortality or flight, sex ratios were heavily skewed toward women, *mestizaje* was more marked. In Mexico, the total number of mestizos and mulattoes, who probably comprised about 5 percent of the population in 1650, made up more than 33 percent of the population by the end of the colonial period.[6] In the late eighteenth century in regions such as Argentina, Chile, and Colombia, mestizo peons and small farmers were the largest group of rural inhabitants.

Much race mixture took place without the formal sacrament of marriage. Indeed in some rural districts of Latin America clergy made only sporadic visits to their rural flocks. By European standards, Latin America was remarkable because of its extraordinarily high incidence of free unions and illegitimate births among mixed blood, white, and slave populations. Félix de Azara traveling through the rural districts of Paraguay in the late eighteenth century remarked as to the casual living arrangements of the mestizo inhabitants while doubting that there were any women over the age of eight in the entire region who were still virgins.[7] Traditional Indian communities reflected very different patterns. Here the proximity and control of Catholic clergy and/or the values of these societies worked to encourage young men and women to marry and have children within legitimate unions. As a result Indians who lived in clerically supervised mission towns formed the most married of all ethnic groups, and illegitimacy rates were only between 1 and 4 percent.

The vast rural society that developed throughout Latin America was far from uniform through time and space. Although large haciendas would become the hallmark of much of central and northern Mexico and highland Peru, another important system—the plantation—emerged in the seventeenth century when the Portuguese in northeastern Brazil found the perfect crop—sugar—and the perfect labor force—African slaves—to begin large scale production for the world market. Variations of this system spread along the tropical coasts of Latin America during the next two centuries. While the crop might change from region to region (cacao in Venezuela, sugar and cotton in coastal Peru, sugar and cacao along the Gulf Coast of Mexico), the labor force (enslaved black workers) and the close dependence on world markets never varied.

In other regions of colonial Latin America small- to medium- scale farming coexisted alongside larger haciendas. These properties, farmed by individual owners, renters, cash tenants, sharecroppers, or squatters, were used either for subsistence farming or to provide small excess production for local town and city markets. Still other zones of Latin America were in the hands of small producers who dedicated their time and labor to producing an exotic crop in widespread demand. Among this group were the tobacco farmers of Cuba and Paraguayan producers of *yerba mate,* a herbal tea much in demand in Buenos Aires, Chile, Peru, and southern Brazil.

More remote regions were involved in the ranching of European animals: sheep and cattle in northern Mexico; horses, cattle, and oxen in the *sertão* of Brazil; and horses and cattle in the llanos of Venezuela. In the Argentine pampas an estimated 48 million cattle roamed wild by the end of the eighteenth century; these herds were periodically harvested for their hides, tallow, and horns. Cattle also supplied the meat processed into jerky, an inexpensive source of protein for slave populations.

Ranching often predominated close to the frontier, zones of interpenetration between European-mestizo and nomadic Indian society. Over time frontiers moved, advancing or receding in response to population pressures, strategic decisions, shifting alliances, and access to exploitable land and labor. While neither the settled rural regions nor the frontier were egalitarian societies, the frontier developed its own distinct social forms and life-styles, in which the relative distance from centers of viceregal power bred independence, valor, and self-sufficiency.

There were, therefore, several rural societies in colonial Latin America—the plantation society, the society of large haciendas and that of

Fig. 1. A jungle cat hiding in a tree. Baltasar Jaime Martínez Compañón y Bujanda, *Trujillo del Perú.*

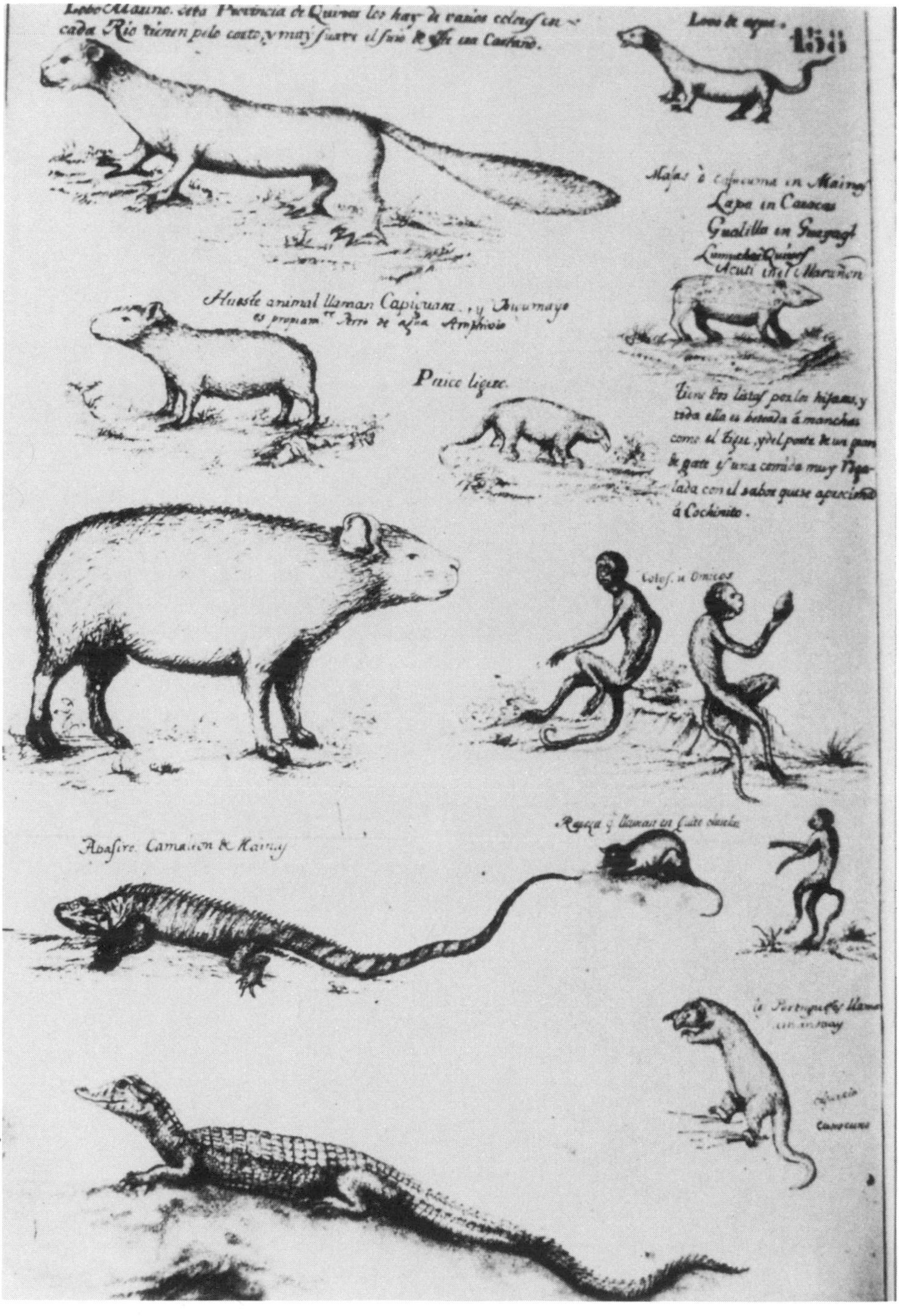
158
Lapa en Caracas
Acuti en el Marañon
á Cochinito.

Fig. 2. Puma. Drawing by José del Pozo (Madrid: Museo Naval).

Fig. 3. *(Opposite:)* Four-legged creatures. Drawing attributed to José Guio (Museo de América, Colección Bauza).

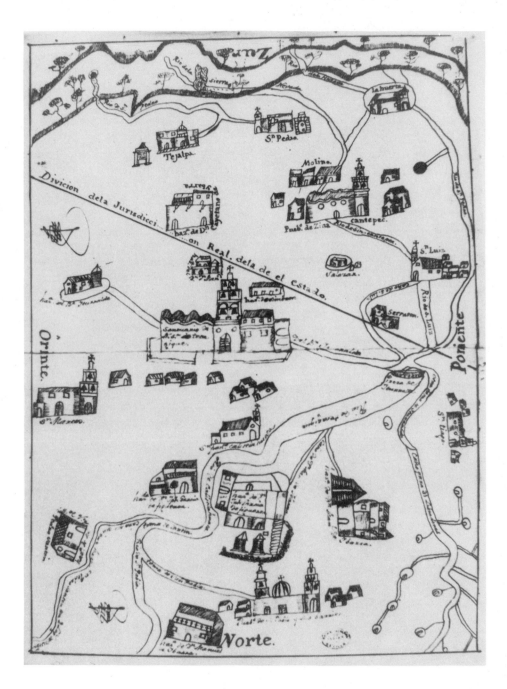

12

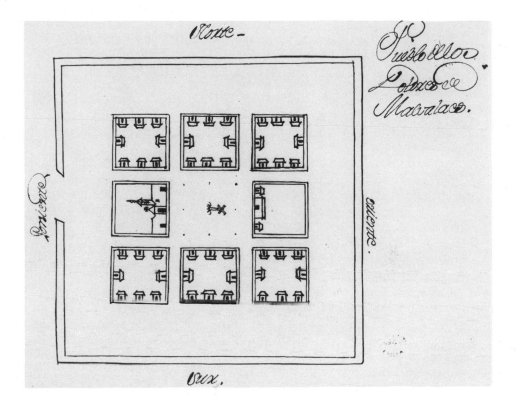

Fig. 4. The town of Dolores de Malvalaes. (A.G.I., Mapas y Planos, Buenos Aires 232).

Fig. 5. *(Opposite:)* Map of the San Pedro district rivers showing the towns and haciendas in the vicinity, Toluca, 1757. (A.G.I., Mapas y Planos, Mexico 735).

traditional Indian communities, the ranching society of the plains, and the society of small landholders who produced basic foodstuffs such as wheat and meat, as well as tobacco and herb tea (*yerba mate*). Depending on the region, population density varied widely, from 0.4 inhabitant per square kilometer of the mid eighteenth century Argentine pampas to 23 inhabitants per square kilometer in the province of Guanajuato in New Spain (Mexico). These rural worlds also ran the gamut from great wealth to great poverty.

In the pre-Columbian heartland of Latin America—Mexico and altiplano Peru—rural districts consisted of Spanish-owned haciendas, Indian communities, and mestizo towns. Indian communities remained a central feature of the landscape, but they were forced to change in order to survive the increasingly onerous demands on their land and labor resources. In specific zones such as the Bajío of Mexico or the Cochabamba Valley of Alto Peru, large segments of the Indian population no longer lived in communities but rather were tenants and laborers in haciendas and *estancias*.

Rural people also inhabited a world of great architectural diversity, although in general rural construction was never as opulent as urban buildings. Both secular and religious rural architecture used local craftsmen and local materials. In regions poor in forests such as the north of Mexico or the plains of Argentina, use of wood in construction was minimal and adobe (sun-dried bricks) was the material of choice. Many churches, like the large rural homes built for wealthy landowners, featured walls made of stone and adobe. Originally roofed in timber covered with thatch, they were eventually reroofed in red-glazed tile. But not all rural inhabitants were privileged enough to reside in houses of solid adobe with tile roofs. Many of the poor lived in small huts whose roofs and walls were made of straw.

Buildings, while based on Iberian design, were often modified in response to American needs. In areas of Mexico and Central America, for example, fortress churches featuring an open-air nave, large outdoor plazas surrounded by high walls, arched gateways, and four corner chapels evolved during the sixteenth century. While the churches themselves might be relatively small buildings, they opened on one or more sides to a large, often elevated square, allowing a small number of clergymen to preach to large numbers of Indians. In highland Peru rural churches were frequently built with balconies that served the same purpose.

The rural world of colonial Latin America was a world of continuous physical movement of people. There were several reasons why rural people moved. Most migrants were rural laborers searching for jobs, Indians escaping from tribute payments, or blacks and mulattoes fleeing slavery. Poor city and country folk left for the frontier in search of land, economic opportunities, or anonymity. Geographical movement could be either permanent or temporary, voluntary or coerced, from one rural district to another, or from countryside to town or city. Indians subject to the *mita* made annual treks from their rural communities to the mines. More permanent migration of Indian populations was also a major feature in certain rural areas of Latin America by at least the end of the seventeenth century. In Alto Peru for example, one-third of the population counted in the *numeración general* of 1683–84 was no longer living in the province in which they had been born.[8]

The rural colonial world did not exist in complete isolation from the urban one. Indeed the links between urban and rural society and economy were extensive. The elite of Latin America often moved back and forth between their rural haciendas and their urban townhouses. But they were not the only segment of society that was periodically mobile; merchants, petty traders, vendors, unskilled and semi-skilled laborers, Indians and mestizos, not to mention muleteers and others in the transportation industry, moved between the two worlds. Peasants also participated in local markets or fairs in nearby towns where they sold their surplus subsistence crops, animals, and household production such as coarse textiles and wax. In this way small rural producers, both men and women, became petty urban traders for one day a week. Rural inhabitants—Indians and peasants—also made their way to larger towns and cities to avail themselves of royal justice. The surplus production of the rural sector—food, and textiles—flowed to urban markets, while tribute made its way into the royal coffers located in principal cities, and agricultural tithes supported urban cathedrals and religious institutions. (See Figs. 4, 5.)

The movement of people, goods, and specie took place in a world of long distances and difficult communication and transportation. Goods moved along rough roads in oxen-drawn wooden carts or on mule back. While communication and transportation improved during the eighteenth century, aided in part by the establishment of a system of royal post houses, land transport was always costly and slow. For example, it took at least three months to travel from the pampas of Buenos Aires to Jujuy in the foothills of the Andes. Water transportation was faster and cheaper, allowing those plantations, haciendas, and ranches with access to rivers a clear advantage in marketing their produce.

The rural world was also extremely sensitive to the effects of natural disasters. In mountainous regions, there were periodic volcanic eruptions and earthquakes. Although much of Latin America lies within the subtropical belt, to the north and south of the Spanish colonial empire frost and hail occasionally produced crop destruction. Most abnormal weather patterns were related to the effects of too little or too much water—drought or flooding. Natural disasters were often exacerbated as scarcity and famine gave way to epidemic disease.

Although the eighteenth century was a period of increased agricultural production in many regions of Latin America, there is strong evidence that living conditions worsened for large sectors of the rural population during the latter part of the century. Late colonial population growth brought new pressures on rural resources, increasing competition for land and social instability as it created a surplus of labor among rural producers. In central Mexico the growth of large estates and a shift from corn to wheat production resulted in rising rents charged to tenant farmers by landowners, declining wages, mounting evictions, and growing marginalization of rural people. In addition, regional overspecialization in a lucrative crop could quickly lead to crisis conditions. In Oaxaca, for example, when a shortage of rainfall in 1779 caused crop failure and the death of livestock, inhabitants of ranches and cochineal-producing zones found themselves in dire straits.[9] Drought and famine produced widespread suffering in the Mexican Bajío in 1808–10. Even more disastrous were the widespread famines of 1749–50 and 1785–87, produced by crop failure following a year of poor harvest. Both of these crises affected the subsistence level of the rural population in much of Mexico. Indeed the famine of 1785–87 has been called the greatest social catastrophe to occur in central Mexico since the sixteenth century.[10] Furthermore, repeated disruptions of colonial trade in the 1790s worsened the economic situation of those rural inhabitants engaged in producing agricultural goods for export.

Mexico was not the only region to suffer recurring rural food crises. Crop failure caused by weather and possibly exacerbated by population pressures and overused land also afflicted areas of South America. From 1720 on, several Andean regions experienced persistent drought conditions. The Cochabamba region in Upper Peru suffered severe food shortages in 1783–84 and again in 1803–04. Between 1800 and 1805 several areas throughout Upper Peru reported loss of crops and livestock and famine conditions. In general the rural poor bore a disproportionate share of the social and economic costs of these disasters.

In addition, changes in land usage caused rural dislocations in specific regions. In the Río de la Plata region, especially along the New Littoral, open range land was converted into private ranches thereby limiting the access to land for the rural poor as well as curtailing the nomadic life-style of gaucho families. Moreover, the militarization of late colonial society tended to increase the government's control of rural people and exacted militia service from them as well. On the other hand, in Venezuela an increasingly diversified rural economy expanding into coffee, sugarcane, tobacco, and livestock production created new opportunities and increasing demand for labor.

As we have seen, rural society was neither static nor uniform. Indeed, it varied greatly from region to region, and from century to century. The following original essays deal with the structural features and social groups of colonial rural society. Each presents an overview of the complex society that developed in colonial Spanish and Portuguese America. The first three chapters in this book focus on broad systemic and institutional features of the colonial rural world, which affected all social groups, creating the parameters of the physical and economic world in which rural people lived and worked. Arnold Bauer details the economic conditions and constraints of rural production, concentrating on trade, market, credit, and labor. Eric van Young paints a vivid picture of the material conditions of rural life. Juan Carlos Garavaglia's chapter on rural ecosystems reveals the varieties of crops, animals, and tools found in colonial Latin America.

The next five chapters concentrate on the major social groups to be found in the rural setting. Stuart Schwartz looks at the evolution of the landed elite, in the main, descendants of Spanish and Portuguese settlers. Below these landowners on the colonial rural social ladder were the clergy, usually also descendants of Europeans. John F. Schwaller examines the roles of both regular and secular priests and their change over time. Lowell Gudmundson focuses on other members of the middle groups, including local bureaucrats, small storekeepers, peddlers, muleteers, and owners of small landholdings. These groups included both Europeans and peoples of mixed race, primarily mestizos and mulattoes. Still farther down the socio-racial ladder of rural colonial society were the Indians who survived primarily in the highland regions of the Spanish colonial empire and the African slaves imported into the region. Herbert Klein discusses the lives of the enslaved people of color forcibly transported from Africa to the lowland plantations of Latin America to produce tropical crops for the world market. Cheryl Martin explores how, not notwithstanding demographic disaster and tribute extraction, indigenous people were able to hold on to their communal property and defend their traditional way of life. In the final essay, Ward Stavig discusses the reaction of Indians, Africans, and other dispossessed peoples to their powerlessness and the ways in which they came to challenge their social, economic, and political situation.

By presenting these essays and a list of additional readings on each subject, we hope to contribute to an improved understanding of the richness and complexity of research on the rural reality of colonial Latin America.

Notes

1. Alexander von Humboldt, *Political Essay on the Kingdom of New Spain* (New York, 1972), 139. Von Humbolt was speaking of Mexico, but the same could have been said for all of Latin America.

2. Philip D. Curtin, *The Atlantic Slave Trade: A Census* (Madison, Wis., 1969), 268.

3. Richard Morse, "The Urban Development of Colonial Spanish America," in Leslie Bethell, ed., vol. 2 of *The Cambridge History of Latin America*, (Cambridge, 1984), 89.

4. Dauril Alden, "The Population of Brazil in the Late Eighteenth Century: A Preliminary Study," *Hispanic American Hispanic Historical Review* 43, no. 2 (May 1963): 193–96.

5. See, for example, Enrique Florescano and R. Pastor, eds., *La crisis agrícola en México, 1785–1786*, 2 vols. (Mexico City, 1981); Moisés González Navarro, *Cinco crisis mexicanas* (Mexico City, 1983). For the data on Sacasa

and Acasio see Enrique Tandeter, "Crisis in Upper Peru, 1800–1805," *Hispanic American Hispanic Historical Review* 71, no. 1 (February 1991): 35–71.

6. von Humboldt, *Political Essay on the Kingdom of New Spain,* 37, 86.

7. Félix de Azara, *Viajes por la América Meridional [1781–1801]* (Madrid, 1969), 285–86.

8. Brian M. Evans, "Census Enumeration in Late-Seventeenth-Century Alto Perú: The *Numeración General* of 1683–84," in David J. Robinson, ed., *Studies in Spanish American Population History* (Boulder, Colo., 1981), 38–39.

9. Brian Hamnett, *Politics and Trade in Southern Mexico, 1750–1821* (Cambridge, 1971), 63-64.

10. D. A. Brading, *Haciendas and Ranchos in the Mexican Bajío* (Cambridge, 1978), 185.

CHAPTER ONE

The Colonial Economy

ARNOLD J. BAUER

Any economy is formed through time and space. This simple truth provides our first approach to an understanding of the multiple layers and varied regions of colonial Spanish America. Just as in the case of Western Europe, the rural history of Spanish America is also "stratigraphic": that is, the "contributions it receives from every century or group of centuries, and from every millennium, are not wiped out but merely overlaid . . . by the contributions of subsequent centuries."[1] Thus at the end of the colonial period, pre-Hispanic notions of planting cycles uneasily coexisted with scientific information provided by the "Economic Societies" of the Enlightenment. For a century after the Mexican conquest, silver and cacao coins rattled together in the same pockets and even today in Mexican markets the ancient, Moorish *almud* remains a measure in a metric world. Animal-drawn plows were introduced everywhere in America but hoe agriculture persisted (and is still present) alongside European practice. In Chile, for example, the Andean horticultural *chacra* complements European cereals and livestock. Deeply held values of reciprocity that predate the Spaniards and the Incas as well, continue to influence economic transactions in the central Andes. During three centuries of Spanish rule, European economic culture became dominant and leached into the native substrata, but it is also true that indigenous forms persisted and continue today to seep to the surface.

The importance of the European invasion, the nature of the underlying native culture, and the intermingling of historical times varied across space, which is to say that there were (and are) strong regional differences in Spanish America. Let us begin with a discussion of certain features of Mesoamerica and

19

later compare that with the Andes. Both zones embraced large economic spaces; each contained several interconnected regions. They have enough in common to make comparison useful and "sufficiently striking differences" to make comparison fascinating.[2] Regions such as Chile or the Spanish Main, peripheral to the core areas of colonial Spanish America, will be brought into the discussion when appropriate.

The Formation of Regional Trade and Markets in the Economic Space of New Spain

At the time of the conquest of Mexico, an alliance of three city-states in the Valley of Mexico had subjected much of Mesoamerica to tributary status. This meant that the flow of goods such as precious feathers, cotton cloth, and cacao was encouraged by force—through merchants backed by state power—from subject peoples and transported on the backs of men to the great intermontane Valley of Mexico. There, in several of the larger towns but especially in the great market center of Tlatelolco, these tribute goods mixed with the local produce of thousands of peasants and artisans and were exchanged through barter or via the rudimentary monetary system of copper pieces and cacao beans. It appears that much of the produce requisitioned by the Triple Alliance (or more commonly, the Aztecs) from such distant regions as present-day El Salvador eventually found its way to Tlatelolco. Both Hernán Cortés and Bernal Díaz saw this great marketplace in full operation guided, in fact, by Moctezuma himself, only a few days after their triumphal entry into the lacustrine capital and they were mightily impressed. Cortés thought the main plaza, filled with foodstuffs and merchandise, was "twice the size of Salamanca's." Bernal Díaz, with his eye inevitably closer to the ground than his haughty captain's, lists in detail the rope, sandals, honey, timber, salt, and hides along with male and female slaves "as many as the Portuguese bring Negroes from Guinea." Although Tlatelolco was surely the largest of Mesoamerican markets and greatly enriched by the inflow of tribute goods, we should have in our mind's eye a picture of a widespread market economy turning around a series of local marketplaces (tianguis) throughout the larger settlements in the Mesoamerican landscape where peasants and artisans laid out the products of their work.

In exchange for the exotic produce of the tropical lowlands, long lines of specialized human carriers (tamemes) transported more refined goods such as metalwork and fine pottery from the center and also, as one historian puts it, "talked the lowland inhabitants into buying largely worthless plateau delicacies" such as algae cakes, sacks of lake flies, and potted ducks.[3] Because there were no draft animals, exchange was mainly limited to items of high value in relation to weight, but it is also true that under pressure of famine large quantities of bulky goods such as maize were moved on human backs. Obviously the relative value of goods—that is "prices"—were closely calculated. Cortés noticed that "everything is sold by the piece or by measurement, never by weight" and reported that the measures themselves were closely controlled by overseers in the markets. Bernal Díaz thought that all goods were measured against various lengths of thin goose quills of gold dust, but a more common measure of value, and one that persisted into the later sixteenth century, was provided by cacao beans, the standard currency of the day.

While Cortés and Bernal Díaz were describing this economy, they and their countrymen were also beginning to transform it, first by changing the system of values so that things previously worthless began to have a "price," while at the same time such things as the previously coveted *chalchihuitles* (semiprecious decorative stones) lost value. The invading Europeans began by imposing a forced demand for goods ranked high in their value system, most particularly metals considered "precious," but also food they considered civilized. During the subsequent three centuries the invaders and their descendants developed a European, or more properly, Hispanicized, sector in the larger economy which, if designed at the beginning to stand alongside the native system, soon spread outward from cities and mines to penetrate and eventually absorb most of that economy. If there is anything the newer research agrees upon, it is that miners, merchants, landowners, and any number of petty entrepreneurs were keen to truck and trade and turn a profit. Parallel to all this, and indeed deriving from the European demand for products to their taste, the conquerors introduced equally important changes in the rhythm and remuneration of work in their efforts to create a labor as well as a commodities market. Let us explain briefly how this came to be and then try to visualize how this economy, especially the rural economy, actually worked on the ground in its mature phase, by the last third of the eighteenth century.

In the first two decades after their arrival in Mexico and Guatemala (the 1520s and 1530s), the Spaniards endeavored to extract native foods and labor services through the *encomienda*. The invaders also were quick to introduce European livestock and plants, but they were not successful in persuading the local population to grow wheat; moreover, olives and vines take time. In short, the creation of a European food regime could not be accomplished overnight. So in these early years we are in the presence of a command economy at one level while underneath a thousand daily acts and the buzz of native markets went on pretty much as before.

By the mid sixteenth century, the discovery of extensive silver deposits, the steady increase in European immigration, and the development of European towns and cities created a growing demand for goods, and especially for those familiar and bulky foods that could not be satisfied by imports. At roughly the same time, European pathogens devastated the native population, allowing their depopulated lands to be distributed to Spaniards. There now emerged new elements in a segmented and jaggedly integrated market for commodities and labor in which compulsion remained present for both.

European livestock were the most visible introduction in the American landscape and in this fenceless land with few predators, cattle, sheep, pigs, and horses multiplied like mad. Native people eventually saw the value of sheep and goats (chickens quickly became a native staple), but cattle and horses remained largely in the European sector with the exception of those raised by mission Indians for sale to markets in the mining towns. They grazed destructively onto the cultivated fields of both tropics and highlands and then spread into the more arid lands of the near and far north. Meat, hides (someone has called the seventeenth century the Age of Leather for its high demand in the mines), and tallow produced by Europeans became important items of European consumption. After initial scarcity their prices fell in the late sixteenth century and remained generally lower than comparable prices in Europe. A better example of production and exchange in the European sector of the economy can be seen in the emerging market for wheat and wheat flour.

Although the Spaniards did not turn up their noses at tortillas or the humble spud while on the march to Tenochtitlán or Cuzco, they quickly insisted upon "proper" foods, fundamentally the Holy Trinity of Mediterranean agriculture—wheat bread, olive oil, and wine—once they were settled. Two of these of course are necessary in small quantity for the Mass, and through the consumption of familiar foods, Europeans undoubtedly sought also to reinforce their own identity in small islands of urban settlement within the vast sea of conquered natives. They certainly preferred wine to pulque and pork and beef to turkeys or grilled dogs. Above all the Spaniards insisted on having, if not like Don Quixote "pan de trastrigo," at least proper bread made from wheat.

The Spaniards initially tried to get native people to grow wheat by making it part of the tribute requirement. This policy had scant success any place in Mesoamerica, but the plan seems to have been somewhat more readily accepted in the Andes. As we shall see, the same was true for European livestock. From the Indian point of view, European cereals seemed inferior to maize. The latter can be planted among stumps and rocks and steep hillsides while wheat requires the clearing of the entire surface of the field. Maize may be left ripe in the fields so the harvest may be spread over several months while wheat requires concentrated labor in a critical two-week period. Maize may be stored on the cob and is less susceptible to rot and weevils. Above all, maize yielded up to ten times more than wheat measured in proportion to seed and perhaps one and a half times as much in terms of area sown or labor time. Finally, wheat required the plow and draft animals and the sickle or scythe, all of which were absent in aboriginal America.

Wheat was consequently introduced haltingly into New Spain and came to be concentrated in a handful of intermontane basins, particularly Puebla-Tlaxcala, Toluca, the Bajío, and Guadalajara, as well as the Valley of Mexico itself. This is because wheat is a more demanding mistress than promiscuous maize. It does well and makes better bread when grown in cool climates, but it will not tolerate frost in the later growing season. It is susceptible of rust and stem rot in damp or excessively humid climates while summer rains may flatten the standing grain and hail will shatter the kernels. In the first years following the conquest, the Spaniards, wrestling with unfamiliar climate and crop cycles, planted their wheat in the Mexican spring. It grew during the summer rains and then was harvested in the dry autumnal and winter months. This practice had two major disadvantages: Such a calendar had to attract Indian workers just at the time they were busiest with maize; secondly, it ran afoul of the uncertain and often destructive weather mentioned above. For these reasons, spring planting was gradually abandoned and the schedule shifted to autumnal planting and winter irrigation; because harvest now could run into the early summer rains, large investments in storage sheds were required. Spaniards also insisted on their Mediterranean threshing practice of treading out the grain (rather than the northern European practice of flailing), which required the presence of large numbers of horses, usually mares, and abundant pasture lands. On a Jesuit-owned hacienda in Puebla for example, seventy-seven horses were kept for threshing the harvest of 100–124 acres. On the Guadalajara estate of Huejotitlán there were 540 acres in wheat and many of the 2,380 horses listed in the inventory were used for threshing.[4]

As the Hispanicized segment of the population grew over the course of the colonial centuries and wheat bread became both a prestigious and dietarily satisfying food, European settlers withdrew from the attempt to force the introduction of wheat upon the native population and instead took steps to insure their own domination of its production. Wheat farms doubled and tripled in size and wheat became a demesne crop, cultivated not by tenant farmers, sharecroppers, or peasant families as it often was in the Old World and as maize was (and is) in the New, but rather directly administered by the estates employing a service tenantry and wage-earning day laborers. The cost of workers and the need for draft animals and storage, horses and pasture for threshing, all increased the price of entry for potential competitors.

In time, European settlers and their descendants also began to move into maize production, but haciendas could offer competition to the multitude of small native producers only under extraordinary circumstances. When drought or frost caused the peasant sector to exhaust its supplies early, the large granaries on the estates enabled a few large producers to hold maize off the market until the inevitable high prices brought profits. The two great cereals, then, led to a dual culture in the countryside: Wheat was produced on irrigated, centralized, and directly supervised estates and circulated primarily in the Spanish, or Hispanicized, sector of the economy. Because little wheat was grown for subsistence or self-consumption and because of its high value relative to weight (wheat brought up to ten times more than maize in eighteenth-century Guadalajara, for example), it was traded across regions. Most wheat entered the market, and its prices reflect fairly accurately local and even interregional supply and demand. The same was true for several other commodities.

European goods had long entered Mexico and Guatemala from the transatlantic trade. Until the early eighteenth century these goods, including European cloth, wines, iron products, and luxury items, were hauled up from Veracruz to the annual fair at Jalapa and laid out for the scrutiny of merchants throughout the realm who then paid for them in cash or solid credit. The great mines that lay along the spine of the Sierra Madre—the names of Parral, Fresnillo, Zacatecas, Durango, Guanajuato, and Taxco ring with the sound of silver—together with the burgeoning capital at Mexico City, drove a multipolar economy that, as in Peru, created a large interrelated economic "space."[5] Across this space, credit was advanced, goods sold for money, and prices governed the flow of trade. Thousands of sheep were driven south from Coahuila to the textile mills of Querétaro, wheat and flour from Atlixco (near Puebla) found markets in Mexico, indigo and cochineal that earlier flowed from Soconusco and Oaxaca to Tenochtitlán were now sold in Europe and on the China trade. The European imports already mentioned moved on muleback across this space. At the same time, thousands of workers from Guatemala to New Galicia migrated from one job to the next, prepared to sell their labor for a daily wage. (See Figs. 6–8.)

No doubt the workings of this economy touched the lives of many people, even those in the shadow of the great haciendas or in remote villages. So when we now begin to talk of another economy, one based on subsistence and local markets, the reader should not see in this description a simple-minded "dual economy" or sharply divided "modern" and "traditional" or even "capitalist" or "feudal" sectors, because the Hispanic and native worlds were always, to a certain degree, interdependent. But in the words of Woodrow Borah, "[T]here were two populations with different patterns of consumption, this is, a Spanish world wishing to eat wheaten bread, oil, meat and wine; to dress in European clothing made of wool and silk; and to live with European furniture in houses built according to European standards; as against Indian worlds living on American products such as maize and in South America, manioc, potatoes, etc., wearing native American clothing of cotton, agave, and in South America, wool from cameliods, and living in native-style huts or houses furnished in native fashion." Because of the differing patterns of consumption, he concludes, "there were different kinds of markets for each ethnic group."[6]

Local Markets and Exchange in New Spain

Underneath the monetarized and fairly integrated layer of regional markets lay the production of innumerable villagers and hacienda workers who produced much of their own food, pots, and clothing. Much of this was not traded in any market, regional or local, and consequently not measured by prices. Villagers and hacienda workers produced for their own consumption, bartered at local markets, and rarely received a wage in hard coin (*moneda sonante*) but more commonly in rations, access to land, or credit made by their employers against advances in cloth, maize, needles, or ribbon. Although some enterprising householders carried whatever remained after consumption to market, surplus was more commonly extracted by compulsion, through the twin devices of tribute and tithe. Because the workings of this lower economy were less visible to crown officials and observers than the interregional market, less is known about it. Recent research, however, provides at least a rudimentary picture of this more humble social landscape, which was increasingly submerged in the rising tide of a more Hispanicized or Europeanized economy.

Whether based on the pre-Hispanic settlements or the *congregaciones* of the sixteenth century, village-dwelling people in Mesoamerica endeavored to preserve their way of life where possible and adapt when necessary to colonial rule. In economic terms, the Holy Trinity of Mesoamerican food—beans, maize, squash—supplemented by chiles and the marvelous chicken, a gift of the Europeans, remained the subsistence items. Pots, homespun cottons and, with the coming of sheep, woolens, wooden trays, beeswax, and a range of other items were the staples of local markets and consumption.

The tithe, ordinarily a tax of one-tenth levied against agricultural production and one-tenth of the annual increase of livestock, was collected for the church either directly by clerics or indirectly through contractors. The tithe was collected in kind; that is, villagers were assessed a certain number of bushels of grain or head of livestock, which was then collected and put up for sale. The cash proceeds went to the diocesan church (the secular clergy) but the produce itself, usually purchased by a local merchant, landowner, or official, entered the larger, regional market. The tithe thus served to force commodities out of the communities into larger commercial circuits. In the more isolated regions such as the western Guatemalan highlands, the Franciscan and Dominican friars extracted surplus from the Quiché Maya not through the tithe (the religious orders were not entitled to tithe income) but from personal service (*servicio*) and in the form of commodities called *ración* (chickens, pigs, maize), which were then sold on the market to raise clerical revenue.

The tribute or head tax levied by the crown on adult men was also used to extract commodities out of the lower economy for circulation in the upper. A village with a hundred *tributarios,* for example, would have been liable in the eighteenth century for around five hundred to eight hundred pesos a year. Since little silver actually circulated among the villagers, the Indian governors working in conjunction with the crown officials, accepted payment in kind, sold the produce for cash to the local merchant (often a landlord as well), and after deducting certain overhead costs, passed the proceeds on to the district governor (*corregidor*) to fulfill the tribute obligations. The merchant in turn (who to complicate things ever further, might be the *corregidor* himself) sold the maize, wool, and cochineal to the mines, cities, or the export trade. The reader will notice that because tithe and tribute were used to extract commodities from the village economy, little money was returned to the villagers. To be sure this description does not apply to all people and places; nor was there a single type of "villager." At times, tribute collection was "farmed," that is, the right to collect it was put out for bid to Spanish entrepreneurs or officials who in turn sold the produce on the market to realize a profit. Of course many enterprising communards and private small farmers (*rancheros*) produced their own surplus and offered it for cash sale; others sharecropped on the larger estates to gain additional income. Nevertheless, if there was not a solid floor between the two economies we've sketched here, there was at least a coarse mesh screen.

The other principal element in the rural landscape, apart from villages and loose clusters of *rancheros* were, of course, the large estates, which came to be known by the seventeenth century in Mexico as haciendas. Although Spaniards or their descendants were often the owners, in Oaxaca, for example, or throughout the Andes, the native elite also had extensive holdings. The private estates stood, Janus-faced, at another intersection of the two economies. The hacienda's external front faced the cities and mines and the larger world. Its owner sought credit at interest, shifted from one crop to another in reaction to prices, sold produce for cash, and aimed for profits; in short, he acted like the quasi-capitalist entrepreneur he was. But toward his workers, toward the internal front, he was a semi-feudal seigneur, or if not so grand, a penny-pinching employer.[7] His main aim was to avoid any payment to anyone in money. Rudimentary tools, harness, and rustic furniture were made by resident artisans, and the workers themselves were mainly paid in commodities they themselves produced, funneled, together with such urban niceties as needles, coarse sugar, or a length of ribbon, through the hacienda store. In many cases, the estate had its own crude textile mill (*obraje*) as well. Goods were advanced against the promise of future work or used to attract residents in times of labor scarcity. The landowner paid his workers' wedding and baptismal fees and asked for work in return; in those cases where workers were inscribed as tributaries on the estate rolls, the owner paid the tribute tax in money or in kind for his workers and again, extracted labor services in return. (See Fig. 9.)

Work and Labor Markets in New Spain

Whereas the various pre-Hispanic kingdoms endeavored to wring an agricultural surplus out of their subject peoples, the European invaders aimed to gain control over the labor power of the conquered and turn their energies to the construction of public, or more commonly, ecclesiastical buildings; to silver mining; and the production of European crops, animals, and commodities. From the mid sixteenth century, those requiring laborers petitioned crown officials, who had begun to regulate the newly reconstituted towns, for Indian workers.

We can visualize the new regime by imagining the experience of such a town as Acámbaro, one of the first congregations, in what is now the state of Michoacán in west-central Mexico. Here as elsewhere, the crown official made a count of all households and the tributaries (a tax unit was a man between the age of eighteen and fifty) within them. Let us picture a given day in say, 1604, when a certain variable fraction—perhaps one-seventh—of the eligible men would have been required to present themselves in the central square. The crown official, working with the native caciques or newly installed leaders of the Indian town government, assigned these men to various tasks. We can imagine a group of twenty sent to work on the vast drainage project at Huehuetoca, a public project designed to reduce flooding in Mexico City; fifteen others may have been assigned to help construct the Franciscan convent in Valladolid; a contingent of thirty might have trekked northward to the mines of Guanajuato; and groups of five to ten allocated to local landowners. These workers took turns, depending on the task, laboring for weeks or months; and in principle they were to be paid—in coin—"in their own hand." Two reales (one-quarter of the Spanish peso) came to be a widely imposed statute wage.

One can quickly see in these arrangements the absence of a free labor market yet something less than a completely forced labor system. We should also notice that in the beginning only a small part (frequently no more than 5 to 6 percent at any one time) of the total population was drawn into this system of *repartimiento*, or "distribution," as it generally came to be known, and actual practice varied considerably from the idealized picture just presented. Let us pose a number of seemingly ingenuous questions: Why did employers have to force native people to work? Why could not miners or landowners or church architects simply have passed the word that workers were needed and offer wages sufficient to attract them? Or alternatively, if coercive power were available, why pay any wage at all? Although it is true that some work, especially underground mine work, was unattractive to most people, white, black or Indian, and although conquerors and conquered held different economic values (remember that the invading Europeans were bent on directing the energies of an essentially agricultural people to rather more industrial rhythms), it is still true that almost from the beginning, the Europeans discovered that the natives would work for the proper inducements. In other words, there was a wage or remuneration sufficient to draw people into the labor market. But because force was present, because the people had after all, been conquered, employers did not have to pay a market wage, which judging from those cases where a market did function, seems to have been from three to four times greater than the statute rate of two reales. Underneath this, many employers held the belief that men would not respond to incentives and "having no needs" would not stick to the job once a target income was obtained, and thus they pushed hard for compulsory labor. Finally, a mine operator or landowner or textile mill owner wanted workers when he wanted them, not just when the end of planting or harvest made them available. The combination, then, of state-directed coercion with a statute wage aimed to satisfy all parties. It provided workers when workers were needed in those activities deemed essential to the success of the European enterprise at a wage the employers were prepared to pay. *Repartimiento* separated potentially powerful *encomenderos* from their workers; while at the same time the crown's insistence on pay was a step in the direction of its overall policy of eventually creating an integrated labor market.

The collapse of the native population brought pressure to bear on these arrangements. As more and more European (or culturally European) entrepreneurs clamored for a shrinking labor supply, the ethnic leaders—caciques and *indios principales*— previously exempt from tribute and consequently from the labor draft, were now included in it; mine operators had to offer shares of ore to attract workers, and landowners held out the offer of land and rations in order to secure a stable labor force on their *labores* and haciendas. In this scramble for hands, certain sectors of the economy now moved toward a more fully integrated labor market. By the last third of the eighteenth century, for example, a large, mobile corps of independent, hard-bitten, by now mostly mestizo, salaried mineworkers cut the ore and extracted the metal that produced Mexico's Silver Age. Thousands of wage-earning construction workers built the impressive aqueducts of Querétaro and Valladolid, labored in the eighteenth-century boom in ecclesiastical construction, and put up the houses of the rich in the colonial capitals. Several observers noticed an increase of migratory workers in agriculture. At this level—in mining, construction, and seasonal rural work—by the last half of the eighteenth century we are in the presence of something approaching a labor market. These people are mainly paid in money and are "free" in the liberal sense of the word. At the same time, the persistence almost everywhere of the magical "two reales," which began as a statute and became a customary wage for unskilled workers, indicates the weight of habit and convention in the economy as well as a certain amount of mutual bargaining that accompanied late-eighteenth-century population increase.

Wages and Prices

Let us ask again, What was the nature of this colonial economy? Can it be explained in conventional terms of supply and demand, that is, in terms of population and market forces? Historians have argued that population provided the "overmastering" explanation for social change: Population increase meant higher prices and lower wages while the reverse was true in times of plague and demographic decline. In New Spain's "century of depression" (the seventeenth century), however, the great epidemics might have increased the wages paid to construction and mine workers, but there is no good evidence that it did. This is because workers were usually remunerated with a mix of coin and ration. Even when the wage is expressed in monetary terms it may in

Fig. 6. Alpaca. Anonymous painter. (Madrid: Museo Naval).

Fig. 7. Sixteenth and early seventeenth-century Spanish pieces of eight minted in America.

Fig. 8. Traveling Wagon in a Pontano (Morass). E.E. Vidal, *Picturesque Illustration of Buenos Ayres and Monte Video...* (London: 1820).

Fig. 9. Map of the hacienda of San Pedro Tenayaque, 1786. (A.G.I., Mapas y Planos, Mexico 714).

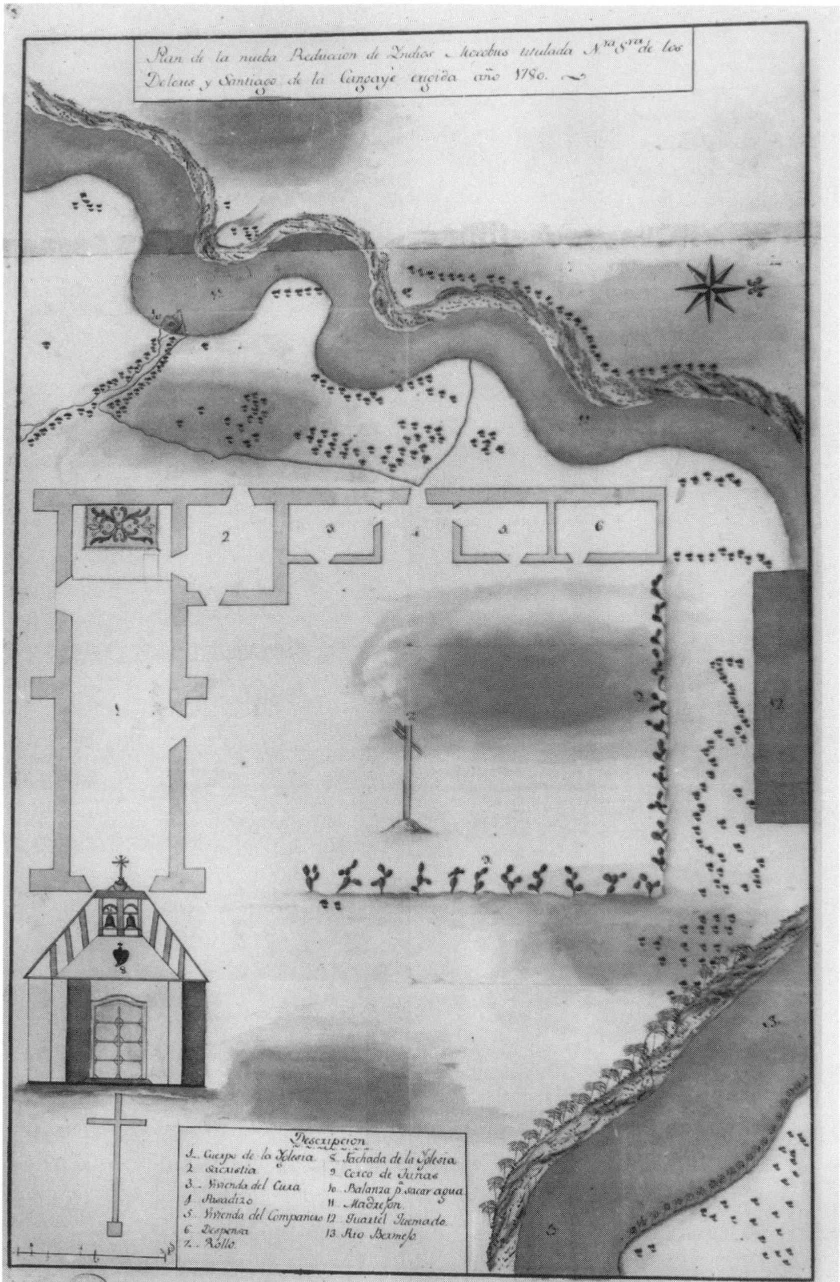

Fig. 10. Plan of the new Mocobí Indian reduction...1780. (A.G.I., Mapas y Planos, Mexico 714).

fact have been paid only on account. Two reales a day (six pesos a month) remained remarkably constant as the statute and conventional wage for unskilled workers throughout the period and, indeed, well into the nineteenth century (and not only in Mexico but also in many places throughout Spanish America where costs of food varied widely!). As long as the ration of maize remained constant, workers remunerated in this way were insulated from changes in the price level. Many other people in this predominately rural world scratched the earth for their own subsistence, so while maize prices may be a valid measure of the worth of interregional trade, and certainly reflect general conditions of supply, they indicate less accurately the daily, on-the-ground well-being of the mass of rural population. Supervisors and skilled artisans are more visible in the archives and here again, their wage seems essentially static even when market prices for cereal vary widely.

W. W. Borah thought it possible that labor scarcity drove landowners in the seventeenth century to offer greater incentives in the form of land and rations in order to attract tenants to the estates while at the same time endeavoring to hold them on the job through the device of debt peonage. He also made the point that given the presence of a crown-organized system that forced village tributaries into mines and other demanding tasks, many communards saw the hacienda as the lesser of evils and even as a protected haven.[8] Whatever the actual mechanisms, in the seventeenth and eighteenth centuries, the Mexican hacienda began the business of acquiring its labor force, which culminated in a golden age of exploitation in the later, liberal, nineteenth century. Recent opinion tends to play down the importance of debt peonage in this process during the colonial years, in part because landowners "pined in vain" for the kind of state support available, by contrast, in the serf regimes of Eastern Europe. In Spanish America, landowners or their local administrators, wrangled endlessly with village leaders, with the priest, with the impotent and venal *corregidor* over questions of boundaries and pay and deference. In the end, bargains were struck and accommodations reached. All of course in a society where the patron held the right end of the stick but nevertheless had to tread quite softly. Only such a picture can explain the long endurance of colonial arrangements.

If ordinary wages are difficult to calculate, and in any case mean little in an economy that is only partially monetarized, we must also be very clear about just what it is that "prices" measure. They indicate the value of imports and goods and food such as cloth and wheat traded across regions or in urban markets. And of course they measure the changing value of silver itself; the upward trend of prices in Bourbon Mexico, for example, reflects in part an increase in the money supply. When prices from, say, Chile, Mexico, and Peru are compared, we are given some indication of supply elasticity in agriculture and broad macroeconomic trends. But prices are essentially set by the local production of goods and by the number of people who actually go to the market. As Ruggiero Romano has insisted more than once, if only 10 percent of agricultural produce goes to market, then the price "reflects the economic history of that 10 percent" and only in a most indirect way, the value to consumers of the other 90 percent.[9] As population recovered in the later eighteenth century from the depths of the demographic catastrophe, an increasing percentage of consumers were white and mestizo, generally city dwelling and consequently dependent upon the market. Prices therefore reflect not just an increase in population but in a specific kind of population.

In eighteenth-century Mexico there is evidence for a general rise in the level of prices brought about by a sharp increase in the money supply as the mines of Guanajuato and Taxco poured forth a torrent of silver, and by a rising demand for maize, not only as food for workers but also for the thousands of mules in mining and transport that consumed an inordinate amount of grain. At the same time, there was little if any increase in worker productivity in agriculture. The new crops, rotations, and techniques that became common practice in seventeenth- and eighteenth-century European agriculture were not transferred to colonial Spanish America. All of this seems to have eroded the well-being of the evermore numerous popular classes and contributed to the explosive outburst against colonial rule in 1810.

Markets and Economic Space in The Andes

In contrast to the conquistadors of New Spain, who were fascinated by the great marketplace of Tlatelolco and noticed the hum of commerce in provincial towns, the first Europeans in the Andes are mute on this subject. But without trade, at least as Europeans understood it, how could one explain a land where the "mountains and uplands whitened with flocks; the valleys [were] teeming with the fruits of a scientific husbandry; the granaries and warehouses filled to overflowing"?[10] Working with the records of mid-sixteenth-century Spanish accounts, scholars have found that the social grouping in which people were organized (*ayllu*) was not spatially defined as settlements of contiguous dwellings but rather as an "archipelago of ecological niches" scattered through several elevations, in which the inhabitants endeavored to bring under their control a wide variety of crop and pastureland and for that matter, even maritime resources. Thus, members of the same *ayllu* might have access to fish on the desert coast, maize in mid-elevations, potatoes or other tubers further up, llamas and alpacas for meat and wool on high-altitude pastures and coca from semitropical terraces beyond the *cordillera* in the Amazon drainage. Members of *ayllus* strove for self-sufficiency, and although llama trains might have linked the various niches in each *ayllu* there was little exchange among different *ayllus*. In each community, lands were set aside and worked by members to yield a surplus to the state and the cult; widows, orphans, and the poor were also provided for. Where trade served to redistribute goods in Mesoamerica, that function was assumed by the Inca state in Peru. The important caste of *pochteca* (long-distance traders), so noticeable in Mexico, were consequently absent in Peru. More recent research, it should be admitted, has somewhat qualified this picture, which seems most applicable to the south and central highlands. It is clear, for example, that local markets flourished in Quito, in the far north of the kingdom, and merchants there, or *mindala*, seem similar to *pochteca*.[11]

After the conquest, the rise of the mining economy at Potosí, and the establishment of stable Spanish settlement, the crown dispatched Francisco de Toledo as viceroy of Peru (1569–81) with the main purpose of organizing the native rural population in European-style communities to supply the Spanish sector of the economy with food and commodities and to establish forced labor regimes to supply the workers for the mines. We shall look first at the resettlement of the native population and the development of interregional markets in the Peruvian "space" and then at the labor system.

Spanish enthusiasm for the reduction of rural Indians into European-style communities arose with the first contacts in the Caribbean. The policy was carried forward in New Spain and, postponed by the turmoil of civil war, haltingly introduced in Peru. Not until 1571, under the implacable hand of Viceroy Toledo, did this "colossal undertaking," involving at least a 1.5 million people, get underway. Although frequently excused in moral terms (the Spaniards believed that Indians living in remote hamlets "got drunk and fathers became involved with their daughters or brothers with sisters with no restraint of any kind"), resettlement above all aimed to make it easier to Christianize the native people and organize them so that commodities and labor could be extracted for Spanish enterprise. Towns in the familiar grid plan were laid out, church construction began, and a jail as well as a building where the Indian town council would meet were built. In the years following Toledo's decrees, the Andean vertical "archipelagos" of several "ecological floors" were compressed into settlements where people lived side by side. In the district of Moquegua and Arica on the south coast of Peru, for example, 226 hamlets were reduced to 22 new towns. The native leaders first offered Toledo an 800,000-peso bribe to stall the program and when that was rejected, dragged their feet in resistance so that by a century later, many had drifted back to a more dispersed settlement pattern. But many Toledean settlements stayed put. Wheat and European livestock were more readily accepted here than in Mesoamerica, no doubt because Andean people were already familiar with quinoa (a milletlike, high-altitude Andean cereal), llamas, and alpacas. Also unlike in New Spain, where the European capital was directly superimposed on Tenochtitlán-Mexico and the occupation much more pervasive and obliterating of native culture—except in such off-the-track places as Oaxaca or the Maya highlands—in Peru the indigenous structure and its ethnic leaders remained much more intact. Thus, rather than being "destructured" or actually "vanquished," the Inca and their descendants resisted, survived, and accommodated themselves as unequal partners in the colonial world. (See Fig. 10.)

Agricultural production from the new settlements yielded a generous surplus for the rapidly expanding colonial economy. Local markets now became more prominent, and *corregidores* and *kurakas* organized trains of human carriers and then later, llama and mule caravans to move goods. Coca production increased perhaps twentyfold in the century following the conquest. All of this was forced upward, into the Spanish economy through compulsion: Once again, tithe and tribute were payable in coca, sheep, maize, llamas, wheat, and potatoes, and these products were sold for money onto the interregional market by local merchants who were, not infrequently, the local *kuraka* or *corregidor* as well. At the same time, shrewd native entrepreneurs, most often, *kurakas,* seized the new opportunities in this "world turned upside down." One of the best known was don Diego Caquí, *kuraka* of Tacna in southern Peru. He acquired lands, sold wine to Potosí, had three ships for coastal trading, and a net worth in the 1580s of some 260,000 pesos, a fortune by any standard.

While produce from below was being pumped into the larger circuits of trade through colonial exactions and native entrepreneurship, the spreading influence of the greatest silver mining complex in the world at Potosí began to draw into itself and absorb the production from far more distant regions. By the late sixteenth century, Potosí already had a population of some 120,000 and it grew to 160,000 a few decades later. To supply the burgeoning market of this economic space, the specialized products of distant satellite regions came into existence, attracted by the powerful magnet of the Potosí-Lima axis. Spanish landowners planted wheat in the temperate valleys of Cochabamba and exported it to Potosí; other Spaniards pushed into the frontier of northern Argentina—below Tucumán and Córdoba—to raise mules and sold thousands to the mines; from even farther away Chilean landowners sold wheat to Lima while the fabrics from *obrajes* or large textile mills of Quito also circulated on the Lima-Potosí axis.

There are two points to make about this trade. First of all, the silver mining of Potosí can no longer be understood solely as an "enclave" economy in which metal was extracted and most of it then directly remitted to Europe either as taxes or to pay for imports. Potosí generated market linkages throughout the "Peruvian space," as we have seen above, and perhaps 60 percent of all silver remained in the colony to pay for the goods and services consumed by the mine.

The second point is that although an interregional colonial market mediated by merchants, credit, money, and prices was created and consequently touched the lives of people from Quito to Santiago, it did little to transform the relations of production between the entrepreneurs and workers in those subregions; or at least it did not transform them in the direction of monetary payment, incentives, or greater independence. In Chile, for example, the owners of large agricultural estates in the central valley had taken onto their properties a number of poor Spaniards and mestizos. At a time when the land was mainly used for pasture, these tenants, described in the documents as "renters," were permitted to graze a few animals and help with rodeos while recognizing their personal tie with the patron.

As the Lima market for wheat increased, land became more valuable, more hands were needed for cultivation, and the landowner stepped up the amount of service required. Instead of occasional labor during roundup or slaughter, each renter was required to supply an able-bodied man all year round to help with planting, plowing, or irrigation. In time social stratification increased. Landowners became more wealthy and fastened their hold on the land. The tenants, faced with the alternative of expulsion, accepted the increased service requirement. They were referred to less and less as "renters" and more and more as *inquilinos,* a term still used. The *inquilinos* produced wheat, which was sold for money on the Lima market, but received in turn a handful of toasted flour (which they themselves had produced) and the right to remain on the landowner's property. In Quito, responding to the Peruvian market, large private and clerical landowners installed impressive textile mills on their property (the Jesuit mill at Latacunga, for example, had four hundred workers). The labor force was drawn from residents on the estate who were required to split their time between their usual chores and work in the *obrajes.*

On the coast above and below Lima, Jesuit plantation owners responded to the new markets by buying more black slaves to produce sugar and wine for sale in Potosí. Here as elsewhere in Spanish America, landowners sold on the market for cash but stoutly resisted the use of coin within the estate. Once again slaves, like hacienda workers everywhere, were fed and clothed by the maize and cloth that they themselves produced.

Finally, the practice of forced consumption also drove peasants into interregional markets, not only in the Andes but throughout much of Spanish America. With the decline of Spain in the seventeenth century, offices in the overseas bureaucracy were offered for sale to raise crown revenue. *Corregidores* purchased their positions from the crown by borrowing money, most often, from Lima merchants. To repay their debts, the *corregidores* acquired advances on credit of cloth, mules, and iron goods from the same merchants and then, taking advantage of their position as administrators and judges became merchants as well, forcing their merchandise down the throats of the Indian peasantry in their jurisdictions. The villagers paid for the goods in scarce coin or more commonly in kind—in maize, llamas, wool, or wheat—which was then sold by the *corregidor* for cash. This abusive practice yielded substantial profits to Lima merchants and *corregidores* alike and also contributed to the Tupac Amarú revolt that rocked the southern highlands in the later years of colonial rule.

Mita and the Labor Market in Peru

Just as in the case of New Spain, the European invaders of Peru insisted on access to unpaid native labor through the *encomienda.* Every one of the 168 Spaniards present at the capture of Atahualpa in November 1532, for example, received an *encomienda,* although of course the number of tributaries in each one varied widely. The *encomienda* of an early entrepreneurial conqueror, one Lucas Martínez Vegaso, included nearly two thousand Indians in several clusters, stretching from Arequipa into what is now northern Chile, who provided labor for several enterprises including wheat farming, silver and gold mining, and textiles. By 1560 there were some eight thousand Spaniards in Peru, about a third of whom "were involved in encomiendas or lived in the houses of the 480 encomenderos." Just as in New Spain, the crown was determined to separate the conquistadors from the native population. The indelicate handling of this matter, however, cost the Spanish viceroy his head and nearly cost Spain its Peruvian colony as some settlers rose in revolt under Gónzalo Pizarro in defense of their *encomiendas*. *Encomienda* subsequently remained important longer here than in New Spain (and there were far more native holders of *encomiendas* here than there) even though Viceroy Toledo had little sympathy for the *encomenderos* (and even less for rapacious *kurakas*). Only by the mid-seventeenth century did the *encomienda* dwindle to insignificance.

In the first years following its discovery, silver was extracted from Potosí in the same way that it was mined in other parts of the Spanish New World: Spanish supervisors paid wages in the form of a share of the product to attract voluntary workers and forced *encomienda* workers into the more onerous tasks below ground. As the shafts deepened and ore quality declined, the labor supply began to contract through the effect of epidemic disease and flight. It became clear that the wages the mine operators were prepared to pay would no longer attract sufficient workers to the mines. One of Toledo's major assignments was to maintain and even increase the flow of silver from Potosí. In this he was assisted by an important technological introduction and his own talent for organization. Silver was originally extracted from the rich ores, lying near the surface of the great "silver hill" through smelting. With the introduction around 1570 of the mercury amalgamation process, lower grade ores, including those previously discarded, could now, if sufficient hands were available, be made to yield silver.

Toledo began by demanding approval for a new forced labor policy from an assembly of learned clerics and crown officials in Lima. With "his conscience eased by this vote," the viceroy organized a labor draft for the newly discovered mercury mine at Huancavelica (just inland from Lima), which required that one-seventh of the adult male population from Jauja to Huamanga (around three thousand men) work underground in return for a wage of around two reales (including ration), far less than the amount necessary to attract voluntary workers. The term *mita*, a Quechua word for the Inca practice of requiring labor for the common good, was now used to describe the Spanish system of forced labor. Three years later, the viceroy turned his attention to Potosí itself. Now at full production, the Spanish operators required some forty-five hundred men working at any one time. In a series of ordinances issued in 1574, Toledo ordered an inventory of the human resources in an area stretching six hundred miles, from Cuzco to the present-day Argentine frontier. The census revealed some ninety-five thousand eligible men—not counting *kurakas* and *kurakas'* sons—and one-seventh of these were made liable for duty in the *mita* of Potosí at a statute wage of roughly two reales a day. Each settlement or newly constituted *ayllu* (the usefulness of the Toledan reductions now becomes apparent) was assigned a quota and the *kuraka* was responsible for delivering men for the *mita.*

During the first few years thousands of Andean peasants, often accompanied by their wives, pack animals, pots, and food for the journey (which could last three months) were forced into mine labor at Potosí. One colonial observer, noticing the crowded roads and trails, wrote that it seemed as if "the whole world were on the move." Yet, before long, demographic reality, ingenious Andean resistance, and limits to the coercive power of the crown all became apparent. Epidemic disease shrank the labor pool, and many villagers in the vast catchment area of the Potosí *mita* fled, taking refuge in more remote zones or seeking shelter on Spanish estates; many others found ways to buy their way out of *mita* obligations. By the turn of the sixteenth century, less than two thousand workers (called *mitayos*) were supplied by the *mita* to the mine operators. They were assigned to work underground in the lengthening and dangerous mine shafts, and additional workers for the stamping and ore-processing work aboveground were hired from the large number of uprooted people now crowding into Potosí. They, however, demanded and were paid from three to four times more than the statute wage received by *mitayos.*[12] Why was this done and how were the mine operators able to do it? To understand the evolution of the Potosí *mita,* let us backtrack from the mine and follow the roads back to the villages that were subject to the *mita* levies.

Let us imagine a town on the road beyond Puno toward Cuzco such as Tinta or Sicuani with an obligation of, say, fifty men for the *mita.* Twenty of these, let us further imagine, might have been informed by the *kuraka* that it was their turn to serve and like their brothers in neighboring towns set off for Potosí. But the remaining thirty may choose to buy their way out by paying some forty or fifty pesos each. This ransom was partly paid in scarce coin but more commonly in kind—in animals, wool or maize—to the *kuraka* who then sold the produce for cash, kept a portion, and sent the rest in coin to an individual in Potosí who in turn distributed the money to mine operators. They took the money and hired workers at something approaching the market wage. In this way, the *mita* provided a certain number of real workers to Potosí and a larger number of "Indians in coin" (*indios de faldtriquera*) in the expression of the day. By the mid-seventeenth century the amount paid in ransom to the mine operators amounted to nearly as much as the silver they produced. To put it another way, Toledo's forced labor system resulted in the Andean peasantry subsidizing a wage labor system at Potosí.

None of this would have been possible, of course, without the collaboration of the *kurakas,* a class that was more quickly coopted by the Spaniards in New

Spain (except in such out of the way places as Oaxaca) and eliminated altogether in other places. These ethnic leaders stood between the invading Spaniards and the native mass in Peru, transmitting demands and complaints from one group to the other. Like the priests, they were cultural mediators and economic arbiters. In Peru, the survival of the ethnic leaders also served to keep alive the memory of the pre-Hispanic Inca past, indirectly fueling every major social upheaval with a belief in an earlier age of justice and glory.

The Ecclesiastical Economy in Spanish America

From the very beginning of the Spanish occupation of America and lasting throughout the period of colonial rule and beyond, the Catholic church, or more properly, the various agencies of the Spanish church in the Indies, had a profound economic effect on Spanish America. Most discussion of the church has concentrated on its heroic work of evangelization, its prodigious building of convents and cathedrals, and the gradual establishment of a vast organization that provided to the conquerors and conquered alike whatever services of health, education, and welfare that existed together with the sacraments that punctuated colonial life. Underneath all this, however, was a vast economic system that penetrated every layer of colonial life and reached into the most remote corners of Spanish America. This economy, the ecclesiastical economy, generated the revenue that made the church's work possible.

The various agencies of the church energetically promoted economic activity. At the same time that more than one priest traded or managed a textile mill, various religious orders ran large plantations and haciendas, and cathedral chapters and convents lent money at interest. Not only that, hundreds and thousands of masons, carpenters, glass makers, and stonecutters were hired by the church; far more, in fact, than were employed in any other kind of public works. When the Condesa de la Selva Nevada pushed for the construction of a Carmelite convent in Querétaro in the late eighteenth century, her agents pointed out the obvious social benefits not only of forty young women filling the air with prayer but of the construction and skilled jobs that would thereby be created.

As in early modern Europe, the clergy's economic role encompassed providing a particular kind of service. "In most respects the contribution of the clergy to a community is not different from that of psychiatrists in modern societies . . . and the priest often also performed those functions which we now regard as belonging to the schoolteacher and the doctor."[13] Because it was almost wholly responsible for health, education, and welfare, the church played a positive economic role in the service sector and even helped support the social infrastructure. As Professor Cipolla concludes, "From an economist's point of view, a good or service has no absolute utility, only the utility attributed to it rightly or wrongly, by the consumer."

One of our main questions here is whether, and to what extent, the church impeded economic development or growth. Or, put slightly differently, how great an economic burden did the church represent for colonial society? Apart from some lay entrepreneurs who viewed the church as a competitor, this was not a question that led to sleepless nights in many colonial beds. During these centuries, the church and its values permeated colonial society at all levels, its function inseparable from the state. Our query betrays the preoccupations of our own secular age.

The Sources of Clerical Income

Let us look first at the sources of church wealth and revenue, keeping in mind that the church was not a single institution. We should remember the two fundamental divisions between secular and regular clergy (parish priests and members of religious orders) as well as the innumerable agencies and dependencies that in the course of centuries grew up around the church, including the Inquisition, lay brotherhoods, hospitals, and *colegios*.

Of all the income available to the secular clergy, the tithe came to be, by the end of the eighteenth century, the most important and reliable source. Originally, and before the unanticipated variety of American crops and animals were classified, the crown decided that only those products on which the tithe was levied in the archbishopric of Seville (the original metropolitan of the American bishoprics) should be liable for taxation in the Indies. To these categories were gradually added such native American products as maize, cotton, tobacco, and cochineal plus all livestock and domestic fowl. The usual tithe rate was 10 percent but this the crown occasionally lowered, particularly in the eighteenth century, to promote key exports such as sugar, cacao, or indigo. Despite continual conflict over who should pay the tithe—the missionary clergy, for example, urged that the burden not fall on the very native American people they were trying to convert—revenue from that source increased, and by the end of the colonial period, constituted a major source of the secular clergy's income. The bishoprics of Michoacán, Puebla, and Caracas, for example, each produced around 350,000 pesos a year in the later eighteenth century compared with around 20,000 in the 1620s. Since revenue from the tithe was affected by the prices of agricultural produce, the cost and effectiveness of collection, and the changing diocesan boundaries, the amounts collected are imperfect indicators of agricultural production but they do show what the church in fact received.

The distribution of tithe income reflected the inequalities in colonial life, present in the church as well as in civil society. Work in the episcopal archives of Michoacán, for example, shows that out of a net tithe income of 333,827 pesos in 1787, the bishop himself received some 88,000; the cathedral chapter consisting of the dean, four dignitaries, ten canons, and twelve prebends took

145,000; while the remainder was assigned to the crown, the construction of churches and hospitals, and the ever spreading clerical proletariat of poor priests in provincial parishes. Thus, "the purpose of the tithe was to support an episcopal capital and sustain the celebration of the liturgy in all its splendor . . . in short, the agricultural production of the entire region paid to maintain the daily liturgical celebration. One of the accounts shows a cost of 3,250 pesos a year for candlewax."[14]

Another important source of church income was clerical fees and alms. Following European precedent, the parish church established schedules of fees for the administration of the sacraments to the faithful. A common funeral in the mid-eighteenth century cost fourteen pesos for a "Spaniard," a peso or less for Negroes, mulattoes, and mestizos, while Indians in theory paid nothing. One peso was also the common fee for baptisms. Clerical fees ranged from modest sums for simple burials and weddings to impressive amounts for the rites of the elite. The heirs of Isabel de Zúñiga, a clearly exceptional landowner near Cuernavaca, paid 1,076 pesos for her funeral. Many haciendas in Spanish America had a chapel for the circuit priest and often the landowner paid his workers' clerical fees and then required them to work off the amount.

Clerical fees provided a fundamental source of income, especially at the parish level, but given the nature of that income and informal accounting, it is difficult to calculate the overall volume. Referring again to the bishopric of Michoacán in the eighteenth century, parish income varied from 5,182 pesos in the prosperous town of Zitácuaro to around 1,000 in the Tarascan Sierra. At the same time, a fairly rich Peruvian parish such as Palpa (Ica) took in around 1,000 in fees. And each bishopric, of course, included many such parishes.

In addition to clerical fees the church had other sources of income. Parishes received income from the innumerable rural lay brotherhoods (cofradías). In the provinces, these often might provide sacks of maize or a few chickens for the parish priest as well as fireworks and firewater for Saint's Day celebrations. Their volume is impossible to quantify; we can only observe that it was substantial. We know for example that the Sanctuary of our Lady of Chiguinguira in Colombia got twenty thousand pesos a year in the form of donations and alms. Gifts and bequests added to church wealth. Few members of the colonial elite failed to include the church in their final testament. At times an entire hacienda or plantation together with its black slaves was left to the church.

The most important way the church involved itself with rural colonial economy and society was through its own ownership of real estate, its claims on the income of other property owners, and lending money at interest. Here we must look carefully in order to sort out the church's positive as well as negative role—we are speaking here in economic terms—in colonial economy.

From 1535, when the crown sent out the first of several decrees that forbade the acquisition of land in America by any "church, monastery or ecclesiastic," until the end of the colonial period, all branches of the church in fact amassed an enormous amount of property. The secular church owned estates, mills, and factories as well as many urban properties. Many of these they usually let in long-term leases to private entrepreneurs, content as a rule, with a 5 percent yield. The amount of actual land held by the secular church has been greatly exaggerated, but as we shall see, it came to have substantial claims on the income of others. In fact, the regular clergy were the main clerical owners of haciendas and plantations through Spanish America. Not eligible to receive tithe income and dependent upon the scant support offered by the crown while at the same time attracted by the unprecedented opportunities the New World offered for evangelization, the orders quickly took measures to assure a constant and reliable income. Like the seculars, the orders generally leased out their properties and received produce and cash for their convents and some of their missions.

With the arrival of the Jesuits the ownership of clerical property acquired a new dimension. From humble beginnings in Lima (1568) and New Spain (1571), the Jesuits came to acquire hundreds of the best sugarcane plantations, haciendas, vineyards, and textile mills across the map, from Chile to Baja California. Unlike the other orders, the Jesuits managed their own properties and made them into models of well-run and productive estates. Although we have good counts on the total number of properties held by the orders, it is hard to tell what part of the total land they represented. Research on Ecuador indicates that the Jesuits alone owned over 10 percent of the total agricultural land of that region. The Jesuits' fifty estates plus those of the Mercedarians, Augustinians, and Dominicans must have amounted to at least that share of central Chile, and we know that the church was wealthiest of all in New Spain. The matter must remain quantitatively inconclusive, but we can say that the church in its various manifestations was an important property owner in colonial Spanish America.

Perhaps more economically important than property in Spanish America was the widespread, tangled, complex, and baffling network of claims that the church held on the income of private property owners. We refer here to what contemporaries called pious works, *capellanías, censos, memoriales,* terms which no longer exist or have changed their meaning in the past three centuries. Let us see if we can understand how this aspect of the ecclesiastical economy developed by imagining a more or less representative section of the colonial Spanish American landscape, such as the hinterland of Puebla, highland Ecuador, or the environs of Arequipa or Córdoba.

As private property became established in the later sixteenth and early seventeenth century, almost all owners sooner or later felt an obligation to the church. If a daughter, for example, chose (or had chosen for her) a clerical vocation, her landowning family was expected to guarantee her maintenance. The same was true if a son entered the clergy, if one wanted to guarantee a series of Masses for a deceased relative, or provide for oil or candles. Because landowners were usually short of cash or coin, or because they were reluctant to part with real money, they generally "imposed a burden" on their property, calculated in monetary terms but involving no cash outlay, to guarantee an annuity for the daughter in the convent or for the payment for Masses. If, for example, a hacienda was worth 100,000 pesos, its owner might impose a *censo* of 10,000 pesos and stipulate that an annuity of 5 percent on that amount would be paid as dowry for the convent daughter. Then every year an agent of the Mother Superior would knock at the hacienda gate requesting 500 pesos in money. If a son entered the priesthood a similar burden was imposed to yield revenue to the appropriate branch of the cathedral chapter; upon his death, the landowner might impose yet another *grávamen* or obligation to pay for the support of a special chapel. In the sense of obligation to pay interest, these can be called mortgages with the important difference that landowners never received loans in money. In this way, the estate (or urban property) became progressively burdened with obligations to the church. The obligations could be redeemed by paying the entire capital amount to the church, but, of course, because of the original problem of cash scarcity, they rarely were. Since the obligations were made in perpetuity, they went with the property when it was inherited or sold. Subsequent owners in turn usually imposed their own obligations. It takes little imagination to see that by the end of the colonial regime, a great many properties were encumbered to the church. To return to our earlier example, the hacienda worth 100,000 pesos might commonly be burdened with obligations of 60,000 or 70,000. Thus, if the estate yielded a 5 percent return on investment (a quite typical yield) or an annual income of 5,000 pesos, between 3,000 and 3,500 of that would go to the various agencies of the church, leaving the owner with 1,500 or 2,000 pesos. If he chose to sell the estate, the buyer would pay 30,000 or 40,000 equity and assume the clerical obligations. Thus a colonial landowner may have had thousands of acres and hundreds of workers from whom he enjoyed deferential treatment but only the scantiest cash income.

The hypothetical case we have just discussed is amply confirmed by colonial documents. In the 1790s, in the district of Cholula (south-central New Spain), the haciendas, *ranchos,* and mills had an assessed value of 788,942 pesos; there were clerical obligations on 550,564 of that. Recent research shows that the haciendas in the district of Tepeaca carried ecclesiastical obligations of two-thirds of their value, one—San Mateo—assessed at 38,000 to 39,000 pesos actually had burdens to the church worth 53,000.[15] In Ecuador it was difficult to find a single property, urban or rural, that was not burdened with *censos* in favor of one religious house or the other. The same was true of Chile and Venezuela, where clerical obligations affected almost all rural and urban properties.

Now to complicate matters, the church not only received payments from the obligations we have just discussed, it also lent money at interest. These two functions have often been confused or collapsed into one so that in an older view the church was seen as a much more important bank than in fact it was. Nevertheless it is clear that the church was an active moneylender. Several agencies of the church, or associated with the church, lent money. These included the richer urban lay brotherhoods, the Inquisition, and individual clerics. Two sources were especially important: the *Juzgado de Capellanías* within the cathedrals and the female religious orders. Both of these lent substantial sums (thirty thousand, forty thousand, eighty thousand pesos at a time) at usually 5 percent interest to those borrowers with enough property to guarantee the loan with a mortgage. This, of course, meant that the church generally lent to the colonial landholding elite. The relative importance of the church within the overall credit market is difficult to determine. Even though church lending increased in the later eighteenth century, the quickening pace of the Atlantic economy meant that nonecclesiastical capital, supplied primarily by merchants and miners, also increased and in time became a more important source of credit to agriculture than the church. Nonetheless, convents in Arequipa, Santiago de Chile, Charcas, Cuzco, and Córdoba were all active, although on a fairly modest scale in the colonial money market.

The Burden of the Ecclesiastical Economy

Let us now return to our original query in this section: How great a burden was the church on colonial economy, and did its presence negatively affect economic performance? We have seen first of all that the church was an active producer. Wine, wool, wheat, and sugar from its many estates were sold on the market and must be added to any calculations of what we might call Gross Colonial Product. Many individual clerics were productive businessmen who traded, lent money, and ran textile mills. And, of course, several agencies of the church acted as banks as they accumulated capital and then lent it, mainly to landowners, at interest. All of this contributed to economic growth just as did the efforts of private landowners and merchants. Moreover, the church, although a substantial landowner, actually owned no more land in Spanish America than it did in Western Europe. While landed property of the church tended to be reduced from the sixteenth century on in Europe, this development did not take place in Spanish America until the last third of the eighteenth and, especially, in the nineteenth centuries.

More important than landholding in Spanish America were ecclesiastical taxes, a persistent flood of voluntary donations, and above all, the claims that the church established on the income of others through the devices of *censos, capellanías,* and pious works. If we recall that the tithe took 10 percent off the top of all agricultural production and that the church claimed, if it did not always receive, in addition 5 percent annuities on probably half of the capital value of all rural property, we can understand that to a great extent agriculture supported an ecclesiastical, not a private or crown, economy. Moreover, unlike most crown revenue, which was sent to Spain, almost all ecclesiastical revenue remained in America. This helps explain the absence of public works in Mexico and Peru compared with the tremendous weight of ecclesiastical construction. With the exception of two or three impressive aqueducts and massive fortifications along the maritime route, the crown invested little American wealth in the country. Roads barely existed; ports were rudimentary; even the buildings that housed the royal bureaucracy were meager affairs. The same can be said of the country houses of the colonial elite. There was nothing in Spanish America remotely resembling the great rural palaces of Eastern or Western Europe. Private hacienda and plantation houses were rustic; the best were built by the Jesuits. There were a few moderately impressive private townhouses in the colonial capitals, but they lay in the shadow of the great convents and churches. Everywhere, in town and country, ecclesiastical construction dwarfed the efforts of crown and private builders.

Was the heavy weight of the church detrimental to the colonial economy? As in early modern Europe, the clergy provided goods, capital, jobs, and many services, not easily quantified but still of social value. While the church used part of its income to provide teachers, counselors, and preachers desired by colonial society, a great deal of the capital it accumulated financed a lavish life-style for the upper clergy and a tremendous eighteenth-century surge in ecclesiastical construction, neither of which notably promoted further economic production. We can also easily imagine the inhibiting effect that clerical taxes and heavy annuities had on private rural entrepreneurs who, by the end of the colonial period, began to see that they had become "merely administrators of the income of others."

Why did Spanish-American landowners, miners, and merchants voluntarily support the church so lavishly, almost to the point of their own economic suicide? Why did nearly all properties bear heavy obligations to the church? Why, in the last third of the eighteenth century, did two great silver miners in Mexico put their fortunes into the gorgeous churches of La Valenciana and Santa Prisca? Why, compared to other places in the eighteenth century, was there so much "baroque piety" and so little "de-Christianization"? These are other large questions and their discussion goes beyond the bounds of this chapter but it seems to me that those who suggest that the greatest energies of landowners "were not oriented to make a fortune but to spend it" in order to safeguard their fundamental values of honor and piety, are on the right track.

In colonial Spanish America, a society impregnated with the values of the Counter-Reformation, a good way to safeguard those values was through consumption: through visible donations and obligations to the church; through the imposition of thousands of censos, capellanías, and pious works. At a more humble level in this society, a peasant community's yearly saving could be displayed in one glorious explosion of fireworks in celebration of the local saint. Perhaps it is this juxtaposition of social time, the persistence of baroque values into the world of Adam Smith, that provides the best explanation for what we, the spiritual descendants of that austere Scot, are inclined to perceive as rural backwardness.

Conclusion

Can we conclude that this peculiar multilayered and hybrid economic culture created by the interplay of indigenous and European elements accounts for Spanish American "underdevelopment"? Were three centuries of colonial rule economically detrimental for this part of the world? If we seek an explanatory path for Latin American poverty and isolation must it inevitably lead, as it does for the people of García Márquez's Macondo, to the rotting shell of a sunken Spanish galleon? The creole leaders who fought Spanish armies for independence in the early nineteenth century had no doubt on this score; nor did Anglo-American Protestants who saw the dead hand of the Catholic church weighing too heavily on the spirit of capitalism; and of course, the dependency theorists of the 1960s largely explained the melancholy state of Latin American economies as a result of their unequal relations with Spain, England, and the United States.

While reflecting on these questions it may be useful to pose counterfactual hypotheses: Suppose, for example, that the Pizarro rebellion had been successful in the mid-sixteenth century and Peru had separated from Spain then rather than 300 years later. Would we have had a more integrated and harmonious nation in place of the racially segmented and oppressed colony? Or suppose that Catalan merchants rather than adventurers from Extremadura with "seigneurial visions dancing in their heads" had led the sixteenth-century conquest; or that a Castilian cleric, not Martin Luther, had nailed the famous theses to a Spanish church door so that tight-lipped Puritan families and not zealous priests might have walked ashore at Veracruz. Or let us pose the ultimate counterfactual hypothesis: Suppose Columbus had lost patience in the Sargasso Sea, thrown up his hands and returned to Palos to let Anáhuac and Tawantinsuyo develop their own history. Would they all be better off? We cannot, of course, rewind and play it again with different actors, but speculation on these or other possibilities may help us understand what actually happened.

Notes

1. E. LeRoy Ladurie, *The Territory of the Historian*, trans. Ben and Sian Reynolds (Chicago, 1979), 79.

2. Friedrich Katz, "Commentary," in Nils Jacobsen and Hans-Jurgen Puhle, eds., *The Economies of Mexico and Peru during the Late Colonial Period, 1760–1810* (Berlin, 1986), 143–49.

3. Friedrich Katz, *The Ancient American Civilizations* (New York, 1972), 212–13.

4. Eric Van Young, *Hacienda and Market in Eighteenth-Century Mexico* (Berkeley, Calif., 1981), 214–25.

5. Carlos Sempat Assadourian, *El sistema de la economia colonial* (Lima, 1982), 110–20.

6. Woodrow Borah, *Price Trends of Royal Tribute Commodities in Nueva Galicia, 1557–1598,* vol. 55 of *Ibero-Americana* (Berkeley, 1992), 5.

7. Pablo Macera, "Feudalismo colonial americano: el caso de las haciendas peruanas," *Acta Historica* (Szeged, Hungary) 35 (1971). The essay by Stuart Schwartz in this volume relates the large estate owner's concern with self-sufficiency to the values of honor and independence, as well as to economic considerations.

8. Woodrow Borah, *New Spain's Century of Depression,* vol. 35 of *Ibero-Americana* (Berkeley, 1951), 3–4.

9. Ruggiero Romano, "Some Considerations on the History of Prices in Colonial Latin America," in Lyman Johnson and Enrique Tandeter, eds., *Essay on the Price History of 18th-Century Latin America* (Albuquerque, New Mexico, 1990), 57.

10. William H. Prescott, *The Conquest of Peru,* vol. 1 (New York, 1847), p. 1095.

11. John V. Murra, *Formaciones económicas y políticas del mundo andino* (Lima, 1975); see also, Murra, "Existieron el tributo y los mercados antes de la invasión europea?" in Olivia Harris, Brooke Larson, and Enrique Tandeter, eds., *La participación indígena en los mercados sur andinos* (La Paz, 1987), 51–64.

12. Peter Bakewell, *Miners of the Red Mountain: Indian Labor in Potosí, 1545–1650* (Albuquerque, 1984), 123-126.

13. Carlo Cipolla, *Before the Industrial Revolution: European Society and Economy, 1000–1700* (New York, 1976), 81.

14. David Brading, "El clero mexicano y el movimiento insurgente en 1810," in A. J. Bauer, ed., *La iglesia en la economía de América Latina, siglos xvi al xix* (Mexico, 1986), 135.

15. Juan Carlos Garavaglia and Juan Carlos Grosso, "Mexican Elites of a Provincial Town: the Landowners of Tepeaca (1700–1870)," *Hispanic American Historical Review* 70, no.2 (May 1990): 266.

CHAPTER TWO

Material Life

Eric Van Young

In the middle of a fresh summer's morning on 21 August 1752, the Spanish magistrate of the district of Etzatlán and La Magdalena, in New Spain, was called to the rural estate Labor de Rivera near the town of Ahualulco, about forty miles west of Guadalajara. At about five o'clock that same morning the estate administrator, don José Leandro de Siordia, who was also the brother of the owner, had been brutally killed. The magistrate duly took testimony from a number of witnesses, sent four *peones* (laborers) to the ramshackle little jail in the town of Ahualulco as material witnesses and possible accessories to the crime (they were later cleared of all suspicion), and eventually made his determination in the case: murder. But by that time the killer was nowhere to be found, having added insult to injury by stealing his victim's horse and riding off into the morning.[1]

In 1752 Ahualulco was a sleepy little village of a few hundred souls in which the death of José Leandro de Siordia must have been a topic of conversation and gossip for some months after the event. There simply was not much else to talk about except the weather and the state of the crops and livestock. The entire parish of Ahualulco contained perhaps two thousand people, mainly Spanish and mestizo, most of them living on the rural estates, smaller *ranchos,* and hamlets scattered about the jurisdiction. A good part of the area's inhabitants, probably including the four hundred or so Indians who lived there, were resident laborers on the half-dozen haciendas that dominated its economy. The estates and ranches in the district, including the hacienda Labor de Rivera, produced cattle, maize, and a little wheat. In the general agricultural expansion of the late eighteenth century, the hacienda's population was to rise to some two hundred or so permanent laborers and their families, but in

1752 there were perhaps a few dozen laboring families at most. In Ahualulco and the surrounding hamlets a good deal of simple weaving of textiles was done on hand looms; the town was famous for the quality of the saddles produced by its few resident artisans; and there was still a little desultory open-pit silver mining activity in the neighborhood, a holdover from palmier days. In the middle of the eighteenth century, and even as late as 1800, the area was known for the quality and extent of its wooded lands, which boasted abundant forests of pine, oak, and cedar. Just a few miles to the northeast, in fact, the wooded hills around Tequila were already becoming denuded because the distilling industry there required enormous amounts of firewood and charcoal to keeps its stills producing the famous local firewater. Agriculture was the lifeblood of the entire area, and the wealthiest men and families were those who owned the land.

On that August morning, after a two-hour horseback ride over a topography roughened by wooded hillsides, deep canyons, and a sinuous road, the magistrate reached the Labor de Rivera, whence he had been summoned by the victim's sister. He arrived to find José Leandro's body stretched out on a reed mat (*petate*) in the one-room house of Tomás Aquino, one of the estate's resident laborers, with a large crowd of people gathered around talking in hushed tones of the sudden and tragic events of the morning. José Leandro's elder brother José Luis, the actual owner of the Labor de Rivera, was absent that day on one of his other rural properties and did not arrive in time for his brother's funeral. The victim's body was wrapped in a blue cloak with a handkerchief draped over the face and was found upon inspection to have several deep stab wounds. From the highly detailed but kaleidoscopic testimony of several witnesses, it is possible to reconstruct with some precision the circumstances of the crime.

At about five in the morning, while it was still dark, don José Leandro had arrived on his rounds of the estate laborers' homes at the dwelling of José Clemente Lorea to wake him and summon him to work. José Clemente's wife, Juana Isabel, told the administrator that her husband had already left for the fields. José Leandro then went to the kitchen of the house (in a separate structure at the back) to light a cigarette at the stove and shortly returned to ask Juana Isabel who it was that was sleeping, wrapped up in a blanket or cloak, by the still-warm stove. She replied that it was José Tomás, a laborer often employed during the preceding two years on the estate, a bachelor who had lived for much of that time in the home of José Clemente and his wife. Don José Leandro had discharged the man from the estate's employ about a week earlier (for reasons unspecified) and was clearly chagrined to find him back again. He went back to the kitchen and woke José Tomás, challenging him brusquely with the words: "Tell me, man, didn't I kick you off the place and settle our accounts?" The man jumped up from his place on the floor, answered "I came back because the boss sent for me!" and without so much as another word drew from his clothing a long dagger (*terciado*) and stabbed his interlocutor repeatedly. Threatening to kill Juana Isabel if she ran for help, José Tomás made good his escape on the victim's horse. In the meantime don

José Leandro, mortally wounded, stumbled into the patio of the neighboring house of Tomás Aquino, another estate laborer (and Juana Isabel's brother), where he sat down heavily on the ground and was described in his death agony by Tomás Aquino as slipping first to one side, then the other. Another man, summoned by the shouting, was sent up to the owner's house (*la casa grande*) to fetch help, but the younger Siordia brother must have died in the interim. José Tomás's motive for the crime was never actually made clear, though presumably it was anger over his firing. The records of the case do not indicate if he was ever brought to justice.

The Siordia murder case is inherently dramatic and interesting, as such occurrences almost always are, for a number of reasons. It draws us across nearly two and a half centuries onto the common ground of several transhistorical, basic human emotions—anger, fear, shock—which we today experience no less than our ancestors, and we get both an aesthetic and emotional jolt when we contemplate such things. It also provides us with a more rarefied, sociological sort of glimpse at the bonds that held a traditional society together—kinship, residence patterns, and labor—and the conflicts—personal animosity, class resentment, perhaps ethnic tension—that were never far beneath the surface. But to the eye of the interested social historian or other observer, the Siordia murder case also presents a good deal of detail about how people lived in colonial Mexico two and three centuries ago, and even, by extension, how people were likely to have lived elsewhere in Latin America. We can glean some idea of what some rural working people at the time wore locally (produced cloaks and blankets), what they slept on and where (reed mats, on earthen floors), what sort of objects they habitually handled (cigarettes, weapons), how their houses were laid out (one room, cooking area separate), and so forth. This is my theme in the present chapter: the partial reconstruction of how people lived, in the material sense, in the area we now call Latin America over a period of about three centuries, from the advent of the Europeans at the start of the sixteenth century to the violent end of formal colonial rule (in most places) by about 1825.

Before we embark on that reconstruction, however, it seems appropriate to make a few general remarks about the importance of the study of material life as a window into social history, culture, and the mentality of a bygone era. The most obvious of these observations is that "things" matter immensely to all but the most disconnected human beings. We are, of course, ourselves material objects and understand much of the animate and inanimate world around us through projections, metaphors, and analogies between the "I" and "not-I," all of them rooted in the complex maze of language. Beyond this, however, material objects mediate between us and the environment, including other human beings. This begins with food (milk from the maternal breast, the first extra-uterine form of sociability) and goes on to embrace the pleasures of art (paintings, musical instruments), the consolations of religion (places of worship, ritual objects), the camaraderie of the tavern (intoxicants and the vessels they are consumed from), tenderness of the hearth (fire-tending tools and cooking pots), and the distinctions of rank (clothing, houses, carriages, and up to and including the ownership of other people as objects).

The importance of material life—of material objects, their symbolic and emotional meanings, and the social relationships in which they were embedded—was no less true of colonial Latin America than of our own day, but people's attitudes toward objects themselves were probably considerably different. I say *probably* because, as it turns out, it is rather difficult to find out how people felt about material objects—not just what they owned, in other words, but what they valued (though the two are obviously related). In any case, to delve into this wide historical question we must put ourselves into an archaeological frame of mind and guard against anachronistic transpositions of our own modern perceptions and attitudes onto people of past times. A few examples will serve to illustrate ways in which attitudes about the material world, most especially the world of man-made objects, may have changed over the last two hundred years or so, distancing us from the rural Latin Americans of 1525 or even 1825.

When one goes into a museum today, for instance, and sees the common household objects of even two centuries ago, one may be struck by their crudity—the rough surfaces, the asymmetries, the primitiveness of their design. Partly this is the effect of survival through time, of wearing and use by many hands, but also it is the result of their mode of manufacture: They were handmade. Aside from some textiles, almost all the material objects the average rural Latin American of two centuries ago saw around him or her would have been made by craftsmen in small enterprises, or even at home. Metallic objects were reasonably rare and expensive, molded plastic, cast metals, and machine-tooled steel absent completely, and most things were made of cloth, vegetable fiber, leather, wood, stone, adobe, fired clay, and occasionally of iron. Therefore, the homogeneity of factory-made objects would also have been missing, since hand manufacturing inevitably leaves signs of unevenness and outright imperfection. One interesting implication of this would be the way in which one person's possessions, such as tools, furniture, and even other objects like books, would quickly stand out from another's and acquire a sense of individuality and identity with the owner/user, the very opposite of the sense of material disposability found in alienated, modern post-industrial society.

On the other hand, things "in general," as a class of experience, and the power to acquire them, may well have had different meanings to a Latin American villager of the sixteenth, seventeenth, or eighteenth centuries than to a modern Latin American urbanite. People of that era led a pretty pared down material existence relative to us. In much of the modern industrialized world it does seem to be the case that the very multiplicity of material objects and the easy access to them we enjoy has made them *more*, rather than *less*, important. Objects for us may be more important indicators of power, social status, validation, and self-worth, among other immaterial concepts, than they were for our ancestors. But for us certain possessions (especially high-priced consumer durable goods) may represent proportionately *more* of our lifeblood than for them. Take, for example, our houses. For most middle-class homeowners today the value of their living places represents a number of years worth of labor, and its takes us a large part of a lifetime to amortize the loans that get us into these structures to begin with. For most ordinary Latin American country people of the colonial period, living under conditions of fairly simple building technologies, a few weeks work with adobe, stone, wood, and thatch would have sufficed to produce the average dwelling. What might this say about the affective attachment of people of that time to their houses, in contrast to us; not to their house*holds* (a rather different concept)—that is, their families or their homes—but to their houses as physical objects? The relatively inexpensive and simple reproducibility of dwellings suggests that the mystique of walls (adobe), floors (earthen), and roof (probably grass and wood) may have been less compelling for them than for us. (See Fig. 11.)

Finally, it seems likely that objects in early modern Latin America mediated between individual and community in ways now lost to our contemporary sensibilities. In a society of relative scarcity in which modern bourgeois notions of the comforts of home and consumerism were virtually unknown, and in which certain ideas about sociability were shared between indigenous American and Mediterranean cultural traditions, much of nonwork life was lived outside the house, in public spaces, examples being religious expression, gossip, and politics. One concomitant of this was a much stronger identity of individual with the local community than prevails in most modern societies. Thus, amongst the most highly valued material things two and three centuries ago in rural Latin America would have been constructed central spaces—village plazas, for instance—and the objects that filled them—churches, modest civic buildings, sacred and ritual artifacts. Country dwellers from the poorest villagers to members of local elites took much pride, for example, in the construction and decoration of their churches, in much the same way that we are told medieval Europeans did. Certainly modern cities have their symbols of urban pride, but one often has the feeling that these are more the offspring of civic boosterism than of a deep identification between individual and community. In the rural Latin America of the colonial centuries, the individual/community nexus was much stronger, and part of the symbolism of that bond was constituted by material objects felt in some sense to be owned by all.

Rural Diet, High and Low

Had the unfortunate don José Leandro de Siordia survived the morning of 21 August 1752, what would he have eaten for breakfast in the *casa grande* where help was so desperately but futilely sought even as he was dying? And what meal would Juana Isabel have prepared in the little kitchen off the back of her modest house had not the morning quiet and her domestic routine been so violently shattered? It should come as no surprise that down the hill in the workers' quarters the meal would have centered around maize, mostly in the form of the common tortilla, as it did for large parts of the Mexican urban population, as well. The killer José Tomás and probably all the rest of the estate's work force would have eaten cold or slightly rewarmed tortillas from the previous evening's meal, perhaps seasoned with a little chile pepper and salt, perhaps not. Fresh handmade tortillas were, and remain today for their devotees, about as close to gustatory heaven as one could hope to approach whilst in mortal form, but their preparation two or three times a day (they have a very short half-life) required back-breaking labor of women. The shelled maize had first to be steeped for several hours in lime-water, then pulverized on a specialized stone grinder (*metate* in Mexico), the dough (*masa*) patted out and cooked on a round, flat clay griddle, generally over some sort of open fire, and all by female hands.[2] With the tortillas to ward off the chill of even a summer morning at central Mexican altitudes (about five thousand feet above sea level in this case), the humbler sort of people in the workers' quarters might also have drunk *atole,* a thin maize gruel flavored with available sweeteners such as honey or semi-refined sugar, and still today, even in large cities, a welcome source of warmth, calories, and sweetness on chilly Mesoamerican mornings.

The main element in the rest of the day's meals would almost certainly have consisted of copious amounts of tortillas, both at midday and in the evening. These would have been accompanied by beans (*frijoles*), probably in a watery pot-liquor, possibly with the addition of (or replaced by) squash of some sort and small quantities of tomatoes, onions, or other locally produced garden vegetables. Meat, mostly in the form of beef, might have been eaten at the midday meal occasionally, and chickens on festive occasions, raised by Juana Isabel herself along with a pig or two on the land around her house. In fact the records of rural estates in Mexico from an early period show that beef (sometimes mutton or pork) formed part of the weekly rations of laborers and other dependents, if not in large amounts, though it is my impression that for most laborers meat rations tended to decline or even disappear in the later colonial period. As condiments, Juana Isabel would regularly have had in her house salt, various types of chile peppers, semi-refined sugar (*panocha*) of local manufacture, and possibly tiny amounts of more exotic items such as black pepper or sesame seeds, purchased with the small cash resources of a laboring family. At midday and evening all this was washed down with a cup or two of the ever-present pulque, a mild intoxicant made from the fermented juice of a variety of agave cactus (other varieties of the same plant produced the distillates tequila and mescal).

As a nutritional regimen in general, and allowing for large seasonal, geographic, social, and cultural variations even within Mesoamerica, this maize-centered diet probably provided adequate amounts of calories for most purposes—people's basal metabolic needs, prevailing work habits/demands, physical reproduction, and growth. This diet might include things like chunks of sugarcane to be gnawed on while working in cane fields or refineries, or wild fruit such as the ubiquitous Mexican prickly pear (*nopal*), eaten even today by peasants as they make their way through their daily work routines or amble around the countryside on their domestic errands. But this diet was low in certain sorts of vitamins, proteins, and especially animal fats, and could tip over into outright deprivation or famine conditions, as it did during the roughly decennial subsistence crises that hammered Mexico right up until the eve of independence from Spain in 1809–10, and which were known to occur with a somewhat less regular periodicity in other areas of the New World as well. This nutritional scenario and accompanying reduced immunological capacities may partly explain, in turn, why bouts of epidemic disease scourged large areas of Spanish America even during the eighteenth century, well after centuries-long exposure to Old World diseases could have been expected to reduce their epidemiologic virulence.

To return to the Labor de Rivera, what could don José Leandro have expected to eat on that long-ago August morning, had he not encountered José Tomás? He, too, would have breakfasted on maize tortillas, supplemented by the same condiments being eaten down the hill in Juana Isabel's house. In addition he would have drunk a steaming, frothy cup of chocolate, and also have munched a small amount of cheese or, if particularly hungry, some cold meat. If the estate produced wheat and there were an ambitious cook in the kitchen of the big house, wheat bread, alongside tortillas, might have formed part of his meal even at breakfast, but it was people in cities—even the working poor, including Indians—who were more likely to eat bread regularly. At midday he, his family, the more important estate retainers, and the occasional visiting local dignitary or other guests dined on tortillas and bread, with additional increments of meat, *pozole* (corn and pork porridge), or soups, cheese, fruit (at that time of year peaches and melons, but little in the way of fresh vegetables), and sweets. Then, as now, the best and most varied produce made its way to the table of urban consumers, leaving in its wake a relatively simple selection of foods. Don José Leandro usually washed down this fare with pulque, or if the family were prosperous, some imported Spanish brandy or wine. Later in the evening he supped on a light meal composed of the same foods as at lunch, perhaps embellished with chocolate again and more elaborate forms of the maize-centered cuisine. (See Figs. 13, 14.)

The maize-based diet, of course, though it embraced all of Mesoamerica, extended to much of South America (parts of the Andean area, tropical northern South America, and even Brazil), and eventually invaded substantial stretches of the Old World from southern Europe through Africa to east Asia, was not the only Latin American nutritional regimen in colonial times. The other three major ones were potatoes, manioc, and wheat. Potatoes were indigenous to the Andes and imported to the Old World, where by the eighteenth century they had become a dietary staple among European peoples as diverse as the Irish, French, Germans, and Russians. The starchy, tuberlike manioc root (also known as cassava, yucca, or tapioca), widely cultivated in tropical areas such as the Caribbean and lowland Brazil, had to be processed into a dried flour to be edible, since in one of its raw forms it contained potentially lethal quantities of hydrocyanic acid. But it could be produced plentifully in tropical zones and stored in the ground for long periods of time, thus increasing even further its striking adaptability. Columbus brought wheat with him in the form of hardtack on his initial voyages, and large quantities continued to be imported throughout the early sixteenth century, along with other fixtures of Mediterranean cuisine such as chick peas, beans, salt fish, cheese, vinegar, olive oil, and wine. Wheat, though more delicate and yielding less than maize, could adapt to temperate growing conditions and evolving agricultural systems in the New World, so that by the end of the sixteenth century the colonies were self-sufficient in it. These basic sources of calories were supplemented with other cereal or cereallike starches that nourished both men and beasts, several of them—rice, oats, barley, lentils, chick peas—native to the Old World, and some—for example, quinoa, a ricelike grain from an Andean grass—indigenous to the New.

As for most sedentary farming populations, even in our own age (certainly in the Third World), a starch-based diet has been the norm and meat consumption a relative rarity, with certain exceptions. In the Latin American case exceptions were found in certain regions. Seventeenth-century Brazil, for example (especially in the interior zones of the northeast, which emerged as a complement to the coastal sugar plantation sector), developed a cattle-based economy in which rural people used leather for everything and ate meat (and sometimes little else) as often as three times a day. Similar situations developed somewhat later on the Argentine pampas, the llanos of Venezuela, and the semiarid plains of large parts of northern Mexico. The relative abundance of animal flesh after 1550 or so was a novelty for the sedentary villagers of the former Aztec and Inca heartlands. Whatever the case, by the late colonial period there is substantial evidence that in some areas (Mexico, for example) population pressure and relatively inelastic agricultural productivity tended to raise meat prices faster than grain prices, thus shifting the popular (mostly rural) diet away from the former and toward the latter.

In the Andean highlands quinoa flour, prepared in the form of small griddle-cakes, primarily substituted for maize, though the latter was also consumed roasted. A sort of freeze-dried preparation called *chuño* made the most of the nutritional and preservational properties of the sturdy potato, while several varieties of beans and gourds complemented the central starch in the Andean diet. European-introduced beef and other sorts of meat (including the flesh of native cameloid species such as the llama and alpaca) were eaten in the form of the sun-dried strips called *charqui* (in English "jerky" or "jerked beef"). Another mammal indigenous to the Andes, the guinea pig (not really a pig but a rodent), had been domesticated during the pre-Columbian period and was much prized for food. While Mexican rural people drank pulque, Andean country dwellers guzzled *chicha,* also a fermented intoxicant, made from germinating maize kernels rather than cactus juice. Corresponding to the Mexican tequila and mescal were the Andean distillates *pisco* (from wine grapes)—by late colonial accounts a favorite among rural Indians when they could afford it—and *guarapo,* made from sugarcane. Indigenous Andean country dwellers made much use of the native coca plant and its stimulating properties, chewing its leaves to combat the lethargy-inducing effects of life and hard labor at high altitudes, and bequeathing to the modern world a distinctly mixed blessing. While Mexicans of all classes were inordinately fond of their chocolate, and all Latin Americans later of New World–produced coffee, South Americans from Argentina to the Andes during and after the colonial period drank copious amounts of mate, a tealike potable decocted from *yerba mate,* commercially produced on a large scale from about the seventeenth century in the area of Argentina and Paraguay, and traded over long distances.

In the big houses of Andean haciendas, and in the homes of landowners and the better-off sort in the zone's provincial towns and villages, diet overlapped with the more modest cuisines of peasant villagers and Indians in much the same way it did in Mexico, not becoming sharply distinct from them until the latter part of the nineteenth century. Elite diet was richer in animal protein and fats, wheat-based starch dishes, and overall culinary complexity, emulating—to the degree that the raw materials were available—the eating habits of Lima and other coastal cities. The famous stews (*pucheros,* also prepared in Mexico) and soups (*chupas*) of the coast and the narrow Andean lowlands were based on beef, mutton, pork, fish, and shellfish, supplemented with wheat, maize, and potatoes. To the east, in Portuguese Brazil, diet for rich and humble alike centered not on wheat, which did not do well in most areas because of the climate, but rather on manioc and maize along with sweet potatoes, peanuts, beans, fish, and the flesh of scrawny cattle raised in the interior and driven to the coast to be slaughtered. From the seventeenth century, the African cuisines associated with slaves began to influence Brazilian eating habits in significant ways; crops like bananas and okra were introduced, leaving their permanent stamp upon the country's diet.

Considerations of material life touched not only free Indian peasants and (for the most part white) landowners, but also the millions of black African bondsmen brought across the Atlantic to labor in the New World. Scholarly controversy has raged for decades as to whether the slaves' life was bitterer in city or country, in Anglo, Portuguese, or Spanish America. What is fairly clear, however, is that in the name of cost-effectiveness masters fed their slaves as little, as simply, and as cheaply as possible. Colonial manuals suggesting to slaveowners the optimal care and maintenance of their human chattels prescribed one sort of standard for food rations, common practice (judging by high slave mortality rates) entailed a less generous one. In late colonial Mexico, for example, the nominally prescribed diet of slave field hands on sugar plantations overlapped significantly with that of free Indian villagers, consisting for the most part of maize, some meat, salt, chile, and other items varying from estate to estate, but which might include sugar, honey, and tobacco. Slaves also probably grew some garden crops around their houses, and while there is no evidence that this reached the extent of the famous "provision grounds" of slaves in eighteenth-century Jamaica, it may have occupied a significant place in slave subsistence strategies. For colonial Brazil the evidence is quite consistent that slaves were not adequately fed by their owners, and that they ate everything they could get their hands on, including rats culled from the cane fields. Much as for free people, the central starch in the slave diet consisted of manioc, supplemented with rice and bananas. They very rarely ate fresh meat, more often salt meat or fish. On the coastal farms and plantations of colonial Peru, maize was the staple of slave diet, supplemented with wheaten bread, fish, plantains, sweet potatoes, the cheapest possible cuts of meat, and small amounts of tobacco and rum to dull the pain of a life of constant labor and degradation. Late-sixteenth- and seventeenth-century records in some areas reveal startlingly large prescribed rations of meat or fish and bread (respectively two and three pounds per adult per day), but whether these were honored is very doubtful.

In bringing to a close this discussion of food as an aspect of material life, I would like to make some brief remarks relating technology, diet, and social status in colonial Ibero- America. It is perhaps obvious, but nonetheless worth remarking, that people two and three centuries ago lacked a wide range of modern food-processing technologies that we take very much for granted (and some of which take their toll on our health): freezing, chilling, freeze-drying, vacuum-packing and tinning, chemical preservation and irradiation. Take for example such a simple thing as ice, available directly or indirectly today even in much of the Third World. Modern food technologies have tended to even out, at least to some degree in the industrialized world, changes in the overall food supply due to seasonal variation and perishability. Indeed, the perishability problem contributed greatly to culinary limitations and transportability across even relatively short distances. Items that we take for granted, such as certain dairy products and beer, for example, were not often accessible—even assuming sufficient income on the part of potential consumers—because of their short shelf-life and had to be produced locally or not at all. Long-distance trade in foodstuffs, therefore, was closely limited to commodities that would not spoil (for instance, grain), or to high-unit-value items like distilled drinks, mate, sugar, salt, tobacco, and coca.

In the absence of modern food technologies, therefore, the interplay of seasonality, perishability, and high transport costs would probably have imposed something like a natural ceiling on the sorts of food that would differentiate rich and poor, Juana Isabel's from don José Leandro's tables. In terms of the relationship of social status to food consumption, most consumers, whether city or country dwellers, would have had some access to highly desirable forms of animal protein and fats, for example, but social distinctions and culinary differences would have influenced how much they consumed. On the other hand, the variability across social classes and ethnic boundaries of clothing and other nonfood consumer products would have been greater than with dietary elements because of the easier preservation and transportability of the former.

Fig. 11. Indian thatched huts (jacales): (A) hipped roof (B) peaked roof.

Fig. 12. Town and country houses built by the Indians of Tezpetlaoztoc for their encomendero.

maxime autem illis abundat *Gustimala*. Hæc ille.

10   Sed antequam pleniorem hujus arboris deſcriptionem proſequamur, à *Fr.Xime-nez* jam ſæpius à nobis nominato, acceptam operæprecium fuerit, ramum arboris cum integro fructu hic apponere.

Indigenæ harum regionum (inquit *Ximenez*) ante Hiſpano-rum adventum, *Cacao* fructibus loco numiſmatum utebantur, hodieq; multis locis uſurpant. Ex iiſdem potum ſuum confi-ciebant, vini ignari, licet non 20 paucis locis vites, ſed ſilveſtres, naſcantur: Eſt autem *Cacahua-quahuitl* arbor magnitudine & foliis aurantiæ, ſed majoribus (*Herrera* comparat Caſtaneæ frondibus :) fructus illius eſt longus & ſimilis peponi, verum ſtryatus & ruſus, qui dicitur *Cacahuacintli*, plenus illis *Cacao* nucibus (quas ſupra exhibui- 30 mus) quæ diviſæ ſunt in duas partes æquales & bene compo-ſitas atque conjunctas; teneri ſunt nutrimenti, ſaporis inter dulcem & amarū medii, tem-perie nonnihil frigida & humi-da. Quatuor, quantum potui obſervare; hujus arboris reperiuntur ſpecies. Prima vocatur *Cacahuaquahuitl* quæ omnium maxima eſt & copioſiſſimos fert fructus. Se-cunda ejuſdem nominis, mediocris magnitudinis, frondes & fructus ferens longe mi-nores. Tertia appellatur *Xuchicacahuaquahuitl*, adhuc minor, cujus fructus exte- 40 riori parte magis ruber, interiori cæteris ſimilis. Quarta omnium minima: ideoque *Tlalcacahuaquahuitl* dicitur, id eſt, humilis ſive pumila *cacao* arbor, quæ fructum fert omnium minimum, licet colore nihil differat à cæteris. Omnes autem hi fru-

Fig. 13. Description and illustration of a cacao tree. Joao de Laet *Novus orbis seu Descriptionis Indiae* (Ladguni: Elzevieros, 1663).

CLACHIQUERO

Fig. 14. Mexican peasant collecting sap from the maguey plant. Carmen Sotos Serrano, *Los pintores de la expedición de Alejandro Malaspina*, (Madrid: Real Academía de Historia, 1982) fig. 444.

Fig. 15.
Mexican Indians.
Drawing by Felipe
Bauza. (Madrid:
Museo de America)

Fig. 16. Realejo women.
Drawing by Juan Ravenet.
(Madrid: Museo de America)

Fig. 17. Examples of Indian dwellings. Jean Baptiste Debret, *Voyage pittoresque et historique au Brésil* (Paris, 1834–39).

Clothing

The face of the slain don José Leandro was described as being draped with a handkerchief, his body wrapped in a blue cloak. As to the handkerchief, in the absence of other evidence to the contrary we may assume it to have been either printed cotton or silk, if the former of Spanish or Mexican manufacture, if the latter possibly from Spain or East Asia. At a guess the "cloak" was of wool, dyed with indigo or another natural colorant, and of local manufacture (though it might have come from Querétaro or another major textile center). This was the typical outer garment, with regional differences, of men of widely varying ethnicity and class in the Latin American highland zones from Mexico to southern South America, though white men of elite status tended rather to imitate prevailing European styles. The cloak had a number of names—*frazada, manga, sarape, poncho, ruana*—according to local usage and whether it had some sort of sleeves, was slit halfway down the middle, or simply had a hole for the head. Generally woven of sheep's wool (or even of alpaca or llama hair in the Andes), the garment was very adaptive in the temperate-to-cold highland climates, serving a number of purposes, from covering to blanket to protection in a fight. This versatile male apparel could be bought by country people at some great distance from the point of manufacture, assembled locally from cloth produced in the textile workshops (*obrajes*) of the Andean highlands or central Mexico, or made entirely with local materials and labor (Indians in far northern Mexico, for example, made *frazadas* from the wool of their own flocks). The costume of Mexican rural farmers and laborers of modest means was likely to be completed by loose cotton pants and shirt, leather sandals of home or local manufacture, and a broad-brimmed hat woven of straw or some other vegetable material.

This costume was quite stable over long periods of time, and remarkably similar across the greater Latin American area, though it would obviously have varied according to climate and available raw materials. In fact there is little evidence, judging by the case of Mexico, that it changed significantly in many rural areas until well into the twentieth century, with the advent of North American–style factory-made clothing. For peasant men in the Andean highlands everyday dress was very similar: heavier woolens—of such a weight and weave as to keep out cold and rain—replacing cottons at higher, colder altitudes. Leggings were wrapped around the lower leg for much the same reason. One engraving of a Chilean rural scene at the close of the colonial era by a foreign traveler with a good eye for detail (iconographic evidence underlies much of the treatment in this section) shows an obviously mestizo carriage driver wearing a tall, brimmed hat of some indistinguishable material (probably fiber), a patterned *ruana* fitting so closely about the torso that no shirt is in evidence, breeches to the knee, and a sort of half-shoe with metal spurs affixed to the heels, while the two white men inside the carriage are obviously in European-style dress. In geographical areas where cattle culture dominated the economy, such as northern Mexico, the Venezuelan and northeast Brazilian interior, and pampean Argentina, boots, leather breeches, hats, and other leather clothing would have played a larger part in the wardrobe. In lowland tropical areas, on the other hand, clothing obviously needed to be lighter, cotton was much more adaptive than wool (and in fact tended increasingly, because of aesthetic and health considerations, to capture much of the clothing market all over Latin America in the later colonial period), and outer garments might be abandoned entirely and footwear reduced to a minimum. As for the tropics, iconographic evidence from seventeenth-century Brazil shows slave men shirtless, in loose, knee-length pants, occasionally with headbands; and women dressed more elaborately in skirt, petticoat, blouse, and bodice, all of coarse cotton homespun.

Rural women in general, it would seem, even in the poorest of circumstances, dressed somewhat more elaborately than their menfolk, though as between rural working women and their elite urban sisters there was a universe of distinction. Indian women in the Andes tended to clothe themselves very simply, in dark-hued woolen dresses (the somberness possibly alleviated by a brightly colored fringe or other decorative motif) with short sleeves and knee-length hems, their legs bare and feet shod in thonged sandals. Atop this ensemble they wore the nearly universal loose cotton or wool blanket and a straw hat. In colonial Mexico, by all accounts, common female dress was somewhat more elaborate, though this would of course vary with individual and family economic resources. Again, bare feet or sandals were the rule for most rural women, but patterned skirts of wool or cotton might cover several layers of cotton petticoats, and blouses be overlaid with the traditional shawl (*rebozo*). The female outer garment, whether blanket or shawl, wool or cotton, shared the versatility of its masculine counterpart, serving as covering, carrier (for infants, objects), and quite possibly as sleepwear. (See Fig. 15.)

Rural dress, for reasons that we have mentioned, almost certainly marked off more obviously than diet the distinction between Indian and non-Indian, poor and rich, and was influenced at its upper reaches to a much greater degree by urban and European fashion. Choice of clothing was governed, of course, not only by ethnicity and economic resources, but also by occupation and the weather. But in general terms, for men the whiter and wealthier the individual, the more closely his costume would tend to approximate "European" styles; and this would have held true across the New World, probably producing an elite male dress much more homogeneous than that for nonelite men. This might mean undergarments of silk or linen as opposed to none at all, woolen felt rather than fiber hats, closer fitting pants or European-style knee-breeches in place of loose peasant garb, and leather boots instead of open footwear. Judging by the scant evidence we have, a white landowner was much more likely to wear a European-style short jacket with sleeves than a poncho while directing the work of his laborers. In fact, so synonymous did the man's sleeved jacket become with whites that during the Mexican wars for independence (1810–21) *chaqueta* became a derisory slang expression used by insurgents and their sympathizers to refer to royalists in particular or even whites in general. To take but one illustrative example, an itinerant Spanish merchant from western Mexico was wearing at the time of his death in 1733 a long, European-style overcoat with silver buttons, a short white jacket, blue pants of bombazine (a fine, corded cotton, most often figured), silk hose, and European-style shoes.

For rural women, as for men, the elaborateness and richness of dress increased directly with ascent up the socio-ethnic ladder. Late colonial female dress for women of the upper social strata was notably European in its style compared to that of peasant women, and was functionally more elaborate, including specialized dress for lounging about the house, riding, attending church, and entertaining. Depending upon means, age, social pretension, and individual taste, women could be expected to don more or less elaborate silken undergarments, chemises, hose, cotton petticoats, and European-style dresses. These were usually long-sleeved and of floor length and moderate décolletage. Outer wear consisted of full capes, fine cotton shawls, and lace *mantillas*. In eighteenth-century Peru, rural women of upper social standing must have worn some more modest variant of the female costume typical of Lima, central to which were the *saya* (a close-fitting skirt) and *manto* (a mantled overgarment), believed in combination effectively to disguise women and therefore discourage flirtatiousness and sensuality, but actually known for its suggestiveness. These items of dress were liberally, even excessively, decorated with an abundance of lace (especially from Flanders if means permitted), and complemented by the *mantilla* and *rebozo*. At higher, colder altitudes, such as the former Inca capital at Cuzco, the lighter fabrics of the coast (cotton, linen) were replaced with wool. Still, New World fashions often provoked negative comment from more fashion-minded European travelers. The further one ventured from a major metropolitan area, the more rustic and backward-looking even elite dress might appear. An illustration of a group of obviously upper-class men and women in the patio of a substantial Chilean country house, the men dressed in tall hats, short capes, knee-breeches, hose, and shoes, the women costumed demurely in long, somber dresses and shawls, has about it a distinctly archaic look, as though they had just stepped out of a European domestic painting of the sixteenth or seventeenth centuries. The venue of this scene (a late-eighteenth-century country house) suggests the next stop in our tour of the colonial material-scape—rural architecture; but first a detour to a country store.

A Commercial Interlude

Consumer items that colonial rural people could not grow, collect, or make for themselves might come to them through a number of channels. While commerce itself lies outside our theme, the range of options in the acquisition and use of material objects, and how and where they were acquired, certainly lie within it, I would maintain, since these circumstances were likely to affect how people felt about "things." Two of several major conditioning factors here were distance and consumer income.

An important variable that affected the range of material goods accessible to Latin American country people of the humbler sort was what geographers call "the friction of distance": that is, high transport costs where roads were generally bad, travel and trade often risky (subject to bandit or hostile Indian attacks and other disruptions), animal traction the major means of transport, and commercial profits on many items of common consumption too low to make their commercial sale worthwhile. In general this situation would have reinforced strongly the tendency of many sorts of goods in daily use to originate locally. Take, for example, the wood so much used for construction, farming implements, furniture, and above all for fuel. Settled farming populations tend over time to denude forested lands and even smaller woody vegetation, so that the work required to provide fuel for cooking and heating tended to increase and the cost of that fuel (stated either in cash equivalents or labor) to rise concomitantly. Certainly there is evidence of this in some areas in colonial Latin America, such as in the Valley of Mexico and its northern extensions even in early colonial times.

On the other hand, distance per se was not the only factor in access to goods. Some fairly isolated areas, of which the best examples are mining complexes (not agricultural, certainly, but nonetheless rural in the sense of being outside urban centers), may actually have enjoyed better access to a wider range of manufactured items and some foodstuffs, though at proportionally higher prices, than rural areas in closer proximity to cities. During most of its long history, for example, the great silver mining complex at Potosí in what is today Bolivia—a zone located at such high altitude that little can be produced there except mineral ores—functioned as a magnet for material goods of all sorts because of the sheer purchasing power and wealth concentrated there, energizing South American trade circuits stretching over thousands of miles. The same was true of many of the northern mining zones of colonial Mexico. Parral (in Durango), for instance, enjoyed during most of the seventeenth and eighteenth centuries a constant influx not only of locally produced basic foodstuffs, but also of textiles and other manufactured goods.

Of course, to be within the ambit of such wide-ranging commercial circuits was not necessarily the same as being able to purchase what they brought into reach. This depended not only on taste and consumption requirements, but also upon prices for purchased goods and the movement of real wages (what people's incomes could actually buy at constant prices). These factors impinged, in turn, both on people's living standards in the short run, and on their expectations (certainly those of working people and peasants, the majority of the rural population) of what they would own or consume during their lifetimes. This, in turn, influenced their worldview and attitude toward material life in fundamental ways. In terms of prices for basic consumer items, there is substantial evidence to indicate that the cost of living for working families in southern Peru, for example, may actually have fallen between 25 and 35 percent in the years from 1680 to 1820; something similar may have occurred in Brazil during the first half of the eighteenth century.[3] Standards of living— that is, what rural people were actually able to consume—did not necessarily improve under such conditions if money wages did not improve at the same time. The fact is that we simply do not know enough about rural wages at this point to make much of a statement one way or another for most of Latin America. This is somewhat less the case with eighteenth-century Mexico, where it is rather clear that rising prices for maize and other items of popular consumption, combined with largely stagnant money wages, produced a fall in the purchasing power of rural working people of something on the order of 25 percent over the course of the century. This meant that over time a larger proportion of family income was spent on the bare necessities—food, rent, clothing, taxes—and a smaller proportion on the purchase of small amenities and luxuries, including manufactured items. Income distribution in Mexican society as a whole was probably pushed toward the upper rungs of the social ladder, as access to material goods and life expectations for the popular classes in both country and city degraded.

Still, even taking all this into account, the range of consumer items available in country stores to rural people of all classes was fairly impressive, though variable according to time and place. On the sparser end, for example, the rather pared down, backwoods life of rural Argentina in the late eighteenth and early nineteenth centuries supported small general stores (*pulperías*) that might have functioned to some extent as centers of gaucho conviviality (especially if they sold alcoholic beverages), but were poorly stocked. An English traveler of the 1810s found the following articles for sale:

> a little *canna,* or spirit distilled from the sugar cane, cigars, salt, onions perhaps, and so near the city bread, but farther in the interior, this last article is not to be procured; so that the traveler, unless he carry bread with him, must live, like the country-people, on beef alone."[4]

In the countryside near Caracas in the late eighteenth century, on the other hand, such stores stocked, among food and other consumer items alone, various alcoholic drinks, sugar, cacao, maize, bread, biscuits, flour, rice and beans, bacon and other pork products, salt, candles, firewood, and soap. Detailed inventories of the stocks of three modest mercantile establishments in Mexico, separated by nearly 150 years in time—two in the northern mining district of Parral (1641), one in the western central farming town of Cocula (1770)— overlap to a great degree and show an impressive array of material goods available to rural consumers.[5] Among the inventoried items were a large variety of foodstuffs, ranging from grain, beans, lentils; to chocolate, spices, salt, and

dried fish; ready-made clothing and yard goods of both domestic and imported origin (Chinese, Spanish, French); tools, kitchen implements, pottery
from Puebla, harness, containers of various sorts; and paper, steel, and religious objects (crucifixes, reliquaries, rosaries, and medallions with images of
the Virgin or St. Christopher). Most of the items were of local or Mexican
provenance, with a small but significant proportion originating in Europe or
East Asia via the Spanish Manila trade.

If the consumer could not (or would not) go to the goods, the goods might
come to him or her. A similar but somewhat reduced range of consumer items
was available to country people through itinerant traders (*mercaderes
viandantes*) who traveled the backroads of Latin America from Brazil to
Mexico well into modern times. As it happens, one such merchant met a fate
similar to that of don José Leandro de Siordia in the same area about twenty
years earlier. Don Juan de la Escalera, apparently a European Spaniard, was
murdered by a person or persons unknown on a country road near Ahualulco
in 1733, his chest traversed by a single fatal sword thrust. The inventory made
of his property included a good deal of ready-made clothing, such as several
types of stockings for both men and women, blouses, *rebozos,* petticoats, jack-
ets, waistcoats, and even a wig, in addition to much yardage and sewing material, from large quantities of French lace, Chinese ribbon, Portuguese thread,
raw silk and silken thread, cotton cloth from Mexico, to pins and buttons. Also
among Escalera's stock were hardware and household items such as folding
knives, brooms, hoes, and raw indigo dye, as well as a respectable quantity of
jewelry, religious items, and gewgaws, including coral, enamel, and other
beads, earrings, copper rings, silver reliquaries, rosaries, and combs. Completing the picture were a limited number of nonperishable food items, among
them cinnamon and cacao beans. (See Fig. 16.)

There were yet other channels aside from direct purchase with money
through which colonial country people might acquire material goods, and it is
not unreasonable to suppose that the mode of acquisition affected people's
attitudes toward their role as consumers in general, and toward the things
they acquired in particular. Though colonial economies were far from "natural" (that is, economic systems in which goods changed hands through trade
and barter, rather than through the intermediacy of money), all over Latin
America rural people in particular were very often paid, at least in part, in
things rather than cash. Take, for example, the rural laborer Nicolás García,
whose wages on the Hacienda Santa Cruz (again in the neighborhood of
Ahualulco, Mexico) are noted in the estate administrator's accounts for the
years 1747–49. During this period, in addition to basic food rations including
maize and meat, García received (partially in lieu of his nominal money wages,
and in addition to small amounts of cash) a saddle, large amounts of cloth, a cape,
a hat, some petticoats, a quantity of tobacco, and meat and other foodstuffs. In
addition, he took part of his wages as payments to a tailor (presumably to make
clothing from the cloth he also received) and in the value of a baptism for a child.

This kind of arrangement, we may imagine, tended to personalize the colonial economy in ways unfamiliar to the impersonality of money transactions in highly commercialized modern societies. Aside from important economic implications for the colonial period (such as economic premiums for property-owners who controlled the distribution of goods through estate stores [*tiendas de raya*]), there are some interesting social implications, as well. First, the payment of wages in kind by master to laborer may often have been conflated with ritual expenditures by the landlord for such things as religious celebrations, and the fact that the material subsistence needs as well as the *immaterial or spiritual* needs of dependent rural people were met from the same source may have acted somewhat to soften class and ethnic lines in the colonial countryside; had all wages been paid in money, this would not have been the case. Second, such arrangements limited consumer choice to some degree, since what might have been spent on other items had the wherewithal been received as cash wages was instead received directly in the form of a fairly limited range of items, thus undoubtedly forming people's ideas about what they could or could not own, and how they felt about the range of consumer goods possibilities in general. Finally, in the case of large parts of the rural population in the colonial period, we are looking at passive rather than active consumers, at people whose consumption of material goods was both constrained and socially embedded in ways unimaginable to modern consumers who stand alone in the marketplace.

Housing

The nature of Tomás Aquino's and Juana Isabel's house is only hinted at in the account of the murder that took place there, but we are probably not far wrong in thinking it much like other humble rural housing pictured and described in travel and other accounts, its design and construction likely to have changed little over the course of the colonial period and even into the nineteenth century. The main dwelling—earthen-floored, low, of one story, and windowless—would almost certainly have been limited to a single room constructed of simple building materials obtainable locally, most likely of crude, whitewashed adobe (sun-dried mud-and-straw) blocks and some sort of thatch roof supported on wooden cross beams or a central pole. If the stove (itself a simple, low structure of stones or adobe, fueled with wood or charcoal)—the house's only site of cooking and source of heat—was in the main structure rather than in a lean-to at the back, there may have been a hole in the roof for the escape of smoke, though at times the smoke simply exited out the door, blackening the walls and ceiling over the years. In the tropical lowlands of Mexico and other areas, adobe construction might be replaced by the more adaptive bamboo or other light materials for walls and palm-thatch roofs. For the really poor, hut walls could be constructed of closely set organ cactus (as they still are today in some places) and roofed with some sort of thatch. The value of these humble dwellings was very low whether owned independently, or rented, or received as a perquisite by estate laborers. For example, while the elaborate *casa grande* of don José Prudencio de Cuervo near the Mexican town of Tequila was evaluated at nearly eight thousand pesos in 1811, the thirty-six huts (*jacales*) of his permanent resident labor force were valued at only two pesos each (about two weeks wages for a rural laborer at the time). Interiors were uniformly simple, unadorned, and relatively barren. Fanny Calderón de la Barca described the homes of Indian peasants in central Mexico in the nineteenth century in much the same terms we have used above, adding that they typically contained small altars with simple religious icons, crude pottery, religious images decorating the walls on occasion, and personal possessions (clothing, cooking utensils, tools) hung on hooks in the walls.

In the Peruvian sierra, Indian peasants constructed their houses out of materials similar to those used in Mexico—adobe (which helped to retain the interior heat) and thatch—with the difference that the shape was round, igloolike. The scarcity of wood in the high mountains meant that heating and cooking relied on the burning of animal dung (as in India and other areas of the world today). The more prosperous peasant might have several different buildings for living, cooking, and storage. As in Mexico, interiors were sparsely furnished, most personal possessions either hung on the walls or stored in wooden trunks. Chairs and tables were virtually unknown, beds would have consisted of low wooden platforms covered with blankets and ponchos, and people sat on the floor. In colonial Brazil the housing of rural working people was similarly simple. The slave quarters (*senzalas*) on Brazilian sugar plantations consisted of mud-walled, thatched huts or simple rowhouses, of lighter materials but otherwise of similar construction to those on Mexican estates, and similarly low in value. All over Latin America, climate permitting, such humble dwellings would have had small gardens planted around them. (See Fig. 17.)

It should come as no surprise that we know a good deal more about the housing of the wealthy and powerful than of the poor and humble. The images we have of the baronial splendor in which great colonial landowners lived— *hacendados*, *fazendeiros*, *estancieros*, depending upon mother tongue and local usage—turn out to be largely exaggerated or simply incorrect. Certainly there were great rural houses that bordered on the luxurious, and wealthy landowning clans might own elaborate townhouses for their frequent sojourns to the provincial and viceregal capitals, but for the most part the *casa grande* was built for functionality, spaciousness, comfort, and even defense rather than conspicuous show. Building materials would have overlapped in kind substantially with those of more humble constructions, relying basically on adobe, complemented with stone, tile for roofing, stucco for the adornment of walls, carved wooden beams and the occasional paneled interior. Multiple rooms, spacious but simple, were laid out off Mediterranean-style central courtyards, connected by colonnaded corridors; a variety of functionally specific outbuildings completed the picture. (See Fig. 12; compare Fig. 11, p. 53.)

Take, for example, the *casa grande* on José Prudencio de Cuervo's hacienda alluded to above. The 1811 inventory enumerated a main living room (*sala*), a master bedroom, and ten additional rooms, all well roofed; a chapel licensed for Masses; a variety of attached rooms dedicated to storage, soap-making, and sugar-making; a central great patio with grain storage bins; and enclosed orchards with fruit trees. It is interesting to note that relative to the valuation of nearly 8,000 pesos placed upon the house, the furniture and religious objects in the chapel were inventoried at 300 pesos, while all the furniture and other items in the house itself were evaluated at only 245 pesos. Indeed, the sparseness of decoration, furniture, and possessions in general in elite houses in the Latin American countryside from Mexico to Brazil evoked constant, somewhat bemused comment from late-colonial and early-nineteenth-century travelers. Maria Graham noted this same characteristic in substantial rural houses of the middling sort in early-nineteenth-century Chile, emphasizing the wide and gracious verandas so well suited to the temperate climate and a life lived largely out of doors, but also commenting on the lack of windows (making for a perpetual gloom in interior rooms) and the plank rather than stucco ceilings, a concession to the frequent earthquakes of the Andes.

The same problem of seismic instability plagued Peru, and house-builders took account of it in employing such techniques as leather thongs to fasten beams in place of nails and light partitioning walls. In the words of one modern authority, buildings in earthquake zones were supple to the point of being "cartilaginous." In a substantial country house in southern Peru, one late-colonial traveler noted that the family's beds were strategically placed beneath interior arches four to six feet thick as a precaution against earth tremors. A French traveler of around 1800 described a country house with a colonnaded courtyard and very large, high-ceilinged rooms, the bedrooms windowless and wooden shutters used in the main living areas to close the unglazed openings. The whole was furnished very simply with pieces of local manufacture, primarily of wood, leather, and horsehair, with a good deal of silver tableware in evidence, and occasional tapestries or paintings of religious or genealogical motif adorning the walls.

A Brief Look at Other Items in the Material-Scape

In closing, I would like to devote some very brief attention to two aspects of the rural material-scape: the disposition of private goods in wills, and the community ownership of religious icons.

Testaments from colonial Mexico survive in abundance in the registers of small-town notaries and court records, though generally they relate to people of modest means on up the social scale, and very seldom to the working poor. To cite but a few examples, we have a cluster of wills from the Guadalajara area, in western Mexico, dating from the eighteenth century. Matías Suárez, a modest rancher from Poncitlán, near Lake Chapala, and a native of Tenerife, in the Canary Islands, died in 1720. His testament listed in detail his livestock and its money value, an African slave or two, his land, and outstanding debts owed him by local people. His personal property consisted of some silver pieces, a modest amount of furniture, a few religious paintings, and his clothing, saddles, and arms. Nicolás Méndez Vallesteros, a small-scale sugarcane farmer, died at the nearby town of San Cristobal de la Barranca in 1758, leaving a will that enumerated his horse-operated sugar mill, attached lands, and livestock. It also listed in considerable detail his agricultural tools, even down to the weight of several hoes and other implements. Don Juan de Olivares, another middling farmer from the area, died in 1775 and detailed in his will the disposition of his carpentry tools, a pair of breeches "of blue Castilian cloth," and the branding iron he left to a local religious brotherhood. Even more modest was the personal property of don Manuel Sánchez Lomelin, a small farmer from Tequila, who listed under personal property only his carpentry tools ("as this was my trade"), a few agricultural implements, his saddle, and arms.

The evidence of these and other similar documents suggests a number of tentative conclusions, none of which are in themselves very surprising, but all of which bear emphasis. First, they reinforce the impression of a fairly sparse material existence even amongst those rural people of modest to middling means, be they Indian or white. Second, such documents tend to indicate the value of the exotic, particularly those items with a European provenance— Juan de Olivares's tender evocation of his blue Castilian pants illustrates this—worth almost certainly attached to the mystique of the mother country itself (with affective value heightened by high price) and social status. Relatedly, the punctiliousness one sees so frequently in listing items like saddles and arms, particularly by rural people of a middling status, had a good deal to do with their effort to reinforce their own social position by setting themselves off from the sea of darker, poorer people around them. This emphasizes for them (as for us) the symbolic value of material things in addition to their use value. Finally, although a certain amount of private property must have been disposed of through extra-testamentary means, the emphasis in the wills themselves is overwhelmingly on the disposition of *productive* property, even among personal possessions. We thus see enumerated items most easily convertible to cash value (readily resalable) or costly to begin with, but along with them the simple tools and equipment, livestock, and other things necessary to production in the rural framework. This implies more of an ideology of "producerism"—a belief in the value and virtue of productive labor—than we might otherwise imagine if we were to take too literally the stereotypical wisdom about patterns of work, leisure, and consumption in traditional agrarian societies or in the contemporary Third World.

Moving from the sphere of private to that of public, or communal, property closes the argument about how colonial people viewed the world of man-made objects and provides at the same time a bridge from that world to the next. Apart from the lands held in common by most rural (especially Indian) communities in the colonial period, the most important publicly owned material items would have been sacred objects, starting with their chapels and churches, the altars and other sacred furniture therein, and extending through religious art to locally venerated icons such as figures of Jesus, the Virgin, and the Saints. Contestation between social groups over the physical possession, ownership, or meaning of these objects could unite communities or tear them apart, since they were construed as symbols of community identity and of the special relationship of a locality to supernatural (divine) forces. There must also have been some sense in which the icon—the material object—owned the community members/believers, rather than the other way around, since the divinities associated with such objects offered special protection to their worshipers. To cite some examples, the "kidnapping" and/or destruction of religious statues is known to have occurred in cases of land conflict between Indian peasant villages and neighboring landowners or even other villages. The clear assumption in such violent confrontations was that if the symbol and protector of village identity could be removed, the community itself might be weakened or even exterminated. In one interesting case, village factions united against the local priest in Atlautla near Mexico City in 1799 when he attempted to sell out of the pueblo's church an altarpiece dedicated to Our Lady of the Sorrows, leading to a near violent confrontation with local Spanish authorities and the reinforcement of village solidarity in the process.

To close with a last illustrative anecdote, we may cite the case of the riot that took place in the town of Cuauhtitlan, a few miles to the north of Mexico City, in December 1785. A rumor had been circulating for some days among the area's Indian parishioners that the local priest intended to repair a much-venerated effigy of the Virgin Mary, which the Indians of the town claimed as theirs and the Spanish inhabitants as theirs. The Indians maintained that altering the body, robes, or especially the face of the statuette was a sacrilege, while the priest insisted the icon was desperately in need of repair because the hollow body had become a nest for rats that were steadily gnawing through the clothing. In the course of this controversy a violent riot was triggered in which the homes of several local Spaniards were sacked or destroyed and the priest himself chased from the town. But where, we may ask, did the locus of divinity actually lie? For the Indians, apparently, it lay in the material object itself, and for the Spaniards in the less literal, representational connection between object and divinity. Harking back to some considerations raised at the beginning of this chapter, the anecdote emphasizes the role of material objects as symbols of group and/or community solidarity. Beyond that, however, it underscores the multivalent quality of material life, and the objects that constitute it, as mediating not only between humans and the natural world, but also amongst human beings, and even between them and their conceptions of the supernatural.

Notes

1. The archives consulted for this essay were Biblioteca Pública del Estado de Jalisco, sections Bienes de difuntos, Manuscritos catálogados, and Archivo Judicial de la Audiencia de la Nueva Galicia; Archivo del Arzobispado de Guadalajara; Archivo de Instrumentos Públicos, Guadalajara, sections Tierras and Protócolos notariales; and Archivo General de la Nación (Mexico), sections Criminal and Clero regular y secular.

2. It is interesting to note that long after hand-operated and then electric- or gasoline-powered corn grinders (*nixtamal* mills) became available in rural Mexico in the nineteenth and twentieth centuries, men in particular pressed their womenfolk to continue the age-old, labor-intensive methods of grinding maize, insisting that mill-prepared dough did not have the same taste. One modern scholar had pointed out that this was a socially acceptable way of controlling women's labor-power and actions in a society still strongly patriarchal in tone, and in which characteristically strong ideas about female chastity and honor prevailed. Arnold Bauer, "Millers and Grinders: Technology and Household Economy in Meso-America," *Agricultural History* 64 (1990): 1–17.

3. See the excellent articles on Peru and Brazil, respectively, by Kendall Brown and Dauril Alden, in Lyman L. Johnson and Enrique Tandeter, eds., *Essays on the Price History of Eighteenth-Century Latin America* (Albuquerque, N.M., 1990).

4. E. E. Vidal, *Picturesque Illustrations of Buenos Ayres and Monte Video . . .* (London, 1820), 67, cited in Jay Kinsbruner, *Penny Capitalism in Spanish America: The Pulperos of Puebla, Mexico City, Caracas, and Buenos Aires* (Boulder, 1987), 2.

5. The Parral stores are described in Peter Boyd-Bowman, "Two Country Stores in XVIIth-Century Mexico," *The Americas* 28 (1972): 237–51.

CHAPTER THREE

Agrarian Technology and Changing Ecosystems

Juan Carlos Garavaglia

Part of any discussion of the rural dimensions of a society is a consideration of the ecological impact of humans on the land they inhabited. What were the relationships between man, land, crops, and environment in colonial Latin American? What were the principal technological changes contributed by the Europeans, and how was this technology adapted to the American landscape? How did various social groups compete for the use of land? These are some of the questions this essay will answer.

For purposes of comparison, a number of concrete examples have been chosen from two dramatically different regions: the Río de la Plata and central Mexico. The former is characterized by an abundance of fertile land and a low population density; the latter is characterized by precisely opposite conditions. This contrast both enriches the analysis and allows for an exploration of the variety of relationships between people and environment in colonial Latin America.

Ecosystems and Agrarian History: Some Definitions

In this work ecosystems are defined as communities of living things involved in reciprocal exchanges that take place within a biological environment, and in turn, actively modify that environment.

Agriculture is a specific type of ecosystem, an agrisystem. The agrisystem is an exporting ecosystem, where the crop produced is the element exported. Destined for consumption "outside" the ecosystem, the crop breaks the continuity of the food chain and thereby impoverishes it. This impoverishment, the

75

result of the harvest, can only be compensated by new contributions to the system. Mankind, from the very beginning of his relationship with plants and animals on their way to domestication, provided a number of responses to the problem of impoverishment. Among these were utilization of surplus harvests of plants and animals, increase in the supply of water through irrigation systems, more effective use of the land, and introduction of complex systems of crop rotation, combining fallowing (a period whereby the land was allowed to rest in order for it to "recuperate" naturally) with the use of vegetables that return to the soil some of the nutrients taken by the crop.

Clearly agrisystems refer to relationships among plants, animals, humans, and the abiotic environment, that is, climactic, soil, and hydrological elements. These elements both modify, and are themselves modified, by human action. In addition there are specialized agrisystems, such as those that center around the cultivation of certain grains ("cereal culture"), fruits and vegetables ("horticulture,") or certain animals ("ranching" and "herding"). In establishing these biological relationships with plants and animals, people simultaneously create a fixed social relationship. This, in turn, modifies, alters, and complicates the dynamic of the ecosystem. The influence of these relations on the ecosystem comprises a substantial part of human history.

Ecosystems in the Río de la Plata

The Cereal/Horticultural Ecosystem of Buenos Aires

To European travelers accustomed to the country life of England or to bureaucrats raised in the north of Spain, the Platine plains appeared to be an enormous space, one empty of humans and full of enormous herds of semiwild cattle. This view has been exaggerated and unduly simplified, but a comparison of this region with that of the Mexican *meseta* or the Andean world does little to dispel this initial impression.

At the close of the eighteenth century, Buenos Aires counted some 40,000 inhabitants. This primarily Spanish population constituted an important market for the fertile surrounding countryside; more than 200,000 Castilian *fanegas* of wheat (or approximately 133,000 English bushels), were consumed in the city each year, as well as great quantities of fruit and vegetables. Another 200,000 *fanegas* of alfalfa went to feed herds destined for urban markets. Mutton and beef, of course, were the central protein components of the *porteño* diet of that time.

As with other colonial cities surrounded by fertile lands, various agricultural concentric circles formed around the city. A belt of mixed fields producing fruit, vegetables, and forage gave way to a second belt, composed of cereal farms of diverse sizes, and a third, more distant ring, where cereal production

Eighteenth-Century Rural Buenos Aires

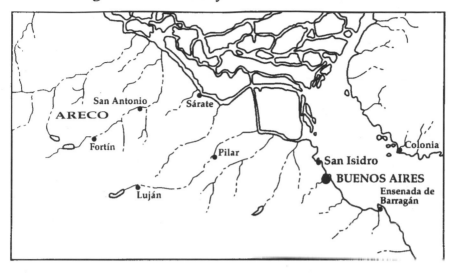

alternated with cattle, horse, sheep, and mule raising on larger properties. Last, in the outer circle, stock raising enjoyed an undisputed reign. The abundance of suitable pasture land in these last two rings was such that mutton and beef were comparatively cheap in relation to other areas of Hispanic America.

San Isidro, a region to the north of the city, was situated between the first and second circles within both horticultural and cereal ecosystems. At the beginning of the nineteenth century, more than five thousand people lived here, working on *chacras* and *quintas* of all types and sizes. At times these estates adjoined one another, but at other times they were separated by living fences formed by plants such as the American aloe (*Aloë*, L.), agaves (*Agave*), or prickly pear cactus (*Opuntia inermis*); fields were also separated by adobe walls, some supplemented by ditches. All types of European fruit abounded, particularly, figs (*Ficus carica*), quince (*Cydonia vulgaris*), peach (*Persica vulgaris*) and apple (*Malus sylvestris*) trees.

Climactically, this was a temperate zone. With frequent rains in the spring and autumn and sufficiently high humidity during the summer, a mild climate marked by distinct summer and winter seasons, and rich, dark meadowland soils (loess and mud), the region was ideally suited for the production of wheat.

At the beginning of the nineteenth century, the rural zone to the north of the city of Buenos Aires produced between 30 and 40 percent of the area's cereal crop and more than 50 percent of the seasonal fruit and vegetables for the Buenos Aires market. That is, some sixty thousand to eighty thousand Castilian *fanegas* of wheat, some eight thousand *fanegas* of barley, two thousand *fanegas* of maize, and less easily quantified amounts of alfalfa, vegetables, orchard crops, and fruit were harvested here each year. Cattle production for the Buenos Aires market was virtually nonexistent, although some twenty thousand cattle, horses, mules, and sheep populated the area.

A brief look at the agricultural calendar can help one understand the complexity of crop production. January, the height of summer in the southern hemisphere, was the month of the late maize sowing (*Zea mays*), timed so that the grain—if not nipped by the morning frosts of May—produced young ears of corn in April and May. Different varieties of beans (*Phaseolus vulgaris*) were also sown at the same time. The relationship of corn and bean production appears to be a legacy of the native past, inasmuch as it is commonly found in historically native agricultural regions throughout Meso- and South America. This is a dual—even triple—relationship (recognizing the ideal nutritional complement of these crops to man), and an association that benefits both plants. The bean climbs up the corn stalk, thus increasing its yield. It also provides an additional dividend, in that it, like all legumes, is able to trap atmospheric nitrogen, enriching the soil and, as a consequence, producing a larger maize harvest. Maize, beans, and squash (*Cucurbita moschata*), all closely associated with each other, were "stalk" plantings, cultivated by placing seeds in small holes and covering them by hand, a direct influence of native planting techniques.

February was the month to sow barley (*Hordeum vulgare*), an fast-growing grass destined for livestock forage. It was scattered in plowed furrows or patches. The ground was plowed again after sowing, and the seed covered and packed by the passage of a light harrow (*rastra*). Barley planting could continue into March, when the first signs of autumn appeared.

April was the month to plant alfalfa (*Medicago*), a leguminous plant grown for forage, which also served as a supplemental vegetable. Once the land was prepared, the seed was broadcast thinly over the field. After a return pass of the plow and harrow, there was another, heavier scattering of seed. Another pass of the plow and light harrow covered the seed.

Although the ideal time for wheat sowing began in June, early planting could begin in May. The wheat cycle is tied to soil moisture, because to begin the process of germination, the seed must accumulate almost 40 percent of its dry weight in water. The earlier one sowed wheat, therefore, the less seed required. Early preparation of the fields also prevented giving free rein to the weeds that might later choke the young shoots. If sowing were left until the end of July or August—winter—a greater "charge" of seed would be needed to produce the same yield. Wheat required the same time to mature as barley. It was sown in patches and furrows, then covered by a pass with the plow and lightweight harrow.

The major sowing of maize for grain began during September and October, just as the first buds of the southern hemisphere spring appeared. Again, corn complemented beans and squash. In addition the peanut, another legume which performs a function similar to the bean, could be planted. None of these seeds—each a heritage of the pre-Hispanic indigenous tradition—were scattered in the European manner; they were planted in mounds. In October, early spring in the southern hemisphere, the days began to lengthen, and wheat, like all winter grains a plant of long days, grew quickly, but the late frosts of September and October could adversely affect flowering and setting—the most delicate stages in the life of this grass—and thus threaten the crop.

November was the month set aside for the preparation of the threshing floor for wheat and barley. The floor was carefully cleaned and packed down by the threshing mares. It had to be prepared before the harvest in order to avoid any waste when the grain was threshed.

December is the beginning of summer, and the month in which the harvest, the central and most labor-intensive activity of the agricultural cycle, began. Depending on latitude, temperature, and amount of summer rainfall, the harvest extended until the middle of February. The threshing and storage of grain followed.

This complex cycle was not found in all of the region's cultivated lands; this degree of intricacy characterized only a fraction of its farms. The mixture of horticultural and cereal-growing aspects in this ecosystem, however, was not unusual; in San Isidro, as would later be the case in many areas of Europe, activities were intermixed, and it is neither easy nor useful to separate them. For the owners and renters of small properties, one activity complemented another. The same sort of complementary production was found on large estates.

Some large *chacras* could be truly imposing. In 1799 the estate of don José Luis Cabral, for example, measured almost 6,000 *varas* (approximately 558 acres or 226 hectares). With a frontage of 1,000 *varas* and a depth of one league, the land was surrounded on all four sides by a cactus fence. Within this irregular parallelogram, there was a grove of peach trees, another of willows (*Salix*), and two of *tala* (*Celtis spinosa*) and thorn trees (*Pyracanthata*). A number of houses and other structures were also located within the *chacra*. Valued at more than ten thousand pesos, the fences and trees represented more than 55 percent of its worth. The estate's value was directly related to its productive capacity and to its proximity to an urban market, where its harvest of cereals, orchard crops, and fruit could be sold. In addition, another important source of income for this type of estate were payments in agricultural goods made by tenant farmers. In 1819, on another large *chacra* in San Isidro, twenty-six tenants supplied a total of 187 *fanegas* of wheat from their year's harvest as rent. When added to the owner's harvest, and the yield the tenant farmers realized from the property, the total wheat harvest of the *chacra* was about 600 *fanegas*.

As in all of Spanish America, the agricultural implements used on these farms were quite poor. Plows were generally very simple, and had only one iron blade. They were more closely related to the Iberian plow than to the heavier, wheeled type. There is no mention of a moldboard in the few extant references. (See Figs. 18, 19.)

Metal was used for sickles, axes, and shovels. Some hoes with metal parts appear in inventories, but these, as well as the rakes, pitchforks, and harrows were, except for their cutting parts, mostly made of wood. The harrows, as in Mexico and in North America, were made from branches tied to transversal sticks. Such use of wood was common in most of the agricultural peasant civilizations of the time. In this vegetable- and cereal-based agrisystem the role of the hoe, the shovel, and the rake was quite important. (See Figs. 20–24.)

One should not be too surprised by the simplicity of the agricultural tools, as they appear to have been appropriate to the functions demanded by agriculture on rich, yielding land with abundant rainfall. It must be remembered that lower levels of technology are not always correlated with technologically "backward" agriculture.

The wheat and barley harvest began with the workers cutting the spikes with sickles. The type of wheat under cultivation was much taller than present-day hybrids and was therefore very sensitive to the wind. It had to be cut quickly, before the slightest threat of a storm. Once armloads of wheat had been gathered and tied into sheaves, they were put aside to await threshing. Threshing was done with teams of threshing mares or castrated stallions moving around the circular threshing floors. When the mares had finished the treading and the grain had been separated from the straw, the wheat had to be winnowed. To do this, one had to wait for an appropriate gust of wind and then, using rustic wooden pitchforks—or, more rarely, winnowing shovels designed for this purpose—the wheat would be shaken in the air, allowing the broken straw to fly outside of the threshing floor. This very ancient practice, recorded since the Classical Era in the Mediterranean world, was the most common way of ending the threshing season.

As can be imagined, the loss of grain was enormous. It began at the very first moment of harvesting, when much of the grain was "beheaded." Although this problem could be avoided by harvesting the grain before it reached its ideal maturation point, grain had to be dry before threshing. More loss occurred when the wheat in the field was lifted onto calfskin slings in order to move it to the threshing floor. At the threshing floor the animals themselves ate some of the grain before they began their work. Since winnowing was usually done with pitchforks, a considerable amount of grain flew away with the straw. Needless to say, a downpour during any of these steps would significantly reduce the yield.

One of the most difficult moments for a farmer with few resources came once the grain was ready. The high percentage of humidity within the grain made preservation from one harvest to the next very difficult; storage systems were primitive, and the *Sitophilus granarius* weevil immediately descended like a plague upon badly stored grain. The absence of stone made the construction of the enormous barns such as those in Mexico impossible and, although some granaries were built of bricks or adobe, these storage areas were very scarce.

A Mixed Cattle-raising/Cereal-growing Ecosystem:
San Antonio de Areco

San Isidro was an agricultural area of advanced horticultural and cereal specialization. Further to the northwest was San Antonio de Areco, another ecosystem closer to the traditional image of the Buenos Aires countryside near the end of the colonial period. As we shall see, the activities in this ranching zone were more complex than traditional views suggest.

San Antonio de Areco is in a zone whose biological components differ little from those zones closer to Buenos Aires. Over four thousand people lived in the region at the end of the colonial period. At that time, Areco contributed approximately 20 percent of the cattle and 15 percent of the regional grain production of the entire area. Reasonably trustworthy figures from the same period show that the cattle stock consisted of well over 100,000 head. Areco was then an area specializing in bovine and equine husbandry as well as wheat cultivation.

The most decisive factor in understanding this mixed ecosystem was the abundance of land; indeed the region provides a classic example of its almost unlimited availability. The existence of a frontier where inhabitants were engaged in warfare with the indigenous societies of the plains, however, produced rather definite limits; one could go to the frontier to cultivate a little *chacra,* but one could also lose one's life in the process. Nonetheless, land abundance explains many of this agrisystem's peculiarities. Areco was the frontier in two senses: the divide between white and indigenous peoples, and an agrarian region where whites were gradually incorporating new lands for their direct exploitation.

This region of rolling plains contained very rich pastures. From the middle of the eighteenth century, officials and other travelers in the northern Buenos Aires countryside mentioned the presence of exogenous grasses and leguminous plants spread by animals associated with humans. Included were the great trefoils (several types of the large leguminous *Trifoliae* family), barley (*Bromus unioloides* and *Bromus inermis*), and wild thyme (*Thymus vulgaris*), all of which constituted excellent natural pastures. There were also espartograsses (*Stipa tenacissima*) and various types of rushes (*Juncus inbricatus*) as well as other tall grasses growing in ravines and lowlands. The animals' waste also spread other seeds such as thistle (several genera of the *Carduea* family) and jasmine (*Ammi biznaga*).

The advance of these plants across the plains preceded white settlement; new plants were introduced by cattle and horses fleeing to the interior of the pampas during dry spells. These exogenous animals and plants greatly modified the "original" ecosystem of the pampas, or more clearly put, of the humid pampa steppes. The beneficial effects of large-animal excrement upon the plains are well-known. Firstly, it introduced important modifications in the flora, increasing the grass/trefoil relationship and favoring the hardier grasslike plants. Secondly, it contributed to the development of the earthworm population, a species which had many physiological and mechanical functions in the maintenance of fertility, including aeration and humidification.

Economic operation in the Areco region was based on two types of production entities: the large *estancia* and the medium-sized *chacra*. Cattle farming with some cereal production predominated in the former; in the latter, which lacked the resources to maintain large herds of cattle, the basic activity was cereal production combined with small bovine, ovine, and equine herds.

I have already mentioned *chacras*, although the "open field" units found in Areco were somewhat different from those in San Isidro, since the former possessed a much larger stock of animal capital. María Antonia Melo, who resided in the village of Cañada de la Cruz in 1765 is a typical example of an Arecan tenant farmer with a medium-size holding. The inventory of her *chacra* indicates that she had one slave, two mulatto servants, three plows, thirty *fanegas* of wheat, twelve oxen, the same number of cows, five calves, three hundred sheep, eight stallions, and sixteen mares. Throughout the region, animal capital was more universal, especially when compared to the situation in San Isidro.

An inventory of an *estancia* in San Antonio de Areco allows for closer analysis of large-scale landowning. In 1767 a detailed listing of the land owned by don Joseph Peñalva was made. The frontage of his *estancia* measured 1,500 varas, that is, some 566 hectares or 1,398 acres. Although plots in this region usually measured 1.5 *leguas* in depth, the depth of Peñalva's holding was not specified in the inventory, an omission that reflects the relative abundance of land. Don Joseph also owned a house, a grove with fruit-bearing trees and another planted with willows, a pen, two carts, and their respective pigs and oxen. In addition, the *estancia* had a bucket-well and the ubiquitous bread oven. His property was worth around thirty-four hundred pesos—compared to the ten-thousand-peso value of the San Isidro *chacra*—distributed in land (10 percent), slaves (13.4 percent), and animals (68.8 percent). The animals were in turn subdivided into cattle (1,451 head), horses (386 animals), and sheep (1,446 head).

This example clearly shows that land was the least valuable possession. It also points out the mixed character of these production units. In this region the specificity of the cattle-farming calendar influenced the mixed ecosystem's dynamics.

The two most important undertakings on the cattle-farming calendar occurred when the cows gave birth (August–October) and when the animals belonging to the previous round of births were branded and castrated. The second activity usually took place in July, particularly in the case of free-range cattle. To these two most important activities, the taming of colts (from February to April) and the shearing of sheep during the first months of spring should be added. In addition cattle destined for the production of leather had to be readied for sale in the market, although this task, like the others mentioned below, was not tied to any calendar. Among other chores were the taming of oxen, the periodic cattle roundups in order to avoid the dispersion of

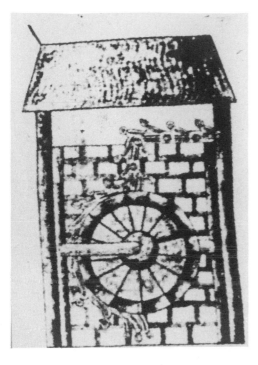

Fig. 18. Waterwheel.

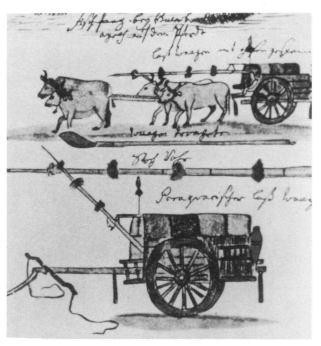

Fig. 19. Wagons.
Drawing by Florian
Paucke, c. 1752.

Fig. 20. Branding cattle. Engraving by Fernando Brambila, c. 1798.

Fig. 21. *(Opposite, top:)* Indians of Mexico City working in the garden of a Spaniard. They are cultivating new plants, and using a wooden spade of prehispanic orgin (uictli), and a Spanish hoe. (Codex Osuna, Madrid: Biblioteca Nacional, c. 1565.)

Fig. 22. *(Opposite, below:)* Uictli (wooden spade) being used in corn harvest. (Florentine Codex).

Fig. 23. Balling Ostriches. E.E. Vidal, *Picturesque Illustration of Buenos Ayres and Monte Video...* (London: 1820).

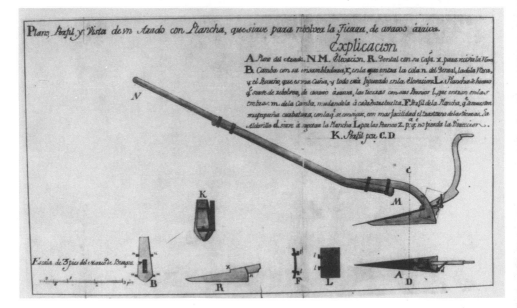

Fig. 24. Side and front view of a new hoe for turning up the ground...1778. (A.G.I., Mapas y Planos, Buenos Aires 117).

the herd (there were almost no fences and wire had not yet been introduced), and the raising and fattening of animals to sell to urban markets and, later, to salting factories.

Branding and the great roundups were the two most labor-intensive activities. Luckily, they did not necessarily coincide with the periods of greatest movement in cereal production: harvesting and, to a lesser degree, sowing. Nonetheless, the two calendars did not always mesh.

There was, in addition, another complex activity requiring a great deal of patience, time, and dedication: mule breeding. It was not always easy to convince a mare to mate with a donkey in order to produce the hybrid mule. To this end, selected stallions were altered so that they were able to bring mares into heat without impregnating them. This surgical procedure was both complicated and delicate. Once the mare was sexually excited, the would-be father donkey finished the job begun by the impotent horse.

The abundance of fertile lands had a great influence on cattle production and wheat yields. Tax collectors often complained that "the farm workers constantly move from one place to another" in search of "new" lands. In other words, the region was developing a peculiar migrant agriculture. The only limitation to the search for new land to exploit was the availability of seed and labor. Another important feature of the region was the relatively low cost of animals—the zootechnical capital—a direct result of abundant land with natural pastures.

The productivity fostered during the first cereal-producing cycles by the spread of legumes such as clover was probably superior to the land's "natural" fertility. The land consisted of well-drained plots (except in ravines and lowlands) with rainfall and climactic conditions very favorable to winter cereal. The custom of building wells with relatively accessible water levels, a system in use from the early days of settlement, allowed the watering of orchards and the upkeep of *chacra* animals during periods of little rain. Although in some places it was possible to find drinking troughs that used wooden or metallic tanks and pails, because of a shortage of wood, most buckets were made of leather.

Farm workers resorted to an ancient method of eliminating weeds and stubble: They burned them. Such dangerous activity was prohibited by decrees of colonial authorities; during a sudden reversal in wind direction, fire could quickly spread to neighboring plots. Early spring was the ideal time for field burning; once the fires had been extinguished, it took less than a month for the first rains to turn the burnt fields into lovely prairies glistening with clover and arrow grass (*Stipa setigera*). Field burning enhanced fertility, as it allowed the spring rains to bury the ashes under the topsoil. Current research on the biological productivity of the North American prairie shows real increases in fertility as a result of burning. But if fires were started when the grain was ripe, the consequences could be disastrous in open fields.

In short, colonial Río de la Plata was a model of a highly productive cattle-raising and cereal-growing agrisystem with great human mobility resulting from almost unlimited land availability in a very naturally fertile biological prairie environment. Precise figures on wheat yield are scarce and barely reliable; a traveler visiting an Areco *estancia* during the first decade of the nineteenth century spoke of yields of one to fifty, that is, fifty kernels harvested for every one planted. Although estimates on cattle yields were also high, they are more trustworthy. At roundup, cattle normally had an annual growth potential of between 20 and 25 percent, depending on the type of pasture, epizootic conditions, and precipitation. Cattle roundups generally included 10 percent male breeders (although some ranchers were recommending the reduction of this percentage); the rest was divided into mother cows and their young female and male issue. Once castrated, the latter were earmarked for urban market consumption. The growth potential of sheep was even greater, while the growth rate of horses was similar to that of the cattle. As we saw earlier, mule breeding was much more complex.

An Ecosystem in Mexico

Cereal-growing Ecosystems of the Puebla Valley

One of the most characteristic aspects of the agricultural milieu of New Spain was the rapid consolidation of the large haciendas and ranches as market-oriented production centers. In the Puebla Valley—in contrast with the Río de la Plata case—land was a scarce commodity over which Indian villagers and *hacendados* fought. Nonetheless, because the arrival of the Spanish resulted in demographic catastrophe for the indigenous population, the struggle for land ownership was barely a factor for well over a century. Friction over the control of land dates from the late seventeenth century, when the native population began its slow numerical recovery; as a result by the eighteenth century the rural universe of the Puebla plateau was ripe with social tensions based on the desire to control land and water resources.

The Puebla Valley is an immense depression located between spurs of the western and eastern Sierra Madre mountains. The western range's highest peaks are the volcanoes Popocatépetl and Itzaccihuatl, each well over 16,000 feet in height. In the eastern range, bordering Veracruz, the summit of the 18,400-foot-high Orizaba Peak is covered with snow all year round. Between 5,900 and 7,200 feet in altitude, the valley boasts a great variety of climactic conditions. It is, however, its temperate region that is most interesting to us; the northern summer is the rainy season, while winter and spring together form a long, dry spell.

Spanish farming habits had a negative effect on the land because of this peculiar hydrological regime. Before the conquest, the indigenous system of exploitation was based on physical labor and hoes but used no animals or plows. The advent of European ox- or mule-drawn plows, with their stronger traction, in combination with the erosive action of rainfall on the slopes, threatened the stability of the topsoil. Between thirty-one and thirty-nine inches of rain could accumulate within a four- or five-month period, during which the force and intensity of the torrents would wash out the sloping plots. On the other hand, the long annual rainless period—typical of all of central Mexico—caused great difficulties in the breeding of some types of livestock such as cattle.

The Puebla Valley agricultural ecosystems were part of a complex structure of great richness and variety. The central portion of the valley, part of the "neovolcanic axis," housed some of Mexico's most important cereal production centers. The two most important cereals grown were maize, of pre-Hispanic origin and crucial to the diet of people and animals, and wheat, which spread quickly through the region after its introduction by the Spanish. The relative abundance of wheat led to its replacing maize as the dietary mainstay of the working classes in some parts of the valley, particularly when the maize harvest was smaller than average or when it failed almost completely. Other important vegetables produced for human and animal consumption included several types of chile (*Capsicum*), beans (*Phaseolus*), peas (*Veza*), broad beans (*Vicia fava*), and barley. There were also some pockets of livestock production, especially swine, sheep, goats, and to a lesser extent, cattle. A peculiar plant, the agave, was grown for the manufacture of a popular, slightly alcoholic beverage called pulque.

The hinterland of one of the subregions dominated by the town of Tepeaca had over seventy-two thousand inhabitants by the end of the eighteenth century. Its approximately four hundred haciendas and ranches produced mostly maize and wheat. Large properties such as haciendas and some ranches harbored vast and diverse production systems. Managers, overseers, and their assistants (*troxeros, rayadores,* and others) had direct use of a portion of the hacienda's land via a partial lease mechanism. In turn, they would sublease part of their land to other producers. Sometimes, the property owners themselves would sublease plots of various sizes. Some of their tenants could in turn sublease to smaller tenants. Finally there were the *gañanes,* permanent indigenous servants who lived on the property and who kept their own plots of different sizes. Members of each of these production units kept their own animals on the hacienda.

Resource availability determined the Tepeaca agricultural entities' productive specialization. In this region there were several great haciendas that produced cereals: maize, wheat, and to a lesser extent, barley. Others produced chile on their irrigated lands, and still others fed swine with the maize, barley, and broad beans grown on-site. The swine were sent to Puebla, the regional capital, where large amounts of pork were consumed. Some were processed into ham, lard, and other by-products to be sold in Puebla itself or in

Late Colonial Tepeaca

Veracruz. This process was a typical example of the conversion of vegetable production into animal protein for human consumption.

The Santa Ana Capula hacienda had twenty-four *caballerías* or approximately 2,470 acres of land. Not all of its land, nor that of the adjoining ranch belonging to it, was of equal quality. Santa Ana had ten *caballerías* "for all types of seed" and eight of "medium quality." The remaining six *caballerías* consisted of inferior land and hills. An inventory taken in 1836 gives us an idea of the exploitation undertaken on the property. Of the hacienda's total value of about twenty thousand pesos—average for the Tepeaca region but significantly less than that of the great haciendas of New Spain of the time—land accounted for almost 50 percent of the hacienda's value. Hydraulic works, springs, and buildings accounted for another 18 percent, and livestock (Santa Ana fattened pigs, sheep, and goats) for 12.8 percent.

When the inventory was taken, the hacienda owned cultivated fields of maize, chile, wheat, beans, and alfalfa.

This example and others demonstrate that as a result of the scarcity of fertile lands in relation to population density, land in the Puebla Valley was a most valuable commodity; this was quite different from the case of the Río de la Plata. The value of hydraulic works or spring water, where they existed, tended to be second in importance, while livestock and implements of production and buildings took last place. In the Puebla Valley buildings were imposing, particularly when compared with those in Río de la Plata. Corrals, threshing floors, stables, water wells and ponds, granaries, and other facilities were made of brick or strong tecali stone; even the most modest buildings were made of adobe.

Tepeaca haciendas averaged between 1,850 and 2,900 acres in size. The most important ones had adjunct ranches that sheltered animals during the worst moments of the dry season and reinforced production capacity by adding agricultural specialties to the hacienda's repertoire. While the inventory value of the valley's haciendas was low to average in comparison to that of other New Spain estates, it was high in relation to size. Tepeaca haciendas were easily worth four times the value of the best Río de la Plata properties of the time.

Although livestock—particularly sheep and pork—were a significant inventory item accounting for about 10 percent of the hacienda's value, the numbers of animals were still minimal when compared to those found on northern Mexican haciendas or Río de la Plata *estancias*. The animal inventory also included plowing oxen and mules, transportation and cargo mules, and sometimes threshing horses and mares. One of the elements that threatened livestock in the region's haciendas was the low sodium content of the soil, especially along washed-out hillsides. Thus, haciendas usually had to purchase "livestock salt" for consumption by the hacienda's animals. Over time this poor zootechnical capital—relative to the amount of tillable land—would have a negative effect because of the resulting scarcity of fertilizer.

Indigenous peoples controlled lands and other resources outside of the haciendas and ranches. Their lands were often of marginal use for the commercial production of cereals, since the Spanish had already appropriated the most productive territories. They did, however, yield a wide variety of foodstuffs. A significant portion of the vegetables and the animal protein—scarce as the latter were—consumed by the indigenous population came from this land, where complex ecosystems thrived invisible to the eyes of a commercialized, European-dominated society.

A plant that played a very important role as an energy source and as an economic resource for large sectors of the population was the maguey cactus (*Agave*). In the Puebla Valley, where some haciendas already had maguey fields, the plant was used by both native people and the Spanish. Thanks to the agave, Tepeaca weavers were able to earn additional income while also using the plant fibers to weave clothing and baskets. Local ethnic lords, an important sector of the old native nobility, still owned a few small plots of land which they farmed. The fencing surrounding these properties usually consisted of great numbers of maguey plants.

The peasants, in addition, planted maize and beans for their own consumption in these small maguey-fenced lots, just as the hacienda farmhands did on the scant land to which they were entitled. The Indians used maximally intensive and integrative—as opposed to extensive—farming techniques, which yielded harvests relatively richer than those of the haciendas. The pre-Hispanic approach to farming, based on household labor, included the ancient traditions of the rigorous selection of individual seeds, the use of digging sticks, the application of detailed weeding and leaf removal as soon as the first corn cobs sprouted, careful shelling, and the cutting back of reeds and leaves, which were then used as kindling or forage for household animals.

Although there are difficulties in obtaining concrete documentary evidence for the preconquest period, most sixteenth-century chroniclers who came into contact with native farming technology registered their astonishment at the abundance it yielded. For the eighteenth-century Indian peasant, whose only sources of wealth were his knowledge and his household's labor force, the preservation of techniques that produced high yields were vital; they often amounted to the difference between life and death. When he was lucky enough to have a few days' water every month (frequently as a result of a struggle against some hacienda) he could also cultivate fruit orchards, tomatoes, and chiles that could be sold in the market.

Many natives who owned little suburban plots located outside of towns and Indian villages had a resource important because of its mobility: small herds of sheep and swine. The sheep fed on the grass that grew on the plots, along roadsides, and on hillsides useless to commercial agriculture. The pigs ate leftovers, hay, seeds, and acorns from the surviving limited forests. Native farmers could either consume the meat of these animals or sell them for quick cash.

Pigs were classified according to how they had been fed; "full-fat" pigs were given fodder, while "half-fat" and "savanna" pigs were nourished with the various foods mentioned above. Pork by-products had enormous dietary importance, since a substantial portion of the animal protein consumed in the region came from lard, ham, and rinds sold in local markets. The supply of these by-products was in the hands of poor Spaniards, mestizos, and Indians, proving that these "inferior" social groupings were of no small economic importance to the area's markets.

Alternating maize, wheat, bean, and barley cycles dominated the agricultural calendar of the Puebla Valley. Although these four crops were fundamental to the region, alfalfa, various types of chile, peas, and broad beans could also be found. Maize, the most important of the area's crops in terms of human and animal diet, began its cycle in May. If the harvest were to consist simply of fresh corn on the cob, the cycle ended in August or September. If grain to feed people and animals was needed, the harvest could be extended until October or November. These dates could vary, since differences in altitude and exposure to sun and wind resulted in microclimactic conditions that affected crop calendars. Variations in the agricultural calendar were related both to various ecological "niches" and to differences among dozens of varieties of maize.

Sometimes there was a close relationship between maize and beans. When the depleting action of maize had exhausted the soil, beans would be planted exclusively during the following cycle. At other times, irrigated haciendas rotated their crops in the following manner: wheat (October–April), beans (May–September), wheat (October–April), and maize (May–September). Another rotation called for the planting of broad beans after several maize cycles; the beans, like maize, were reserved for fattening pigs. Although the productivity of each succeeding maize cycle was lowered, the soil-enriching beans caused subsequent maize harvests to be a bit more abundant.

The wheat cycle was also very important to the entire region. There were three types of wheat crops: "irrigated wheat," "venture wheat," and "rainy spell wheat." The first type, found in almost all of the irrigated haciendas of the time, was planted in October and harvested between April and June. Paradoxically, irrigated wheat was forever threatened by the possibility of rain, particularly as it began to mature. "Venture wheat," as its name implies, was grown in the hope of a rainfall during the dry season and followed the same calendar as irrigated wheat. "Rainy spell wheat" was planted at the beginning of the rainy season in May or June and harvested in October.

The ranches and haciendas near Puebla that could count on ample irrigation and on the fertilizer produced by the sheep being fattened for urban markets would sometimes rotate wheat, maize, barley, and beans. Under this system, barley was planted in October and cut for forage in March or April; the same land was then used for maize, and wheat was planted in October. Thus, a sixteen-month cycle would yield three different crops: one for forage, one for multiple use (animals and people), and one for human consumption only. The rotation of maize and wheat was particularly beneficial in increasing wheat's yield, but even when this yield was aided by constant irrigation, it was necessary to reintroduce beans from time to time as the excessive rotation of grasslike plants would eventually put an end to high yields.

Chile, a very labor-intensive vegetable requiring irrigation and great care, had its own complex calendar. It was planted in nurseries during February and March and transplanted in April and May. In some haciendas, numerous workers would fill earthenware pots from small wells located near the irrigation ditches and carry them to the nurseries' furrows. Nursery-based planting had great advantages; only perfectly developed specimens were transplanted and the sowing of new plants could be organized very precisely. Peasant families, particularly those who had access to irrigation, derived very high yields using this method. This may explain why peasants always took chile to sell in the region's urban markets.

Looking closely at the soil preparation technology in place in the Puebla Valley, we can see that the use of wooden harrows and plows was widespread, at least in large production units such as haciendas. On Tepeaca haciendas mules were used to pull the plows, while small farmers resorted to the hoe. Both wheat and maize required a series of careful steps after planting.

Wheat threshing here, as in the Río de la Plata, was powered by horses. Unlike the unstable threshing floors of the Río de la Plata, however, those of the Puebla Valley haciendas were built of brick or stone. One hacienda, located near Acatzingo, had a brick threshing floor measuring 75 feet in diameter with a 235-foot circumference! Granaries and barns were extremely important to production, since the commercial strategy of the haciendas depended largely on their existence. They were elongated stone or brick structures varying in size, usually very large and almost always covered by a roof. The ruins of some of those enormous buildings can still be seen today.

Barns were crucial to the business plans of the great haciendas because they allowed for storage of grain that could be sold during times of low or nonexistent supply. Since peasants usually lacked conservation facilities even on the rare occasions when they produced surpluses, only haciendas were able to fix grain prices off-season.

Measuring harvest yields is a rather thorny issue. The statements of classical colonial authors such as Motolinía or Agustín de Vetancourt would lead us to believe that wheat yields were very high during the early period, reaching ratios of sixty to one. We must not, however, put our trust in such data; they fail to take into account the size of the plots under cultivation (the surface-to-yield relationship), and are probably the result of the chroniclers plagiarizing each other's information. Scant but more trustworthy data speaks of much lower yields. One well-managed Atlixco hacienda produced an average yield of 12.6 to one for irrigated wheat in a four-year period; during much the same period an hacienda near Puebla planted with "venture wheat," yielded a slightly higher five-year average of 13.1 to one. Although these figures seem reasonable, the problem of surface-to-yield relationship remains, making the study of yields during the colonial period extremely difficult.

In the case of maize, the chroniclers also provide high figures, which are hardly acceptable without an analysis of sources. Maize production, measured with the ancient system of comparing how much grain is produced for each grain sown, always gives higher yields than those of wheat. The comparison is nonetheless problematic for although a larger amount of grain is obtained, maize quickly exhausts the soil. In addition, the nutritional value of maize flour is much lower. During a three-year period, an hacienda near Puebla recorded yields that ranged from 17.5 to one and 155 to one. Although these figures are a far cry from the estimates of some chroniclers and travelers who spoke of 800 to one yields, they are nevertheless quite high. It is entirely possible that the yields from small peasant plots were much higher, although there is no reliable documentary data.

Some Final Thoughts

I will end this essay with some thoughts about the ties between types of consumption and colonial agrisystems in relation to some of the issues discussed above.

Plants are power converters, transforming sunlight into chemical energy. Animals are also energy transformers; herbivores assimilate the plant parts that man is not capable of processing, and turn them into proteins and animal fats that humans can digest. When we consume plants, we derive only a small portion (between 1 and 5 percent) of the energy received by them. When we consume animal protein, we receive only a fraction of a fraction of the energy originally absorbed. Thus, the consumers of animal protein suffer a double loss of energy. Although not all protein is animal in origin, in general animal protein has a higher nutritional value than plant carbohydrates. Nonetheless most societies cannot afford to waste energy and must be content with a diet richer in vegetables than in animal flesh. Energy waste is also, of course, directly related to population density; the lesser the density, the more wasteful per capita consumption can become.

The relation between the Río de la Plata ecosystems and the resulting animal protein consumption offers a good example of the foregoing model. Each inhabitant of the Buenos Aires countryside, or of the city itself, had at his or her disposal an amount of animal protein, mostly derived from cattle, similar to that available today to the inhabitants of rich countries. The convergence of low population density, abundance of fertile lands, and favorable international trade created the peculiar conditions enjoyed by the *porteños* of the time. These conditions also explain why, during four hundred years, the Río de la Plata region was a magnet for a most diverse internal and external flow of migration.

The situation appears quite different when seen from the vantage point of consumption in cities like Puebla or Mexico. Although animal protein was available, its weight was doubtlessly smaller in relation to other dietary components and its sources were much more complex and varied. Hunting and gathering still played an important role in the lake area of the Central Valley where wildlife resources were astonishingly varied: fish, birds, frogs and toads, insects and small crustaceans. In addition, small livestock, especially pork and pork by-products, played an important role in the area, providing an ideal example of the "reconversion" of vegetable resources into animal protein. Most of these vegetable resources were semi-wild and useless to the commercial production of the haciendas. There was no energy waste here; on the contrary, the peasants turned their leftovers plus other "marginal" vegetables into saleable goods that allowed them to earn some cash income.

Things were quite different on the large haciendas that devoted sizable amounts of their maize, barley, or broad bean harvests to the feeding of swine. The San José de Nopalucán hacienda, for example, was largely engaged in swine breeding and fattening from 1693 to 1704. Over 50 percent of its income was derived from the sale of some thirteen hundred pigs at the Puebla market; the rest was divided among maize, wheat, and barley sales to Puebla, Tierra Caliente, and neighboring landowners. One third of the maize produced by the hacienda during this ten-year period was used for pig feed, another for people and animal maintenance, and the remaining third was sold at market. Most of the barley went to fatten the pigs while some was sold and a small amount was used to feed the hacienda's animals. Broad beans were used almost exclusively for pig fattening, and wheat almost exclusively for sales.

In order to become an authentic animal protein factory, the hacienda had to put a complex strategy in motion. Because it devoted so much fodder to the pigs, the hacienda had to send its other animals to watering places in Tierra Caliente during the worst of the dry season in order to keep them productive. In addition, to feed its workers the hacienda was forced to produce maize every year. Further diversification was attempted by producing barley and leguminous broad beans, which in turn enriched the soil exhausted from the overproduction of maize. Thus the city of Puebla's incessant consumption of pork was fed by ecosystems as different as the small farms of indigenous and mestizo peasants and the great breeding haciendas of the Puebla Valley.

Had I analyzed the "floating garden" (*chinampa*) communities of the Mexico Valley, we would have seen other ways in which human societies react to population density in a given environment. Based on water resources developed over the course of several centuries, its inhabitants built a special biotype highly productive in relation to available surface and labor requirements. This productivity was reflected in the Mexico City market, where the maize, legumes, chile, beans, and other products of the *chinampa* area played an important role. Bean consumption was especially important; as we know today, the *Phaseoli* boast the highest protein content of all the leguminous family members. Beans quite adequately replace animal protein in the human diet and thus compensate for their absence.

The *chinampas* continued to be highly productive for many years. The "water policy" introduced by Spain in the sixteenth century, however, progressively depleted the Mexico Valley basin until it was almost completely dried.

In the Valley of Mexico, the transition to European technology produced dire consequences. The use of the planting stick in steep terrain and the *chinampa* system are both examples of integrative techniques. The Spanish, who were more concerned with immediate productivity and with flooding in Mexico City, applied a technology—plows—that turned out to be disastrous for both the environment and the people. In other cases, of course, the technology and products imported by the Spanish yielded high productivity, even though results were not always positive for all the social groupings that made up the complex colonial society.

CHAPTER FOUR

The Landed Elite

STUART SCHWARTZ

Despite images of plundered empires, fabled mines, bustling cities, and bullion-laden fleets, the colonies of Spain and Portugal in America were essentially agrarian societies. In them, perhaps 80 percent of the population resided in the countryside or in small rural towns and derived their livelihood from agriculture and livestock or from the subsidiary activities connected to them. The ownership of land seems an obvious key to power and wealth in these societies, and so it became, but the story of how landowners became so important is a complex one with considerable regional variation in its pace and timing. Agricultural property took many forms—Indian communal villages, municipal commons, small farms, subsistence plots, slave-controlled provision grounds—but eventually the great estates, called haciendas in many parts of Spanish America, cast their long shadows over much of the countryside and over society as a whole. However, the large landowners did not dominate Latin American societies from the outset nor was their stability as a class or their political power always secure.

In some ways we know more about the structure and operations of the great estates themselves than about the men and women who created, owned, and exploited them. To write the history of these people as a social class is not easy because we must take into account not only its formation and internal organization, but also its relationship to other groups and to institutions like the state. Moreover, what the landowners thought of themselves and how they were viewed by others in society are essential parts of this story.

97

From Labor to Land

To the earliest Spanish and Portuguese explorers and conquerors the lands of America seemed to stretch out in unending abundance. Claiming these lands seemed limited only by opportunity, valor, and personal desires, restricted later by royal recognition of the Indians' rights to property. However, what is most striking about the early Spanish settlements is the relative disregard for land or for its legal acquisition. Initial Spanish activities in Santo Domingo, Puerto Rico, and Cuba centered on the search for gold, and that in effect meant control of the Indian population for labor and the exploitation of its agricultural production through a system of tribute. Columbus's second voyage in 1493 had sought to establish Spanish farmers with European livestock, grain, grapes, and olives in the islands, but the prospect for creating a class of Spanish farmers was dim in the midst of the many opportunities for conquest. Instead, the most desired form of property for the Spaniards arriving in the Americas was a grant that gave them control of Indian production and labor. These grants, eventually called *encomiendas,* were the key to the formation of the first elite after the conquest. *Encomenderos* primarily controlled Indians rather than land, but their aspirations, goals, and means of operation set the tone and style that would later become characteristic of the great landowners.

Members of conquering expeditions, especially those close to the leader or from his home province, were rewarded with *encomiendas* and usually with the status of citizens or householders (*vecinos*), which entitled them to a houseplot and the right to serve in newly founded municipal councils. New expeditions were often composed of frustrated men who had failed to get such rewards or whose original *encomiendas* were no longer sufficient because disease, mistreatment, and disruption of Indian culture had reduced the number of their dependents.

Few persons of noble status emigrated from Spain and those who did so were usually of lesser rank, only gentlemen (hidalgos) some of them quite poor. During the sixteenth century, only about 5 percent of the immigrants styled themselves "don," the honorary title signifying hidalgo status. But in the Americas the early immigrants had won the new lands by the force of arms and had fulfilled the traditional military function of the nobility. Thus, they considered themselves gentlemen and deserving of the privileges of that rank. The crown manipulated this drive for social status by promising new immigrants hidalgo status, memberships as knights in the military orders, coats of arms, and the right to entail property. But in reality the crown rarely fulfilled these promises. Instead, Spanish immigrants and members of the expeditions of conquest secured their social position themselves by gaining an *encomienda* and then living the life of a gentleman. In Spain fiscal, juridical, and social divisions marked the distinctions between hidalgos and commoners, but a viceroy of Peru could state in 1582, "In the Indies everyone is a gentleman and this [social mobility] is the thing that most populates them."[1]

Encomenderos were required to maintain horse and arms and to provide religious instruction to their wards, duties well in keeping with the traditional roles of the nobility. Each *encomendero* maintained a household in a city or town surrounded by kin, retainers, servants, and some slaves. While their Indians usually resided in the countryside, the *encomenderos* lived and exercised political control in the towns where they dominated the town councils. Visits to the actual villages held in *encomienda* might be made occasionally, but often a manager (*mayordomo*) and his helpers (poorer Spaniards or mestizos) took on the everyday task of assigning work, collecting tribute, and directing operations, usually in cooperation with Indian headmen or caciques. *Encomenderos* sought to live nobly, without recourse to manual occupation or trade, from the production or tribute of their dependents. However, in order to do so they sometimes turned their grants of Indian labor into complex economic enterprises combining farming, mining, or cloth production, managed with an eye to profit. In this combination, and sometimes tension, between aspirations to nobility and economic gain, *encomiendas* provided an early model for the landholding class.

The Spanish crown, however, was unwilling to see a new semi-independent class of nobility emerge in the colonies. *Encomenderos* eventually became a kind of rentier class. As more Europeans continued to arrive in the New World, they also became an ever declining percentage of the Spanish population. In Mexico, in 1540 one out of four Spaniards held an *encomienda*, but by 1570 that number had fallen to one in twenty. Constant royal pressure and the decline of the Indian population eventually undercut the viability of the *encomiendas* as a basis of wealth.

The *encomienda* persisted longer in more peripheral regions, and in some places like Chile and Venezuela lasted well into the eighteenth century. Despite its decreasing importance, in function and operation the *encomienda* served as something of a model for the landed estates and the *encomenderos*, with their pretensions of nobility and desire for security and gain, as models for the owners of the great estates who replaced or overlapped with them.

From Encomenderos to Estancieros

In theory, based on the right of conquest found in Roman law and on a papal donation of 1493 in which the pope granted the newly discovered territory in the Atlantic to Castile, all lands in the Spanish Indies belonged to the monarch and could be distributed only by the crown or its agents. In the early years especially, town councils also awarded lands to settlers. With rarest exception, the crown did not give up traditional seignorial rights of lordship and justice over the lands awarded to settlers.

The award of a houseplot and *estancia* designed to support the creation and settlement of towns was a first step in the distribution of lands, what might be called the settlement stage. Then, lands further from the centers of Spanish settlement were distributed. Grants often specified the purpose to which the land would be put: wheat, cattle, sheep, pigs, wine, sugar. The size of grants varied to some extent with their purpose (cattle ranches were usually the largest awards), but size also depended on local conditions, availability, the density of the Indian population, and personal or political influence. These grants of land were juridically distinct from *encomiendas,* but in reality *encomenderos* with access to Indian workers were in the best position to develop their lands. Moreover, *encomenderos* also served on the municipal councils that had the right to make land grants so that the interest of that group was favored. Ultimately, there were many more landed properties than there had been *encomiendas,* but it has been suggested that in any given region the "oldest, stablest, most prestigious, and best located haciendas" would have originated in the lands of the original *encomendero* and his family.[2] This was the case, for example, of Hernando Pérez de Bocanegra, who in the 1550s held two rich *encomiendas* near Acámbaro, Mexico, close by his extensive lands obtained by a viceregal grant. Eventually by purchases from the Indian communities of the region and further land grants, he came to control almost all the land of the original *encomiendas* as well as additional properties. A century later the Bocanegra-Villamayor family was still predominant in the region. The creation of haciendas from *encomiendas* was especially prevalent where Indian societies were battered by Spanish demands and demographic loss.

Around these large holdings, often formed first by the *encomendero*-landowners, would be other large properties, medium-sized estates, small farms, or in some places Indian communal lands. In regions like Oaxaca in New Spain, Indian communities were able to hold on to traditional lands in the face of Spanish encroachment, but in many areas private landholding expanded at the expense of communal lands. In general, the result was a patchwork of rural property dominated in many, but not all areas, by the great estates—lay and ecclesiastical.

In the flat lands around Bogotá, *encomenderos* received land grants from the municipal council until the end of the sixteenth century, although the royal high court (*audiencia*) had forbidden such distributions in 1557. The pattern was not surprising since *encomenderos* dominated the council. Such infractions of the law were later "regularized" by the payment of a fee to the government. As the Indian population contracted and Indians were eventually concentrated in villages and assigned communal lands, "vacant" lands became available for award. Between 1592 and 1640 a new series of grants were made. *Encomenderos* were now joined by bureaucrats in the acquisition of these rural properties, and eventually, in the eighteenth century merchants would also become landholders. In this process the area around Bogotá was carved into large rural estates. About 60 to 70 percent of the lands were held in these "haciendas" (a term only used here in the eighteenth century) while the rest were cultivated by Indian communities or small farmers with a few to a few hundred acres. The larger estates might include a few square miles. One, El Novillero, included over 125 square miles.

In central Peru control of Indian labor and tribute first seemed to be the quickest road to status and success. By 1536 about one out of every four Spaniards held an *encomienda*. The richest lived like feudal lords and some controlled thousands of Indian tributaries. Newcomers sought similar rewards but Indian depopulation in the 1540s, diminished tribute, and increasing royal concern over the formation of the *encomenderos* into a potentially independent feudal nobility reduced the awarding of *encomiendas*. By 1555, only one out of every sixteen Spaniards held an *encomienda*. Dissatisfied Spaniards revolted against the crown or even threatened to separate Peru from Spain. The demands were so many that Viceroy la Gasca claimed that rewarding friends was more difficult than dealing with enemies. By 1550, other means of reward such as pensions or salaried positions in the viceregal guard were used to quiet discontent, but by that time Spaniards were already considering other alternatives. For example, *encomenderos* began to acquire land grants, and *chacras* began to develop in the outskirts of Lima. Coastal estates in central Peru produced wine, grain, and livestock for the growing Hispanic market, while those in the northern river valleys cultivated sugar. Livestock ranches at upper elevations provided meat, hides, and wool. The purchase of lands from Indian headmen (*kurakas*), who often had no right to make these sales, helped create Spanish-owned agricultural properties.

Landowners did not simply inherit a desire for the noble life-style directly from *encomenderos*, rather both groups shared in the widely held aristocratic ideals of Hispanic society. Living nobly without recourse to manual labor, surrounded by kin and retainers, and supported by rents provided by dependents over whom a patriarchal authority was exercised, served as the foundation of this ideal. The large landowners often displayed an acute business sense and an entrepreneurial attitude, but the reference point by which they lived their lives and the predominant discourse of their activities were not wealth and profit but family and lineage. Providing for their children and the continuity of their "house" preoccupied their energies and strategies. Owning land figured in the dreams of many like the picaresque hero of the early Mexican novel *El Periquillo Sarniento* (1816) who hoped to amass riches from commerce, buy a landed estate, acquire a noble title, and eventually retire to Spain.[3]

As markets for farm products expanded, land ownership was one way to fulfill this dream. In Mexico, the discovery of silver mines after 1550 in the sparsely populated north-central and northern areas of the colony attracted large number of workers to the mining towns that sprung up. These people needed to be fed, and together with the demand for hides, tallow, and cloth at the mines themselves they provided a market for large estates that developed to supply this demand. The estates were sometimes owned by the same families that controlled the mines. Such was the case of Captain Pedro de Arizmendi Gogorrón who in the seventeenth century took the fortune he made in the Mexican silver mines at San Luis Potosí and invested it first in a smelting and refining operation and then in large agricultural estates. Miners with their own haciendas also had the advantage of producing the meat, hides, tallow, and charcoal they needed themselves. Large haciendas were often relatively self-sufficient in most basic commodities.

In Venezuela the market also played a central role in the development of rural estates. Around Caracas, founded in 1567, control of Indian labor had provided the first basis of wealth and forty of the town's sixty original *vecinos* held *encomienda* grants. For a while Spanish raids on Indian communities to acquire more laborers or slaves for sale was the primary economic activity. By the 1580s, however, a rise in Spanish wheat prices and a market for flour down the coast at Cartagena, port-of-call for the annual silver fleet, moved Caracas's residents to exploit the mild climate of and well-watered land around the city to grow wheat for local consumption and export. A landowning elite based on the wheat trade took control of Caracas and its municipal council.

But whereas the market for flour had brought this class into being, the market could also decimate it. A decline in demand for flour at Cartagena after 1600 threatened the position of the Caracas landowners and moved them to seek alternate crops like tobacco. Eventually, they turned to cacao. Those who held both land and *encomiendas* could best exploit the new crop. In 1635 there were over three thousand Indians employed in cacao agriculture. In the long run, the Indian population was too small to support the expansion of cacao, and it was gradually replaced by large numbers of black slaves on the plantations.

Around the Spanish settlement at Santiago, Chile, founded in 1541, the distribution of land to Spanish colonists was limited at first by Indian occupation. As the Indian population was decimated by warfare and disease, some of these lands were sold. A market in lands began to develop first on the perimeter of the city, and then by 1585, lands as far away as forty miles from Santiago were bought. While Spaniards of different occupations and ranks acquired land, the largest lots, averaging over six hundred acres, were purchased by *encomenderos*.

First sales were made of the small *chacras* of wheat and grapevines that surrounded the town, originally owned by first settlers. These valuable lands were often purchased by merchants and bureaucrats, but the *encomenderos* were more interested in the potentially rich but inexpensive and extensive lands further from the town. These, added to the lands acquired by grant, allowed them to construct extensive ranches and farming estates called *fundos*.

The *fundo* usually contained broad open ranges and a few acres for food stuffs and alfalfa; each had a small resident work force of a few slaves and from the original *encomiendas* thirty or forty Indian families who conducted the annual rodeo and slaughter. The hides, jerked beef, and tallow produced were shipped to Peru. Toward the end of the seventeenth century, Peruvian demand for grain caused the Chilean *fundos* to shift to wheat production, a process that increased the value of the estates and also called for a larger labor force. The workers in the main were mestizos, assimilated Indians, and poor whites who in return for assured labor and some marginal land for their own crops and stock were willing to become resident workers with heavy service obligations (*inquilinos*). The owners' control of land fortified their dominant position. For the large, floating, landless population, seasonal employment under control of the cattle ranchers (*estancieros*) was the only hope for survival, other than banditry or trying to homestead on the Indian frontier in the south. In Chile, by the seventeenth century a group of about two hundred families controlled most of the arable land, which gave them a predominant economic position and a stranglehold on Chilean society. (See Fig. 25.)

Brazil provides a final example somewhat unlike Spanish America but sharing certain common elements. Explored and settled by the Portuguese after 1500, the Brazilian coast offered few attractions. The cutting of logs and extraction of dyewood, the first economic activity, depended on bartering with Indians for their labor. The Portuguese used this same technique to obtain food, so that at first, as in Spanish America, early colonists had little interest in acquiring title to lands. After 1535, a new colonization scheme, the creation of captaincies under lord proprietors (*donatários*), began to change the nature of the colony. The lord proprietors had powers reserved for the state in Spanish America. They could appoint judges and levy taxes as well as found towns and distribute land grants (*sesmarias*) to attract colonists and settle their captaincies. The crown and the proprietor retained certain rights over these lands, but the *sesmarias* served as the basis for colonization.

Grantees were required to build strong defensible residences, maintain arms and munitions, and provide for the defense of others in their vicinity against hostile Indians. This role was somewhat like that of the early *encomenderos* in Spanish America or of medieval European border lords. Little wonder that they considered themselves the "nobility of the land." The distribution of lands in Brazil was most successful where sugarcane had been introduced and capital was available. By 1549, the beginnings of a plantation economy had developed. *Donatários* granted many of the early *sesmarias* specifically for the building of sugar mills (*engenhos*). As in Spanish America, the original land grants were eventually expanded by purchase, appropriation of unused lands, inheritance, dowry, and illegal seizure. In northeastern Brazil a class of sugar planters on the coast and cattle ranchers in the interior emerged as the colony's landed elite. (See Fig. 26, 27.)

The Large Landed Estates

What distinguished the different types of great estates was their extent, the size of their work force, the amount of capital they included, and the quality of their land. Livestock *hatos* or *estancias* had a small number of workers and limited capital investment beyond their herds. Haciendas tended to mix agriculture and livestock, were relatively self-sufficient, needed permanent or temporary laborers, and received periodic infusions of capital. Both *estancias* and haciendas generally produced for local or regional markets. Finally, the market-oriented *engenhos* (Spanish *ingenios*), with their heavily-capitalized machinery and large labor forces often composed of permanent or enslaved workers, came the closest to the modern image of the plantation. On livestock ranches often the stock itself represented the major investment; on haciendas somewhat more was invested in land, credit to workers, and sometimes, purchase of slaves; on sugar-producing properties, the slaves and machinery constituted the bulk of the value. No matter what the mix of capital, all three types served as the basis of landed wealth and social status.

As the large estates emerged, they were often a composite of an original land grant, subsequent *mercedes,* purchases, and perhaps lands acquired by illegal occupation or force, later made legal by the payment of a fee or *composición* to the crown. In Mexico the *composición* of 1591 legitimated many of the early land acquisitions. In New Granada, a *composición* of 1643 was important in the formation of the landowning class. Later, *composición* became a regular process by which title to land could be legalized. The indebtedness and financial difficulties of the Spanish crown in the late sixteenth and seventeenth centuries contributed to its willingness to legitimate titles by payment of these settlements. For the landowning class in the Americas, the *composiciones* enabled it to solidify its position by paying cash.

Each large estate was a story; each had its own history. In 1705 Captain Juan Ortiz, resident of the city of Santa Marta (New Granada) petitioned the town council for a *merced* of about eighty acres of land at a place called Genes Island in the Magdalena River. He later transferred the land to doña María Jimínez who sold it to Juan Antonio de Araújo. In 1710 Araújo's son, Cristóbal, and don Juan Esteban de Padilla solicited a grant of over eight hundred acres on neighboring Pestagua Island to set up a *hato*. A year later Padilla sold his share to Araújo who now held both Genes and Pestagua. Araújo a few years later requested and received yet another grant of over one thousand acres on another island, specifically to serve for the many head of cattle and horses he hoped to accumulate. By 1725 Araújo's widow and his son had to seek a *composición* to legalize the title on these lands against the claims of a neighbor. But the real problem was Cristóbal's promise in his will to leave ten thousand pesos for the founding of a Capuchin convent. When this sum was not paid from his estate, the bishop of Santa Marta brought a suit that eventually forced the sale of all the lands for twelve thousand pesos so that the bequest could be made. Between 1739 and 1748 the buyer, Andrés de Madariaga, by grant and purchase consolidated the properties and added others that bordered them.

By 1755, the lands of Pestagua extended from the mouth of the Magdalena river well inland, and its cattle were sold in both Santa Marta and Cartagena. Other lands were added so that by 1760, when Madariaga's son, Dr. Andrés de Madariaga, established an entail (*mayorazgo*) on the property, the Hacienda San Antonio Rompedero de Pestagua contained over forty-four thousand acres. The land, however, made up only about 10 percent of the property's value, while animal stock composed about 50 percent, and improvements, buildings, tools, and slaves made up the rest. In 1775, Pestagua was valued at four times its original purchase price of 12,000 pesos and it served as the basis for the Madariaga family fortune and position when they became the Condes de Pestagua. In the history of this property we can see land grants, purchases, partnerships, inheritance, legal squabbles, *composición*, the creation of a family fortune, and eventually a noble title. While the establishment and preservation of the family's position was an important goal, the creation and operation of the hacienda seems to have resulted also from an active and acute spirit of enterprise.[4] In fact the two goals of economic success and the building of a family's status and reputation were closely interrelated.

The size and arrangement of a large estate's lands varied considerably. A hacienda's lands were not necessarily contiguous, but there was a tendency to make them so by acquiring intervening properties. Also, over time there was a tendency for the wealthier agricultural families to acquire multiple estates. The variability in size was striking and depended not only on available land or capital but on technology as well. In the Lambayeque Valley of northern Peru, the six sugar-producing haciendas that dominated the region at the beginning of the eighteenth century varied in size from 720 to 3,100 acres. Similar ranges in size could also be found on Brazilian and Mexican sugar estates. Given the capacity of the grinding mills and the difficulties of transporting sufficient sugarcane to them before it spoiled, larger properties were difficult to operate. In ranching, however, especially in barren country, large size was almost a necessity. In northern Mexico where there were few settled Indian communities to compete for land and where much arid land was needed to raise a single head of cattle, estates grew to enormous size. An extreme case is the *latifundio* of the Marqués del Aguayo, which by 1805 included almost 15 million acres of land divided among ninety-five properties, a series of estates about two-thirds the size of Portugal. In contrast, in small agricultural valleys, a few hundred acres of productive well-watered land in the midst of smaller farms or peasant fields might be considered a hacienda.

In Brazil there were similar distinctions according to the large estate's function. On sugar plantations, size was less important than the quality of the soil, access to water power for the mill, and good roads or easy water transportation. Some of the best Bahian and Pernambucan *engenhos* had less than a thousand acres. In the Brazilian sugar industry cane was also supplied to the mills by dependent cane farmers who controlled their own land and slaves. Thus the *senhor de engenho* could draw on the production of lands he did not own or work and the risk of low sugar prices or a bad harvest was shared. The largest Brazilian properties were not the *engenhos* but rather the enormous cattle ranches of the interior where many acres were needed to raise a single head of cattle and where restrictions on the size of land grants were usually ignored. In Bahia, for example, although one to three thousand head on a few thousand acres was common, there were properties with hundreds of thousands of acres. In the 1690s, Domingos Afonso Sertão owned over sixty ranches and farms with a total of over 2.5 million acres. Such "backland potentates" (*potentados do sertão*) were truly masters of cattle and people.

Large property size should not necessarily be equated with a luxurious lifestyle in the countryside. Characteristically, haciendas included a manor house (*casco*) where the owner or his manager resided, sheds, stables, employee houses, improved farming land, pasturage, and equipment. Sometimes the residences were well-built and furnished, but usually such luxury was reserved for the urban dwellings of the elite. There were exceptions as can be seen today in a few still-standing plantation houses in the Bahian sugar region or in the fertile lands near Guadalajara. Clerics sometimes complained about a profligate life-style, and the virtues of hospitality and largesse were highly esteemed by the landowners. Still, wills and testaments indicate that the fortunes of the landowners were usually invested in land, slaves, and stock rather than in clothing, furniture, jewelry, or other kinds of material goods. In fact, it is sometimes rather surprising to see in the inventories of prominent *hacendados* or Brazilian *senhores de engenho* how a European bed, some imported sheets, a lace ruff, and a service of silver spoons constituted the few prized valuables at the moment of death.

Material goods and luxuries were few partly because of the landowners' limited access to capital and credit. They needed funds to develop and maintain their properties, which were used to secure loans and mortgages, but sources were few. Without banks, many in colonial Latin America turned to private creditors. Merchants, and in some places miners, had capital available to lend to landowners. Private lenders often found ways to circumvent the limitations on usury that held interest rates to between 5 and 6 percent. Merchants preferred short-term loans, and they were willing to use the courts to collect their loans and to foreclose on borrowers who defaulted on payments. In areas like Brazil where fluctuations in the international price for sugar made planters especially insecure, access to credit was essential. By 1798 a governor of Bahia calculated that every merchant in the city had ten to twenty *senhores de engenho* and hundreds of cane growers as debtors. Large landowners complained about their debts and about the abuses of their creditors, but they could not survive without access to outside capital.

The other major source of credit for the large landowners was the church.[5] Whereas merchants often made short-term loans and sought to recapture the original capital, religious institutions had a different strategy and were willing to allow the term of the loan to continue indefinitely so long as the interest was paid. These low-risk, low-yield arrangements suited the religious institutions, which were seeking a constant flow of income. Over time, however, despite the benefit of available capital, properties often became encumbered by a number of loans and perpetual liens (*capellanías*) that reduced their value.

The prevalence and strength of large landowners in any region was subject to changing fortunes of the agricultural markets. Among the sugar-growing *hacendados* of Saña in northern Peru the cyclical nature of this process and its sensitivity to debt can be seen. Debts on the Saña estates totaled less than 10 percent of their value in 1600 when markets were strong and new capital was being invested but had risen to 40 percent by 1700 and 65 percent by 1800 as profits fell and family obligations grew. Sometimes a group of large landowners could develop quickly. In Ponce, Puerto Rico, there was only one estate sizable enough to be called a hacienda in 1816, but the arrival of French emigré planters and Spanish immigrants with capital to invest, coupled with a world demand for sugar that kept prices high, created conditions for estate formation. By 1825, Ponce had forty-nine haciendas, thousands of slaves and a new planter class.

The dependence on long-term ecclesiastical loans worked well as long as there was no need to repay the original principal of a loan or the capital value of a *capellanía*. When in 1804 the Spanish government, hoping to raise cash, assumed all debts owed to the church and then required the payment of annuities and the principal of overdue loans to it, landowners were placed in a difficult position. The wealthiest were able to make payments, more marginal *hacendados* were forced to sell. In some regions like Chile that lacked much available capital, few could pay. Even though the crown soon rescinded the 1804 decree, the measure revealed the nature of the credit problem, and it weakened the loyalty of the *hacendados* toward the government.

How much profit did the large estates generate? Although the landowning elite has often been portrayed as a class of great wealth, and it is true that in some periods large fortunes were made, the level of annual profit was more modest. Quantitative studies of Brazilian sugar estates and New Granadan mixed-farming haciendas both reveal a level of profit at about 5 to 6 percent a year, although there were periods of higher gains or of loss. This modest rate of return, however, was considered good enough because of the large volume of production and because of the security and social benefits that accrued to landholding. Even after a series of bad years, the fact that the land market continued to operate and that after failures and bankruptcies others were willing to buy large estates suggests that they were viewed as sound investments and not simply symbols of status.

Scholars still debate the extent to which the "hacienda became a sink through which poured the capital generated in other sectors of the economy," but the acquisition of lands was a common phenomenon and it was unusual to find a family fortune that did not include some rural property. Despite market fluctuations and the constant threat of flood, drought, frost, and pests, land provided a certain security, an asset that could secure loans, and a physical base around which the family could be organized. The relative importance of the landowners' economic and honorific goals has long intrigued historians. There was much about the large estates with their dependent workers under paternalistic control, self-sufficiency for many needs, and seemingly uneconomic control of extensive lands that were often not fully cultivated that seemed to recall the manorial system of feudal Europe. While it is true that large landowners often had a rudimentary idea of bookkeeping and accounting, and that they derived social status and power from their position, recent research has emphasized the economic nature of the large estates. For example, given the poor transportation and distribution network in many areas, regional monopoly of good land and thus of local markets was an effective way of limiting production and thus controlling prices. Thus owning more land than was farmed or grazed to limit production and competition was a rational economic strategy and had a more practical end then satisfying the *hacendados'* desire to gaze upon a lordly domain.

The Landed Elite

Wealth, status, and power defined the colonial elites. Landholding became the symbol of elite status in many places in colonial Latin America and even those who became wealthy through mining, commerce, or governmental office often acquired land as a supplementary basis of wealth and position. Take the case of Antonio de Vivanco who made a fortune in the mines at Bolaños and Zacatecas and invested most of it in rural estates like the ten- thousand-acre Hacienda de Chapingo near Mexico City. It probably makes little sense to speak of the landed elite as a separate social category. People from various occupational groups could buy land and thus become landowners. In León, Mexico, in 1770, for example, the town council was composed of three men born in Spain who were merchants and three American-born whites (*criollo*) *hacendados*. But within a few years two of the merchants had bought haciendas and one of the *criollos* was also a merchant.

The wealthy in León and elsewhere tended to form a single social strata, but deep conflicts could still arise between merchants and *hacendados* on specific economic or fiscal issues such as the setting of commodity prices or financing arrangements. In Brazil, for example, planters sought and obtained the privilege of having their *engenhos* exempted from foreclosure, and they also sought a moratorium on the payment of their debts at various times. These were measures firmly opposed by the merchants who had lent the money to the planters. Membership in the same social class did not remove differences of economic interest.

Government officials and clerics also sought land. A royal survey of the property of all officeholders in Mexico made in 1624 indicated that even by that early date, landed property had become a major source of wealth for the *cabildo* members of Puebla and other major towns. Even priests owned lands as private individuals (to say nothing of the large properties owned by religious orders, monasteries, and other church institutions). Landowning was no guarantee of economic security or of elite status, but it was considered a step toward both.

Fig. 25. Chilean country gentleman and lady. Drawing by Felipe Bauza. (Universidad de Santiago. Biblioteca Central).

Fig. 26. A plantation. Zacharias Wagener, *Zoobiblion: Livro de Animais do Brasil.*

Fig. 27. Sugar cane. M.E. Decourtilz, *Flore pittoresque et medicale des Antilles* (1883).

28. Harvest scene. Baltasar Jaime Martínez Compañón y Bujanda, *Trujilo del Peru.*

How was that step usually made? The two crucial moments in the linkage of family and property were those of marriage and death. Aside from the land grants, usurpation, *composición*, and purchase, rural estates also originated in, and were expanded by marriages, dowry, and inheritance. Women often played an important role in the transfer and maintenance of property. Women were able to inherit properties, and the possession of a good hacienda often became an asset in attracting a suitable husband. Women, often as widows, sometimes controlled large agricultural enterprises. In late colonial Bahia, for example, men owned 80 percent of the properties, but the largest single slaveowner in the region was doña Maria Joaquina Pereira de Andrade, who controlled four sugar mills and a number of subsistence crop farms with a total of almost six hundred slaves. She was not alone and other sugar mills and cane farms were also owned by women. This reality of feminine ownership and management was confronted, however, by an ideology that considered women unfit for such roles. In one Brazilian legal suit in 1800 two siblings accused their mother of mismanaging a property. The children argued that "management by a woman, even an active and efficient one, is as a rule not the best practice." Such attitudes were found throughout Latin America, but the reality of women who took on responsibilities as owners and managers of large estates contradicted them in practice.

Landowning families planned and arranged unions that would not only link their families but unite their properties. In the southern Peruvian region of Arequipa the first generation of the elite made up of *encomendero*-landowners tended to marry outsiders from Lima and elsewhere; after 1600 the elite increasingly married other local landowners including relative newcomers. Patterns in which newcomers sought marriage with the daughter of an established *hacendado* family, or in which two or more children of one family married the siblings of another, or in which cousins were betrothed were common strategies for acquiring and maintaining rural properties. In early São Paulo, Brazil, the relative poverty of many young men moved families to give their daughters large dowries to make sure that suitable mates could be found and that families could maintain control over property. In this way, the patriarchal mantle passed from fathers to sons-in-law, and male heirs were encouraged to seek their fortune on the frontier. Other strategies were attempted. By the mid-eighteenth century in Mexico, a pattern emerged among the landowning merchants in which their haciendas were willed to their American-born sons, but their businesses went to their son-in-laws, the European-born husbands of their daughters who were often also their nephews.

Preoccupation with preserving property and family may have resulted in some peculiarities of demographic and social structure for the landowners as a group. Evidence from the eighteenth century for the wealthy Caracas cacao planters and for the newly emerging sugar planters of western São Paulo indicates a pattern of delayed marriage for men and earlier marriage for women. In both places elite men married on an average between twenty-eight and twenty-nine years old and women around age twenty. The delay of family formation for elite men while similar to the contemporary European patterns differed nevertheless from the majority of the Latin American population. The relatively young age of their spouses had the effect of maximizing reproduction and perhaps insuring an heir. Given life expectancy of around fifty years for men, this pattern also had the effect of reducing the number of property transfers between living fathers and sons since often fathers were deceased by the time their children married. This in turn then created a situation in which mothers and mothers-in-law often fulfilled the "patriarchal" roles as senior members of families at the time a new family was being formed. Finally, this pattern probably gave older uncles and male cousins who often served as estate executors an important role in family and property decisions.

While people of elite status often owned land, landowning as such conferred no special privileges, tax exemptions, or the rights to office that were usually enjoyed by European nobles, nor was there the constant round of public events, celebrations, and private parties and receptions where status could be continually established and compared.[6] Thus the landowners were an aristocracy always seeking to acquire legitimation as a nobility or as members of it by acquiring titles, knighthoods, or other symbols of distinction.

The formation or acquisition of a large landed estate, however, often proved easier than winning those insignia and privileges usually associated with elite or noble status in Europe. Promises to grant titles of nobility or knighthoods in the Spanish military orders, to award the status of hidalgo to those who helped to conquer and settle new areas, or to allow the creation of entails were often made but seldom fulfilled. In the sixteenth century only Cortés and Pizarro, the conquerors respectively of Mexico and Peru, received titles of Spanish nobility. Both were made marquis. In the seventeenth century, the Spanish crown's financial problems resulted in an increase in the granting (sale) of titles. In Peru between 1665 and 1700, twenty-seven such grants were made. The eighteenth century was the great age of ennoblement in the Americas, but even then, the numbers remained small. Through the whole of colonial Mexican history, for example, the crown only rewarded eighty families with noble titles, and at the end of the colonial era, there were fifty titled nobles, almost all of whom resided in Mexico City. The vast majority of elite landholders had to content themselves with a knighthood, a militia commission, or some other insignia of noble status that gave a luster to their position and legitimated their aristocratic pretensions. Here too there was a mix of practical and symbolic motives. In Brazil, membership in a military order of knighthood exempted the holder from paying the tithe (the tax on production owed to the church). This was an added attraction to the planters seeking noble status but also one of the reasons why the crown was reluctant to grant many of these honors. In Spanish America, knights were entitled to similar exemptions.

Militia commissions were a more attainable prized attribute because a commission entitled the holder and his family to the *fuero militar,* the privilege of being exempt from civil justice and only subject to military courts. Militia officers could bear arms and ride horses—traditional signs of nobility—and their uniforms and positions of command reinforced their social position. The benefits were not only symbolic. In Mexico, landowners who commanded militia units sometimes used their troops to mobilize or terrorize workers or to impose their will on Indian communities. While the sons of landowning families sometimes chose a military career, the landed elite preferred local militia units where status counted in promotions and where duties were performed close to home. This pattern had existed since the establishment of militia units, but it intensified during the period of reform in the eighteenth century. By the early 1800s, for example, in Mexico, fifty-four of the eighty or so men with noble titles held militia commissions, while in Bahia, Brazil, two-thirds of all the officers of the militia units were sugar planters. For these men such rank was a logical extension of their social position. When Antonio de Bittencourt Berenguer Cezar applied for a position as a colonel in the Bahian militia in 1786, he justified his promotion both on his many years of military experience and on the fact that he owned three "first class" *engenhos.*

Another symbol of elite status but also one with practical uses was the *mayorazgo.* Among the techniques for preserving wealth and combating the rules of inheritance in Spanish and Portuguese law, which guaranteed each child an equal share and thus threatened to break up properties, the *mayorazgo (morgado* in Portuguese) was a much-sought prize. The privilege of entailing property so that it could not be alienated or subdivided and then making it inheritable by one child, usually the eldest son, in Spain had been granted only to the nobility as a way of preserving a basis for the luster and continuity of the family name, or as the grants read, so "that there remain[s] a greater memory of you and your wife... and that your descendants may be more honored and have the substance to better serve the crown."[7] Yet, few *mayorazgos* were authorized before the late eighteenth century. In central Mexico only sixty-two were created before this date and even at the close of the colonial era no more than a hundred existed. In Chile, a poorer colony, only nineteen have been identified and most of these dated from the eighteenth century.

In the words of Tomás Manuel de la Canal, the Mexican son of a Basque merchant, the entails were sought to avoid the "ruin and dissipation of funds and patrimony . . . causing the despair, outrage, and decline of families."[8] With such security, the holder could assume the obligation of making charitable bequests, supporting indigent relatives, and provide loyal service to the crown. Entails prevented foreclosures on the estate to pay debts. They allowed families to maintain property across generations. Along with good management, adequate markets, and some luck, an entail helped to support and maintain an aristocratic way of life, but it was no cure-all. It had certain disadvantages. Portions of entailed properties could not be mortgaged and thus the opportunity to borrow money was curtailed by these large, integrated assets. Some of the most astute merchants, in fact, refused to tie up their assets in this way. Legal suits by less-favored heirs were not uncommon against the *mayorazgos*. Above all, the ability to dispose of some property in the entail in order to improve the rest was legally restricted. Still, until their abolition in the nineteenth century, the entailed estates represented the most stable kind of property.

While not all entails were large or successful, some of the largest properties and wealthiest families were *mayorazgo* based. In the 1820s, the Conde del Valle de Orizaba in Mexico held an entail that had originated as an *encomienda* in the sixteenth century. In the seventeenth century when the entail was established, the estate had expanded to include almost ninety square miles of lands in the sugar-growing region of Morelos. Over the next five generations other properties and entails were added through marriage so that eventually the *mayorazgo* of Valle de Orizaba included lands producing sugar, wheat, sheep, and grain all over central Mexico. This pattern of wealth and stability was, however, the exception, not the rule.

While the great entailed estates of the most prominent landowners symbolize the power and continuity of the *hacendado* class, the reality for most members was far more volatile. Nonentailed estates were regularly dismembered by inheritance even though siblings might cooperate to run a hacienda or make arrangements to buy out a co-heir. Studies in the Mexican Bajío, Guadalajara, and Morelos; in Venezuela; and in Chile indicate that land was regularly bought and sold, haciendas often changed ownership, and those owners who did not have nonagricultural sources of capital and credit were often particularly vulnerable to failure. A three-generation cycle became proverbial. The founder of the hacienda using energy, influence, and luck constructed the landed fortune, his heir added to it and enjoyed the prestige and security it offered, but by the third generation, the grandchildren frittered away the family wealth by bad management and a profligate life-style. Despite the mythology of wasted lives and fortunes, however, climatic crises and market fluctuations had a significant effect on the stability of the large estates.

The cycle of construction and dissolution meant in effect that the landowning elite remained relatively open and that access to it was always possible by individuals displaying a certain social and economic character. Of the 164 *encomendero-estancieros* listed as the Chilean elite in 1655, only 5 people with the same surnames remained among the top rank of landowners at the close of the eighteenth century. For the most part they had been replaced by northern Spanish, especially Basque, immigrants like the Larraín, Eyzaguirre, and Echeverría families who along with other Spanish immigrants had turned the money made in commerce into land and noble titles. In the Guadalajara region of Mexico, each of eighty haciendas were sold an average of four times between 1700 and 1815; thus each hacienda changed hands approximately every twenty-eight years, although the rate of turnover slowed after 1760 as expanding markets and a better labor supply made hacienda operations more profitable. Similar rates of turnover could also be found in other regions of Mexico.

The Bahian planter class provides an interesting example of an elite with aristocratic pretensions that never became a hereditary nobility or a closed group. Many types of people became sugar planters, from royal governors to men like the "New Christian" (descendants of converted Jews) brothers Pascoal and Dinis Bravo. In rather typical fashion the Bravo brothers came to Bahia as merchants in the early 1600s, began growing sugarcane for others, and finally established their own mill. In the years between 1680 and 1725, about 30 percent of the Bahian sugar planters were, like them, immigrants. True, 70 percent were Brazilian-born, but many of these were the children of immigrants. Plantership was open and acquiring an *engenho* was a step toward elite status. For example, João Lopes Fiuza came from Portugal in the 1690s to work for his merchant brother in Salvador. In 1709 he married his sister-in-law, the daughter of a prominent planter, and thus acquired an estate, Engenho de Baixo, to which he later added another plantation. He continued to combine commerce and sugar planting and by the time of his death in 1741 had served on the town council and had become a prominent member of the Bahian elite.

Men like Lopes Fiuza derived great pride from their title of *senhor do engenho* or lord of the mill, and virtually never called themselves *fazendeiros* (the Portuguese equivalent of *hacendados*). The title *senhor do engenho* in Brazil was equivalent to a title among the Portuguese nobility because according to one observer the *senhor* was "served, obeyed, and respected." Ownership of a sugar mill was not necessarily a sign of noble status, but since nobility depended on how one lived as much as on a formal grant of noble status, *engenho* ownership called for a seignorial life-style with broad control over family, dependents, and slaves. No wonder then that sugar planters thought of themselves as the nobility of the land. Few, in fact, had noble origins in Portugal, and those that did were generally from the *fidalgo* class of the lesser nobility. But in Brazil their predominant economic position made them a local aristocracy, and they came to see themselves serving the same social function as the nobility of Portugal. Women of the planter class, although subordinate to men, held similar attitudes and position among other women. They saw themselves as "moons among the stars" in local society. These were views eventually accepted by others in the colony and by the Portuguese crown, which depended on the loyalty and industry of this class to hold the colony and make it valuable.

Although large landowners were an elite, there was considerable gradation among them. Among the Brazilian planters distinctions could be made between the few traditional lineages woven together by marriage, kinship, and association, which seemed to be able to weather the blows of nature, politics, and struggles over legacies, and those others that strove, usually unsuccessfully, to reach that status. In Bahia and Pernambuco everyone recognized the names of the elite: Bulcão, Aragão, Argolo in Bahia; Rego Barros, Cavalcanti, Albuquerque in Pernambuco. Members of these lineages controlled the best properties and over the generations exercised political and social power in their region. To their ranks others constantly aspired, especially when world demand for sugar was high. By 1820, Bahia had 340 *engenhos* owned by 250 individuals. The few dominant families created an impression of stability, but among the more marginal producers there was considerable turnover. Few broke into the circle of the twenty to fifty families that stood at the top.

This same division could be found in many parts of Spanish America as well. There is good quantitative information about this division from the region around La Paz in Upper Peru (Bolivia) in the decade prior to 1797. At that time, the region had 1,100 haciendas producing food, livestock, and coca leaves. These estates were owned by 719 *hacendados* (124 were women) who had almost eighty-three thousand landless workers *(yanaconas)* under their control. The wealthier *hacendados* who owned more than one estate were only a quarter of the landholders, but they held almost half of the workers. Within the wealthy group, the twenty largest landowners controlled over 145 estates with almost twenty thousand workers. The richest *hacendados* of this province tended to be absentee owners and resided in their townhouses in La Paz. Curiously, here as elsewhere, those who created the image of the rural patriarch and set the standard for the life-style of the hacienda elite were the most likely to be living in a nearby city. Often, they were men like Tadeo Diez de Medina, owner of fifteen haciendas with over seventeen hundred *yanaconas* in the area near La Paz who used the wealth generated from commerce and urban real estate to develop haciendas acquired by dowry and purchase in order to establish each of his children as a landowner.

This Bolivian data show that "the hacendado class was not an undifferentiated elite, but rather a complex layering of both local resident and absentee landlords, of small single hacendado farmers with relatively few Indians, and of multiple owners whose holdings extended over the vast stretches of the province."[9] Other studies have revealed similar patterns. The landowning elite was generally open to all whites and membership in it depended more on wealth than status, although these two attributes tended to coalesce in the top layer of society.

By the eighteenth century in many places in Latin America, the landed elites sought to codify their status and to create an image of themselves as a hereditary aristocracy. Genealogical histories were written or invented to honor and legitimate them. These histories covered over "defects" of birth or purchase of titles and privileges. The fact that a family's ancestor had been among the original conquerors and settlers more than made up for his possible low social origins. In the multiracial societies of the American colonies the landed elite were almost invariably white or accepted as such and that was a necessary attribute of elite status. Indians or mestizos in a family tree were explained away or covered over and new links with recent arrivals from Spain or Portugal tended to reinforce the racial separation between the elite and the mass of the population. The American-born elites, however, remained sensitive about their social and racial origins. Their constant drive for titles, knighthoods, and other emblems of nobility became a cause for ridicule in Europe. But by the mid-eighteenth century, the power of the landowning elite over the American colonial societies was no laughing matter in Lisbon and Madrid. Reforming ministers in Portugal and Spain believed that the power of this class either had to be harnessed to royal interests or broken if the colonies were to remain secure.

Landowner Power and Politics

The landed elites stood just behind the highest royal officials at the apex of the colonial social hierarchy, and despite their varying fortunes, they were usually counted among the richest members of society. The landowners sought to turn their status and wealth into social and political power at different levels. The first layer of their power was expressed in their relations with other landowners, neighboring Indian communities, and dependent workers. While *hacendados* might recognize common interests with others of their class, there are many examples of cases where both the law courts and violence were used to settle disputes and to drive competitors out of operation. Relations with Indian communities in disputes over land and water rights showed a similar pattern of conflict, although at times landowner strategies such as limiting village production were designed to encourage communal Indians to work for the private estates. Sometimes in these disputes Indian communities showed resilience. In eighteenth-century Morelos, the haciendas' dependence on irrigation made them particularly susceptible to sabotage of aqueducts and as a result the landowners were cautious in their dealings with Indian communities. Usually, however, the balance of power rested with the elite landowners.

It was in their dealings with dependent workers that the power of the elite landowners was most immediately seen by the majority of the population. The large estates had a curious double aspect. The old Iberian concepts of nobility led to a life-style that promoted a patriarchal attitude toward dependents, who in the Americas were often racially distinct. Indians, mestizos, free blacks, slaves, and poor whites worked under *hacendado* control in a variety of labor arrangements as sharecroppers, salaried employees, tenant farmers, tenured workers, or bonded servants. These labor arrangements often varied according to the ethnic or racial status of the worker; Indians with one kind of arrangement, free blacks with another, slaves with a third. In some places, work contracts (*conciertos*) regulated the relationship. In the early seventeenth century, for example, on doña Ana de Carrión's hacienda in Mariquita province, New

Granada, Indians and their families received twelve to twenty-four pesos a year, food, and *doctrina* (services of a priest) for work as herdsmen. The overseer of the estate's Indians, Pedro Criollo (probably a free black) received thirty-six pesos in gold, food, and *doctrina* for himself, his wife, mother-in-law, and two children. Francisco Fajardo (a Spaniard or mestizo) received a straight salary of fifty pesos to direct the roundup of the herds. By the eighteenth century in New Granada, these arrangements, which included religious services and food for workers' families, had been abandoned in favor of salaries paid directly and exclusively to individuals for defined tasks to be done in specified periods of time.

The *hacendado* expected deference from workers and support when needed in local disputes. The image of the mounted *hacendado,* greeted on the road by his *peones* who doffed their hats, returned his questions with "Sí Señor, No Señor," and then accepted his parting blessing has become part of the reality and the mythology of the rural landscape. In return for deference and support, paternalistic care and protection was to be provided to the workers. Owners might serve as ritual godparents for workers (in Brazil, almost never for slaves), provide a chapel or the services of a priest, pay for harvest celebrations, provide tools and food, and extend credit. This last "benefit" had a negative aspect for those workers who eventually became indebted to the estate, but debt peonage was relatively limited in the colonial period. In many ways, social relations on the large estates took on an almost medieval tenor of lord and master; however, the owner and his family often lived in a city or town and the resident *mayordomo* embodied the patriarchal contract. (See Fig. 28.)

The large landowners sought to express their power beyond the countryside by the control of important institutions of local government such as municipal councils. Whereas in the sixteenth century, the *cabildos* had been dominated by *encomenderos,* in the seventeenth century *hacendados* had replaced them in many places in Spanish America. Power on these bodies was sometimes shared with miners and merchants, but American-born landowners held many municipal offices.

A similar situation existed in Brazil where the sugar planters dominated municipal life in the seventeenth century. On the town council of Salvador, planters predominated through most of the century although merchants and bureaucrats also shared power. Only when new town councils were developed in the heart of the sugar-growing region, did the planters begin to give ground on the Salvador council, and even then merchants never held more than a quarter of the offices prior to 1740. In Pernambuco, the sugar planter "nobility of the land" had long dominated the town council of Olinda, and when in 1710 the nearby port area of Recife sought to establish its own council dominated by mercantile interests, a civil war erupted. Even in Recife, however, the landed aristocracy also held municipal office. Membership in a municipal council might have practical benefits but it also testified to an individual's status as a respectable and important individual, what the Portuguese in Brazil called a "man of governance," and the Spanish referred to as "the nobility of the city." It was therefore yet another way of establishing elite status.

The *hacendados,* however, had other, informal ways to be heard. Through marriage, business, friendship, and kinship, links were forged with the royal bureaucracy that gave the landowners access to the seats of political power. High court judges, retainers of the viceroys, and other Spanish bureaucrats married the daughters of the landowning class and thus acquired both property and family connections. At the same time, creole *hacendados* sent their own sons to study law and prepare for the royal bureaucracy. By the eighteenth century, many *hacendados* held governmental positions, sometimes in violation of the regulations restricting service to areas outside of one's homeland. The result of this process was creole predominance at many levels of governance and a corruption in government that favored the interests of the local elites. The image of the *hacendado* and the *corregidor,* the local magistrate in charge of Indians, collaborating to exploit native people was often a reality. Spanish reformers who viewed the haciendas as exploitative institutions and argued for a return of Indian lands faced the entrenched interest of the most powerful group in colonial society.[10]

Conclusion

During the late eighteenth century, the Bourbon monarchs of Spain instituted a series of reforms designed to improve government and administration in the Spanish Indies and, by various fiscal reforms and innovations, to increase revenues. The target of many of these reforms were the dominant local groups, and principal among them the *hacendados,* most of whom were creoles. As the creoles were moved out of government offices, old ties of influence were broken, and the landowning class confronted a newly invigorated bureaucracy less inclined to serve local interests. Moreover, measures like the Consolidación of 1804, which called for the repayment of existing loans from the church, struck the *hacendado* class a heavy blow. But the landowning elite showed remarkable resilience in the face of these reforms. Governors soon realized that cooperation of local elites was essential for the overall program of strengthening the empire.

Conditions were also changing. A rapidly growing colonial population, the opening up of trade within the Spanish empire after 1765, and changing opportunities in world markets created conditions in both Spanish America and Brazil for the expansion of agriculture and of landowning elites. In Brazil, government policies and new markets resuscitated sugar in the traditional areas of the northeast, promoted new crops like indigo and cotton, and stimulated the growth of cattle ranches in the southern grasslands. In areas such as Mexico, the *hacendados* benefited from the colony's growth although they continually complained of their poverty caused by bad harvests, high costs, and the indolence of the Indians. These new conditions of trade and market created opportunities for sugar planters in Cuba and cattle ranchers in the Río de la Plata and stimulated the growth of new landowning groups in those areas. Landowners were increasingly willing to express their common interests politically not only in local government, but by appealing to the crown in "representations" for a loosening of trade and tax restrictions.

By the beginning of the nineteenth century, those few critics who began to see the large estate and the maldistribution of land as a cause of colonial poverty confronted throughout Latin America powerful and entrenched landowning classes prepared to defend their social and economic position. During the wars of independence and the creation of national states in Latin America, the landowners emerged in many regions as a predominant economic force and the heirs to state power, anxious to direct the destinies of their new nations, which they assumed to be parallel to their own interests as a group.

Notes

1. Cited in Guillermo Lohmann Villena, *Los americanos en las órdenes nobiliarias (1529–1900),* vol. 1 (Madrid, 1947), xxii.

2. James Lockhart, "Encomienda and Hacienda: The Evolution of the Great Estate in Latin America," *Hispanic American Historical Review* 49, no. 3 (August 1969): 411–29.

3. José Joaquín Fernández de Lizardi, *El Periquillo Sarniento,* ed. Jefferson Rea Spell, 3d ed. (Mexico City, 1966). See the discussion in Doris M. Ladd, *The Mexican Nobility at Independence, 1780–1826* (Austin, Texas, 1976), 8.

4. This case is drawn from Hermes Tovar Pinzón, *Hacienda colonial y formación social* (Barcelona, 1990), 97–102.

5. Bauer, in the chapter entitled "The Colonial Economy" in this book, discusses the types of credit offered by the church and their effect on landowners.

6. This point in made by David Brading, "Government and Elite in Late Colonial Mexico," *Hispanic American Historical Review* 53, no. 3 (August 1973): 389–414.

7. Hayward Keniston, *Francisco de los Cobos* (Pittsburgh, 1958), 115.

8. Quoted in David Brading, *Haciendas and Ranchos in the Mexican Bajío: León, 1700–1860* (Cambridge, 1978), 29.

9. Herbert Klein, "The Structure of the Hacendado Class in Late Eighteenth Century Alto Peru: The Intendencia of La Paz," *Hispanic American Historical Review* 80, no. 2 (May 1980): 200.

10. Such reforms for Peru were suggested by two royal investigators. See Jorge Juan and Antonio de Ulloa, *Discourse and Political Reflections on the Kingdoms of Peru,* ed. John J. TePaske (Norman, Okla., 1978), 154–62.

CHAPTER FIVE

The Clergy

JOHN F. SCHWALLER

In nearly every rural area of colonial Latin America the one certain representative of Spanish domination was the local priest. The clergy's mission of Christianization and the means by which they supported themselves make the priests and friars one of the most controversial and influential rural social groups. The close partnership between church and state, a hallmark of Iberian colonization, was never static. The colonial period in Latin America was marked by a growing dominance of the state over the church.

The Catholic church at first glance seems to be the epitome of a monolithic institution. It actually contained two quite different types of clergy, the regulars and the seculars. The regular clergy included all those priests and friars who were members of religious orders, who took special vows, such as vows of poverty, above and beyond the normal priestly vows of celibacy and obedience, and who lived in accord with a special rule. Because regular clergy were largely self-governing, under the direct authority of their prior or abbot, friars could generate their local leadership; since they also lived and frequently traveled in groups, they constituted a fairly independent unit. This organization meant that the regulars were particularly well suited to the new missionary activity.

The secular clergy were the normal parish priests, subject to the direct authority of a bishop. Rather than live in a cloister, these priests lived out in the world. Although the parish priest could administer the sacraments of baptism, Eucharist, marriage, penance, and unction, in all things, secular priests were subject to the will and authority of their bishop. In Europe, regular clergy was normally confined to monasteries and convents while the secular clergy administered the parishes; in the Americas, because of the early history of missionary activity, both the seculars and the regulars had responsibility over parishes.

The three-hundred year sweep of the colonial period actually encompassed quite different phases in the influence of the clergy. The first period of church activity began with the initial conquest and settlement and continued until 1575–1600. By the last quarter of the sixteenth century the major thrust of evangelization of the Indians had been accomplished and efforts were focused toward the routine spiritual administration of both Spaniards and Indians. The seventeenth century marked another shift, with the gradual transfer of rural parishes from the regulars to the seculars (secularization), and a slow increase in the number of seculars in rural parishes. Many secular clerics did not pursue ecclesiastical careers and instead owned estates, ranches, and enterprises in the mining districts. In addition rural estates under religious control proliferated. (See Fig. 29.)

From about 1740 until Independence in the 1820s the process of secularization ended. At the same time there was a decrease in the prestige of the clergy and of the church as an institution. While the church remained a powerful economic and social force, the monarch came to exercise more absolute control over both the secular and regular clergy. In the first half of the eighteenth century, the king issued a series of decrees that prohibited the construction of new convents and monasteries, limited the number of novices who could be admitted to the orders, and placed limits on bequests to the church. This trend culminated in the expulsion of the Jesuits in 1767. After the expulsion of the Jesuits, the other religious orders and the hierarchy of the secular clergy proved to be docile in their dealings with the crown. As the church and clergy fell under royal domination, the institution lost considerable stature.

The Clergy in the Early Colony

The missionary efforts of the clergy in the rural areas are famous. Although church evangelization throughout Hispanic America was filled with drama, the Mexican experience has received the most study. Friars and other clerics had already been active in the Antilles when the conquest of Mexico thrust the missionaries into a totally new and unforeseen experience: confrontation with more complex beliefs, a highly organized priestly class, and a larger population. The spreading of Christianity has been called the "spiritual conquest." The term is appropriate, for the missionaries needed the same kind of organization, discipline, and order that was needed by any military company. Because the regular clergy had the internal structure necessary to operate in the newly conquered territories, and had received papal permission to administer sacraments independently from local bishops, the spreading of the Gospel most often fell to them. Seculars, on the other hand, tended to follow along as areas were Christianized and settled.

The conquest of the major regions of the Americas provides many examples of the activity of seculars and regulars. In both the conquest of Mexico and the conquest of Peru two principal clerics, one regular and one secular, accompanied the expedition. Serving under Cortés were Father Bartolomé de Olmedo, a Mercedarian friar, and Juan Díaz, a secular priest. Olmedo was Cortés's private chaplain and also responsible for the spiritual needs of the army. Díaz was a member of the expedition in his own right and served as the chaplain for the troops. Both priests played important roles in the missionary activity of the expedition. Díaz baptized the nobles of Tlaxcala, Cortés's first important Indian allies, while Olmedo normally celebrated the Mass when Cortés wanted to provide a good show for the natives.

As the military conquest ended, other priests and friars arrived in the New World to continue the "spiritual conquest." The first organized missionary expedition to Mexico consisted of twelve Franciscans who arrived in 1524. They were followed in 1526 by twelve Dominicans, and in 1533 seven Augustinians arrived. By 1559 the missionary corps had swelled to some 802 religious in some 160 monasteries.

In Peru a similar pattern emerged. The Franciscans there were also among the first missionaries to arrive, along with Dominicans and Mercedarians. All three were established in Peru shortly following the conquest. In 1534 and 1535 the Franciscan order established monasteries first in Quito and later in Los Reyes (modern-day Lima). The first Mercedarians appeared in Lima in 1535, and by 1540 they had established four monasteries in Peru; the same year twelve Dominicans arrived. The first regular clergy to come to Brazil were the Franciscans, but it was the Jesuits, led by Manoel de Nóbrega, who landed at Bahia with the first royal governor in 1549. They dominated the missionary effort in Portuguese America. (See Fig. 30.)

Regular priests were not the only clergy to migrate to the New World; in both Mexico and Peru seculars also began arriving shortly after the conquest. For example, Pedro López de Mendoza arrived in New Spain at about the same time as Bishop Zumárraga (1527), perhaps in his entourage. López worked in the rural areas of what would become three different dioceses—the Mixteca of Oaxaca, Michoacán, and Colima, as well as the mining districts of Taxco and Zultepec—and he learned Nahuatl, the indispensable Indian language for service in central Mexico.

Spreading the Gospel

The process of converting the Indians presented several important obstacles to the friars and priests. The two major problems were those of communication and the sheer size of the native population. To cope with the first, friars learned native languages, coming both to value and criticize the native cultures they studied. In many ways the early missionaries functioned as structural linguists. They listened to the languages, learned them aurally, then copied them down with Spanish letters. Unfortunately, there was not always a close fit between the sounds represented by the Spanish alphabet and those in the Indian languages. While the early linguistic efforts generally fell to the regulars, especially the Franciscans, eventually the secular clergy followed suit. One sure method of securing a clerical position was to learn a native language. The major languages—Nahuatl in Mexico, Quechua in Peru—were even taught in the universities founded in the colonies.

Native languages were important in the spiritual conquest. The first book printed in the New World was a catechism written in Nahuatl, published in 1539 in Mexico. Of the nearly two hundred works published in Mexico in the sixteenth century, no less than thirty-five were in Nahuatl, while other books were in Tarascan, Maya, Otomi, and even Timucuan from Florida. In colonial Peru similar works appeared in Quechua, Aymara, Guaraní, and other native languages. (See Fig. 32.)

Among the authors of works in native languages, two Franciscan friars were exceptional. Father Alonso de Molina, who learned Nahuatl as a child and grew up among the Franciscans, compiled the definitive dictionary, a work so complete that it remains the standard Spanish-Nahuatl and Nahuatl-Spanish dictionary. In addition to this work, Molina also composed a catechism, grammar, and two widely used confessional guides. He also translated constitutions for religious sodalities, papal indulgences granted to various sodalities, the method of praying the rosary, and other doctrinal works into Nahuatl.

The other giant of Nahuatl study in the sixteenth century was the better-known missionary, Father Bernardino de Sahagún. As with Molina, Sahagún's interest in the language came from a deep religious commitment, which lead him to immigrate from Spain and serve as a parish priest in several towns of central Mexico. In the case of Sahagún, this commitment took a curious turn. He compiled a twelve-volume encyclopedia of Aztec lore, religion, customs, beliefs, and history. Written in Nahuatl, this work closely resembles the field study of a modern anthropologist, but Sahagún studied the culture not merely to record or even preserve it, but rather to extirpate it. He wanted priests to know enough about Aztec culture to recognize its features among "Christianized" Indians, so that they might better stamp out all traces of the old culture. Yet much of what we know about the Aztecs we owe to Sahagún.

Such priests were not only found in central Mexico. Similar figures include the Franciscan friar Diego de Landa in Yucatán; another Franciscan friar, Luis Jerónimo Oré; and the secular priest Francisco de Avila in Peru. Avila, an orphan and probably a mestizo, was raised by the Jesuits of Cuzco. Seeking to fight backsliding among the Indians of his parish in the province of Huarochirí, he published a two-volume compendium of sermons in Quechua. Oré, the son of an *encomendero* in the province of Huamanga, learned Greek and Latin as well as Indian languages as a child. In 1607 he published a handbook of Catholic ritual with sections in Aymara and Quechua, as well as Guaraní, Puquina, Mochica, and one of the indigenous languages of Brazil. One of the leading missionaries of the late sixteenth and early seventeenth centuries, Oré seems to have had a certain sympathy for the Indians, while Avila was more antagonistic.

In the contact between natives and Spaniards, not all communication was clear. The spiritual conquest occurred with varying success in different parts of the Americas. Even in areas of large sedentary native populations where the friars learned the local language and conversion became routine, there were difficulties, because the Indian worldview differed so radically from the European. Some Indian practices had superficial similarities to Christian ritual. The friars sought familiar concepts in Indian religions as a point of departure for Christian instruction, but often the resemblance was deceptive and the results produced confusion and a sense of betrayal on both sides. The dialogue between the missionaries and the converts was never a simple exchange of ideas, and much was lost or deformed in translation.

For example, the Aztecs had a ritual of confession, called *neyol melahualiztli*, or "the act of making the heart straight," in which the penitent recounted his sins to the goddess Tlaelcuani, or filth-eater. But the Aztecs' concept of sin was that of impurity or filth caused by outside forces rather than by one's own actions. Furthermore, in Aztec practice it was sufficient to recount one's sins, while in Christianity a priest had to grant absolution and the penitent to pledge to sin no more. Among the Incas, one area of difficulty was their veneration of the mummified bodies of deceased rulers. While Christians believed all who died returned to God, erasing earthly distinctions of wealth and status, the Incas believed death reintegrated humans into a familial network that perpetuated the standing of the lineage. Spanish burning of the mummy bundles probably made the Inca less receptive to Christianity.

There were other problems too. Some of the native cultures of Paraguay lacked the necessary arithmetic concepts to count up their sins. The Tarascans, who dwelled largely in the area that is now the state of Michoacán in Mexico, did not understand the concept of sins of intent. In the end, missionaries complained that some natives did not confess regularly, and that when they did, it was a monotonous repetition of memorized lists of sins, while others clamored for the opportunity to confess, and then did so in exquisite detail, often with notes and visual aids.

One means of bridging the language barrier was the sixteenth-century equivalent of comic strips. This novel idea came from Father Jacobo de Testera, an early Italian Franciscan in Mexico. He used little stick figures to draw out the important features of Christian doctrine, thus creating what are know as Testerian catechisms. Theater was also used to spread the Gospel. Friars used pantomime early on to explain Bible stories. Once they had mastered the native languages they began to present European passion plays, translated into the Indian languages. These plays were extremely popular.

They were so well received that in many communities the natives still put them on, in one form or another, after nearly five hundred years.

The friars also needed to determine the amount of instruction needed for baptism. Should they imitate the ancient church and make the neophytes undergo a long and complicated theological indoctrination before offering them the benefits of the sacraments, or should they baptize them straight away and work later on perfecting their understanding of dogma? Although the friars clearly understood the strength of pre-Columbian religions, they believed the Indians more receptive to the Gospel than other groups with whom they had previous experience, such as the Muslims. Churchmen reasoned that the natives were merely heathens, individuals who had never ever heard the Gospel of Christ, while the Muslims were infidels, people who had heard the Gospel, but rejected it. In most areas the friars baptized first and preached second. One Franciscan lay-brother, Peter of Ghent, is credited with baptizing 100,000 Mexican natives in one day. Provincial Luis de Grã, a Jesuit missionary in mid-sixteenth-century Brazil, baptized 900 Indians in one long, nocturnal ceremony.

Clergy and Parishioners

Once the initial contact was made, and the friars settled into the native villages, the missionary activity became routine. On a regular basis, often daily, the priests convened the natives for indoctrination. Men, women, and children, were trained separately, according to their needs and abilities. Recognizing that the children could be a potent tool in indoctrinating the elders, the friars established schools for children to train them as Christian headmen who would return to their villages and occupy leadership positions in the native social and political order and to serve as examples to their people.

Indian children of the sixteenth century were not educated to become priests, however, for the Spaniards denied them the sacrament of ordination, believing that they lacked enough knowledge of Christian doctrine to become priests. Although there are some legendary exceptions, such as the son of the last king of Michoacán who became a priest shortly after the conquest, in 1555 the bishops of New Spain prohibited the ordination of anyone descended from an Indian, Jew, Moor, or heretic to the fourth generation. By the early seventeenth century, however, some Indians and mestizos were able to acquire enough training and demonstrate enough Hispanic cultural identity to qualify for the priesthood. Thus while mestizos and Indians entered the clergy in the seventeenth and eighteenth centuries, they were culturally more like Spaniards than natives.

In general the Indians did receive baptism, attend Mass regularly, and take the Eucharist several times a year. Many natives received the sacrament of confirmation. Sixteenth-century norms required at least annual confession. Marriage was required although the native nobility often had multiple wives, something the friars abhorred. The priests forced the nobles to recognize their first wife, as the true wife, and abandon the rest. Often the nobles suffered a convenient amnesia and could not remember which came first, allowing them the luxury of choosing the favorite.

In their region, the local priest, whether a secular or regular, came to control the daily life of the rural Indians. The community arose to the sound of the church bell, then went to Mass or indoctrination. From the church they were sent on their way to work in the fields by the priests. The clergy intervened at every important juncture of their life. The labor calendar revolved around ecclesiastical holidays. Early on, royal orders decreed that the natives were not to work on Sunday or important religious feasts, thus allowing the clergy to control free time.

There were two slightly different forms that the ecclesiastical administration of the native village could take. One occurred when the priests accepted the physical location of the village and its outlying communities, and continued to administer the town and hinterland as a whole, often proceeding along a routine circuit. A priest normally served in the principal town of the parish on Sundays and special feast days. He visited outlying villages, on a weekly or fortnight basis. The other type of administration occurred in areas where the officials, either civil or ecclesiastical, chose to relocate the outlying population into a new center. Because the population had been resettled into one village (*reducción* or *congregación*), less time was spent in traveling from place to place.

Tasmalaca, located in southern Mexico, between Mexico City and Acapulco, provides a good example of the duties and attitudes of a typical parish priest. In 1569 Antonio Fernández served the parish, which consisted of four independent towns (*cabeceras*), with a total tributary population of 1,757 and some 4,605 souls regularly confessing.

Canon Fernández lived continually on the move, never staying in any of the towns for more than four consecutive days. Upon arrival in the town he would call the Indians to the church, and there hear confessions, especially from the sick, and say Mass. He would call for all newborn children born since his last visit and baptism them. He would also begin the appropriate proceedings for any villagers who wished to be married and marry those natives who had been prepared on earlier visits. In his conversations he attempted to determine if any one had committed any serious offenses which might require a public punishment. He would then teach the doctrine to all the villagers and test them on their comprehension. They were required to know the four basic prayers (Our Father, Ave Maria, the Creed, and Salve Regina), the Ten Commandments, and the Articles of the Faith, although in some places the sacraments, and a list of mortal sins and Christian virtues were also required. The doctrine was taught in Nahuatl and Latin, but Fernández felt that trying to teach in Latin was a waste of time, and that it would be more reasonable to expect the natives to know the doctrine in their own language and Spanish. For his labors he was paid 230 *pesos de minas* annually by the local *encomenderos* who used part of the Indians' tribute payment to pay his salary.

Although he feared a reduction in salary because of declining Indian population, Fernández did not have an uncritical view of his parishioners. He believed that the greatest problems facing his villagers were public drunkenness and the excesses of the local Indian officials. He also felt that Indian self-government was like the blind leading the blind, and that more clerical supervision and greater access to royal justice were necessary. Although he was the only Spaniard living in the district, he noted that he did not receive any goods from the natives unless he had first paid for them.[1]

The priests' and friars' role in rural society remains a subject of controversy. Instruction in religion, the Spanish language, and mechanical trades or agriculture was a positive feature of the clergy's presence in the countryside. However, critics have accused them of being rapacious and cruel. Records of the *visitas,* periodical tours made by bishops to observe the priests of their dioceses, reflect both visions of clerical conduct.

In September 1609, don Alonso de la Mota y Escobar, a Mexican creole who served in the early seventeenth century as bishop of Guadalajara, set out on a visit of his diocese. Born and raised in the colony, he had learned Nahuatl as a child, a skill he later used in his priestly career. As a youth he spent time in the village of Chiapa, northwest of Mexico, where his father held an *encomienda.* Early in his clerical career, Mota had experience as a parish priest in rural areas of New Spain, as well as in the mining district of Pachuca.

On Saturday, 27 October, Bishop de la Mota arrived in Tlatlauquitepec, five leagues over a bad road from his previous stop. The village was administered by a secular priest, Lorenzo de Horta. In the town the bishop confirmed 790 Indian and Spanish children. Mota recorded that the town, located in a fertile region with a salubrious climate, consisted of 482 tributaries who spoke Nahuatl. During his visit, the bishop officiated at the solemn Mass for All Saints Day, preaching to the Indians in Nahuatl on the immortality of the soul, the nature of Purgatory, and the importance of prayer for the aid of the souls in Purgatory. He praised the priest, de Horta, as an honorable man.

Not all of the curates were as praiseworthy as Lorenzo de Horta. While visiting another village, Iztacymachtitlan, Mota suspended the curate, Pedro de Mendoza, for having illicit sex and engaging in commerce. In the parish of Quimichtlan, Mota found that the local priest had treated the Indians badly, engaged in prohibited trading, and committed other venial sins. Mota suspended him from his office for several months, and fined him.

Colonial chroniclers are another useful source on the priests and friars. One of the most important was the part-Indian Peruvian writer, Guamán Poma de Ayala, who illustrated in gruesome detail many of the depredations that clerics caused among Indian communities.[2] Guamán Poma tells the story of Juan Bautista Alvadán, curate of Pampachire, who demanded that his parishioners each give him a llama. When one, Diego Carúas, refused, Father Alvadán had him bound to an "X" shaped cross and began to burn his sexual organs and anus with a candle. Alvadán tortured other parishioners and took sexual advantage of women in the village, especially unmarried women in the household of one of the village elders. Alvadán was eventually punished and exiled from the territory.

The clergy who helped determine royal policy also displayed the two different faces of the priesthood. Clerics constituted the vanguard of the movement for social justice, as exemplified by the Dominican friar, Bartolomé de las Casas, who after a midlife conversion went on to champion the rights of the native peoples of the Americas. One of Las Casas's most fervent beliefs was that natives be attracted to the faith through peaceful examples. Yet, underscoring the divisions among the friars, an important group within the clergy argued that forceful conversion and use of corporal punishment and imprisonment to enforce regular attendance at Mass were justifiable. The dedicated Brazilian Jesuit, José de Anchieta, wrote in 1563 that "for these people there is no better preaching than by the sword and iron rod."[3]

The clergy's treatment of the Indians also varied from region to region. Exploitation seems to have been more acute in Peru, where there were fewer Spanish priests, settlers, and officials residing in the countryside, and they were less subject to scrutiny and restraint by one another. The priest in both Peru and Mexico constituted an independent authority of theoretically high moral stature who had the potential, at least, to check abuses committed by secular officials and landowners. The clergy, at the same time, felt quite comfortable demanding the services and goods from the Indians deemed necessary to the support of the parish.

Church-Indian relations were even more ambiguous along the frontiers where Spaniards were involved in long and bloody conflicts with native peoples. One of these regions, the Gran Chichimeca in northern Mexico, was inhabited by hunters and gatherers who proved to be far more difficult to conquer and Christianize than the sedentary peoples of central Mexico. Another region was Chile, inhabited by the fierce Araucanians.

In both the Mexican north and in Chile the crown faced a similar dilemma. On the one hand colonists demanded the opportunity to move into and settle the frontier regions. Settlers also asked for grants of *encomienda* so that the native population could provide the labor and materials to build the new society. On the other hand, the friars and others argued that if the Spaniards placed demands on the native population, the Indians would either flee or retaliate. In Mexico, the crown, under viceroys Villamanrique and Velasco II, adopted the policy of peaceful attraction to the faith for which Las Casas had fought, reducing the number of military expeditions against the natives and offering food and trade goods in return for peace and settlement. The policy did not accomplish all of its goals but it did lessen tensions in the Mexican north. Unfortunately, it was never attempted on the same scale in Chile, and the border with the Araucanians remained a battlefront into the nineteenth century.

Sacred Spaces

The physical arrangement of the church and related buildings tells us much about the pressures on the friars and their needs. The typical architectural plan in sixteenth-century Mexico included a church, a small adjacent open chapel, and a very large courtyard on one side. This courtyard, surrounded by a wall, recalled the pre-Columbian temple complexes in which a *coatepantli*, or snake wall, marked off the sacred space. Lacking formal knowledge of construction techniques, and faced with a huge Indian population, the early friars, made the courtyard the church and conducted rituals from the small chapel.

Although the early churches in New Spain were often built very close to ancient temples, seldom were they built right on top of the ruins. The placement of the earliest churches in association with prior religious sites conveyed the lesson that the old religion had died and was destroyed, that Christianity had triumphed, and that the two cults were separate and distinct. After a few generations of natives had grown up in Christian communities, the churches began to be built right on top of the old temples, since presumably the memories of the old religions had faded by then.

Likewise church iconography was initially quite European, although often executed by native workers. Later the iconography became more syncretistic, borrowing from both the Indian and the European traditions. Peruvian artists with little notion of what a Paschal Lamb should look like, substituted a roasted guinea pig, a local delicacy and celebratory food in their depictions of the Last Supper.

The earliest churches were built in a simple unadorned Renaissance style called plateresque. In Peru this simple style was very much in keeping with Inca notions of line and beauty. In Mexico, especially among the Aztecs, there was a much greater emphasis placed on decoration, especially in stone. Thus the churches built in Mexico have details that demonstrate the assimilation of Aztec style into the European architectural vocabulary. At Calpan the main door of the church is flanked by relief-carved stone flower spikes of the maguey cactus, painted red for maximum effect.

The plateresque slowly gave way to the baroque, a highly adorned and ornamented style that in America combined features of Indian and European sensibilities. In the small town of Tonantzinla, near Puebla, for example, the local church provides an excellent example of "Mexican mestizo Baroque." Every inch of the church is covered with ornamentation, including figures of cherubim and seraphim with Indian skin color and features and native dress. Because of the earthquakes that repeatedly destroyed towns in Peru, in the seventeenth century the newer baroque style was more widespread. Again surface ornamentation gave full scope to the mixing of Indian with Spanish motifs. (See Figs 31, 33, 34.)

Fig. 29. Priest forcing Indian woman to weave cloth for free by threatening and beating her. Guamán Poma de Ayala, *El primer nueva crónica y buen gobierno* (Paris, 1936).

Fig. 30. Church and plaza of Realejo, Chile. Drawing by José Cordero. (Madrid: Museo Naval).

Fig. 31. The convent of San Miguel Arcángel, Huejotzingo,
Puebla (Mexico), an example of plateresque rural church
architecture. *Vocabulario arquitectónico ilustrado*
(México: Secretaría del Patrimonio Nacional, 1976).

Fig. 32. Testerian catechism, and below, a transcription of a portion. Miguel León Portilla, *Un Catecismo Náhuatl en imágines* (México: Cartón y papel de México, 1979).

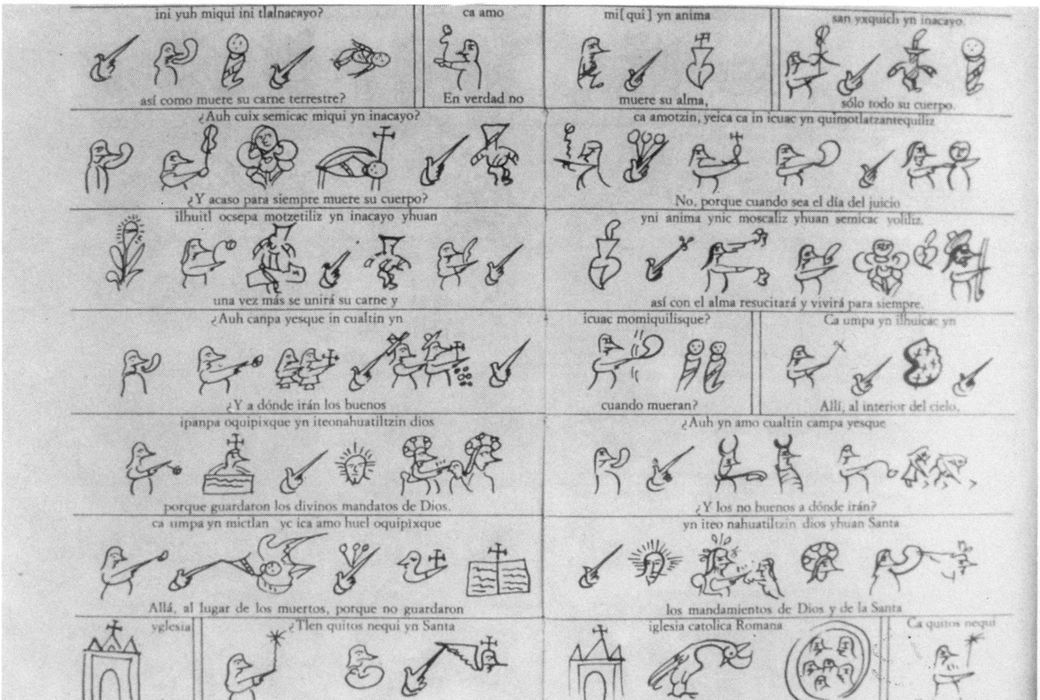

Fig. 33. San Miguel Arcángel, Charo, Michoacán, an example of an early Baroque rural church. *Vocabulario arquitectónico ilustrado* (México: Secretaría del Patrimonio Nacional, 1976).

Fig. 34. Open chapel of the church of Atlatláuhcan. John McAndrew, *The Open Air Churches of Mexico* (Cambridge: Harvard University Press, 1965).

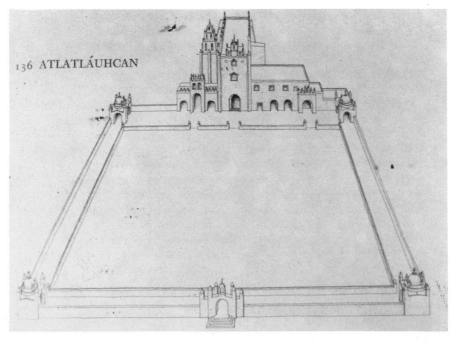

136 ATLATLÁUHCAN

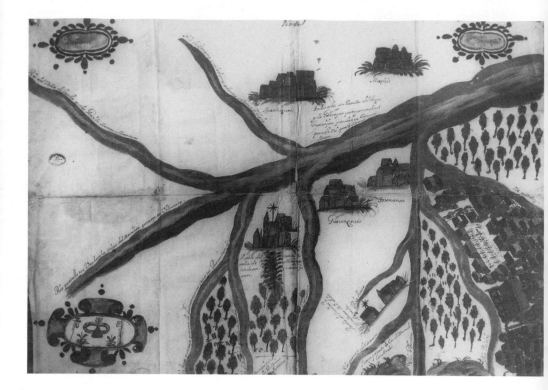

Fig. 35. Map of Franciscan mission territory to the north of Charcas and east of the Andes, 1678. (A.G.I., Mapas y Planos, Buenos Aires 24).

Fig. 36. *(Opposite:)* Plan of a church built in four different Indian reductions by the Governor of Tucumán Province, D. Gerónimo Matorras, 1775. (A.G.I., Mapas y Planos, Buenos Aires 240).

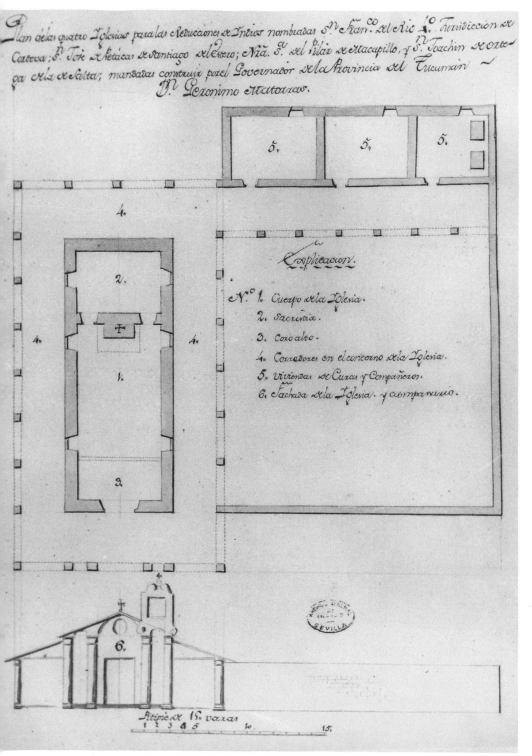

Clergy During the Middle Colony

From about 1575 until about 1740, few major changes disrupted the orderly life of the priests in the countryside, but some important shifts occurred. The most noticeable was the slow growth of the secular clergy and the gradual retreat of the regulars.

Increasingly appointment of priests fell under the *patronato real*, the power granted the Spanish crown to appoint all ecclesiastical officials in the New World. The church in America became a branch of the royal government. All bishops, archbishops, cathedral chapter members, and parish priests were appointed by the monarch, or other royal officials subject to papal approval. Only the parish priests from the regular orders fell outside this scheme, since they were responsible to their religious superiors.

In 1574, in the *Ordenanza del Patronazgo*, the king ordered that all parish clergy fall under the jurisdiction of the local bishop. The same *ordenanza* established a minimum guaranteed stipend, 150 *pesos de minas* per annum in Mexico, which allowed parish priests to live modestly but securely. The *ordenanza* also guaranteed that a priest would hold his office in perpetuity, and that curacies would be filled through competitive exams. Seeking to assure quality and to avoid the whim of a local prelate, these policies determined the course of parish service for the rest of the colonial period.

Up until about 1625, priests did not collect fees from Indians for the performance of routine clerical services, such as baptisms, marriages, and burials. After that, charging fees became routine, and a schedules of fees (*aranceles*) became a common feature of parish life. The reasoning behind this new policy reflected changing attitudes toward the Indians. Initially, Indians had been relieved of the need to pay fees because part of their tribute payment, the head tax paid by all natives, went to support the local parish priest. As the natives became more completely Christianized, it was decided that to better integrate them into the faith, they should be charged for services like any other Christian. With this, rural parishes became far more attractive places to work. The parish priest, in addition to receiving food, fodder for his livestock, and labor for his household, could also collect fees from the native parishioners.

What was the typical career pattern of a secular priest? He usually began his career by serving as an interim replacement in a parish. After a few years he would begin to compete for a permanent benefice in some parish, perhaps a small rural parish, which paid the minimum wage, moving on to a larger rural parish where he would both receive a higher salary and collect significant amounts for marriages and burials. Mining regions too were highly desirable because of their potential for outside income. Eventually the priest might win a large urban parish, or a secure a post as curate of his diocese.

Some clergy occasionally specialized in rural congregations, especially after fees could be charged. Pedro Ruiz Suárez, for example, was a parish priest in Oaxaca in the late sixteenth century. Ruiz refused the prestigious appointment as member of the cathedral chapter of the diocese of Chiapas (perhaps because the pay was nearly nonexistent). He remained in rural Oaxaca until his death in the early seventeenth century.

Other priests moved back and forth from rural to provincial urban settings. Don Joseph Rodríguez, a native of Lima, and son of a local physician, attended the University of San Marcos where he earned the degree of *bachiller* (baccalaureate in the liberal arts). For several years after his ordination he served as an interim curate, in Lima and in some rural parishes. In 1726 he won the curacy of Acas in the relatively remote Cajatambo province. In 1734 he competed successfully for an urban curacy in the city of Huánuco. Although it took him further from Lima, life in a Spanish town offered more advantages than in an Indian village, although he had mastered the Inca language, Quechua, and even taught it in the university. Six years later he competed for the parish of Los Reyes in Tarma province. Although it was a rural parish again, it was reasonably prosperous, supplying Lima with meat and wool. Eight years after that he moved to Pasco in the same province, a larger town with a Spanish population. His last move was to Araguay in the province of Canta, about sixty miles north of Lima.

An important function of many parish priests was to serve as the local ecclesiastical judge (*vicario*) within the church's courts set up to enforce canon law and hear the civil suits of the clergy. The matters handled by the local *vicario* were usually basic questions of faith and morals. Suits against Indians for living together without benefit of marriage were common. The extirpation of idolatry was also an important job for the parish priest. Although Indians were removed from the jurisdiction of the Inquisition, the natives were subject to the supervision of the local *vicario*, and many suits involving Indian idolatry were tried in the colonial period. In general, Peru produced many more cases against Indians for backsliding than Mexico, due to the less intensive conversion effort and the stronger position of the Indian nobility.

Parish priests might also administer agricultural enterprises. Although they were forbidden to participate in menial work or be employed by others, priests owned cattle ranches, sugar plantations, sheep stations, and farms. They were indistinguishable from other Spanish residents in the countryside, except that they supposedly maintained celibacy, were nominally subject to the bishop, and did not pay the tithe.

Clergy During the Late Colony

After many decades of relative inactivity, the religious orders, especially Jesuits and Franciscans, began new and vigorous missionary endeavors in the eighteenth century. The far fringes of the empire felt the impact of these initiatives, notably the far north of New Spain—California, New Mexico, and Texas—and the northern region of Río de la Plata—Misiones and modern-day

Paraguay and Bolivia. Both orders were supported by the crown, which paid the salaries of the soldiers and the missionaries. (See Fig. 35.)

By the middle of the eighteenth century the Franciscans had approximately 125 friars working in the northern missions, principally in Texas, Coahuila, Chihuahua, and New Mexico. The Jesuits operated in Sonora, Sinaloa, Arizona, and the Californias. After the Jesuit expulsion in 1767, the Franciscans took over many of their missions in the Californias, establishing missions in San Diego in 1769 and in San Francisco in 1776. Although the Jesuits in many ways had maintained the northwestern frontier as an active missionary region, the Franciscans emerged after 1767 in control of the entire missionary field.

The soldiers who served the *presidios* tended to come from the lower reaches of Spanish society, and included many mestizos and other mixed-bloods, but the mission friars and priests were overwhelmingly European and included many foreigners. Examples of the non-Hispanic nature of many of these missionaries can be seen among the Jesuits of the Pimería Alta, now part of Arizona. In 1732 the Jesuit missionary assigned to the mission at Guevavi was a native of Bleiburg in the Carinthia district of southern Austria. He was eventually replaced by a native of Lucerne and then a priest born in Zeven in the Duchy of Bremen. In 1741 the only Mexican-born priest to serve this mission arrived. He was replaced by a native of Sardinia, and then a Moravian from the town of Brno. The remaining priests who served till the Jesuit expulsion in 1767 included a man from Evenshausen in German Franconia; a native of Mannheim in the diocese of Cologne, and a priest from Valdelinares in the kingdom of Aragon.

The Franciscans serving along the northern frontier were an equally cosmopolitan group of men. There were very few natives of New Spain among the Franciscans sent to California. Of the 142 Franciscan missionaries who served between 1769 and 1848, only 19 were natives of the New World, 17 of them from Mexico. On the other hand, the Franciscan missionaries of New Mexico in 1776 were overwhelmingly European or American-born Spaniards. For example, in 1776 the missionary at San Jerónimo de Taos was a native of Mexico City, while the missionary priest at Santa Clara, near Taos, was a native of Tuy in Galicia, Spain.

While a handful of missionaries, such as Father Junípero Serra, are revered for their saintliness, the great majority of the friars merely did their job to the best of their ability and have been largely forgotten by posterity. Father Miguel Pieras, born in Palma de Majorca in 1741, was a typical missionary. He entered the Franciscan Order in 1757, also in Palma, leaving for American missionary labor in 1769. His passport records described him as of medium height with scant beard, pockmarks on his face, and chestnut-colored hair. He was a competent preacher and upon arrival in the New World was assigned to the College of San Fernando in Mexico City. In 1770 he was sent to the California missions, arriving in San Diego, then on to Monterrey. Along with a fellow *mayorquino*, Father Buenaventura Sitjar, he founded the Mission San

Antonio. Except for a few brief absences, he spent the rest of his career at this mission in California. By the end of 1793, the year that he retired, he and Sitjar had baptized over two thousand Indians at the mission. Pieras returned to Mexico City in late 1794 and died five months later.

The method of administering the mission parishes in the eighteenth century did not differ radically from practices in the sixteenth century. On major feast days and Sundays, Mass would be said in the village church. Afterward the priest would have the Indians recite the catechism. He might take that opportunity to give a short sermon, explaining some point of doctrine to the natives. Daily he would gather up the unmarried boys and girls and go over the catechism with them, and again he might expound on some point. Several of the churches in larger villages also had religious confraternities associated with them. A few like the Confraternity of Our Lady of Light (*Nuestra Señora de la Luz*) in Santa Fé, constructed its own chapel. The sodality, founded in 1760 by order of the bishop of Durango, eventually grew to 236 members. In addition to collecting membership fees, the group's good financial health was due to a herd of 530 ewes donated by the former governor of the province.

Just as the Jesuits had been active in northern New Spain from the late sixteenth century, so in South America, the Jesuits maintained a nearly constant missionary presence in Paraguay beginning in the seventeenth century. This region constituted one of the most important fields of action for the order, but their results have spawned much controversy. When scholars first began to study the Jesuit missions of Paraguay they perceived them either as outposts under a retrograde communal order dominated by the "black robes," or as a kind of Arcadia, filled with benign fathers and innocent natives, living together in harmony. Neither view, of course, is completely correct.

In this region the Jesuits found two quite different people: the Guaycurú, a nomadic people of the Chaco desert and neighboring territory in what is now eastern Bolivia and part of western Paraguay; and the Guaraní, tribes of seminomadic hunters and gatherers in the more dense forest of the Paraná. Since neither group was sedentary, it was difficult for the Spanish to impose their society on them, yet it was far easier to settle among the Guaraní than the fiercer Guaycurú. Because the Jesuits normally were only able to minister to Guaycurú who were ill from epidemic disease, the Indians associated the sacrament of baptism with the death of the recipient. As a result, the Jesuit mission failed among this tribe.

As in Mexico, the social composition of the Jesuits assigned to South America reflected the diversity of the order. Of the just over two thousand priests who labored in the province of Río de la Plata (including all of Argentina, Paraguay, Uruguay, southern Brazil and Bolivia) until 1767, about three-quarters were European-born, the rest creoles. Among the European-born were men from Spain, Italy, Germany, Portugal, France, Belgium, Austria, Czechoslovakia, and Poland. The majority of the creoles came from regions that are now Argentina, Chile, and Paraguay, but a few came from as far afield as Mexico. As with other Jesuit provinces, only a small number of these priests actually lived in the mission areas.

Within the area of Jesuit *reducciones,* the Society established thirty-one missions: eleven in Paraguay, seven in Brazil, and thirteen in Argentina. As with all other missions, these establishments evolved over time. Since the native populations were primarily hunters and gatherers when the Jesuits began to conduct their missionary activity, it was first necessary to settle the natives. Once settled, the Society often would move the villages several times until they would finally be "reduced" into a mission. (See Fig. 36.)

The mission San Ignacio in Paraguay, for example, was first reduced in 1610 by Father Marciel de Lorenzana with the cooperation of the Indian cacique Arapizandú. In 1628 the site of the mission was moved and renamed the Capilla del Santo Angel, and finally in 1667, moved again to the site of the modern town of San Ignacio. The mission's population fluctuated because of periodic epidemics. In 1702 the mission contained just over 1,000 families, but by 1733 it was reduced to only 388. The population rebounded: in 1750 there were 485 families, and in 1784, 867. The mission supported itself by raising cattle, cotton, and *yerba mate,* a herbal tea favored throughout the region. In 1768 the mission owned well over twenty thousand head of livestock, principally cattle, with some sheep, oxen, burros, and horses. It had two *yerba mate* groves, producing a total of twenty tons of *yerba* annually, and four cotton fields with a total of eighty thousand plants.

Mission villages were well ordered and established along a fairly defined plan. The church occupied a central position in the village, flanked by a residence for the priests. In front of the church was a broad plaza, some two hundred square yards. The natives lived in long houses arranged in rectangular zones surrounding the plaza. Beyond the houses were the garden plots, providing the mission with food, while further away from the village were the farm plots. The villages were usually placed on flat ground, near a river or stream, but not on the flood plain.

In keeping with the martial structure of the Society of Jesus, the internal organization of the missions was quite rigid. The provincial, who lived in Córdoba, presided over all activities in his territory. Under him was the mission superior, residing in Candelaria, and charged with supervising the missionaries. A missionary curate and one assistant was sent to each mission, but especially large missions might have two subordinates. The local missionary curate oversaw the activities of his companion and controlled not just the spiritual life of the mission but the economic life as well. As such he was the administrator for the whole of the mission.

The daily routine of the mission Indians and of the curate was demanding. The natives arose with the sun and spent most of the day working in the fields or workshops of the mission. They were given time at midday for a meal and then returned to work until sunset. The priests arose at 4:00 A.M. in the summer, 5:00 in winter, and one-half hour later attended prayers and Mass. For the rest of the morning they attended to the needs of the village, visiting the work places, houses, and anywhere else they felt called. One of the priests always remained at the church in case of emergency. One hour daily was spent in teaching the catechism to the children of the village; three times a week the curate taught adults, and twice a week he worked with the elderly. From noon until 1:00 P.M. the priests engaged in their own prayers, followed by lunch, during which an Indian would read devotional material. This meal was followed by an hour of rest. The afternoon labor closely paralleled that of the morning and lasted until 7:00 or 8:00 P.M., at which time they had supper. The day ended with another period of prayer.

Since the priest oversaw all aspects of the life of the mission, the Order took pains to safeguard against abuses of power. Curates were frequently called by the mission superior to give an accounting of their activities and likewise were subject to periodic visits. They often rotated among the villages, and in no case remained more than five years in one place. In an effort to train the Indians in self-government, the Jesuits established municipal councils in each mission, with an Indian magistrate, sheriffs, councilmen, and judges, elected annually by the Indians but overseen by the curate. The Jesuits also respected the traditional powers of the Indian community, vested in a chief or cacique. Power was in fact divided among three often conflicting camps, the Jesuits, the Indian council, and the cacique. By the seventeenth century, the Jesuits had embraced the philosophy of attracting the natives by example and through love, but some vestiges of an older more militant philosophy remained. When all other remedies had failed, for example, the society used force in maintaining discipline within the villages.

Because the Jesuits in the Paraguay missions controlled all aspects of life, directly or indirectly, they frequently became the target of complaints from local Spanish colonists and officials. Government officials felt excluded from what they felt was their rightful jurisdiction over the political administration of the natives, believing that Indians should be subject to the supervision of local Spanish magistrates and governors, not priests. Colonists complained because the Jesuits maintained a monopoly over the access to Indian labor as well as land. They also resented the direct competition of the missions with local Spanish farmers and ranchers.

In 1759 the order was expelled from all Portuguese dominions. In the late seventeenth century, the Jesuits had twice been expelled from the Amazon provinces so this exile was not unprecedented but this time it was not revoked. In 1767 the Spanish crown ordered the Society of Jesus to leave all Spanish realms. Individual Jesuits were given the choice to remain in the colonies as secular priests, but very few took that option. While serious disturbances broke out in several parts of the empire, most complied with the royal decree, packed up a few belongings and went into exile in Europe.

The expulsion of the Jesuits and subsequent auction of Jesuit estates had two dramatic effects on the rural areas of Latin America. The sales caused a general depression in rural real estate prices, since a considerable amount of property came on the market in a relatively brief period of time. Since the crown demanded cash payment for the properties, only the very wealthy could acquire these lands. The result was further concentration of more real estate into the hands of a few powerful landowners.

The expulsion also sent a clear message to other religious orders and to the secular clergy: The crown was to be obeyed completely by a church that was only one part of a larger royal bureaucracy. After 1767 the church became far more amenable to the royal will than it had been previously.

Conclusions

In looking at the role of the clergy in the countryside of colonial Latin America, one is struck by the continuity from the sixteenth until the early nineteenth century. In rural Latin America the church could be found fulfilling its missionary or spiritual role, as well as utilizing rural properties for the continued support of its evangelization. Yet the very success of the church in winning converts attracted the critical attention of the state and some colonists. The religious orders found themselves, from the end of the sixteenth century, in a continual dispute with the crown over their presence in the rural parishes. By the early eighteenth century the crown had won, and the parishes fell to the secular clergy. Eventually the rural wealth of the orders and other branches of the church also attracted the attention of the crown. By the end of the eighteenth century, as the crown began to expropriate the rural wealth the church had established, the church clearly recognized the authority of the monarch over its administrative affairs.

The story of the church in the rural areas of colonial Latin America, then, is more than the story of missionaries and parish priests. The church was part of the very fiber of the local economy and played an active role in issues of power and control. The church in many ways controlled life in the countryside, for it was landowner, producer, and consumer. In the missions even the schedule of daily life was controlled by the priests and friars. Through the construction of churches and monasteries, even public works and architecture were deeply influenced by the church. Yet, in the end, the church was but one institution in a highly developed bureaucracy ultimately controlled by the crown.

Notes

1. Luis García Pimentel, *Descripción del Arzobispado de México, hecha en 1570* (Mexico, 1897), 104–12.

2. Felipe Guamán Poma de Ayala, *El primer nueva crónica y buen gobierno,* vol. 2 (Mexico, 1980), 530–645.

3. John Hemming, *Red Gold: The Conquest of the Brazilian Indians* (Cambridge, Mass., 1978), 106.

CHAPTER SIX

Middle Groups

LOWELL GUDMUNDSON

Throughout rural Latin America a small social group, diverse in occupation and race but sharing a precarious position between large landowners and peasants or slaves, could be found. This important group, probably never more than 5 to 10 percent of the population, was composed of smallholders, petty officials, retail traders, and muleteers, and could be found operating in all types of agricultural systems and in widely separated regions. In certain zones, such as the dyestuff-producing regions of northern Central America and southern Mexico and the subsistence farm and ranch country of southern Central America and southwestern Brazil, smallholding predominated, with striking consequences for local social evolution. These middle groups also influenced the development of large estate-dominated agricultural zones, such as the cattle or cereal-producing haciendas in central Mexico, and the *fazenda* and tropical export, slave-based plantations in coastal Brazil. By mediating between dominant and more subordinate groups, they added complexity and also stability to inherently antagonistic, rigidly hierarchical, and polarized social orders.

The intermediate status of smallholders, local officials, and traders gave them an ambiguous position in rural society. Where estate owners and smallholders coexisted, they were both competitors and collaborators; the former when dealing with access to land, rent levels, and harvest divisions or prices; the latter when jointly facing the problems of labor recruitment and discipline vis-à-vis the propertyless. Petty officials in rural areas, such as *corregidores,* their lieutenants, collectors of various taxes, and militia commanders, were in an equally ambiguous and potentially precarious position.

147

They had often purchased their posts from the crown, whose interests they only indirectly defended, and they were frequently in conflict not only with higher authorities but also with their financial patrons. Petty officials had to walk a fine line between the law and folk values in a society in which superior imperial authorities often refused to punish rebellious villagers, even when they had physically abused their rulers in popular outbursts of protest and violence. Moreover, many of these officials were of a social and racial origin not far removed from that of the peasant village society they ruled over. In particular, the backlander, slave-catching authorities of colonial Brazil—the frontline defenders of law and order and European, colonial values—were nearly always of mixed race and low to middling social status.

Provincial merchant groups—retail traders and muleteers basically—benefited from the existing socioeconomic structure and chafed against its more restrictive features. Frequent suits involving these retailers, urban wholesalers, regional landed interests, and the state bear witness to this ambiguous situation throughout the colonial period in all of Latin America. While retail trade was an activity that required some degree of proprietorship and thus status, such traders rarely were to be confused with the upper classes. Moreover, as commercial competitors they were very likely to run afoul of local and regional wealthy interests and to be accused of handling stolen goods.

Muleteering, the lowest of the stations in life to be examined in this chapter, was often considered a respectable avenue to economic mobility for the enterprising elements among the poorer classes. It was also a major source of profit for the merchant and landed owners of the largest mule trains. In a society in which nearly all overland commercial transport was by mule (with relatively fewer cart roads and teamsters), and in which it has been estimated that the shipment of cereal grains within the range of two hundred miles could effectively double unit price, the importance of muleteers can hardly be overestimated. (See Fig. 37.)

Smallholders in the Core Economies

Contrary to traditional wisdom, small-scale agriculture was important within the bread basket of New Spain, the Bajío, and surprisingly, the major core economies of the sugar coast of Brazil. In each case, agricultural production ranged from oppressed tenancy or sharecropping to quite substantial owner-operators contracting their services and selling their produce to still larger landed interests in the region in question. Members of this smallholder group, termed *lavradores de cana* in Brazil and *rancheros* in the cereal-producing regions of Mexico, could be quite wealthy, but typically were not.

In contrast to conditions in the Caribbean, ownership of land and slave labor in Brazil was not severely concentrated in the hands of a few wealthy planters. A typical Jamaican or Haitian plantation of the late eighteenth century might house between one hundred and two hundred slaves, all owned by a single proprietor, whereas the Brazilian mill owner (*senhor de engenho*) would characteristically grind his own cane and that of a number of smaller *lavradores*. These individuals might own their own land, or rent it from the mill and landowner himself, but in either case they each owned slaves. Thus a Brazilian plantation might well have similar amounts of cane to grind and the same overall numbers of slave laborers as a Caribbean plantation, but the land and labor arrangements in Brazil included a mosaic of alternative farm or unit sizes and fortunes.

Early in the colonial period *lavradores* appear to have been composed of poorer whites, disproportionately Portuguese-born, who acted as a sort of rural middle class and who therefore possessed some resources and socio-racial prestige in a racist, slave-based society. By the end of the colonial period substantial numbers of the free colored population had entered the ranks of the *lavradores*, but on increasingly harsh terms, and with limited prestige and diminished productive resources.

As a group *lavradores* crossed many social and gender as well as racial lines. Among their ranks could be found not only the free colored, but Catholic priests, New Christian merchants (suspected secret Jews), and women (perhaps 10 percent of this group). Although a sugar mill might have from five to thirty *lavradores* as cane suppliers/contractors, and rely upon them for up to half of the cane output, turnover was often high and contracts both verbal and arbitrary. Landowning *lavradores* paid 50 percent of their crop in milling charges, and tenants paid an additional one-eighth to one-sixth in land rent, leaving precious little as profit in the best of years. However, despite these pressures and a slow worsening of conditions during the eighteenth century, those who, on average, held at least ten slaves and worked ten to twenty acres of land clearly formed the elite of that middling group of dependents (*agregados*) that grew so noticeably in late colonial Brazil. At the highest end, a substantial *lavrador* such as one Felipe Dias Amaral, deceased in 1804, might leave behind property amounting to twenty-seven slaves, thirty-five oxen plus other livestock and carts, a house, and pasture and cane land totaling some sixty-five acres. *Lavradores* such as these, however infrequent and atypical, were clearly a proto-planter group far more than a rural middle class. Nevertheless, their dual nature and novelty in the planter-dominated social order was suggestively captured by one foreign observer who found them unique "because they possess some capital and they work [themselves]."[1]

These middling producer groups also grew in size in the cereal-producing regions of Spanish America, in particular in the Mexican Bajío. While free (or at least nonslave) labor was the rule here, unlike in the Brazilian sugar districts, *rancheros* also possessed some capital resources even when tenants. Oxen for plowing and mules for transport were the functional equivalent of slaves for the *rancheros* of the Bajío. However, unlike the Brazilian *lavrador*, who was oriented toward an international market in slave labor, both family farmers employing salaried labor and subsistence cereal producers employing only family members with as little as three or four acres of land could be *rancheros*. As market demand grew in the region in the late colonial period, large estates expanded at the expense of *ranchos* and *labores,* reducing many former owner-operators and their children to tenancy, but without ever completely erasing the *ranchero* group. Indeed, their continued presence was perhaps required as the larger farms relied upon the seasonal labor of the poor smallholders who supplemented their meager incomes with planting and harvest earnings. This allowed many of them to hang on to their tiny plots of land longer than might have been the case otherwise. By the end of the colonial period, however, one large estate or hacienda in the Bajío might well equal the land area (thirty thousand acres) held by all the *ranchos* of the region taken together.

The social extraction of *rancheros* varied enormously. Poorer "Spaniards" could be found side by side with a majority of mulattoes and mestizos, and even some Hispanicized Indians. Likewise, *rancheros*' kin ties and marriages regularly crossed these purportedly racial lines of division within colonial society, much as was the case with the *lavradores* in Brazil. Similarly, great differences in wealth characterized this group. Tenant *rancheros* ranged from commercial entrepreneurs to sharecroppers living barely beyond subsistence.

Among the landed (and among wealthier tenants) the key indicator of wealth was the number of oxen and other livestock. While land ownership might be as paltry as five acres without livestock, truly rich *rancheros* controlled as much as one hundred to one thousand acres and dozens of oxen as well as mule teams. Even as the haciendas put increasing pressure on the land, those *rancheros* who still had oxen for plowing could expect to make a decent living as a tenant or sharecropper. The most successful *ranchero* family could continue the slow process of wealth accumulation, but the general *ranchero* pattern, owing to the relatively egalitarian laws of inheritance and the "remorseless fertility of their womenfolk," was of downward rather than upward mobility.[2] (See Figs. 38–40.)

The more substantial among the *ranchero* group enjoyed a status exemplified by the de la Fuente family of Concepción in León, Mexico. By 1734 Blas de la Fuente owned a mule train shipping silver from Guanajuato to Mexico City. He owned 130 mules (and the equipment to outfit 80 of them) and a herd of 176 brood mares for mule-breeding, while managing some 735 acres of land, over 400 of which had been cleared for ploughing. De la Fuente was worth an estimated 7,378 pesos, although he had total debts of some 2,400 pesos. No one might mistake Blas de la Fuente or his descendants for a lordly *hacendado,* but neither would they confuse him with his many employees and dependents. De la Fuente, along with *rancheros* only slightly less wealthy, formed a critical intermediate group in the countryside throughout the late colonial period in core areas and economies of Latin America.

Smallholders and Colored Cloth

Further south in Mexico, in the Valley of Oaxaca, and throughout northern Central America (Guatemala and El Salvador), another variant of widespread smallholding developed. Based on the production of two forms of dyestuffs, cochineal and indigo, Oaxaca, and later the areas surrounding Guatemala City, came to specialize in the export of scarlet-colored insects collected from cactuslike plants that were in great demand by English and Northern European clothing manufacturers of the eighteenth and nineteenth centuries. In this activity the customary relationship was one of merchant creditor advancing funds to the local political boss, or *corregidor*. He, in turn, would finance production of Indian villagers and Hispanic cultivators alike, often using very coercive and abusive practices while doing so. While neither of these communities necessarily held all land resources privately, they did carry on export production on a small scale, something of a rarity for the colonial Latin American export trade. Relatively few large-scale Hispanic properties existed in these areas during the colonial period, and the control of villager labor and production was the source of most of the wealth of upper-class Hispanics.

The predominance of Indian communities and populations in these areas and activities varied enormously. While perhaps 90 percent of the population of the Oaxaca region and the northwestern Guatemalan highlands was Indian, there was more variety in Guatemala. Around the capital city, where most of the cochineal was produced, the proportion of Hispanics was much higher, reaching a majority in some settlements to the east and southwest of the capital. For example, in 1804 fully 997 of 1,761 families in Escuintla and Guazacapán were non-Indians as compared to other regions such as Chiquimula, where roughly one-quarter of the population of over 5,000 families were non-Indian.

The situation of non-Indian cultivators varied as much as their overall numbers. In the district of Escuintla, among the Hispanic population 577 individuals owned land while 602 rented from municipal authorities. In Chiquimula, 1,307 owned land and 1,667 rented. Several areas of Guatemala were at least partially Hispanized both socially and economically, but there was a bewildering array of farm sizes and tenure arrangements.

Hispanicized smallholding within the captaincy-general of Guatemala emerged most clearly in El Salvador. Already by the mid eighteenth century over half of San Salvador's population was non-Indian and the majority of the indigo produced came from the Hispanic component of a population which, by 1804, reached perhaps 200,000 in the area of San Salvador and its jurisdiction alone. Here, some 1,905 Spaniards and *ladinos* owned land, while 5,185 rented, often from Indian villages, and 7,936 worked as laborers and artisans. The dynamism of this indigo economy is suggested by the fact that in 1797 the *alcabala*, or sales tax of San Salvador, produced nearly the same amount as the local Indian head tax, while in the Indian heartland of Guatemala the head tax was 3.5 times the *alcabala* receipts. Likewise it has been estimated that between 1811 and 1815 nearly two-thirds of the tithe income (collected from marketable, largely *ladino*-produced goods) of the Kingdom of Guatemala came from San Salvador alone.

Indigo producers engaged in a nonlabor intensive, annual crop cycle, whose most elaborate stage was that of processing the plants in centralized vats, drying and then packing them for shipment during the first months of the year. Indigo was shipped on muleback, a journey that included a stop in Guatemala City and then a perilous 120-mile trek to the Atlantic coast. Transporting the crop to the port could take over two months.

Indigo producers were regularly referred to as either *finqueros* (farmers, owners of *fincas* or small farms) or *poquiteros* (little ones, in regard to the amount they produced) by their merchant lender/supplier associates in Guatemala City. It has been estimated that between one-half and two-thirds of all indigo production came from these *poquiteros* by the 1780s. They received trade goods and small advances of cash, in the form of *habilitaciones,* at the start of each production cycle, but owing to the control and purchasing practices of the major traders based in Guatemala they usually remained indebted to their suppliers. This relationship was highly exploitative and ridden with conflict. One quip of the time had it that the producers of indigo were "adorned with prices" by the merchants of Guatemala "that keep us more naked than adorned." An observer from San Salvador protested to the crown that the Guatemalan merchants conspired to keep indigo producers in a "state of Algerian slavery."[3]

Smallholders on the Frontier

On the semitropical fringes of the Iberian empires in the New World, in areas such as southern Central America (Nicaragua through Panama) and southwestern Brazil (São Paulo in particular) to name but two, another form of smallholding emerged and made a substantial contribution to the social evolution of these regions. Here Iberian settlement was so thin and precarious that colonization, administration, and land tenure functions were often combined in one and the same individual or family. Similarly, the overwhelming abundance of land and extreme scarcity of labor made private ownership of precisely measured and extensive tracts of land irrelevant for local power holders and settlers.

In these areas a system of private appropriation of relatively modest homesteads emerged, either along roads and riversides or in the immediate vicinity of any provincial villages. Along with these modest holdings came the more or less indiscriminate use of the surrounding countryside (back from the road or river or in the hinterland of the village) for impermanent planting breaks, natural pasture, and hunting/gathering activities. Such a novel development of an Old World village pattern adapted to the conditions of the semitropical New World and its often precarious settlement.

It was not until the later colonial period that land came to have much intrinsic value in these societies. Only with the increasing commercialization of economic life, and the more rapid increase in population after the mid eighteenth century, did the more or less ambulatory and impermanent cultivation schemes of these areas change in the direction of stable settlement and private ownership of all land. These settlements, made up of people who were of mixed race but culturally Hispanic, borrowed quite heavily from Native American society in both material culture and social organization. They practiced slash and burn agriculture as well as "exchange" labor (reciprocal provision of common labor among kin groups) for clearing and construction. Likewise, they often practiced cousin marriage and matrilocal residence (new unions taking up residence with or near the bride's parents) to bind the various clans of the area together.

Prior to the full privatization of land resources in the late colonial period or thereafter, *Paulista* and southern Central American settlements were basically a series of interrelated clans with customary land use rights and obligations rather than proprietors, large or small, in the strictest sense of the term. Their control of land resources on the nearby frontier meant that inheritance patterns could remain relatively egalitarian, although daughters and sons-in-law often received the homestead while sons were expected to either marry into a neighboring landed clan or establish their own dwelling along the expanding frontier. In such a land-rich, labor-starved setting, slaves, cattle, and control of kin networks rather than land itself were the real sources of wealth.

In both southern Central America and São Paulo, colonial settlers continually attempted to enslave a highly resistant Native American population. Whether by the famous *bandeirante* settlers and slave raiders of early colonial São Paulo, or by the more infamous Pedrarias Dávila and his successors in Nicaragua, Costa Rica, and Panama, slave raiding under the guise of "rescue of souls" formed a similar pattern through at least the early eighteenth century. Whether referred to as sergeant major, captain major, lieutenant, or simply expeditionary leader (terms such as *capitão-mor, sargento-mor, mestre de campo* in Brazil, *capitán mayor, sargento mayor, alférez, lugarteniente* in Spanish America, as well as leaders of specific expeditions or *entradas*), such slave raiding entrepreneurs terrorized the backlands of Native American refuge, from Talamanca and the Mosquito Coast in Central America to the interior of Minas Gerais and Matto Grosso in southern Brazil. At the same time, they were the most likely figures to dominate the clan-based cliques that came to control productive enterprise, taxation, and trade within the newly incorporated colonial regions.

With such a highly militarized structure of colonization and settlement in areas of so little direct importance to crown officials, it is perhaps not surprising that administrative and military functions were combined. Leading clans provided both militia and civil administrative leadership as needed. With such preeminence came the power to reward themselves and their followers with fairly modest land grants or purchases in the areas being settled.

Perhaps two examples of such successful settlers and petty officials will make clear the origins of smallholder society on the semitropical periphery. In eighteenth-century São Paulo, the wealthiest resident of the village of Nossa Senhora de Penha e Franca was Captain Major Manuel Dias Bueno. Of the thirty-six households in the settlement in 1765, at least one-third, usually the wealthier residents, had kin ties to the Dias Bueno household. Similarly, in other villages of São Paulo, a small number of families consistently dominated the ranks of petty officialdom and were to be found among the wealthiest households in their respective districts or villages.

In the extreme isolation of early-eighteenth-century Costa Rica similar processes of clan-based settlement took place. Alférez and Teniente de Gobernador Sebastián de Zamora and his son Sargento Mayor Antonio Aurelio de Zamora were in charge of an area west of the colonial capital of Cartago, used primarily for pasturing cattle. The younger Zamora subsequently requested that 945 acres of land be sold to him, which he then parceled out among his associates and subordinates in lots of about 100 acres each. Out of this initial appropriation would come the place names of most of the district of Santo Domingo, but there was no significant attempt to fence or delimit properties very precisely. As late as the 1820s and 1830s the properties claimed by the descendants of the Zamora and other founder clans would include home sites and cattle pens, but also as many as a dozen disparate planting breaks and natural pastures in the untitled surrounding countryside.

Smallholders on the rather remote periphery of empire were substantially different from those of the core economies. They were the local equivalents of a dominant group, subordinated only to the crown officials and leading merchant or landlord groups of frequently distant seats of power. In their own bailiwicks their power extended virtually as far as the meager resources of the region itself permitted. This power was certainly nothing to rival that of Brazilian sugar mill or Mexican estate owners, but it was also far removed from the station in life of their poor settler neighbors and dependents.

Tax Men and Traders

While not always as overlapping as were the civil and military administrations of colonial São Paulo and southern Central America, trade and tax collection posts rarely strayed far from each other. Indeed, in much of rural colonial Latin America those who held administrative posts were heavily involved in commerce; administrators often owed the funds with which they had purchased their posts to merchants whose goods they traded at a profit.

Fig. 37. Mexican mule drivers. Carl Nebel, *Voyage pittoresque et archeologique dans la partie la plus interessante du Mexique* (Paris, 1836).

Fig. 38. Buenos Aires ranch hand, c. 1794. By Juan Ravenet.

Fig. 39. Cowboy and woman from Tucumán. Anonymous eighteenth century artist.

Fig. 40. Estancia (Farm) on the River San Pedro. E.E. Vidal, *Picturesque Illustration of Buenos Ayres and Monte Video. . .* (London: 1820).

Fig. 41. Convoy of Wine Mules. E.E. Vidal, *Picturesque Illustration of Buenos Ayres and Monte Video. . .* (London: 1820).

Fig. 42. Map showing the way-stations along the main post road in the Río de la Plata, 1804. (A.G.I., Mapas y Planos, Buenos Aires 253).

158

The *corregidor* and *alcalde mayor* were the persons most often identified with simultaneous taxation and trade functions. Those who held these essentially interchangeable posts with control over village Indian populations were expected to extract both tribute and labor from their charges while forcibly selling them trade goods. The institution by which they did this, the infamous *repartimiento de comercio* or *mercancías,* allowed them to establish quotas for consumption of occasionally useless and always overpriced European goods by Indians under their authority. In non-Indian districts such officials could control long-distance trade and taxation, although they were not able to extort forced labor and head taxes from a non-Indian population. Not surprisingly, in light of these abuses, *corregidores* enjoyed the lowest of reputations among both commoners and would-be reformers of the colonial system.

Corregidores and *alcaldes mayores* were most important in the dye-producing areas of southern Mexico and northern Central America. Here they were quite openly the direct representatives of the leading export merchants vis-à-vis the villagers who produced the dyes. That the *corregidor* was little more than a provincial merchant acting for the wholesaler in Guatemala City is suggested by the fact that the capital city merchant customarily paid the taxes into the treasury which the *corregidor* nominally had collected. The taxes were in effect a fee paid to the government for the privilege of trading with the Indians (providing goods and money as advances against cacao, indigo, thread, or cloth).

And it was here as well where some of the most bitter and violent conflicts would take place. Because of his more or less openly compromised position, well-known depredations in the community, and dissimulations to his superiors regarding the payment of the taxes he collected, the average *corregidor* in Oaxaca, Guatemala, or El Salvador could not always be certain of the support of the crown he represented. Officials in such a position had to walk a fine line between provoking popular rebellion, meeting payment schedules to one's merchant creditors, accumulating individual profits, and collecting sufficient crown revenue to avoid prosecution for malfeasance at the end of a tour of duty. Not all *corregidores* proved to have the requisite talents, although a few did accumulate impressive fortunes in a relatively short time.

During the cochineal boom in Oaxaca in the 1770s Ildefonso Sánchez Solache, *alcalde mayor* of Zimatlán-Chichicapa in the Valley of Oaxaca, signed a promissory note for sixty thousand to seventy thousand pesos in advances to village Indian producers. In this case, the money was forthcoming from one Manuel Ramón de Goya, a merchant resident in Mexico City, and was used to advance goods and supplies to the producers. Eventually, the official would reap a profit from three distinct operations that, in each case, involved underpayment or overcharging of villagers by about 30 to 50 percent: first for their consumer goods and supplies, then in the purchase price of both cochineal and cotton, and finally in the spinning of cotton cloth by Indian women.

Such exploitative relations could lead to local rebellions and protests. Throughout the Oaxaca region leadership in the anti-*corregidor* protests was often provided by women. In 1719 Mariana, a tall, scar-faced Indian of Santa Lucía led a mob against officials sent to measure community lands. After cutting the measuring rope, she took on one of the Spaniards in hand-to-hand struggle, held up a bleeding arm to spur on her compatriots, and led the rock-throwing barrage that drove the outsiders back to Oaxaca City.

Whether led by women or men, entire communities were usually punished collectively for violent outbursts since it proved nearly impossible to establish individual leadership or responsibility. Moreover, when the motives for action were sufficiently clear, the crown might well single out a few individual scapegoats for its wrath and lashes, levying none but the most symbolic of punishments on the village as a whole. Such leniency was based on the fear of destroying the productive, tax-paying capacity of the village, as well as a certain contempt on the part of the Spanish authorities for collective decision-making. As one such official put it, the Indians behaved as the English might, because "everyone rules, including women and children."[4]

In Guatemala and El Salvador during the late colonial period a similar arrangement obtained, with the *corregidores* in the indigo zones of El Salvador working quite openly for the largest Guatemala City merchant of the time, the Marquis de Aycinena. Here as well the charge was frequently heard that the manipulation of prices left producers near bankruptcy. In Guatemala, however, there was an even more openly extortionist layer of bureaucracy applied to the Indian population. Allegedly owing to fears of crop shortages and famine, the colonial authorities created a new group of salaried officials, the *jueces de milpas* or corn-planting judges, to insure that Indian communities planted sufficient food crops for the kingdom. The real function of this group was to control trade in marketable commodities, and thus provide yet another means of parasitical income for petty officials cum traders, but this unique institution was, thankfully, restricted to the Indian heartland of Guatemala within Central America.

In areas of more limited commercial opportunities the imagination of enterprising *corregidores* was taxed even further. In the far south of Central America, in the Nicoya Peninsula of Costa Rica, a small Indian community had traditionally been governed by some of the more destitute and ill-fated of Iberian officials. Its only commercial possibilities were to be found in cotton dyeing (with indigo) and spinning, and a limited pearl diving business. During the three decades between 1780 and 1810 there were repeated legal wrangles over mistreatment of Indian residents, involving the burning of homes, several whippings, and at least one death. One accused *corregidor,* Feliciano Francisco de Hagedorn, simply disappeared rather than face near certain civil or criminal charges. The dismal prospects of these late colonial authorities can perhaps best be explained by the precedent of an earlier *corregidor,* the Spaniard Gabriel de Santiago y Alfeirán, who had been whipped and sent off in chains by rebellious villagers in December 1760. While he was eventually reinstated in his post by the crown, the villagers were not severely punished for their actions and the limits of *corregidor* impositions remained clear to both Santiago y Alfeirán and his successors.

In the central valley of Costa Rica the usual relationship of petty officials dependent on leading merchants could also be seen, albeit with some unique distortions given the poverty and isolation of the area. When the crown briefly in the 1780s gave the province the tobacco production monopoly for Central America, the official in charge, Manuel José de Zea, was the only legal purchaser of tobacco for export north. Chronically short on cash, and in any event hoping to make some money on his own selling imported cloth, Zea turned to a leading local merchant, Antonio de la Fuente, for short-term loans as well as friendship. Zea found that those selling him their tobacco either refused to buy cloth from him or bought only on credit against future tobacco harvests. He bitterly complained in personal letters to de la Fuente that "the Devil only knows where their cash ends up." De la Fuente and his fellow importers, now barred from legal exporting of tobacco, were both the source of Zea's consternation as well as his financing. Local merchants such as de la Fuente became so brazen in their claims for autonomy that, shortly before Independence in 1821, they refused to restrict their purchases to Guatemalan-supplied goods, arguing with a frankness bordering on treason that English goods (via Jamaica) were available to them in Panama and were a better bargain.

Representatives of the royal administration had a great deal of latitude of operation and interpretation. However, they were not always of a social and racial extraction associated with such independence and power. In the slave-raiding frontier regions of Brazil and Spanish America, expedition leaders were most often the mixed-race descendants of unions resulting from earlier campaigns. Their material culture and often even their language was surprisingly similar to the very groups they preyed upon for saleable human captives. Even in the more mundane activity of (runaway) slave "catching" in Brazil, backlander officials were drawn from similar lower-class groups. The early-nineteenth-century British observer, Henry Koster, claimed that "the men whose occupation it is to apprehend runaway negroes are almost without exception, creole blacks; they are called 'capitões-do-campo' [field captains, subject to the authority of a Captain Major of the nearest city]." Koster was puzzled by the ability of local residents to reclassify in their own minds all such "officials" as white rather than black or mulatto, as well as their quizzical response of, "Can a Captain Major be a mulatto?"[5]

Those who carried on provincial trade activities without the formal advantages of office, or worked for those who did, were likely to have an even more precarious position in the social hierarchy. However, their numbers were always quite large and, for some, enterprise and transport associated with long-distance trade could lead to considerable upward mobility and wealth.

Nonofficial traders were always at risk of offending either tax men, competitors, or the local elite of the regions they traded in.

Provincial merchants who were not also officials were of basically three types. At the top of the scale were those few traders, owners of shops or *pulperos* in provincial towns, who were self-financing and did not work for a single wholesaler or supplier. Next were the itinerant peddlers working on consignment for urban wholesalers. Finally, some urban *pulperos* also traveled a circuit in the countryside buying and selling goods. All three varieties of rural merchants faced their most serious problem in financing the purchases of their customers in a cash-starved economy, a dilemma they solved in a number of ways, including the taking of items in pawn as guarantee.

Whether forming partnerships or *compañías* with big-city merchant houses, as was often the practice in more dynamic commercial areas of Mexico and northern Central America, or acting as mere consignment agents and peddlers on their own account on the far fringes of empire, traders offered a surprisingly wide variety of goods. A peddler's stock in the hinterland of Guadalajara in Mexico might include small quantities of food grains, tallow, soap and candles, dry goods, cloth of all kinds and origins, religious objects and books, knives and kitchenware, spices, buttons and pins, harnesses, occasionally firearms and powder, some iron goods, hardware, bedding, and perhaps some of the finer liquors. All this the trader hoped to exchange for silver or some other readily transportable commodity, such as liquor or animals.

In late-eighteenth-century Costa Rica itinerant merchants tended to concentrate their offerings in cloth and clothing from both Guatemala and Europe, raw cotton for spinning, gunpowder, iron and iron goods, and mercury for small-scale silver mining. They exchanged these goods for silver, tobacco, brown sugar in loaves, livestock, and foodstuffs, to be moved north for sale in Central America, or south to Panama in order to purchase European goods there.

One such peddler was the Panamanian Lorenzo Guillen, resident of Costa Rica during the 1780s. He basically worked on consignment for a larger Panamanian merchant, Miguel Núñez del Arco, who occasionally resided in Costa Rica and operated some small trading ships along the Pacific Coast. Guillen had a list of outstanding accounts with some 718 customers over a nearly two-hundred-mile-long area from the Central Valley to the Nicaraguan border region. The average balance owed Guillen in these accounts was a mere 135 pesos and most transactions involved cloth for brown sugar or livestock rather than the silver which was in such short supply locally. Guillen and several other "foreign-born" merchants of the period were defamed by their Costa Rican commercial competitors in racial terms, accused of being mulattoes if Panamanians or *zambos* (mixed African/Indian) if Nicaraguans.

Indispensable to the merchants' efforts were the skills of Hispanic muleteers who, by the thousands, moved goods and people across the landscape. Mule-based transport was the norm throughout colonial Latin America, despite the use of carts and wagons in a few areas such as the Argentine pampas and for some Mexican silver mining routes. Extraordinarily broken terrain, unpredictable volume of trade in boom and bust economies, and high value to weight ratios of the goods traded all conspired against the use of known forms of more elaborate transport technology. Even in Mexico, where substantial improvements were made in road and transport facilities to handle the early colonial silver shipments, most traffic outside of the Valley of Mexico had reverted to muleback by the end of the colonial period. (See Fig. 41.)

Despite the apparent primitiveness of the means of transport, muleteering was both highly profitable at times and capable of moving surprisingly large quantities of goods with thousands of animals. Wealthy ranchers and miners, as well as enterprising *rancheros,* put their available funds into this activity with the hope of substantial profit. Owners of mule trains spanned the entire social and racial hierarchy of the times, from free blacks to "poor" Spaniards. Although someone with as many marital and commercial illegalities to his credit as the Mexican mulatto bigamist Juan Vázquez had little expectation of acquiring landed property, many a mule-train driver was already a landowner and some of the largest estate owners and miners also ran teams. A fair number of *rancheros* became rich in boom periods for transport.

The volume of mule-carried goods also could reach impressive levels as could the numbers of mules bred for transport. In the sixteenth and seventeenth centuries, Costa Rica and Nicaragua sold large numbers of mules to Panama for the transshipment of Peruvian silver across the isthmus. Later, in the eighteenth century, Central American mule traffic included shipping indigo from El Salvador and Nicaragua to Guatemala and then on to the Atlantic coast, cotton and cloth from north to south, tobacco from Costa Rica north, and a brisk trade from Guatemala north to Mexico, in addition to the movement of European import goods from the Atlantic coast inland. (See Fig. 42.)

The value of Central America's annual export trade was about 2 million pesos per year in the 1790s (400,000 pounds per decade per year), with indigo exports by weight in the range of 300,000 to 1 million pounds, all moved by muleback. In Costa Rica alone, the tobacco trade at its zenith in the 1780s occupied over three thousand mules, surely only a small fraction of the numbers needed in Guatemala and El Salvador. As the physician in charge of the hospital in Santiago de Guatemala in the late seventeenth century complained, either the blacksmiths' shops or the hospital would have to be moved, as the incessant hammering in shoeing mules for the dry season trip to the coast was making life intolerable for patient and doctor alike.

The trip from Guatemala to the coast was accomplished with mule trains of up to several hundred animals, each carrying between 250 and 400 pounds divided in packets balanced on either side of the beast. The difficulties of the trip can hardly be overstated, even in the best of circumstances. For those unable to make the trip in the dry season (January to March) the journey could become a nightmare. One of the worst parts of the route passed over the Mico

Mountain on a trail in disastrously poor condition. This commercial lifeline of Guatemala and Central America, responsible for provisioning much of the world's indigo market over the preceding half century, was described by one fairly well prepared British traveler in 1825 as follows:

> It took us eight hours of hard labour to pass the mountain.
> ... The few plains which occurred were deep glens in which the animals found no footing, but plunged along, for the most part in beds of mud. In the slopes they sometimes got fixed in with their baggage in the narrow defiles of the rocks, or foundered, with all four legs so deeply stuck into the cavities as to render them incapable of all exertion: in such cases, the muleteers disburden the animal, and with their united efforts extricate it from its thraldom. Every step is a labour: each leg is pulled out of one hole, even in the harder plots, and placed on the edge of another into which it slips down by aid of the lubricating mud upon the surface; and in many instances the poor animal rests upon its chest or its belly, the hole being too deep for its legs to fathom.[6]

Another British traveler of the early nineteenth century, John Mawe, described an equally perilous muletrack over the Serra do Mar of southwestern Brazil in similarly distressing terms. The road ascended gorges and mountain sides in tortuous bends, with such steep gradients that it became necessary in a number of places for a rider to dismount and pull his mule "up incredible slopes, over bare rock, or through dense forests." At one point it took Mawe fully four hours to cover a distance of only six miles. "Roads" such as these led later Brazilian observers to ruefully admit that "Brazil's roads equaled in precariousness, the worst in the world."[7]

Men with the special talents to overcome obstacles such as the Mico Mountain and Serra do Mar were indispensable to merchants and landlords alike. How much greater their prestige and income should they own the animals as well. Muleteers were drawn from a wide range of groups with radically divergent prospects in life, but they all had in common a certain enterprising independence that marked their life-style and reputation in society.

Conclusion

Middling people in the colonial Latin American countryside have only recently begun to emerge from the long shadows of their more powerful landed and their more numerous laborer and peasant neighbors. They have remained relatively anonymous, owning partly to their widespread illiteracy and the contradictory nature of their ties to their social superiors and inferiors. This ambiguity was more clear for the small landholders who competed with the sugar mill owners or the *hacendados*, but also collaborated with them to control the local laborers. Ambiguity also characterized the relations of traders, tax collectors, militiamen, and petty officials with other social groups.

A variety of racial groups formed the middle group. Some were creoles, others were racial mixtures, such as mulattoes or mestizos, while Indians and blacks were also to be found in some jobs. Even occupations thought to be monopolized by Indians, such as cochineal growing, were practiced by creoles as well. Finally, uncertain economic prospects was a notable middling group trait. Transport or farming might promote upward mobility, but these peoples' story was a tale of modest gains, tenacity, a very few spectacular ascents and far more frequent falls. Although a lack of cohesion definitely marks the middle group, one feature of their lives is common to all: They bridged a social and occupational gap, and held colonial society together.

Notes

1. Stuart B. Schwartz, *Sugar Plantations in the Formation of a Brazilian Society: Bahia, 1550–1835* (Cambridge, 1985), 303, 312.

2. David A. Brading, *Haciendas and Ranchos in the Mexican Bajío* (Cambridge, 1978), 150–64.

3. Figures come from Juan Carlos Solórzano, "Haciendas, ladinos, explotación colonial: Guatemala, El Salvador, Chiapas en el siglo XVIII," *Anuario de Estudios Centroamericanos* (Universidad de Costa Rica) 10 (1984); and Miles Wortman, *Government and Society in Central America, 1680–1840* (New York, 1982); while quotes are taken from Troy Floyd, "The Guatemalan Merchants, the Government, and the Provincianos, 1750–1800," *Hispanic American Historical Review* 41 (1961): 92, 102.

4. William B. Taylor, *Drinking, Homicide, and Rebellion in Colonial Mexican Villages* (Stanford, 1979), 116, 123.

5. Henry Koster cited in Robert Conrad, *Children of God's Fire: A Documentary History of Black Slavery in Brazil* (Princeton, 1983), 211–12.

6. George Alexander Thompson cited in Franklin Parker, *Travels in Central America* (Gainesville, 1970), 93–94.

7. Richard P. Momsen, Jr., "Routes Over the Serra do Mar: The Evolution of Transportation in the Highlands of Rio de Janeiro and São Paulo," *Revista Geográfica* (Rio de Janeiro) 32, no. 58 (1963): 35–36.

CHAPTER SEVEN

Blacks

HERBERT S. KLEIN

Introduction

The countryside of Latin America was home to a complex mosaic of peasants living in self-governing communities, small peasant farmers living on their own and rented lands, and free and slave workers engaged in large-scale commercial agriculture. Although not the dominant labor force in subsistence or local and regional markets, enslaved workers were the single most important group of laborers attached to export commercial agriculture. Africans and slavery were virtually synonymous with the production of sugar, coffee, cacao, and cotton. At one time even coca leaves were produced by African slaves, although tobacco, a slave crop in North America, tended to be a small free-farmer crop in Latin America. Enslaved workers were important in gold mining, especially of the placer variety, and could also be found working as muleteers and rural artisans.

Because of its crucial role in the production of colonial agricultural exports to Europe, slave labor flourished under European rule in the New World. In the course of five centuries Latin America would become the destination for some 10 million to 15 million African slaves. Despite the general use of African slaves, their relative importance and type of labor differed within each colonial area and even from region to region. This chapter will deal with the economies that absorbed these slaves; the manner in which enslaved persons organized their social life; their relations with the free population, both white and colored; the types of social ties formed with other blacks and with whites; and their manner of resistance, emancipation, and cultural adaptation to the New World environment.

The history of blacks in Ibero-America is a complex story, embracing the evolution of labor systems, social relationships, commercial networks, and the transformation of African language, religion, and art. None of this would have taken place, however, without a demand for slave labor in New World enterprises. Because American economic demand determined slaves' nonvoluntary arrival in America, this chapter will begin with an overview of the rural economy. In North America, there are many slave narratives and interviews with former slaves that are invaluable windows into the slave experience. Such is not the case for Ibero-America. That is why we need to rely more heavily on indirect sources, many of them quantitative, for our understanding of Ibero-American slave life.

The Slave Economy

The few thousand Iberian conquistadors were too few in number to carry out the physical labor required to fulfill the gigantic expectations they brought with them from the Old World and, in any event, unwilling to do manual work in their new farms, mines, and ranches. At first the existence of a large Indian population promised an abundant supply of labor. The Spaniards encountered two regions—Mesoamerica and the Andes—where the labor of peasants could be effectively exploited by tapping traditional, preconquest, imperial Indian tax and government structures. As a result, in the central continental provinces of the Spanish American empire the need for non-Indian laborers, whether free or slave, was relatively limited. Where virulent European diseases caused serious Indian depopulation, however, or where the Indians were not willing to be drafted for routine labor, or where there simply were no Indians, the conquerors turned to slaves. Given the relative abundance and productivity of Africans, and their comparatively low price, it was to these latter that the Spaniards and Portuguese turned to develop their export agriculture.

At the same time, improved domestic wages and increasing labor market alternatives within Europe and even Asia meant that Spanish and Portuguese poor and peasant workers were reluctant to cross the Atlantic to make their fortune and were ultimately too costly to import, even under the indentured system later used by Northern Europeans to populate their colonies. Though skilled and unskilled metropolitan urban workers and government officials did migrate, they were insufficient to govern the Indian peasant masses or to populate the major cities developing in the New World. In this context, it was natural for the Iberians to turn to slave labor, and the dominant slaves in late-fifteenth-century Europe were the Africans.

Africans were the cheapest available slaves at this time because the Portuguese had opened up the West African coast. Though all European and Middle Eastern peoples had experienced slavery and no single religious group was exempt from its scourge, by the sixteenth century sub-Saharan African workers had replaced Jews, Moors, and Christians as the dominant group in the southern European slave markets. Increasing church interference with the European trade, growing resistance of Islamic peoples to European expansion, and the abundance and cheapness of Africans brought by sea contributed to this shift. The growing efficiency of the Atlantic slave traders, the dependability of African middlemen in supplying slaves, and the stability of prices helped define Africans as the available slave labor of the sixteenth century.

Because of their rapid conquest of the American heartland and discovery of enormous mineral wealth, Spaniards were the first Europeans to have the capital to import slaves. Thus the earliest years of the Atlantic slave trade drew Africans primarily toward Mexico and Peru. Forced African migrations began with the first conquests. Cortés and his various armies held several hundred slaves when they conquered Mexico in the 1520s, while close to two thousand slaves appeared in the armies of Pizarro and Almagro in their conquest of Peru in the 1530s and in their subsequent civil wars in the 1540s. Spaniards found their need for slaves constantly increasing. This was especially true in coastal Peru, a rich area, ideal for such European crops as sugar and grapes, but one that lost a progressively higher proportion of its population to European diseases.

The need for slaves within Peru increased dramatically in the second half of the sixteenth century as Potosí silver production came into full development, making Peru the wealthiest zone of the New World. To meet this demand, a major slave trade developed, especially after the unification of the Portuguese and Spanish crowns from 1580 to 1640 permitted the Portuguese directly to supply Spanish American markets. At first most of the Africans came from the Senegambia region between the Senegal and Niger rivers, but after the development of Portuguese Luanda in the 1570s, important contingents of slaves from the Congo and Angola began arriving.

Initially African slaves tended to be concentrated in urban areas, but new economic roles opened up for them at the margins of the Indian rural society. As early as the 1540s, Africans in gangs of ten to fifteen slaves were working gold deposits in the tropical eastern cordillera region of Carabaya in the southern Andes. Even though these local gold fields were quickly depleted, almost all later gold mining was done by African slaves, working alluvial deposits in tropical lowlands far from Indian populations.

Although the large plantation, employing several hundred slaves, is the best-known center of slave life, in fact, a great variety of enterprises relied on enslaved workers. On the outskirts of Lima, for example, African slave families worked in nonplantation agriculture such as gardens, orchards, and grain-producing farms. In rural areas up and down the coast, sugar estates, vineyards, and more mixed agricultural enterprises were to be found. On average these plantations in the irrigated coastal valleys, especially those to the south of Lima, had around forty slaves per establishment, but sometimes the larger estates could reach a hundred slaves. The major wine- and sugar- producing zones of the seventeenth century, such as Pisco and the Condor and Ica valleys employed some twenty thousand slaves.

Along with lay people, Jesuits were important owners of slave-based plantations after 1600. Their estates were found throughout Peru. In the tropical valleys of the northern and southern highlands, Jesuit slave estates specialized in sugar. These interior plantations, like those of the coast, were relatively small. Production was for the Peruvian market and a relatively limited Pacific coast trade, and the dominant characteristic of commercial slave plantation agriculture in Peru—both for Jesuits and lay planters—was its mix of products. Beef cattle ranching was also a specialty of the African slave population, and slaves, along with free Indians, were also prominent as muleteers throughout Peru.

The second major zone of slave importation into Spanish America in this early period was the Viceroyalty of Mexico, which from the first moments after the conquest had African-born (*bozales*) and European-born (*ladino*) slaves in the armies, farms, and houses of the Spanish conquerors. As in Peru, the first generation of slaves probably numbered close to the total number of whites. They were also drawn heavily into the sugar and European commercial crop production in the warmer lowland regions, which were widely scattered in the central zone of the viceroyalty. These sugar estates were usually quite small, with the average size approaching the forty slaves per farm arrangement in Peru. Several hundred slaves were to be found in the largest sugar estate of the Cortés family in the 1550s, but this was the exception.

In Mexico, enslaved Africans were initially important in the silver mining industry. By the second half of the sixteenth century major deposits of silver were discovered in the northern fringes of the viceroyalty, in areas with few settled Indians. Given the immediate need for labor and the relative availability of African slaves, they were quickly brought to mining camps to undertake the first work of exploitation. Thus the mines at Zacatecas, Guanajuato, and Pachuca initially used large numbers of slaves to perform all types of mining tasks, both above and below ground, but especially to move the ore to and from the mills. In a mine census of 1570, some thirty-seven hundred African slaves were listed in the mining camps, double the number of Spaniards, and just a few hundred less than the Indians. At this point they represented 45 percent of the laboring population. But the increasing availability of free Indian laborers, who quickly migrated to these new settlements, lessened the need for more expensive African slave laborers. By the 1590s, the slaves in the mining camps were down to a thousand workers and represented only one-fifth of the combined African and Indian labor force. They were now confined to less dangerous aboveground tasks. By the first decades of the seventeenth century they were no longer a significant element in the mining industry.

The lesser importance of Mexican slavery was well reflected in the growth of its slave population. In 1570 there were an estimated twenty thousand slaves in all of Mexico, and at their peak in 1646 the total slave labor force reached only some thirty-five thousand. These slaves represented less than 2 percent of the viceregal population, in both periods. In contrast, the number of slaves in this same period within the Peruvian region had reached close to 100,000, where they represented between 10 percent and 15 percent of the population. Though the Peruvian slave population would stagnate in the next century, it would not go into the severe decline shown by the Mexican slave population in the eighteenth century. By the last decade of that century, Peru had close to ninety thousand slaves, while Mexico had only six thousand left.

In both regions, however, the 1650s marked the end of the great period of massive slave importations. By 1650, Spanish America, primarily Peru and Mexico, had succeeded in importing from the earliest days of the conquest some 250,000 to 300,000 slaves, a total which would not be repeated in the next century of colonial growth. By the end of the seventeenth century, African slavery in the Spanish American colonies was in retreat in most rural areas. Never a dominant institution in Mexico and Central America, its economic importance declined even further as the native American populations recovered from their initial contact with European diseases and began to expand on a steady basis. In the South American continent slaves were still heavily engaged in commercial agricultural production, but even here the trade in enslaved Africans was slowing and the local slave populations were beginning to decline. As yet, the Caribbean island possessions of Spain had small populations of slaves and only modest plantation agriculture.

In the continental colonies of Spain, by the beginning of the eighteenth century, only in the specialized sugar-producing regions of coastal Peru and Veracruz in New Spain (Mexico), and in the cacao plantations of Caracas (Venezuela) could African slaves be found engaged in agriculture in large numbers. Selected mining centers, such as the placer gold mining region of the Chocó in northern New Granada (Colombia), also used African slaves as the exclusive labor force. But these were the exceptions, and by the end of the seventeenth century, it looked as though slavery was a dying system of labor. But in other regions of the Americas, it had gained new life.

The major demand for African slaves after 1650 came from Portuguese America and the marginal lands the Spaniards had previously neglected, above all those in the Caribbean. In these areas with no stable Indian peasant populations to exploit, and with little or no alternative exports in the form of precious metals, the turn toward commercial agricultural production for European markets led inexorably to the massive importation of African slave labor to work the fertile soils of the tropical lowlands. The first of the European powers to develop this system were the Portuguese, who took possession of the eastern coastline of South America in the early sixteenth century. Their example was avidly followed by others.

In the case of the Portuguese, there was less metropolitan constraint in enslaving Indians than with the Spaniards. The decentralization of power in local Tupí-Guaraní societies, and their previous freedom from systematic peasant labor, made them less easy to exploit through noncoercive labor arrangements. They were enslaved but their labor, initially abundant, eventually proved too scarce, unreliable, and costly to guarantee the necessary agricultural work force. Between 1530 and 1580, the devastating effects of European disease on the Indian population was a significant reason that the colonizers looked toward Africa for workers. Because the Portuguese already had extensive experience with African slaves in their Atlantic islands, and through their ties to native African suppliers of slaves had access to these workers, once the decision was made to fully exploit the Portuguese American colony, the turn toward African workers was only conditioned by the availability of capital for importations.

Within thirty years of first discovering Brazil, the Portuguese became convinced that full-scale exploitation of Brazil was imperative for the safety of their entire overseas empire. French competition and brief occupation of the coast showed what might happen otherwise. Portugal's experience in the Atlantic islands demonstrated that sugar was the ideal crop to guarantee the existence of a profitable colony, and from the planter's standpoint, the enslaved African workers were an ideal labor force. This decision was greatly aided by the fact that the Portuguese dominated the Atlantic slave trade at this time and could easily and cheaply deliver slaves to America.

Enterprising colonists had begun to plant sugar as early as the 1510s. But it was not until the 1530s that systematic production began. Two zones quickly became the centers of sugar production: Pernambuco and Bahia. By the 1580s Pernambuco already had over sixty mills (*engenhos*) producing sugar for the European market, while Bahia had some forty mills in production. The two zones produced about two-thirds of all the sugar in the continent. Rapidly becoming Europe's prime supplier of sugar, the northeastern mills of Brazil soon evolved into far larger operations than their east Atlantic island predecessors. With excellent soils, the most advanced milling technology, and close contact with the expanding Dutch commercial network, Brazil dominated sugar production in the Western world by 1600. Sugar became the crucial link between Portugal, Africa, and Brazil. (See Fig. 43.)

Though enslaved African workers were imported from the beginning, the slave trade became massive after 1570. By the mid-1580s Pernambuco alone reported two thousand African slaves, comprising one-third of the captaincy's sugar labor force, while enslaved and free Indians made up the rest. With each succeeding decade the percentage of Africans in the slave population increased. By 1600 probably just under half of all slaves were Africans, with some fifty thousand Africans having arrived in the colony up to that time. In the next two decades the Indian slaves progressively disappeared from the sugar fields, and by the 1620s most laborers on sugar estates were black. The first half of the seventeenth century brought continued growth for the Brazilian sugar industry. With the introduction of new milling techniques in the second decade of the seventeenth century, the costs of production were reduced considerably. By the 1630s and 1640s Africans were arriving in much greater numbers to Brazil than to Spanish America. Whereas Brazil would absorb a migration of some half a million to 600,000 slaves from Africa up to 1700, some 350,000 to 400,000 slaves would arrive in Spanish America in these two centuries.

The middle decades of the seventeenth century would prove to be the peak years of Brazil's dominance of the European sugar market. It was this sugar production monopoly that excited the envy of other European powers and led to the rise of alternative production centers. Crucial to this new plantation movement would be the Dutch, who until then had been firm partners of the Brazilian planters. But their revolt against the Spanish eventually made Portugal an enemy as well. By the 1630s the Dutch took Recife, Brazil's premier sugar port and center of the province of Pernambuco, the colony's richest sugar plantation region. The next step in this competition was to deny Brazil access to its sources of African slaves. The Dutch West Indies Company temporarily seized both the Gold Coast (El Mina) and Angola in the late 1630s and early 1640s.

The direct Dutch intervention in the trade in enslaved Africans and in American production affected sugar output and the slave system in both Brazil and the rest of America. When expelled from Brazil in 1654, the Dutch became the source for the tools, techniques, credit, and slaves that would carry the sugar revolution into the West Indies, thereby terminating Brazil's monopoly position in European markets and leading to the creation of wealthy new American colonies for France and England.

Brazil's monopoly position was destroyed, but the growth of European consumption, the excellent quality of Brazil's best grades of clayed white sugar, and the demand in the home and imperial markets guaranteed that the Brazilian plantations were still a major force in the world market. Although accounting for only about 10 percent of New World sugar output by the middle of the eighteenth century, Brazil was still the third most important American source (after Saint Domingue and Jamaica). But, although sugar cultivation provided the initial impetus for the trade in enslaved Africans to Brazil, other economic sectors aggressively competed for this work force. By 1700 Brazil's economy had expanded into gold and diamond mining on a grand scale. For mining, as for sugar, the Portuguese used African slave labor and increased their intake of enslaved Africans to over twenty thousand per year by the end of the eighteenth century. The newly colonized interior mining province of Minas Gerais quickly became the largest slave province in Brazil with a population of 150,000 Africans by 1800. Government and monopoly company efforts also succeeded in turning the northern province of Maranhão into a world producer of cotton based on slave labor. These new uses of slave labor guaranteed that eighteenth-century Portuguese America remained the single largest slave colony in the Americas. Its one million slaves were found everywhere in Brazil, working in almost every occupation rural and urban, and was drawn from peoples from every major zone of West Africa.

The entire American slave system received a rude shock with the successful slave rebellion in Saint Domingue in 1791, the most productive sugar producer of the time. The immediate result of the revolt was a major reaction by the masters and planters against slaves and free colored everywhere in America. Draconian legislation restricting slave and free colored rights was temporarily introduced in most regions. Because the slave revolt and the subsequent warfare destroyed the plantations, Saint Domingue/Haiti was no longer a significant producer of sugar and coffee. This also had a profound effect on the growth of these slave-produced crops in the other American regions. For Cuba and Brazil, the elimination of the previously dominant Saint Domingue coffee industry gave both colonies the opportunity to enter into this new and profitable market. It was Cuba which first took maximum advantage and with the help of exiled French West Indian planters and their slaves, Cubans made sugar and coffee the major products of the island. By the first decades of the nineteenth century, the sugar industry of northeastern Brazil (Bahia and Pernambuco provinces especially) was also revived, while coffee became important in south-central Brazil, particularly the provinces of Rio de Janeiro and São Paulo.

Rural Slave Life

African slaves were not unique in either the work they performed, nor in their lack of control over their own lives. Like other workers at the low end of the social scale, they were caught between the need to satisfy their employers, yet preserve a sense of identity and worth in their own terms. But slaves were more lacking in ties to kin, community, and land than were other workers. While all low-status workers were deprived of these connections compared to the middle and upper classes, the enslaved Africans endured the greatest loss. This paucity of ties originating outside the work relationship set the slaves apart even from freedmen performing the same types of jobs.

Indeed, it was the greater absence of these linkages that made slaves so desirable in the preindustrial world. Masters could use their slaves at far less cost in reciprocal obligations. Slaves were also the most mobile labor force available. The Africans, who came from multiple linguistic groups and regions in Africa, faced the very difficult task of being forced to adapt to European norms and languages. Nevertheless, many did so, and also, through their experience in slavery, created new, Afro-American forms of kin, community, and culture.

The social life of enslaved Africans was dramatically influenced by the plantation system. The economics of plantation management tended to create a uniformity of social and economic relations common to all plantations in the colonies. One of the most striking of these common characteristics was the high percentage of the slave population that was economically active at all ages. Those with the misfortune to be part of the slave system worked for longer periods during their lives than free workers.

The unskilled field laborers were organized into two or more levels, or "gangs." The first gang consisted of younger children, convalescing adults, mothers who had recently given birth, and older persons. This group tended to do lighter agricultural labor. The major, or "great gang," was made up entirely of healthy adult slaves, usually between eighteen and forty-five years of age, who did all the heavy planting, cleaning, cultivation, and harvesting of the crop. Surprisingly, women made up at least half of the major gang. Sexual differentiation only occurred in the distribution of nonagricultural skilled occupations, such as carpenter or sugar master, which was the exclusive preserve of males. While three-quarters of the women on the plantation were to be found in the field gangs, less than half of the men were located here. A tenth of the men were assigned to the work of the refineries and the rest were in skilled trades. (See Fig. 44.)

From the purely economic standpoint, slave labor was probably one of the most efficient labor systems then operating in the Western world, in the sense that it actively employed approximately 80 percent of the entire population (compared to 55 percent among peasants today). From small children to aged persons, everyone was assigned a task deemed commensurate with their physical abilities. Older men and women cared for or trained infants and children, or had simple cattle tending or guarding tasks. All children worked, starting with weeding tasks at about age eight and gradually moving up the hierarchy of field gangs during their youth.

Masters used force and privileges to achieve compliance from enslaved workers. Strict supervision and punishments helped overcome the natural resistance of human beings to working as slaves. The use of whips and other corporal punishments, and the constant threat to use them may have been more important than any positive rewards of leisure, extra food and clothing, or rights to cultivate small plots of land and sell part of the produce. Both negative and positive types of incentives were constantly available and used.

The distribution of tasks on the plantation shows both consistency across crop types as well as some surprising differences from classic images of the plantation. While there was some variation depending on type of crop, soils, and location, the structure developed for sugar did not differ too significantly from that found in coffee, cotton, tobacco, or cacao production. Between 50 and 60 percent of the total slaves were engaged in field labor. An additional 10 percent of the workers were involved in milling and refining the sugar, while less than 2 percent were servants in the master's household. Another 8 percent were involved in the transport of crops to market. The rest were too young or too old to work. Nonsugar estates had fewer skilled workers because of the lack of any refining activity, but the actual ratio of field hands to total slaves, however, differed little from the sugar estates. On a typical nonsugar plantation, under 60 percent of the total slave labor force were to be found in the field gangs.

The exploitation of women as well as men is seen in the lack of sexual differentiation in labor tasks, and also in the prices and rents planters were willing to pay for slaves. Slave prices of unskilled and healthy male and female slaves remained equal until early adulthood, when male field hand prices rose about 10 percent to 20 percent above female prices. This differential then declined as slaves passed their prime working years. These changing price differences appear to reflect physical abilities that only differed markedly in the age categories that owners considered most valuable. Rental prices for unskilled field hand slaves also followed these patterns quite closely, although they tended to reflect pure physical output potential more. This price structure was identical in all thriving plantation societies, during all periods of slavery in the American colonies and republics.

In Latin America the normal plantation averaged around fifty slaves. These slaves were usually grouped into families and housed in slave quarters—sometimes in communal barracks, but more often in small houses. The slave "villages" were ruled over by slave drivers and white overseers, but they had as a basic unit the family—most often not recognized as such in legal or church documents—but nevertheless an effective social unit. In turn each household had a family plot, and it was not unusual for the slave families to supply most of their own food needs during the year from the production on their own plots.

Some 30 percent of the rural slaves in eighteenth-century America lived in these "factories in the field," but the majority were usually owned in smaller units. More than 60 percent worked in nonplantation agriculture and tended to be in small family establishments closely supervised by their white owners, or were workers on their own in small plots producing foodstuffs for the local urban markets. Other slaves lived on haciendas where they frequently worked alongside Indians and free people of color. The 6 percent or so of the slaves who were still in mining at the end of the eighteenth century had a varied existence, from the very strictly controlled all male *cuadrillas* in New Granada to the more independent diamond and gold prospectors in the Brazilian hinterlands. (See Fig. 45.)

Though all slaves were at the bottom of the social order, their status was not all equal. In societies like Mexico and Peru where there was a large Indian population, slaves looked down on the Indian peasant population as a lower order. More importantly, in all slave societies certain types of occupations conferred more status, power, and autonomy than others. Slave supervisors on the plantations tended to have higher status, but so did some occupations without management responsibilities. In the coffee plantations of Saint Domingue and Brazil, for example, the muleteers who carried the crop to market were considered a particularly independent group. Regardless of their occupation, slaves

Fig. 43. Refining sugar cane. Gulielmi Pisonis (Wilhelm Pison), *De Indiac utriusque re naturali et medica libri quatuordecim...* (Amsterdam: Elzevinos, 1658).

Fig. 44. Black woman and child. Zacharias Wagener, *Zoobiblion: Livro de Animais do Brasil.*

Fig. 45. Black slaves cutting wood. Jean Baptiste Debret, *Voyage pittoresque et historique au Brésil* (Paris, 1834–39).

in rural areas or towns who lived alone and paid their owners a rent, or slaves who worked as muleteers, sailors, and other occupations related to communications and an independent life of travel, were equally privileged. In such a system, domestic servants did not stand as high because of the strict supervision to which they were subject, although they fared better in economic and health terms than unskilled field workers. House servants often held a special ability to mediate demands between the slave quarters and the master's house.

Even in rural areas of Spanish and Portuguese America, slave rentals were common. Most skilled artisans were rented out by their owners, who could be anything from widows living off their rent to institutions and free artisans bringing in extra income. Often the skilled and semi-skilled slaves maintained themselves and simply rented themselves, supplying their owners with a fixed monthly income and absorbing their own expenses for housing and food. It was common to rent most unskilled slaves to free persons who paid maintenance costs, a rental fee, and sometimes even wages from which rental fees were deducted. Thus a complex web of direct ownership, rentals, and self-employment made the slaves for hire an extremely mobile and adjustable labor force.

Everywhere slaves worked harder and lived under poorer conditions than others in their respective societies. For this reason they consistently had the lowest life expectancy of any group in society. They were also far more likely than other groups to suffer work-related accidents and other health problems because of constant and excessive labor. Slaves born in America had an average life expectancy at birth of somewhere between the mid twenties or lower thirties, and for those who had survived the critical first five years of age, life expectancy was in the mid thirties to lower forties. The mortality rates of creole slaves (crude death rates in the mid forties per thousand range) more nearly approached that of the local free populations, although even under the best of conditions, the slave rates were invariably higher. At the same time, creole slave birth rates were high enough (crude birth rates in the upper forties and lower fifties per thousand population) to compensate for the high death rates and produce a positive growth of the slave population. But the heavy forced migration of Africans, and the distortions in their age and sex (75 percent of the slaves arriving by ship were males and 80 percent were adults), combined with higher mortality rates among the African-born, had an overall negative impact on growth. The positive growth rate among the creole slaves was outweighed by the high mortality and overall low fertility of the enslaved population born in Africa.

Afro-American Social Life and Culture

African slaves came from a variety of tribes and linguistic groups and shared few common ties. Only color and status bound the slaves together. In the New World, enslaved workers were forced to create their own culture, making selective adaptations of those African traits best suited to survival in their new home, and abandoning or modifying those that did not work in the American setting. For example, African men in the New World were forced to give up hunting and warfare and the culture that these pursuits had engendered, and instead engage in full-time agricultural labor. On the other hand, the enslaved sometimes succeeded in maintaining cultural values. In African societies knowledge was also an important granter of status. In America, many male and female Africans who were part-time religious, health, and witchcraft specialists continued to hold high status within the slave community, although they were completely unrecognized by the master class.

Likewise with regard to cultural life, the preservation of African culture was difficult when the traditional ways of transmitting it were disrupted by forced migration and slavery. Enslaved populations were forced by their masters to adapt to Iberian norms. For most slaves accommodation was a necessity, but despite oppression and continued frustrations in the lack of control over their own lives, enslaved Africans throughout America worked out their own variations of the dominant culture. In all societies slaves devised family norms unique to their New World environment, even in the face of illegality and forced breakup of families through sales. In many cases naming patterns and kinship arrangements were distinct from the dominant white and free society, as were rules of communal organization. They also slowly created their own variation of the local cultures in which they lived.

The creation of special Afro-American cultures was the unique work of African slaves, and most especially of the unskilled masses who made up the majority of the enslaved workers. The sources for Afro-American slave culture were a complex amalgam of African, American Indian, and lower-class European beliefs, combined into uniquely adaptive cultures. From developing special dialects of the European languages to new forms of musical and artistic expressions, the slaves tried to establish a semi-autonomous existence for themselves. Nowhere was this more evident than in their religious expression. The creation of alternative churches and religious brotherhoods guaranteed an important space for the slaves within the religion of their masters. Nor were African and creole slaves reluctant to practice non-Christian religions in the secret of their own homes and quarters. In every society syncretic African-based religious movements were created, often hidden under Catholic norms, but more often in total isolation from the religion of the masters. These religions could be as formal as Islam and lead to such events as the Malé slave revolts of Bahia in the 1830s, or as syncretic as Voodoo, Santaria, Umbanda, and a host of other African-originated beliefs. Often enslaved Africans retained only selective aspects of their original religions. Those religious deities associated with agriculture, lineages, clans, and state structures could not be maintained in the New World because these ties had been destroyed by the Atlantic crossing and slavery. But those deities and rituals related to the individual and the immediate family in terms of life and death were given added impetus. In Brazil and the West Indies, especially in relatively isolated plantations with large African populations, Afro-American cults came to dominate the lives of the slaves.

In Catholic Latin America, the resulting Afro-American religions tended to blend in with folk Catholicism and receive some support from the established church. Religious brotherhoods took the slave and free colored populations and more thoroughly integrated them into Iberian religious practices. Brotherhoods dedicated to Our Lady of the Rosary, St. Anthony of Catagerona, St. Ephigenia, or St. Benedict tended to be found in urban settings, but as early as 1589 Jesuit missionaries formed brotherhoods for black slaves working on the sugar plantations of Pernambuco, with the express object of improving spiritual instruction. In Latin America slaveowners used Catholicism to teach enslaved workers the virtues of patience, humility, resignation, obedience, and fear. While nominally converted to Catholicism, the slaves repeatedly identified Christian saints with major African deities; through a process of syncretism and acculturation, the saints came to have a dual identity for the black population.

Although most slaves lived in family units, legal marriage was the norm for only a few families. Master opposition as well as the scarcity of clergy and the cost of the sacrament made it difficult for the enslaved to marry. Slaves could also marry free people of color if they had the approval of their owners. In 1699 for example, Catalina, a black, thirty-eight-year-old slave and wife of Manuel de Rueda, free black, her six children (ranging in age from eighteen to three), and her grandchild were all living in the *ingenio* de San Miguel de Almolonga in the Jalapa district of Veracruz.

Afro-American culture as it emerged tended to develop in the small black villages that made up the world of the large plantations. A growing sense of community was reinforced by the way in which slaves were housed on plantations. The field hands and most of the skilled slaves lived in what were often miniature African villages. Slaves usually constructed their own homes of mud and straw, which they grouped around a communal area. Slaves largely organized themselves in these homes in terms of families, with separate living arrangements for unattached men and women. The provisioning grounds that slaves were allowed to tend on Sundays and holidays were also organized by family.

Slave women began having children quite early, and it was common for women to engage in premarital intercourse until the birth of the first child. Women usually settled down into a monogamous relationship after bearing their first child, and in most cases the father of the second child was the father of all later children. This behavior was not much different from that of the lower classes of free society in Latin America. Nonetheless the high death rates of slaves and the impact of sales and forced separations probably led to more serial "marriages" and the emergence of a larger number of stepfamilies than among the free population.

Slaves also used other means to find affection and social support and to establish ties of association. Like other groups in colonial society, they used the tradition of naming godparents for their children to create ties of ritual kinship. Slaves named other slaves as *compadres,* and the African-born demonstrated a preference for ritual sponsors from their own "nation." In Brazil, African-born slaves also viewed their relationship to those who had been brought to the New World on the same ship as a recognized kinship link. African ethnicity, language, and religion also created powerful ties, as did membership in Christian religious brotherhoods.

Slave Resistance

Given a labor system based on force, on the lack of rights, and even the denial of family and kinship, it was inevitable that rebellion, resistance, and escape were part of the experience of many rural slaves. From the simple act of shirking tasks and destroying farm implements to the more extreme gesture of burning crops, killing masters, and running away, slaves expressed their hostility to the system or to especially unusual and harsh conditions.

Throughout the Americas, communities called *quilombos* (Portuguese) or *palenques* (Spanish) were founded by runaway slaves. These maroon communities were usually located on the unpopulated frontiers or in the mountains unsettled by Spanish or Portuguese colonists. Between 1614 and 1826 at least thirty-five such communities were reported in the region of Bahia. Some *quilombos,* like the famous Palmares settlement in seventeenth-century northeastern Brazil, reached several thousand members, but most maroon villages contained a dozen or so families. Many maroon communities not only managed to survive for several years, they also staged hit-and-run attacks on white planters and their property. In 1576, for example, a group of maroons established in an area called Cañada de los Negros threatened Spanish settlers in the town of León in Mexico. Three years later maroons were reported to have taken over ranches and haciendas at Chichimecas, Almería, and Tlalcotalpa. Moreover, though free persons of color were constantly employed to track down these fugitives, as many runaways obtained freedom as were caught by slave hunters.

Rural maroon communities were not the only place of escape. In Latin America, with its high percentage of free persons of color by the late eighteenth and early nineteenth century, it was not unusual for escaped slaves—especially those with some skills—to pass themselves off as freedmen, or even as slaves having the right to hire themselves out as contract labor. Escaping the plantations, they sought refuge in the mines or the cities. For example, the Cuban-born slave, tailor José Maria Andrade, was declared a fugitive in 1814. It was charged that he carried "false papers claiming that he is looking for a master and renting rooms, when he does not outrightly claim that he is free."[1] In the same year another slave named Eusebio de la Cruz was sought as a fugitive by his master.

He "is a friend of dancers, accustomed to going about in filthy condition, a shoemaker by trade, who although he may have a license, is a fugitive slave."[2]

Uprisings of slaves on individual plantations were not uncommon in colonial Latin America. In 1789, for example, a group of slaves on Engenho Santana, a large plantation in Ilhéus, south of Bahia, killed their overseer and seized some machinery before running off to found a settlement in the forest. Outright rebellion although less common, occurred in sixteenth- and seventeenth-century Spanish America. As early as 1522, African slaves working on plantations in Santo Domingo slaughtered their masters and destroyed crops in an attempt to create an African republic. The threat of rebellion as well as armed maroon incursions forced all societies to maintain militias to protect themselves. Of the slave rebellions that occurred in Latin America, only the Haitian rebellion of 1790 can be considered an unqualified success, in that it freed the slaves and led to the destruction of the plantation system.

The Free Coloreds

No matter how much social or even economic space was created for enslaved Africans in America, slavery was still a hated institution. Short of rebelling or running away, the only alternative for escape was through manumission. Slave society in Latin America permitted slaves to be manumitted from the very beginning. The Spanish and the Portuguese accepted the legitimacy of manumission because it was the norm in Roman law and was deeply embedded in Christian piety and practice. In a pattern common to all of Spanish and Portuguese America, free blacks and mulattoes appeared from the very beginning of the conquest and colonization period, some of them even coming from Spain itself. This population grew slowly in the sixteenth and seventeenth centuries, and always faced restrictions on freedom uniquely applied to the group because of its origin and color.

The practice of manumission began when masters piously freed their slaves, or fathers their children, or faithful service was rewarded with freedom. Self-purchase arrangements for slaves also developed early. Throughout the colonial period the Iberians not only continued to accept and support the traditional patterns of manumission, but also actively accepted and codified the route of self-purchase that had grown up in customary practice rather than metropolitan codes. Free persons of every imaginable racial combination continued to reside in rural Latin America, where they often formed ties of concubinage, marriage, and godparenthood with black and mulatto slaves. Interesting examples from haciendas in Morelos, Mexico, suggest that free men of color were just as likely as their female counterparts to have slave spouses, although by law their children, as the children of a slave mother would be born into slavery.

Although manumission was more frequent in urban areas where slaves had more opportunity to gain income and were more cognizant of their rights, manumission was also practiced with some frequency in rural settings. Although some old and infirm slaves were manumitted, the average age of the manumitted in a sample of almost seven thousand cases registered in Salvador de Bahia between 1684 and 1745, was just fifteen years of age. In addition Africans were represented among the *libertos* (manumitted) in roughly the same ratio as in the total population. Between 40 percent to 60 percent of the ex-slaves purchased their freedom, and another third had been granted theirs free and unconditionally by their masters. The remaining 10 percent to 20 percent of the manumitted slaves had been granted conditional freedom; they were usually required to serve for a stipulated period of time before claiming their liberty. Two-thirds of the manumitted were women (from 60 percent to 67 percent), and few were found to be more than forty-five years of age.

As a result the free colored group continually received a dynamic, heavily female, and relatively young element in its midst. The reproductive rates among the free colored population were thus consistently higher than among the slaves. Not only were the creole freedmen reproducing themselves at a positive rate of growth, but they were receiving a steady stream of ex-slaves who tended to have high reproductive rates, that is, younger and fertile women.

When self-purchase was the road to manumission, there was a high proportion of black African-born. The recipients of gratis manumission tended to be creole-born mulattoes. Clearly the racism of the master class was reflected in their choices when freeing slaves. This preference explains the high ratio of mulattoes in the ranks of the free colored, compared to their numbers within the community of slaves. Women were also more likely to be gratuitously freed than men, but among those who purchased their freedom, there was an even distribution of women and men.

Once freed, the ex-slaves entered at the lowest strata of the society. Even skilled slaves usually came into the free population with their savings exhausted by the self-purchase act. Nonetheless these same persons mortgaged future savings by purchasing their spouses and children in order to free them. In only rare cases did masters grant their ex-slaves any income or support in their life of freedom, even if they were the children of the white master. Because of this pervasive poverty, the free colored in all American slave societies typically had the highest mortality and disease rates among the free populations.

In every region and every craft, free black and mulatto workers were employed alongside slaves. In colonial Mexico, freed persons hired themselves out for work on ranches, farms, and in the mines. Often discriminated against on racial grounds by whites competing for the better jobs, they nevertheless were to be found at all levels of artisan society. In some cases they were paid wages equal to white workers, in others they were paid less even than the rental wages of the slaves. Neither favoring manumission nor opposing it in any systematic way, colonial Latin American society allowed the normal operations of the market to lead to manumission and put no social constraints on free mothers or fathers manumitting their children. With self-purchase arrangements allowing skilled slaves to buy themselves and their families out of slavery, and with a steady stream of children and women freed by masters conditionally and often totally, a very large population of free colored arose and actively participated in the free labor market.

The more mobile the freedmen, the more discrimination he or she faced; and the more unsettled the times, the more they were signaled out by the whites as a threatening element. Free blacks and mulattoes were disproportionally found as convicts in Spanish and Portuguese American jails, galleys, and factories. But the society was too desperate for their labor to prohibit them from actively competing for jobs and from attempting to rise out of the lower classes.

The decline of slavery as an institution in the continental colonies after the 1650s, did not mean that Africans or their descendants disappeared from these regions. Just the opposite was the case. By the end of the eighteenth century, free coloreds outnumbered slaves in almost all the mainland Spanish colonies, and their numbers continued to grow, both as products of the original African population and in admixtures with the resident white and Indian population. Thus by 1800 free colored numbered 650,000 compared to just 271,000 slaves in all the Spanish colonies.

Even in those colonies where slavery remained strong, the free colored population grew rapidly by the end of the eighteenth century. Thus Brazil's 1 million slaves lived alongside 400,000 free colored. In the Spanish and Portuguese colonies free coloreds made up a third to a half or more of the total Afro-American population. For a variety of reasons related to cultural, political, and economic patterns, the Iberians were more comfortable with a free colored population then their contemporaries from northern Europe.

Nonetheless, racism was a part of every American system that held African slaves and this did not disappear when blacks and mulattoes became free citizens and economic and social competitors. In the Iberian context this racism blended with racist ideologies that originated both in the Castilian and Portuguese conquest of Jews and Moors in the Old World and the conquest of the American Indians in the New. New Christians and American Indians were denied the right to practice certain professions, to be admitted to many civil and ecclesiastical offices, and in many respects were treated as second-class citizens. With such a stratified system already in operation, it was inevitable that the distinction of race would also be applied to free colored persons in an invidious manner.

In all Latin American societies, a three-tier color system was the recognized method of racial classification. Thus in contrast to North American societies, mulattoes were perceived from the beginning as a distinct group. Mulattoes in both the Portuguese and Spanish American colonies were listed in all legal documents as such, often organized their own autonomous religious brotherhoods, and most important of all, were recruited into their own militia units separate from the free blacks. In all Latin American colonies, the free black and mulatto companies made up a major part of the local military forces. These troops were mostly used to suppress local rebellions—including those of slaves—and to defend their colonies against foreign invasion. They could also be sent to defend other colonies, as occurred with mulatto militia units from Cuba. Though the crowns of Portugal and Spain did everything in their power to keep race an important marker in colonial society, miscegenation guaranteed that racial lines would blur at the edges. This meant, for better or worse, that class criteria often replaced phenotype as the best way to define a person's color category. As a result, passing from one racial group to another became far easier. For example, *brancos da terra* or "local whites" became a euphemism in Brazil for dark-skinned whites who made up a part of the economic elite. Although black continued to be a despised category, the definition of who was black became an ever more complex question. Although prejudice was pronounced, the practice of discrimination in the Latin American colonies was far less clarified than in the North American context.

Conclusion

African slavery in rural Latin America was thus a complex labor system that encompassed a wide variety of forms. Enslaved Africans lived on properties ranging from large plantations to small farms. Slaves were the dominant labor force in the major agricultural export colonies (Brazil from the sixteenth century and the Spanish West Indies from the end of the eighteenth century) and an important minority within all of agriculture. In the Spanish American continental colonies they served in a more limited role, involved in commercial agricultural, but producing for local and regional markets. In all of these Latin American colonies slaves were set apart from other workers because of their relative lack of ties to the community. Nonetheless the enslaved Africans developed their own alternative cultural systems and tried to establish their own identities within the harshness of slavery. Unlike the English and French, in the Spanish and Portuguese colonies manumission was never fettered, and by the end of the colonial period colored freedmen often were as numerous as slaves. Moreover the greater acceptance of syncretic religious belief also allowed for both a more important role in the religion of the masters and the ability to develop Afro-American religions that would survive oppression to emerge as semi-autonomous religious churches in the post-emancipation period. Finally, although prejudice predominated and the manumitted entered the lowest ranks of the free society, the patterns of mobility experienced by Afro-Americans in Latin America were far more open than those in the Anglo-Saxon world.

Notes

1. Herbert S. Klein, *Slavery in the Americas: A Comparative Study of Virginia and Cuba* (Chicago: University of Chicago Press, 1967), 161.
2. Klein, *Slavery in the Americas*, 161.

CHAPTER EIGHT

Indigenous Peoples

CHERYL ENGLISH MARTIN

On the eve of European colonization most people of the Americas lived in rural areas and devoted the bulk of their energies to subsistence activities. Over the course of many centuries they had devised technological strategies and forms of social organization appropriate to their local surroundings. Natives of the interior Mexican plateau and the central Andes lived in dispersed hamlets whose inhabitants might number a few hundred or at most a few thousand. Their agricultural techniques reflected centuries of experimentation and inventive adaptation to particular environmental conditions. Everywhere farmers developed sophisticated systems of irrigation to optimize use of available rainfall.

Along the lakeshores of the Valley of Mexico, they scooped up rich underwater soil to form highly fertile artificial islands, or *chinampas*. Farmers in the highlands of present-day Peru and Bolivia took advantage of the steep Andean terrain, where sharp differences in altitude produced a variety of micro-environments within relatively short distances of each other. They pastured llamas and alpacas on the high, often frozen plains above eleven thousand feet, grew potatoes and other tubers at slightly lower altitudes, and used the warm, still lower valleys to cultivate peppers, avocados, cotton, and coca leaves. These and other forms of intensive agriculture enabled the people of central Mexico and highland Peru to support large populations as well as the apparatus of the Aztec and Inca states.

Elsewhere indigenous subsistence techniques took simpler forms that were incapable of sustaining elaborate political, military, or ceremonial hierarchies. The area that eventually became northern Mexico and the southwestern

United States included the sedentary, adobe-dwelling Pueblos of the upper Río Grande Valley, as well as semi-sedentary groups, such as the Tarahumara of present-day Chihuahua, who combined hunting and gathering with rudimentary farming, and lived in small, scattered *rancherías*. Still others eschewed agriculture altogether, constantly moving in search of edible plants and game. Among the Araucanians in Chile, patterns of environmental adaptation ranged from the semi-sedentary in the north to exclusive reliance on hunting and fishing in the south. In Brazil the Tupí hunters had an arrow suited to each type of fish or game; those with a knob at the tip were used to daze birds or monkeys.

European Settlement and Indigenous Rural Society

Although the Spaniards who arrived in the sixteenth century erected their headquarters either on the ruins of indigenous cities, as in Mexico, or in capitals of their own creation, as in Peru, European settlement profoundly affected even those Amerindians who lived in the most isolated rural hamlets. For many the most obvious effects of Spanish colonization were biological. Because natives of the Americas lacked immunity to Old World diseases, Spanish colonization set in motion a demographic disaster with far-reaching political, social, and economic repercussions.

Other biological and technological changes further transformed rural life in Spanish America. Cattle and horses damaged crops, while their grazing contributed to soil erosion. At the same time most indigenous people modified their subsistence strategies to include selected European plants, animals, and artifacts. In the sixteenth century the Chichimecas of northern Mexico and the Araucanians of Chile adopted horses and European weapons, while developing new modes of guerrilla warfare to exploit the weaknesses of the heavily encumbered and slow-moving Spanish armies. The Araucanians fended off enemy cavalry by lengthening their traditional pikes and attaching Spanish sword blades to the ends. By 1600 they reportedly had more horses than the Spanish settlers in Chile, and they had even incorporated worship of horses into their religion. Although Spaniards succeeded in subduing the Chichimecas, in the seventeenth and eighteenth centuries Apaches and other groups became expert mounted warriors who slowed the northern advance of Spanish settlement. In Chile, the Araucanians thwarted European colonization south of the Bío Bío River.

More sedentary people crafted a judicious mix of tradition and innovation in response to Spanish colonization. While continuing to cultivate maize and other customary crops, many added Old World fruits and vegetables to their diets and learned to raise chickens, pigs, sheep, and goats. For example, by 1580 the Indian villagers of Oaxatepec in central Mexico boasted well tended orchards of figs, oranges, limes, and quinces; later they learned to produce sugarcane and bananas for sale in local markets. Following the Spanish settlement of New Mexico in the late sixteenth century, the Pueblos enthusiastically adopted European fruit trees and animals. Even when they rebelled against Spanish rule in 1680, they ignored their leader's suggestion that they destroy these cultural symbols of colonial domination.

Systems of Forced Labor

Most indigenous people also felt the European presence in the form of new demands placed upon them. Enslavement began in the Caribbean, and despite legal prohibitions forbidding it, the practice continued more or less openly in northern Mexico, Chile, coastal and interior Brazil, and other frontier areas well into the eighteenth century. Santa Fé merchants routinely shipped captured Apaches south to Chihuahua along with salt, hides, piñon nuts, and other New Mexican staples. Many of these captives were young children; owners of haciendas, mines, and silver refineries paid the cost of their "ransom" from a "pagan" way of life and received in return a claim on their labor. Though in theory the terms of their service were limited, in fact many of them worked as virtual slaves for the remainder of their lives. They were bought, sold, and bequeathed to heirs as chattel. In 1729, for example, Gaspar Macías of Chihuahua contracted with a New Mexican soldier to procure two young Indians in exchange for two well-trained horses and an embroidered saddle. In New Mexico and elsewhere, this trade usually counted on the active encouragement or open participation of local Spanish officials, who rationalized their conduct by arguing that continued Indian attacks on Spanish settlements morally justified the taking of captives and other reprisals. In the Amazon, the argument that Indians captured in intertribal wars were legitimate slaves was long used by the colonists.

Various kinds of exploitation awaited those who lived in the areas that had formed the cores of the Aztec and Inca empires. Borrowing on Hispanic practice in the Caribbean and indigenous tribute systems, Hernán Cortés established the *encomienda* in Mexico immediately after completing the conquest, and soon other conquistadors carried this institution to Central and South America. Under the terms of the early *encomienda,* individual Spaniards received the right to exact labor and tribute from the Indians of a particular community. *Encomienda* service drew both men and women temporarily away from their home villages. Men worked in mining, construction, and agriculture, while women served as cooks, maids, and wet nurses in *encomenderos'* households.

Meanwhile, those who stayed behind in the Indian communities labored to provide a broad range of commodities demanded in tribute by the early Spanish *encomenderos.* For example, villages around Cuernavaca in central Mexico, held in *encomienda* by Cortés himself, furnished not only such traditional Aztec tribute items as textiles and food, but also supplied charcoal, rope, and cooking utensils. Indians delivered some commodities to the *encomenderos*' representatives daily, supplying other items at longer intervals. In 1547 the people of Nestalpa, a village north of Mexico City, were assessed two chickens, four loads of maize, fodder for horses, and four loads of wood each day. Every eighty days they also provided twenty petticoats, twenty shirts, and four loads of blankets. (See Figs. 46, 47.)

Hoping to prevent the emergence of the *encomenderos* as a neofeudal nobility, King Charles I of Spain (1516–56) made repeated efforts to curtail the *encomienda*, and tried to limit the obligations of *encomienda* Indians to the simple payment of tribute. The king's measures modified but did not end the exploitation of native peoples of the New World. Indians removed from *encomienda* grants now delivered tribute—commuted first to maize and later to cash—to agents of the king himself. Whether paid to the crown or to an *encomendero*, tribute demands proved increasingly burdensome with the passage of time, as periodic reductions in each community's assessment failed to keep pace with population decline.

Moreover, the king could not prevent the extension of the *encomienda* to new frontier areas that fell under Spanish control in the decades that followed the original conquest of central Mexico and Peru. The promise of an *encomienda* proved to be the only incentive capable of luring Spaniards to less lucrative territories on the northern and southern fringes of the empire. From 1598 until the Pueblo Rebellion of 1680, *encomenderos* formed the backbone of the elite in New Mexico, while Spanish governors in Chile retained the right to issue new *encomiendas* into the eighteenth century. Because Indians in many frontier areas lacked surpluses of material goods that they might have yielded in tribute, they continued to fulfill their obligations by performing labor for their *encomenderos*. In Chile, as in many parts of northern Mexico, they worked in mining, agriculture, and domestic service.

In northeastern Mexico the *encomienda* even extended to nomadic, hunting-and-gathering Coahuiltecas. *Encomenderos* in seventeenth-century Saltillo received permission to exploit the labor of one or more bands or extended families. Each year they rounded up "their" Indians and set them to work, most often harvesting maize or wheat. During those portions of the year when the *encomenderos* had no need for labor, they allowed the Indians to revert to their traditional way of life. The *encomenderos* thereby escaped the need to provide for their workers' subsistence year round, and acquired a vested interest in the survival of band culture. To assure the workers' return the following year, many *encomenderos* retained women and children, ostensibly as domestic servants, in fact as hostages. Successive generations of intermittent contact with Spanish society produced individuals capable of functioning in both worlds; such people frequently became the leaders of their bands.

In central Mexico and the Andes, the numbers of *encomenderos* gradually declined with the passing decades, and labor obligations to *encomenderos* officially ended by the mid sixteenth century. Royal agents quickly devised new methods of tapping indigenous muscle power to meet the needs of the emerging colonial society, however. Beginning in the 1540s in Mexico, forced labor drafts sent periodic shifts of nominally compensated Indian workers to mines, Spanish agricultural estates, construction sites, and a variety of public works. These *repartimientos* continued in much of central Mexico until the 1630s and in some cases for many years thereafter. Drafts for the silver mines of Taxco, for example, continued well into the eighteenth century. Similar arrangements also survived on Mexico's northern frontier until the late colonial period.

Forced labor characterized colonial society in the Andes as well. In 1573 Viceroy Francisco de Toledo organized the notorious *mita* in the Andean highlands of Peru and Bolivia. Far more onerous than the Inca system after which it was modeled and named, Toledo's system, which required men to travel hundreds of miles to grueling jobs in the silver mines of Potosí, in present-day Bolivia, or to the mercury mines of Huancavélica, Peru, endured for the remainder of the colonial period.

All of these labor obligations profoundly affected the communities from which laborers were drawn. Although long accustomed to supporting indigenous local and imperial rulers, Indians found that in certain respects the demands of their new masters seriously disrupted the customary fabric of life in their villages. Seasonal agricultural drafts pulled men away from their own crops at crucial points in the growing season, increasing the burden on those who remained in the villages. It therefore became more and more difficult for them to accumulate surplus crops to tide them over lean years.

The Potosí *mita* proved especially damaging to traditional ways of life. This system typically required men to be absent for a year or more and occupied at least one-seventh, and often as much as a third, of a community's men at any given time. Many young males fled their villages as they came of age for *mita* service. Those who went to Potosí often took their families with them, and many died before completing their assignments. Still others chose to remain in Potosí as wage laborers, rather than return to the relentless grind of tribute and forced labor in their native communities. Finally, workers who did return home brought little cash for their efforts, despite regulations stipulating that they be paid for their labor.

The temporary or permanent absence of so many people disrupted work patterns and social relations in the indigenous communities of the Andean highlands. The *ayllu*, a traditional organization of many households that for centuries had formed the basis of society, depended on cooperation among all of its members. Community members worked together in agriculture and other tasks, and a typical *ayllu* also exploited a variety of ecological niches by scattering its members in colonies located several days' journey from the home community. Colonists on the coast processed dried fish, edible algae, and guano, while those sent to forested areas made wooden implements. Other settlements specialized in crafts such as pottery making and metalworking.

Well-organized caravans then distributed each colony's produce throughout the *ayllu*'s dispersed components.

Through carefully coordinated efforts, then, traditional communities effectively utilized the many local resources of the Andean environment. Such arrangements crumbled as the *mita* claimed its human quota. People who stayed behind felt little incentive to perform labor for those who might never return. Meanwhile, many men entered the cash economy to earn the money that would buy them exemption from *mita* service. As a result, community reciprocity and self-sufficiency eroded.

Moreover, large numbers of *mita* workers chose to settle in communities other than their own after their terms of *mita* labor. Known as *forasteros* (outsiders), these men were denied *ayllu* membership in their new homes. Even though they often gained access to community lands through rental or through marriage to local women, they remained outside of traditional cooperative relationships. Until the eighteenth century they also avoided payment of tribute and liability for additional *mita* service. As a result, households headed by *forasteros* accumulated greater wealth than those of *ayllu* members, further straining the old ideals of community solidarity and reciprocity.

Throughout central Mexico and the Andes, labor and tribute obligations also placed local indigenous leaders in an unenviable position. They bore primary responsibility for seeing that their communities met tribute and labor demands, and often had to surrender personal and community assets or face imprisonment if unable to cover unanticipated shortfalls. Although they invoked their traditional authority to elicit cooperation in meeting the quotas, they found that their subjects no longer respected their legitimacy. In pre-Hispanic times people had perceived a reciprocity in the demands placed upon them. In exchange for goods and services yielded to their rulers, they had expected material or cosmic returns—food from the emperor's personal granaries in time of famine or appeasement of an angry god. Now the surpluses they surrendered to their leaders seemed to serve only alien purposes, and they saw little reason to heed requests for help in meeting labor and tribute assessments. Local rulers in turn felt increasing pressure to protect themselves by appropriating community resources and exploiting their subjects as much as possible.

Evangelization and Family Life

The efforts of missionary clergy to convert the Amerindians to Catholicism further altered community life under Spanish rule. Most Indians had long been accustomed to expanding their pantheons to accommodate new deities when they were conquered by others, but the Spanish clerics demanded a total rejection of indigenous belief in favor of Christian ritual and practice. Although they never converted as thoroughly as the friars would have liked, many people at least superficially accepted baptism and other outward signs of Catholicism. Especially in Mexico, where the evangelization campaign began earlier and with greater clerical enthusiasm than in Peru, Indian laborers built hundreds of magnificent churches, many of which stand to the present. For many villages, the size and splendor of the church came to stand as a symbol of corporate community identity.

As they converted to Christianity, Indians abandoned their old religious calendar in favor of the seven-day week and the Christian liturgical cycle, adjusting markets and traditional festivals accordingly. Men known as *fiscales* took responsibility for maintenance of church buildings, while others served as sacristans and singers at religious functions. Pragmatic considerations evidently furnished a strong incentive for assuming these ritual duties; men who served as church functionaries could often claim exemption from forced labor drafts. For example, in 1763 at least thirty men in the small village of Satevo in Chihuahua evaded *repartimiento* service by participating in liturgical events or working on the rural properties belonging to their church.

Evangelization and other consequences of colonization brought major changes to family life, gender roles, and social organization in the indigenous communities. Although the missionaries' insistence on monogamy most directly affected the native nobility, they sometimes broke up multigenerational households in order to facilitate tribute collection, thereby undermining cooperative labor arrangements based on an extended family. Franciscan missionaries in New Mexico also imposed European gender roles on the Pueblo people. Viewing building construction as a masculine occupation, they assigned to Pueblo men the task of making and maintaining adobe bricks, a job traditionally performed by women. In coastal Brazil, Jesuit missionaries required Tupí men to farm, although traditionally women had planted the manioc cuttings while men were responsible for hunting. Indian resistance to working in sugar mills was based partly on its violation of gender-based occupational roles. (See Fig. 48.)

Wills written by central Mexican Indians in the sixteenth and early seventeenth centuries suggest something of an improvement in the socioeconomic status of women in the aftermath of Spanish conquest. The abundance of land following the great epidemics of the sixteenth century evidently permitted the distribution of available wealth more equally within the nuclear family. As a result, women may have found it easier to accumulate property, while recourse to Spanish courts helped them retain their claims. Meanwhile, liaisons with Spanish men offered women another possible avenue to better their personal fortunes.

In other ways, however, evangelization and colonization seem to have undermined the status of indigenous women. The breakdown of the Peruvian *ayllu* seriously weakened women's economic and social position, for example. Andean concepts of reciprocity had emphasized the complementarity and equal value of male and female labor. Women had borne primary responsibility for weaving, cooking, child care, and many tasks associated with agriculture; plowing and warfare were considered men's work. Because tradition had recognized women's domestic chores as vital contributions to community life rather than as private services performed for the personal comfort and convenience of their husbands, women had enjoyed corresponding benefits. Customary patterns of inheritance had included the transmission of land and other resources from mother to daughter as well as from father to son. As the *ayllu* gave way to less well integrated forms of social organization, however, women's access to prestige and property declined.

Evangelization also eliminated the ceremonial roles assigned to women in indigenous religion. Again, the changes were particularly marked in Peru, though present also in Mexico. The Andean principle of gender complementarity had extended to ritual life, as women presided over cults dedicated to female deities. Because Christianity offered few functional alternatives to these duties, women were officially relegated to the sidelines of the new liturgy. Still, with so many men absent on *mita* service, women assumed considerable responsibility for the clandestine maintenance of traditional rites. Sometimes they retreated to the barren and remote high plateaus, or *punas,* to carry out indigenous observances far from the punishing scrutiny of missionaries. (See Figs. 49, 50.)

Evidence also points to the diminished power of women in the Christian nuclear family as it was constituted by the Spanish missionaries. Evidently the clergy encouraged women to marry at earlier ages and thereby to devote a greater portion of their lives to bearing and rearing children. Missionary teaching may have also reinforced, and perhaps even exaggerated, traditional concepts of female subordination. Some clergy may have imparted an explicitly misogynistic message to their converts; the manuals used by priests in hearing Indian confessions emphasized women's tendencies toward infanticide, abortion, and neglect of their wifely duties. Moreover, abundant evidence shows that in the villages of central and southern Mexico wives were frequent targets of family violence. Perhaps Indian men, unable to challenge new overlords or their traditional rulers, vented their frustrations within the domestic context.

Changing Patterns of Settlement

If the effects of evangelization and colonization extended to the most intimate of personal relationships, they also altered even the physical configuration of native communities. The dispersed pattern of settlement characteristic of most indigenous groups clashed with European Renaissance notions of proper social organization, which equated "civilization" with urban, nucleated communities. Pragmatic reasons also dictated a need to reorganize the native population into more compact units. People scattered about in tiny hamlets too easily escaped the scrutiny of evangelists and tribute collectors alike. Consolidation of the remaining population into miniature replicas of Spanish villages, each complete with a parish church and town hall arranged around a central plaza, a grid pattern of streets, and an elected municipal council, therefore became a major goal of official policy.

In the 1540s missionaries in Mexico sponsored the first *congregación,* or resettlement campaign, moving people from outlying areas into more substantial and accessible villages. Thirty years later Viceroy Toledo carried out a more sweeping consolidation in Peru. In the province of Huarochirí, for example, he concentrated a hundred hamlets into just seventeen villages. For parts of present-day Bolivia, then known as Upper Peru, the effects of Toledo's plan were more drastic still; some 129,000 Indians from nine hundred settlements were "reduced" into just forty-four communities.

Following Toledo's example, civil and ecclesiastical authorities again reorganized many communities in central Mexico at the beginning of the seventeenth century. Meanwhile, Jesuits and other priests who ventured to the remote frontiers of Spanish America gathered nomadic or semi-sedentary Indians into compact settlements where they could learn Christian dogma, new agricultural techniques, and the rudiments of European socio political organization. In Paraguay and adjacent regions of Argentina and Brazil the Jesuits established an impressive network of missions that included more than 100,000 Indians by the eighteenth century. Other missions were much more modest in scope. Tarahumara missions in northern Mexico, for example, were small communities that closely resembled the congregated pueblos of sedentary peoples to the south.

Spanish and Portuguese colonists repeatedly complained that the Jesuits shielded their charges from labor drafts and other contacts with the outside world, but the Jesuits sometimes compromised. The Tarahumaras were subject to periodic labor drafts that sent them to work in mines, silver refineries, and other enterprises. In the Maranhão and Pará provinces of Brazil, one-third of the mission Indians were required to work for the settlers.

All of these resettlement programs brought changes that extended far beyond new forms of physical layout and civic architecture. The concentration of people into more compact villages probably facilitated the spread of epidemic disease. Moreover the grouping of Indians from several different locations into a single unit required a reshuffling of local leadership that inevitably shunted aside some claimants to office. Planners of the *congregación* in Mexico selected the most important communities to be *cabeceras,* or head towns, to which smaller nearby villages, called *sujetos,* were to be subordinate. In so doing they imposed a greater degree of hierarchy among settlements than had in fact existed in indigenous society.

In frontier regions the creation of mission-pueblos for one group might result in the displacement of others. In the mid seventeenth century, for example, Jesuit missionaries in northern Mexico moved Conchos Indians to make room for the newly congregated Tarahumaras in western Chihuahua, probably because the less sedentary Conchos fell under the jurisdiction of the Franciscan order.

Not everyone cooperated fully with these officially mandated resettlements. Some, like the villages of Anenecuilco in Morelos, Mexico, stubbornly refused to move, and in fact used legal recourse to win exemption from the *congregación* decrees. Others outwardly complied but retained memories of their old homes; sooner or later they or their descendants moved back. A group of Andean Indians reportedly offered Viceroy Toledo a bribe of 800,000 pesos in an effort to persuade him to abandon the resettlement program. Although the viceroy refused to back down, as early as the 1580s people in highland Peru were reverting to their original settlements, propelled by the added incentive of avoiding *mita* service. Those settled into mission-pueblos on the northern frontier of Mexico also showed little inclination to stay put.

While coping with the all of these changes, Indians in many places also confronted challenges posed by the very presence of Spaniards and other non-Indians who lived in close proximity to them. Beginning in the sixteenth century and often accelerating thereafter, Spaniards began accumulating rural property in locations that were attractive for agriculture and accessible to markets in their burgeoning cities and mining centers. At first these embryonic estates posed relatively little threat to the well-being of indigenous rural communities. In fact, the severe population decline often left village leaders and individuals with surplus lands, which they readily sold to aspiring *hacendados* or donated to convents and monasteries. When the indigenous population finally began to grow again—in the mid-seventeenth century in central Mexico, later in other areas—agrarian conflict often intensified.

In some areas, particularly in Chile, the combined effects of population decline, relocation, and the growth of Spanish rural estates brought the complete disappearance of many indigenous villages. The rapid development of commercial haciendas in the Cochabamba Valley of eastern Bolivia hastened the decline of the *ayllu* and brought greater acculturation than in other parts of Upper Peru. Some locations, such as Oaxaca in southern Mexico and the Yucatán Peninsula, offered relatively few attractions to tempt would-be *hacendados,* and indigenous landholdings remained substantially intact. Elsewhere, native communities survived through shrewd strategies based on carefully measured amounts of compromise, resistance, and clever manipulation of the Spanish legal system.

Compromise and Resistance

From the sixteenth century forward the Spanish kings and their New World representatives lent support to legislation designed to shield Indians from excessive exploitation. Laws stipulated that no Spaniard, black, or other non-Indian were to reside in indigenous communities or hold lands within a certain radius of the villages. Furthermore, officials could not grant lands to non-Indians without first verifying that no harm would result to Indians in the

Fig. 46. "How an animal is taken from the poor old man to pay for the tribute." Guamán Poma de Ayala, *El primer nueva crónica y buen gobierno* (Paris, 1936).

Fig. 47. June, the month of digging up potatoes. Guamán Poma de Ayala, *El primer nueva crónica y buen gobierno* (Paris, 1936).

Fig. 48. Indians of Cumaná, Venezuela. (Archivo General de Simancas, M. y
P.D.IV–90).

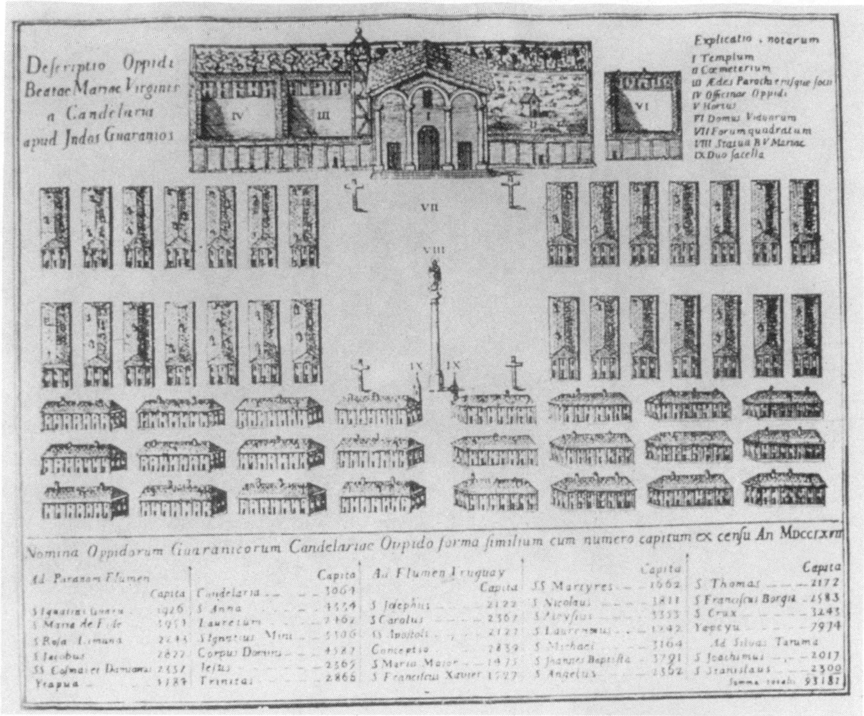

Fig. 49. The Reducción of Candelaria showing (1) the church (2) the cementery (3) the priest's home (4) the offices for the administration of the town (5) the orchard (6) the widows' residence (7) the plaza (8) the statue to the Virgin (9) two chapels. Joseph Emmanuel (José Manuel) Peramás, *De vita et moribus Tredecim Virorum Paraguayacorum* (Faenza, 1791).

Fig. 50. Indian Woman of Monterrey, c. 1790. Drawing by José Cordero. (Madrid: Museo de America).

Fig. 51. Rounding-up wild horses, c. 1752. By Florian Paucke.

surrounding area. Although these and other protective measures often went unheeded, they provided indigenous people with a certain amount of legal ammunition to defend their interests in court.

Colonial archives are replete with bulky files of litigation pursued by Indians to protect their lands and rectify other abuses. Accustomed to presenting written petitions in Aztec courts, the people of central Mexico readily adapted to Spanish legal procedure. Community spokesmen from as far away as the pueblo of Cochiti in New Mexico, traveled to Mexico City to present their cases to the viceroy when he presided over weekly sessions of the General Indian Court, a judicial forum devoted exclusively to indigenous concerns. Exercising their right as vassals to present petitions directly to the king, a few even journeyed to Spain. Hundreds of others looked to local Spanish officials for help.

Representatives of indigenous villages carefully measured their lands and prepared their briefs. They took great pains to obtain—even resorting to forgery when necessary—and guard the written titles and brightly colored maps that documented their claims. Their petitions typically asserted that they had possessed their community lands long before the Spanish conquerors had set foot on American soil. Most often they used the phrase "from time immemorial" to describe the antiquity of their titles, but in 1776 the villagers of Pazulco, a tiny and impoverished hamlet in what is now the Mexican state of Morelos, worded their petition in a way that mocked the entire process of dating claims with reference to the European calendar. They presented a document certifying that certain lands had been theirs since the twenty-third day of March in the year 100,990 B.C.!

Without question villagers were at a disadvantage when pitted against wealthy and well-connected *hacendados* who could easily bribe a judge or intimidate a plaintiff. What is perhaps surprising is that they won their suits as often as they did; clearly the Spanish legal system afforded them an effective instrument with which to protect at least some of their community assets. At the very least, they might wear down an adversary through years of protracted litigation. Indians' recourse to Spanish law carried its price, however, for in every appeal to the courts they tacitly accepted the legitimacy of the colonial state. Nonetheless, through generations of trial and error, they crafted strategies of economic, political, and cultural compromise that further helped them defend their lands and their corporate identity as Indian communities.

Many communities, for example, found ways to insure that proximity to large haciendas did not inevitably spell a village's extinction as a landholding unit. They formed symbiotic if unequal relationships with neighboring estates. Long after the disappearance of forced labor arrangements in agriculture, landowners continued to recruit temporary, paid workers from the surrounding area to help at times of planting and harvesting. The *hacendados* perceived a vested interest in maintaining nearby settlements as handy reservoirs of seasonal workers, but they had no desire to pay workers during those months when their labor was not needed. The ideal solution, from the landowners' point of view, was for villagers to retain sufficient lands to support themselves for part of the year, but not so much that they could get by without resorting to part-time labor on the haciendas.

Such reciprocal arrangements between haciendas and villages owed as much to structural barriers to hacienda expansion as to any calculated design of landowners. The amount of land an estate could effectively use remained limited by the state of agricultural technology, the size of local and regional markets, and available means of transport. Although Indian communities bore a substantial portion of the cost of reproducing the temporary labor force employed by the haciendas, they also earned cash to help them pay their tributes, the legal fees incurred in the defense of village assets, and expenses of local festivals that helped reinforce collective community identity.

Economic Activity

Rural Indians also supplemented their income by producing cash crops and artisan goods. A certain amount of their participation in market activity was forced upon them by colonial officials through a mechanism known variously as the *reparto de efectos* or the *repartimiento de mercancías*. As chief local agents of the colonial state, rural magistrates known as *corregidores* or *alcaldes mayores* regarded the Indians of their districts as a captive market. Goods sold through the *repartimiento,* usually at inflated prices, included mules and other items vital to village economies, as well as imported luxuries of little practical utility. In some areas local officials also required Indians to sell them textiles, cochineal, and other indigenous products, which they then remarketed at substantial profits.

Indian peasants also engaged voluntarily in trade. Accustomed to the thriving markets of preconquest times, people in central Mexico adapted rapidly to the colonial commercial economy that emerged in the sixteenth century. Most villages adapted or developed local craft specialties, selling these wares in regional markets. Though renowned as silversmiths in pre-Hispanic times, the people of Azcapotzalco in the Valley of Mexico turned to bronze work, producing bells, door hinges, and nails. Some valley communities, such as Xochimilco, specialized in woodworking, while still others marketed pottery, hats, woven mats, and countless other articles. Throughout the colonial period communities close to major Spanish cities and towns also found a ready outlet for their surplus agricultural produce. Villagers from present-day Morelos, for example, regularly traveled to Mexico City and to the silver mines of Taxco to peddle their fruits and vegetables.

Although the transition to a market economy represented a more pronounced shift from pre-Hispanic ways in Peru, local hereditary rulers, known as *kurakas,* had already displayed considerable entrepreneurial initiative by the 1540s. *Kurakas* set up coca farms and served as intermediaries in a kind of putting-out system, in which Indians under their jurisdictions wove cloth for sale to Spaniards. For at least a generation or two after the conquest, *kurakas* could marshal a work force for these enterprises by invoking their traditional claims to commoners' labor, and they used significant portions of their profits to meet tribute obligations and buy exemption from *mita* service for community members.

Until the end of the sixteenth century, market activity slowed the erosion of *ayllu* self-sufficiency in Peru, as many communities accumulated considerable cash surpluses during this period. By the 1620s and 1630s rural Indians were purchasing many commodities that they had previously produced for themselves, including indigenous staples such as coca and maize, as well as candles, cloth, and alcoholic beverages. Meanwhile, with the gradual deterioration of traditional community reciprocity, the *kurakas*' endeavors turned more and more toward increasing their personal profits. In time they became rural entrepreneurs scarcely distinguishable from the petty Spanish merchants who hawked their wares in cities and hamlets throughout the empire.

Village Political Life

If the economic activities of rural indigenous communities revealed constant readaptation to changing circumstances, so too did the evolution of internal political life in the villages. From the outset of colonization, European political philosophy assumed the legitimacy of hereditary leadership, even among people considered to be pagans. Moreover, pragmatic considerations—how to govern a large population that despite the ravages of epidemic disease vastly outnumbered the Spanish conquerors and settlers—dictated a policy of relying on native intermediaries. Therefore at the local level the founders of Spanish colonialism delegated substantial power to traditional leaders while dismantling the Aztec and Inca states.

The municipal governments that Spaniards set up in Indian communities drew heavily at first on indigenous ruling groups, known collectively in Spanish parlance as *principales*. Resembling Spanish town governments, elected *cabildos* (municipal councils) varied in size with a village's population and included one to four *alcaldes* (magistrates), two or more *regidores* (councilmen), and usually a jailer, a constable, and a scribe. Spanish policymakers also created the office of local governor or *gobernador,* which had no counterpart in Iberian institutional models. The *gobernador* presided over meetings of the *cabildo,* and together he and the council bore responsibility for collection of tributes, administration of local justice, supervision of religious observances, and allocation of community lands. At first Spanish officials typically reserved the office of *gobernador* for the highest hereditary ruler in a given locale—the *kuraka* in the Andes or the *tlatoani* (plural, *tlatoque*) in central Mexico. In frontier areas, Spanish authorities erected similar local governments among people newly "reduced" to "civilized" life in settled villages, even though they found it far more difficult to identify hereditary rulers among groups who had lacked elaborate political superstructures.

In theory *cabildo* offices and even the position of *gobernador* rotated annually among local elites, following elections that were subject to veto by parish priests and local Spanish officials. In fact, epidemics and other circumstances often so reduced the number of *principales* that *cabildo* seats circulated among just a handful of individuals. In one town in the Valley of Mexico, for example, only thirteen eligible candidates contended for a total of seven offices in 1569. In many places, hereditary chieftains retained control of the governorships for generations. For more than thirty years in the seventeenth century, one man was continually "reelected" as *gobernador* of Cuauhtitlán, north of Mexico City.

Time gradually severed the initial connection between hereditary leadership and local political office, as enterprising upstarts found frequent opportunities to capture control of local political office. Moreover, hereditary rulers risked banishment from their positions if they failed to behave as Spanish authorities dictated, and a judiciously proffered bribe or other favor could persuade an *alcalde mayor* to manipulate an election. By the eighteenth century mestizos, mulattoes, and even an occasional Spaniard came to occupy political posts in many Indian communities, some through completely fortuitous circumstances, others by way of legitimate inheritance from ancestors who had intermarried with Spaniards and blacks.

The rate at which traditional rulers lost ground to newcomers varied considerably from place to place. In many parts of central Mexico, the *tlatoque* forfeited control of the office of *gobernador* within the first generation of colonial rule. Deprived of legitimacy under the new political order, they found it increasingly difficult to claim the perquisites attached to the traditional positions they still held. In eighteenth-century Oaxaca, hereditary rulers—now called caciques, a term indigenous to the Caribbean that Spaniards had transferred to Mexico—still enjoyed substantial economic advantages, though their political power had diminished considerably. Many Peruvian *kurakas*, on the other hand, continued undisturbed in their hold on local office.

The extent to which indigenous officeholders adopted European philosophies and practices of government remains subject to debate. With the passage of time and the increasing acculturation of the native population, memory of old ways certainly dimmed. Nevertheless, Spaniards probably assumed a degree of political acculturation in native peoples that in fact never occurred. Under the guise of their new Spanish titles and to some extent conforming to European bureaucratic practice, Indian officials often retained pre-Hispanic usages. Village *cabildos* throughout central Mexico used the European alphabet—but the indigenous Nahuatl language—to keep careful records of their transactions. Although members of town councils in Spain represented no particular geographical jurisdictions, *cabildos* in the Cuernavaca region of central Mexico continued as before to guarantee local subdivisions a role in government by selecting *alcaldes* and *regidores* from designated areas. In postconquest Yucatán, appointed *gobernadores* displaced those who had traditionally governed the Maya villages. By the eighteenth century, local leaders had reverted to using the customary Maya title of *batab*, exercising a kind of lordship over their communities that far more closely resembled pre-Hispanic practice than any European style of governance.

The struggle between continuity and change also affected the political participation of indigenous women in the Cuernavaca district. Although men had held a monopoly on high-level office in the Aztec empire, noblewomen had apparently exercised at least a limited amount of local political influence. Following the conquest, Spanish notions of proper conduct severely reduced but did not entirely silence the voice of female *principalas* in Cuernavaca. Despite the apparent deterioration of women's position within the nuclear family, some women, especially wives, widows, and sisters of *gobernadores* and *principales*, continued to play active roles in community politics even as late as the eighteenth century. A woman named Francisca María Josefa, for example, led a major political faction in the village of Tepoztlán during the first three decades of the eighteenth century. Scattered evidence, still largely unexplored by historians, suggests that from time to time other female *principalas* and *cacicas* tried to exert influence over local politics. Such assertive female behavior proved far more disquieting to Spanish officials than to their Indian counterparts. *Alcaldes mayores* and other representatives of the colonial state often attempted to discredit outspoken Indian women by casting aspersions on their sexual conduct.

Historians differ on the question of the relative vitality of Indian town government as the colonial period advanced. Some evidence shows that by the end of the sixteenth century Indians in the Valley of Mexico showed little enthusiasm for participation in community affairs. In the Sierra de Puebla in central Mexico, progressively fewer men coveted the office of *gobernador* as the years passed. On occasion colonial officials even resorted to appointing outsiders recruited from a cadre of "professional *gobernadores*" who moved from one post to another as any other colonial bureaucrat. On the other hand, some village *cabildos* in Cuernavaca and elsewhere remained viable through the eighteenth century.

Religious Observances

Regardless of the vigor of their political institutions, most villages found an alternative source of local solidarity in religious organizations, called *cofradías*, that sponsored devotions and festivals on important church holidays, especially the annual feast of the community's patron saint. Villagers financed *cofradía* activities through wages earned in outside employment and by tilling or renting out lands that had once supported rituals in honor of indigenous deities. As time passed *cofradía* treasuries often supplanted the impoverished *cajas de comunidad,* or community chests, as major repositories of village assets.

Originally sponsored by the missionary clergy, the *cofradías* often departed from official orthodoxy in favor of a more autonomous expression of indigenous sensibilities. Indians usually excluded non-Indian residents of their communities from participation in the *cofradías.* Whenever possible they also tried to restrict the role of parish priests to the liturgical functions that served as necessary but definitely secondary introductions to the processions, dance, and generalized merrymaking that the Indians preferred to plan and carry out for themselves. Much to the dismay of the clergy and colonial authorities alike, clear vestiges of pre-Hispanic observances mingled freely with Christian custom in these celebrations. In many parts of Mexico, for example, Indians marked Catholic feasts by indulging in ritual consumption of the indigenous fermented beverage *pulque.* On these occasions as in pre-Hispanic festivals, celebrants showed their devotion by becoming as intoxicated as possible. In the Sierra de Oaxaca and elsewhere, Indians also staged secret religious observances that bore no relation to the Christian ritual calendar. Such ceremonies regularly featured the use of mushrooms and other customary hallucinogens and the sacrifice of turkeys, dogs, and other small animals.

For the most part, however, the religious life of Indians increasingly reflected a new and creative synthesis that was neither European nor pre-Hispanic but rather an expression of indigenous cultural autonomy. For example, Christian custom set aside the Feast of All Souls (2 November) as a day on which the faithful offered prayers to help the souls in purgatory win release from their suffering. Indigenous people in many parts of colonial Latin America, especially in Mexico, enthusiastically adopted this "Day of the Dead" as one of their most important community celebrations. They marked the occasion not only with masses on behalf of the souls in purgatory but also with remembrances of their departed ancestors reminiscent of pre-Hispanic observances. Even today their descendants continue the tradition of placing food and other offerings on the graves of loved ones each 2 November.

Indians on Haciendas

As time passed growing numbers of men and women left the villages to escape labor and tribute obligations, the petty tyranny of local officials, and the mounting pressure on community lands that resulted as the population began its partial recovery from the early colonial epidemics. Many migrated to Spanish cities, the men to jobs in construction and other menial tasks, the women to work as domestic servants and food vendors. Many others, however, opted for permanent positions on Spanish-owned haciendas and smaller rural properties. In some places persons living on these estates eventually came to comprise the bulk of the rural Indian population. In Chile, for example, many villages north of the Bío Bío River were abandoned as Indians settled permanently on haciendas.

Working conditions of those who settled on the haciendas varied considerably. On estates possessing more lands than their owners could effectively cultivate, peons might gain access to small plots for their own subsistence. A fortunate few garnered other perquisites and even found that governmental authorities upheld their claims to these entitlements. On the other hand, few employees received wages in cash; even if their jobs carried nominal salaries, they were often paid commodities or in credits entered into their overseer's account book to offset advances that had been made to them.

Although most hacienda workers remained chronically in debt to their employers, and landowners often ignored laws that forbade the automatic transfer of indebted peons when properties were sold, the degree of bondage that such "debt peonage" entailed has been a subject of scholarly debate. Traditional studies emphasized the manner in which indebtedness bound workers and their children to perpetual servitude. More recent work has pointed out that peons often fled without paying, and that credits extended to workers in advance of their employment reflected their bargaining power rather than the coercive force of hacienda owners. Many employers in fact expected to write off a certain portion of their workers' debts and accepted the expense as a necessary if bothersome cost of doing business.

Colonial authorities were inconsistent in their responses to the permanent movement of Indian peasants to haciendas and other rural properties. Certainly they found it easier to collect tribute and round up quotas for forced labor drafts when Indians remained in their villages under the authority of *gobernadores* and Spanish officials. At the same time they understood that the food supply of Spanish cities and mining centers depended on the produce of haciendas. Viceroy Toledo of Peru therefore permitted the survival of *yanaconaje,* a pre-Hispanic institution that removed Indians from their *ayllus* and bound them to individual lords. He stipulated that any Indian who had worked for a *hacendado* for at least four years could not leave the estate at his own volition or that of his employer. (See Fig. 51.)

In the late seventeenth and early eighteenth centuries, authorities in Mexico also showed a willingness to arrest the movement of Indians from the haciendas, especially if they could gain the landowners' cooperation in forcing workers to continue paying their tributes. Commercial agriculture in such widely scattered areas as Morelos, Guadalajara, and Oaxaca declined during the years from about 1650 to 1750, tempting workers to abandon the haciendas. A royal order issued in 1687 therefore permitted *hacendados* to bind workers against their will, even if they owed nothing. In return, landowners were expected to continue extending certain paternalistic benefits to their permanent employees. In fact, governmental decrees could do little to impede the out-migration of workers from bankrupt haciendas that no longer needed their labor.

Such periodic reversals in hacienda fortunes weakened the hold of large estates in the countryside, allowing indigenous communities to regain access to land, water, and human resources lost during times of hacienda ascendancy. Some workers who left the haciendas undoubtedly sought paid work in major cities or mining centers, but many others took up residence in nearby villages, and some reconstituted pueblos their ancestors had abandoned in the forced resettlements. Peasant agriculture flourished as the haciendas' demands for land and water declined. In the early eighteenth century, as hard times halted sugar production at the hacienda Pantitlán in Morelos, residents of the neighboring village of Oaxtepec enjoyed exclusive use of water they had once shared with the hacienda, and they expanded their own production of fruits, vegetables, and even sugarcane accordingly. In other cases villagers were able to rent tiny parcels of land at nominal rates from *hacendados* who had drastically curtailed sugar production.

Demographic and Cultural Change in the Late Colonial Period

A clearly discernible trend toward greater Hispanicization marked the history of most rural communities by the seventeenth and eighteenth centuries. Though royal officials had historically attempted to segregate Indians from the baneful influence of outsiders, favorably situated villages attracted non-Indian settlers as early as the sixteenth century. By the eighteenth century, residents of Spanish, mestizo, and mulatto descent outnumbered Indians in numerous communities throughout central Mexico, and in some villages in Yucatán and Peru. Many of the Tarahumara mission-pueblos on the northern frontier of Mexico had also evolved into mestizo communities by the late colonial period. For example, by 1785 the population of the former mission of Santa Isabel in Chihuahua numbered 491 persons, of whom only 58 were Indians.

Most non-Indian residents of Indian communities were small-scale farmers or petty merchants; a few were artisans. They acquired house sites and village agricultural lands through a variety of means. A few gained access to community lands through their own or an ancestor's marriage to an Indian woman. Some were descended from early settlers who had purchased lands in defiance of prohibitory legislation, others rented parcels from *cabildos, cofradías,* or individual Indians, while still others rested their claims on nothing more than their long-term occupation as squatters. Although many tenants tried to evade payment of rents, those who did pay provided the communities with a certain amount of revenue. Village leaders used these funds to line their own pockets, to support *cofradía* celebrations and other community functions, or to pay schoolmasters who taught Indian children basic Christian dogma and their ABC's.

Because the Indian *gobernadores* and *principales* controlled allocation of community lands, non-Indian residents found it advantageous to cultivate ritual kinship ties (*compadrazo*) and other links with them. Hoping that these relationships might in turn foster their own entrepreneurial ventures, Indian leaders often provided their allies with choice land allotments. Meanwhile, in central Mexico and other favorably situated places, the growth of hacienda-based commercial agriculture in the second half of the eighteenth century exacerbated long-standing land and water disputes. Certainly the non-Indian residents held a vested interest in helping the *gobernadores* defend community assets against encroachments of neighboring haciendas. However, any victories that such partnerships might have won meant little to Indian commoners, whose access to village lands steadily diminished as their non-Indian neighbors grew in numbers and influence.

Sometimes village leaders also succumbed to the temptation of making self-serving compromises with neighboring *hacendados* and other influential persons. Don Alberto Reymundo de Alva, who served as *gobernador* of Yautepec in Morelos in the 1760s and 1770s, invited local officials and hacienda administrators, including at least one peninsular Spaniard, to serve as godparents to his children. He even attempted to join the *hacendado* ranks himself, erecting a sugar mill on lands he rented from the community. He later transferred those lands to a neighboring landowner in lieu of repayment of funds he had borrowed in order to buy a new bell for Yautepec's parish church. Alva also exploited his personal friendship with the *alcalde mayor*'s deputy in an effort to avoid repaying other personal and community debts.

Spanish officials in the late colonial period actively encouraged the expansion of hacienda output, and the growing presence of non-Indians in the rural villages no longer clashed with royal policy. Especially after 1750, the Bourbon kings of Spain abandoned their Habsburg predecessors' traditional, though poorly enforced policy of isolating Indians in their communities. Instead they promoted the teaching of Spanish and tried to encourage broader Indian participation in regional economies by attempting to terminate the monopolistic *reparto de efectos*. A few royal advisers even recommended the abolition of tribute, to free more resources for the purchase of manufactured items. Policymakers now also believed that Indians could learn valuable skills and behavior from non-Indians living in their midst. In short, governmental policy had turned in favor of a thorough acculturation of Indians.

Concern for acculturation of rural Indians also extended to those who lived on haciendas and ranches. In 1785 Viceroy Bernardo de Gálvez of Mexico issued the Bando de Gañanes, which undermined the power of *hacendados* to bind workers permanently to their estates. Designed to create a mobile labor market, Gálvez's decree also reflected official concern that prolonged confinement to a single hacienda might work against Indians' acculturation by isolating them from the economic and cultural mainstream. The Bando de Gañanes complemented other late colonial efforts to integrate Indians more fully into the larger society.

In other ways, however, residence on haciendas often accelerated the rate at which rural Indians assimilated to Hispanic ways. Working under Spanish and creole overseers, and side by side with mestizos and mulattoes, they acquired at least a modicum of Spanish, which also became a lingua franca among speakers of different indigenous languages. Many also learned European techniques of livestock raising and agriculture. Indians working on the sugar haciendas of Morelos in Mexico, for example, eventually mastered the complex process of sugar refining.

From the sixteenth century forward and especially during the final century of colonial rule, the indigenous communities of rural Spanish America experienced sweeping cultural and demographic change. Numerous so-called "Indian" villages in fact became mestizo communities of small farmers and rural artisans, while many hacienda residents simply became functional mestizos who bore evidence of their indigenous heritage only in their physiognomies. In time miscegenation with blacks and mestizos blurred even the biological distinction between Indians and non-Indians on the haciendas and in the villages.

Even in the face of these compelling challenges, however, clearly identifiable features of indigenous ceremonial life and social relations endured through the end of the colonial period. Except for the *alcalde mayor* or his deputy, the Indian *gobernadores* and *cabildos* exercised the only formal political power in the villages. Despite the presence of sizable non-Indian populations, legally these villages remained "Indian" *pueblos,* still entitled to special protection under Spanish law, and local leaders did not hesitate to invoke these privileges whenever the occasion warranted. Though successive generations of Indians born and reared on haciendas often lost touch with the cultural traditions of the villages, others evidently maintained some ties with their home communities. In central Mexico during the late colonial period, there were many instances in which residents of a particular hacienda joined forces and obtained official recognition as an Indian village, complete with the customary land allocation and other benefits that such status conferred.

Conclusion

Despite persistent efforts of indigenous peoples to assert some form of cultural autonomy and to preserve their subsistence base, the history of rural society in Spanish America from the sixteenth century to the present can be seen as a chronicle of continuing, though imperfect, Hispanicization. This process usually relegated ethnic Indians to the margins of society. Three centuries of colonial rule set a process of marginalization of indigenous people in motion. Sometimes deliberately, sometimes unwittingly, civil and ecclesiastical agents of the Spanish empire adopted policies that tore apart the fabric of indigenous life from the intimate recesses of the household to the highest levels of political administration.

Yet the cumulative effects of Spanish colonization and subsequent political and economic change never fully succeeded in eradicating indigenous peoples or their culture. Colonial subjects struggled against enormous odds to preserve functional elements of indigenous culture and social organization. Within the admittedly formidable limits defined by their status as conquered peoples, they fashioned creative strategies to improve their unenviable situations.

Colonial Indians appropriated and adapted for their own purposes some trappings of European material culture while rejecting others. Especially during the first two centuries of colonial rule, they retained elements of indigenous religious and political tradition under the guise of outward conformity to Spanish practice. Moreover, they succeeded in identifying those features of the colonial political and economic order that they might use to their own benefit. In so doing, of course, they tacitly acknowledged the legitimacy of colonial rule and made concessions that seriously undermined the internal cohesion of their communities, but nonetheless they assured their personal and collective survival.

CHAPTER NINE

Conflict, Violence, and Resistance

WARD STAVIG

At first glance the colonial Latin American countryside seems more notable for its tranquillity than for its violence, and it is true that until the late eighteenth century order was maintained in most places without the presence of an army. However, rural colonial society was far from bucolic. As research probes ever deeper into the lives of rural peoples, and as understandings of conflict alter, life in the countryside, though certainly not always aflame with rebellion, appears to have been fraught with deep structural violence and punctuated by violent disruptions of daily life.

In rural colonial Latin America, especially in regions that had been the heartland of the Aztec, Maya, and Inca civilizations, the vast majority of rural peoples were Indians. Hence, this discussion of rural conflict focuses primarily on native peoples; however peoples of European, African, and mixed descent (for example, mestizos, mulattoes, *zambos*) are also discussed.

This essay divides the violence that touched rural peoples into three sections. The first section takes up the trauma and turmoil of the conquest and its unsettling aftermath. The second part focuses on conflicts over the personal and religious values of Indians and Spaniards that went to the heart of belief systems and reflected deeply held convictions. The final section examines the growing political and social violence in rural areas in the late colonial period as Indians, creoles, mestizos, and others began to question and challenge Spanish authority.

The colonial Indian chronicler Guamán Poma de Ayala, despairing over the violent changes wrought by the European conquest, referred to his world as a world turned upside down— "el mundo al revés." However, the multiplicity of Indian peoples who inhabited the New World when the first Europeans arrived did not necessarily live in peaceable kingdoms. The Inca and Aztec empires had expanded over the countryside by force, and to the conquered peoples at first it made little difference that the battle axes of these imperial armies cut with obsidian or flint instead of Toledan steel. In addition, the competition for resources and the diverse languages and cultures of the native peoples kept them divided, and often in conflict with one another. Thus, while the colonial period began with the violence of the Spanish conquest, this conquest was imposed on ethnic groups who often had experienced violent conquest, or the threat of such conquest, by other Indians.

After the arrival of the Europeans these tensions remained important and led native peoples to confront or deal with the newcomers not as racially united Indians, but as members of specific ethnic groups or communities. These divisions persisted throughout the colonial period and were enhanced by Spanish policies that further divided Indian society, allowing the colonial government to impose its political will with a minimum of force throughout most of the colonial period. Nonetheless, Spanish colonial policies did do violence to Indian peoples and produced severe reactions against them.

Turmoil and violence did not always take the form of physical confrontations. For instance, changes in ways of life, the enforcement of certain Roman Catholic religious principles, and the impact of disease caused severe problems for native peoples. Physical violence that touched Indians on a daily basis often stemmed from forces within Indian culture. Marital and other personal relationships, differences of opinion, drunken excesses (often during fiestas and rituals), and disputes over land and animals were among the leading causes of murder and assault within Indian communities. Thus, the social and cultural turmoil that affected colonial Indians was complex. Some tensions stemmed largely from the native peoples' relationship with the colonial state, while other violence had origins in internal community tensions. Still other turmoil slowly evolved out of the relationships between European society and the mosaic of Indian peoples and cultures.

As the indigenous population rapidly dwindled, especially in the lowland areas due to exploitation and disease, African people were brought to the Americas to supplement or take the place of Indian laborers. However, unlike most Indians who were legally free, African people were openly subjected to the violence of slavery. The entire slave system was predicated on the use of force to first capture, and then maintain people in bondage. While Spanish law provided slaves with some legal protection, use of violent corporal punishment for major and minor infractions was widespread in America. Plantation slavery, with its search for maximum profits and its rigorous labor demands could be especially brutal.

The Destructive Conquests and Their Aftermath

Untold thousands of Indians died in the armed confrontations that were part of the process of conquest. Nowhere was this violence more evident or dramatic than in the fall of the Aztec empire. When the Aztec capital fell Hernando Cortés wrote that

> such was the mortality among the enemy . . . that on that day more than forty thousand souls were either killed or taken; and such was the shrieking and weeping of the women and children that there was no one whose heart did not bleed at the sound of it.[1]

It was not just the Spanish, however, who had wreaked such havoc. The Aztecs paid the price for their brutal conquests and imperial exactions as their former subjects in the hinterland rose up against them when the Spanish provided the opportunity. Thus, the fall of Tenochtitlán was not only a European conquest, but a rural rebellion against the imperial urban center, and it was a former Aztec enemy, the Tlaxcalans, who were largely responsible for inflicting the slaughter described by Cortés.

In the western region of Mexico, Nueva Galicia, the brutal actions of Nuño de Guzmán, who had already terrorized Indians in the Panuco and Huasteca areas of Mexico, led to a serious challenge to Spanish authority. In 1541 the Mixtón war, as the rebellion was known, broke out while many Spaniards from the region were off with Coronado looking for the seven cities of gold. The rebellion was defeated, but it was also clear that there were limits to the demands and suffering that the native peoples would or could tolerate.

Having learned from Cortés's capture of Montezuma, Pizarro and his men, though greatly outnumbered, sought to achieve victory in the Andes by capturing the Inca. Amazingly, in a few short hours of combat the Inca Atahualpa fell into Spanish hands and thousands of Indians lay dead or wounded on the plain of Cajamarca. This did not bring about the immediate collapse of the empire. It limited combat deaths, however, and immobilized Indian forces, making the conquest more likely. Pizarro's task was also made easier because the empire had been engulfed in civil war, and many peoples, like those in Ecuador, had been forcefully incorporated into the empire not long before the arrival of the Spaniards.

Pizarro had the Inca garroted to ensure there would be no widely recognized leader to organize resistance to the invading Spaniards. In the late 1530s, however, Atahualpa's successor, Manco, placed on the Inca throne by Pizarro to preserve the pretense of Indian rule, rose in rebellion against the Spanish. The rebellion failed, but the Inca and his loyalists fled to the jungle of Vilcabamba where a separate state was established. Never able seriously to threaten Spanish rule, the Vilcabamba state came to an end with the capture and execution of Inca Tupac Amarú in 1572.

The Inca was dead but, as events in the eighteenth century would make manifest, not forgotten. Unlike in Mexico, where the last Aztec emperor did not become part of a cult, legends of the return of a just Inca ruler and a surviving Inca kingdom would later flourish in Peru and serve as organizational bases of resistance and rebellion.

Violent armed conquest was just one of the Indians' travails. Among the conquered peoples a sense of despair and disorder became even more widespread as Old World microbes ravaged indigenous people. This was the world turned upside down that Guamán Poma de Ayala referred to, a world where the natural order of life no longer prevailed. In the first decades after the conquest the feeling of anomie, the sense of chaos, was profound. Old explanations, old gods, old ways of organization and order were challenged and attacked. In this situation some Indians lost their will to live and carry on. In Peru aging former officials of the Inca empire testified that after the conquest "the Indians, seeing themselves dispossessed and robbed . . . allow themselves to die, and do not apply themselves to anything as they did in Inca times."[2]

It is nearly impossible to overestimate the impact of Old World diseases. In the century after initial contact over 90 percent of the indigenous peoples died in many lowland and densely settled regions, for Amerindians had no immunities to the diseases brought from Europe and Africa. The Franciscan Toribio Motolinía, known for his work among the Indians of Mexico in the early postconquest era, noted in the first decades after contact that in many regions over one half of the native peoples died of disease and

> Many others died of starvation, because as they were all taken sick at once, they could not care for each other, nor was there anyone to give them bread or anything else. . . . They died in heaps, like bedbugs.[3]

Dejection, despair, disease, and violence also manifested themselves in a lower birth rate. In the Huánuco region of Peru the average family size dropped from six to two and a half persons following the conquest. In the process the surviving native peoples were further demoralized.

During this period of terrible Indian mortality, few conquered peoples reacted overtly to their tragedy. In Mexico, nonetheless, some native peoples were reported to have tried to inflict Spaniards with epidemic disease by "secretly kneading infected blood into bread dough or placing the dead bodies of victims in the Spaniards' wells."[4] Nonetheless having their world turned upside down left the survivors of the conquests of Mexico and Peru physically and culturally shaken. Their survival was a difficult task in such circumstances.

In peripheral areas of the Spanish Indies such as southern Chile; the Argentine pampas; the jungles of Peru, Bolivia, and Ecuador; the desert of northern Mexico; and the Yucatán, Indian resistance was often more successful than in the centers of empire. In certain regions the lack of economic reward, as exemplified by the dearth of precious metals, discouraged Spanish interest, while the decentralized, semi-nomadic nature of some Indians made them hard to conquer. The martial skills of these native peoples also repulsed or slowed conquest, and the difficult terrain in which others lived or had sought refuge meant that they remained unconquered. The Indians on the periphery often made the Spanish pay a heavy price for their efforts at conquest especially after they adopted the European-introduced horse. Indigenous peoples put up a fierce resistance as mounted soldiers, and in areas such as Argentina, European cattle also increased the food supply, which made it easier for Indians to sustain themselves during period of warfare as well as peace.

Racial and Cultural Conflict

The creation of a new people in the New World, mestizos, a cross between Indians, usually women, and Europeans, usually men, was a visible sign of one of the most fundamental changes wrought by the conquest. A world that was Indian rapidly began to change. Thus in addition to conquest by arms and disease, and in part resulting from it, must be added the biological or sexual conquest that did further violence to native peoples and their cultural norms. Sexual proximity revealed sharply differing beliefs about personal conduct and religious values that touched people on a daily basis.

Although a few Spaniards took Indians as wives in the early years after the conquest, this practice soon diminished. European men were often married when they came to the New World, or planned to return to Spain to marry. In the interim, years might pass but these men did not do without female companionship. Indian and mestizo women became the concubines of European men and often functioned as their wives. Some Indian women assumed this relationship of their own choice. Others, of course, were forced or encouraged into this role. Married as well as unmarried women were taken by Europeans as their lovers or sexual partners without consideration for the women or their families.

Prostitution was not new to the Indian world; both Inca and Aztec society had women of public life, and both groups stigmatized prostitutes. The disruption and the trauma of conquest, and the dislocation caused by colonial economic and labor demands created situations that encouraged prostitution as Indian and European men found themselves away from their women for long periods. In the *tambos* (inns) of Peru, innkeepers kept single women, widows, and married women "and there the women . . . became great whores."[5]

Indian-Spanish prostitution and other forms of interracial sex led to the birth of many children of mixed parentage (mestizos). In the first generations some mestizo children were legitimate or were recognized by their fathers, but the vast majority were not. It was not just their Spanish fathers, however, who did not recognize them. Many mestizo children lost their mothers to disease, but others were either abandoned or were not accepted by Indian society. One Spaniard reported that certain Indian caciques in Mexico used mestizo children "some of whom they sell amongst themselves in a manner of business, much as the Christians do animals."[6] Without family support and often culturally and legally alienated from both indigenous or European society, illegitimate mestizos became known for criminality and violence against settled society, and were themselves subjected to violence by both European and Indian communities.

The conquest and its aftermath constituted a massive assault on Indian cultural mores. How did indigenous peoples respond? Their reactions were deeply influenced by religious beliefs. The pantheism of many Indian cultures, the similarity—at least outward—of certain European and Indian religious practices or symbols, the power of the Christian God as manifested by the conquest, and the desire of the Spaniards to convert Indian peoples to Christianity helped bring core-area native peoples into the Christian fold. For most colonial Indians, however, it was a Christianity tempered by their own cultural and religious beliefs, a syncretic Christianity. The Spanish made determined, sometimes violent, efforts to extirpate the non-Christian beliefs of native peoples. This maintenance of pre-Christian values was not only seen as the work of the devil, but was also interpreted by the Spanish, and sometimes was, resistance to colonial domination.

In the Yucatán Fray Diego de Landa, a sixteenth-century defender and protector of the Indians, demonstrated unusual interest in the native peoples until he discovered the degree and nature of the persistence of Mayan religion. Landa and several of his fellow Franciscans, confronted with a reality different than they had supposed, underwent a metamorphosis and turned into fierce extirpators who even employed torture to root out Mayan religious practices. Feeling betrayed or duped, perhaps challenged by the devil, the Christian shepherds unleashed a reign of terror on their neophyte Maya flock. In three months during 1562 more than 4,500 Indians were tortured and 158 died as a result of interrogations aimed at extracting information about continued loyalty to Maya gods.

The European Catholics had hoped for too much too soon. Too few religious personnel were attracted to the Yucatán to carry out the work of conversion and keep a watchful eye on those so new to the faith. Cultural values and symbols were not so easily changed, discarded, or understood. For the Indians it was easy to combine, confuse, or conceal the true use and understanding of preconquest symbols. Furthermore, local Indian leaders maintained their own power and resisted colonial authority by preserving the pre-Columbian political and religious order or appropriating colonial offices.

Even after the extirpation was underway one Maya religious leader "exhorted his fellow villagers who had gathered to sacrifice a dog . . . to cling fast to their old ways, for 'what [the friars] preached about was not God nor would they stay in the land and they would leave soon . . . and their gods of clay they had there were true gods.'" This was clearly religious resistance with a political dimension.

It was not just idols that were being worshipped or animals that were being sacrificed. It seems that human beings were also sacrificed, and in Christian churches. In the village of Yaxcaba a Maya witness reported being at the sacrifice of a young boy in the church. The Maya elite who conducted the ceremony told the weeping victim, apparently a Christianized Maya, "Strengthen and console yourself because what we are doing to you now is not an evil thing nor are we casting you into an evil place or into hell, but to heaven and to paradise according to the customs of our ancestors." Here resistance to colonialism took the form of challenging the new religious order while preserving the old ways. However, a rift had already appeared in indigenous society between those who had converted to Christianity and those who maintained their old beliefs.

As years passed, many of the beliefs and practices considered most offensive to the Spaniards died out or were accommodated to Christianity in syncretic religious forms. However, even accommodation could take the form of resistance. Christianity became a vehicle native peoples used to organize against colonial authority as well as a religion. For instance, although early Spanish efforts at creating a native priesthood had collapsed, in the Yucatecan community of Sotuta in 1610 a pair of Indians went beyond acting as priests and declared they were pope and bishop.

> They said mass at night dressed in the sacred vestments of the church. . . .
> They profaned the holy chalices and consecrated oils, baptized boys, confessed adults and gave them communion, while they worshipped the idols they put there on the altar. They ordained priests for service.[7]

Religion also became a force of resistance and rebirth in the central Peruvian Andes. In the 1560s a movement known as Taki Onqoy or "dancing sickness," challenging Spanish authority and the Christian God, developed among Indian peoples in the Ayacucho region. It took its name from the vibrant, uncontrollable dancing and singing of those who were believed to have been possessed by Andean gods. Indians believed that local gods had left the mountains, streams, and lakes in which they lived and had entered the bodies of those possessed with the spirit. The leaders of the movement, believing that the combined strength of these groups and their gods would be strong enough to vanquish the Spanish and their powerful God, sought to unite various ethnic groups. The *takionqos,* as adherents of the movement were known, rejected all that was European, including European religion, and sought to create an exclusively Indian world. This was not an Inca revival movement, because local ethnic groups were attempting to restore local rule, not the authority of the Inca empire. To the Spaniards, however, Taki Onqoy was a serious threat. Spanish authorities challenged and defeated the *takionqos* through a campaign that sought, as in the Yucatán, to extirpate what the Europeans viewed as idolatry.

Conflicts between Indians and Spaniards over religion and culture persisted throughout the colonial period, although not at the same intense level as in the sixteenth century. Even though the native peoples rejected some Christian values, the vast majority considered themselves Christians. Their syncretic belief system allowed Indian peoples to deal with (accommodate or resist) problems in the manner that seemed most appropriate to them.

Sexual and marital practices were another area where Indians expressed resistance to colonial authority and sought to maintain traditional practices. To ensure the strength of a couple's relationship, and thereby assure the success of the union and community stability, in Peru Indian marriage had traditionally been preceded by a sometimes lengthy period of cohabitation. After the conquest Indian communities insisted on continuing this custom, fighting to defend a cultural practice that helped maintain their way of life.

The Catholic church usually tolerated casual sexual relations or even more permanent liaisons between people of different social status where marriage was not expected. However, when the people who lived together were of a status or race where marriage was expected, the church objected. As early as 1539 the Spanish made reference to the "diabolical" practice of cohabitation. In the 1570s Viceroy Toledo reported that if an Indian couple did not live together before marriage they claimed that after they married they would not have "peace, contentment, and friendship." Toledo saw the practice as "noxious and pernicious to their conversion and Christianity," and recommended punishment for the offenders. Indians had a very different attitude, objecting to marriages when the couple had never slept together, or believing, as did one spouse, that his virgin bride was "a woman of low condition since no one had ever loved her or had carnal knowledge of her before marriage."[8]

The Catholic church attempted to eliminate this period of cohabitation or "trial marriage," advising priests as early as 1613 to dissuade Indians from the practice. Sermons, confessions, and personal advice were used to encourage compliance, and some priests even tried to force a change in native behavior by locking up young Indian men and women in the church until they agreed to marry. Indian objection to such pressure was strong, and in effective day-to-day resistance they largely thwarted this and other colonial demands that contradicted fundamental Indian values. (See Figs. 52, 53.)

Because of the close linkage of political and religious power in both pre-Columbian and colonial society, it is difficult, if not impossible, to know where questions of faith and culture left off and political struggles began. For example, Indians sometimes brought charges against priests for having sexual relations with women. Some of this Indian protest seems to have been a way of getting back at, or resisting, a priest. In other instances the native peoples appear to have been truly offended by the un-Christian behavior of a priest.

Marriages between Indian couples were, for the most part, quite stable. Nonetheless, honor, jealousy, adultery, and spousal abuse disrupted the private lives of Indians. Domestic violence was widely accepted as a part of married life. As long as the violence remained within personal and cultural bounds, the wife—most often the victim of violence—tolerated the abuse. In the worst cases spousal abuse threatened the lives of some women and killed others.

If abuse became intolerable the wife traditionally fled to her family, the culturally accepted way to end a bad relationship. But to Spanish church and state, legal termination of a marriage was not acceptable in all but the most extreme situations, and they sometimes used their power to enforce the marriage contract. In one such case an Indian woman in rural Cuzco, eight months pregnant, was only able to terminate her marriage after her husband tied her up, nearly whipped her to death, and then fled with his lover.

The lack of legal alternatives to end a bad relationship led some Indians, most often battered women, to escape from their spouses and try to resume a new life elsewhere. If they remarried they ran the risk of being punished as bigamists. One Indian women, typical of such cases, was publicly shamed by being paraded through the streets partially nude while her "crime" was announced. She was then whipped, sent to a convent, and later forced to resume married life with her abusive husband.

Violence between Indian men and women existed before and after the arrival of Europeans, but additional suffering often resulted when Spaniards imposed their values and undermined those of native peoples. Thus, conflict over sexual values, like conflict over worship, led to serious problems. Resistance, both open and covert, was employed by native peoples to maintain their way of life against European encroachment that threatened even the most personal reaches of their lives.

Tensions in rural society were by no means limited to people of European and Indian descent, but were relatively common between and among all racial and ethnic groups. Animosities were frequently expressed in verbal slurs as well as physical violence. For example, if an Indian wished to insult a mestizo he might refer to him as a *zambo* or mulatto. "Thief" was another word of derision used by Indians, while "dog" was a common expression employed by Spaniards to insult Indians. A mestizo in rural Cuzco was first insulted and then attacked by Indian acquaintances; they called him a "cholo dog" and then grabbed him and squeezed his testicles so hard that he "suffered more than a year." Verbal abuse and derision were well-used forms of attack in rural society and could precipitate physical violence.

In regions with a sedentary Indian population, tension between peoples of African ancestry and Indians were common. In rural areas blacks were sometimes the slaves of, or in the service of, powerful individuals and were often used as enforcers. Blacks were frequently viewed by the Indians as abusive agents of colonial authority. Indians also claimed that people of African descent often deceived them and maltreated them in other ways.

In regions where the Indian population was more nomadic, however, relations between blacks and Indians were better. Rural slaves fleeing work in mines or on livestock ranches and plantations frequently found refuge among Indian peoples such as the Amazonian tribes of Peru and the Chichimecs in Mexico.

Banditry, and the violence that sometimes accompanied it, was also an ongoing problem in rural society. While garments, coins, or items of silver or gold might be stolen from individuals or churches, livestock usually was the most frequent target of rural thieves. Rustlers typically operated in small gangs; the stolen animals, though sometimes consumed by the thieves, were sold to buyers who asked few questions and who then resold the animals in more distant markets.

Social bandits, those who used crime as a protest against the state or colonial society, if they existed at all, were exceedingly rare. Most thieves were of the more entrepreneurial sort. Thieves stole from Indians and Spaniards alike, indeed from all elements of society, and were roundly detested. A deep cultural animosity toward thieves existed among Andean Indians, which as we have seen, was reflected in the use of the term *thief* as a word of derision. The Spanish colonial system empowered Indian communities with the partial responsibility of enforcing law and maintaining order. Thus punishment of crime brought the community together and strengthened the colonial system, making the control of crime culturally important.

Where the vast majority of rural population was Indian, the majority of perpetrators, as well as victims, were Indians. The same is true of murderers. Most rural murders were not politically, but socially motivated. The vast majority involved young Indian men, or Indian couples, and alcohol consumption was frequently a factor in the killing.

Thus the colonial countryside was disturbed by a variety of conflicts ranging from cultural tensions to family quarrels, racial violence, robbery, and murder. In the eighteenth century, however, much dissension took on a more political character.

Political Turmoil, Resistance, and Rebellion

As the Bourbons replaced the Habsburgs on the Spanish throne and initiated policies designed to increase revenues and strengthen colonial authority and control, discontent and instability began to spread among many rural creoles, mestizos, and Indians. New and higher taxes were imposed on trade, while native peoples were forced to purchase more goods sold by the district governor (*corregidor*). These policies, combined with demographic growth, led to increasing tensions and politicized resistance.

Challenges to state authority by people of European descent had existed throughout the colonial period, but few such insurrections threatened the state or took place in the countryside. Most were urban plots that were discovered before they fully developed or were easily crushed by imperial forces.

Access to and control over Indians, especially their labor, was, however, an ongoing source of conflict between colonists and their government. In the early eighteenth century this conflict erupted into a *comunero* rebellion when the local elite of Asunción in Paraguay challenged the Jesuits and their control of Indians settled in missions. Beginning in 1717 as a broad-based uprising

Fig. 52. "How the priests force people to marry, and refuse to marry others who request the sacrament." Guamán Poma de Ayala, *El primer nueve crónica y buen gobierno* (Paris, 1936).

223

Fig. 53. "An angry Augustinian friar beats the Indians with no fear of God nor of justice." Guamán Poma de Ayala, *El primer nueva crónica y buen gobierno* (Paris, 1936).

Fig. 54. Overseers punishing slaves. Jean Baptiste Debret, *Voyage pittoresque et historique au Brésil* (Paris, 1834–39).

against an unpopular governor, the comunero revolt turned into a war of the have-nots against the haves, the countryside against the city. Determined governmental action and growing fears of social upheaval eventually caused the revolt to wither by 1731. In 1781 another comunero revolt took place in the region of New Granada. This revolt, like that in Paraguay, began with support among rural and urban groups. Although mestizos and Indians initially played an important role, the revolt was taken over by the creole elite.

Like other revolts of the late colonial period, the New Granada comuneros were protesting Bourbon reforms, not seeking to rid themselves of the Spanish rule. However, when elite leaders agreed to end the rebellion after gaining certain concessions many of the poorer comuneros, including Indians, mestizos, and mulattoes, continued to resist. Their former allies, frightened by the specter of race war, now aided the government in crushing the more popular sectors of the movement and the leaders were executed. But the tensions that had led a broad-based rural movement to emerge and march on centers of power had not disappeared.

For Indian peoples in the late colonial period the struggle for survival was most frequently conducted on a community-by-community basis. The conquest and subsequent Spanish policies reduced the scope of native peoples' identity from larger units such as an ethnic group to much smaller divisions. Most often the community, or even a communal subunit such as the ayllu in Peru or the calpulli in Mexico, was the focus of Indian identity by the eighteenth century.

Constricting identity had important implications for indigenous political actions such as resistance or revolt. Except in very special situations it made it difficult for Indian peoples to organize on a broad scale. This, in turn, meant that there were few possibilities for widespread rebellion against the Spanish colonial system. On the other hand, the reduced scope of identity usually meant greater internal cohesion. Individual communities fought hard, and with tremendous perseverance, to maintain their cultural and communal interests.

A series of reciprocal rights and obligations linked Indian peoples and the colonial state. In exchange for meeting a series of obligations that often varied from region to region, but normally included tribute payment and supplying labor as demanded by the government, the Indians were guaranteed certain rights such as limited access to land and water and the right to control their internal relations.

These reciprocal exchanges and obligations established the cultural dynamics, and the parameters of economic and social life, that defined Indian-Spanish relations. Such relations define the "moral economy." Also important to the moral economy were face-to-face relationships between individual Indians, or Indian communities, and the local colonial authorities who enforced the imperial system. Colonial officials who transgressed the bounds of the moral economy could cause Indians to see the relationship as delegitimized, leaving the official, if not the system, open to attack.

These relations were not carved in stone. They had to be flexible in order to meet changing needs and crises brought on by disasters such as drought, disease, and frost. Nor did the Indian peoples passively accept the obligations imposed on them. They sought to improve their situation, or at least reestablish older and better terms when their situation eroded. In this day-to-day testing of limits, Indians often tried to deceive the state. Hiding community members to lower the tributary population was a common practice. Indian communities also frequently petitioned the government to relieve themselves of state-imposed burdens such as labor obligations. Nonetheless until colonial demands or other conditions threatened fundamental aspects of their well-being, Indian peoples did their best to cope with the conditions in which they lived. Sometimes violence was used by native peoples to reestablish their sense of proper order, but very rarely was the colonial system itself challenged through rebellion.

During the eighteenth century the growth of the Indian population in Mexico and Peru put increasing pressure on communal resources. During periods of population decline land had been sold by the communities or taken by the government, often to meet obligations such as tribute. As the communities grew, it became harder to guarantee access to land—a fundamental cultural necessity for communal Indians. This process can be seen in Andahuaylillas, a community near Cuzco that suffered high mortality during an epidemic in 1720. The government lowered the tribute to reflect the decrease in population, and then sold off excess community lands, reserving what was believed to be enough acreage to assure communal needs well into the future. However, by 1745 rapid population growth left the community with insufficient resources to meet its needs.

The shortage of land did not necessarily lead to conflict with Spaniards or colonial authorities. In the eighteenth century Indian communities often attempted to expand their resources by taking lands from other Indian communities. This was especially true in southern Peru where the native peoples had been more successful in holding on to their lands after the conquest than Indians in Mexico or northern Peru, and where rivalries between communities often ran deep. In the 1780s the community of Layo, typical of many communities in the Cuzco region, was engaged in disputes over property with four different communities, two of which were traditional rivals. Such friction between Indian communities tended to dampen or delay conflict with the state. But as colonial demands increased, the number of confrontations between colonial authorities and native peoples increased sharply in both Mexico and Peru. Much of this violence, however, did not question the legitimacy of the colonial system; rather it was directed at maintaining or restoring an order that was rapidly disintegrating.

During the eighteenth century, a growing number of village protests and tumults in central and southern Mexico and Peru were directed at particular individuals such as *corregidores* or *cobradores* (tax collectors) viewed by the

Indian peoples as having violated the accepted norms of behavior. Indeed, "abusos y excesos" were the words used repeatedly in legal documents to describe the actions of individuals who exceeded the understood cultural and legal limits that guided acceptable behavior.

As population pressure and colonial demands increased, state officials were increasingly perceived as excessive and abusive. Angered by what was seen as growing Indian resistance, some colonial representatives resorted to even more threats and force than normal to conduct their business. The spontaneous nature of the tumults suggests that the Indians were provoked to action rather than having planned their violence.

The importance of personal encounters and face-to-face relations in the rural world were reflected in these revolts, and even in large-scale rebellions. In Peru the leader of one of the most significant colonial Indian rebellions, Tupac Amarú II, testified that he had delayed rebelling because of the relatively good treatment that one *corregidor* had afforded him. Typically these revolts or tumults were local in character, spontaneous, of short duration, and directed against individuals. Seeking to maintain or restore an existing order, they did not include mestizos or creoles (as was often the case in larger-scale rebellions). Generally the rebels were not harshly punished.

A case representative of these village tumults involved the Indians of Cusipata (Cuzco) who killed a mestizo tax collector, an especially abusive official who had beaten and imprisoned the local cacique. Members of the community had turned first to the local priest for aid, but even the priest was afraid of the *cobrador*. Without further hope, the Indians, fearing for the life of their cacique, decided to rescue him from the *cobrador*. They entered the tax collector's house, killing him in order to remove their cacique.

After the incident the local priest testified both to the good character of the cacique and the evil ways of the *cobrador*. No action was taken against those involved, for in view of the excesses committed by the tax collector the incident was apparently seen as justified. By going beyond the bounds that governed colonial relations, the tax collector had lost legitimate authority; hence, neither the Indians nor the Europeans viewed the killing as a challenge to or protest against colonial authority as a system. The violence did not spread beyond the borders of the community. After the incident, Cusipata, like most other villages in which revolts occurred, settled into its former routine, its moral economy restored.

Widespread rebellion against all non-Indian people only occurred when native peoples believed the colonial system threatened their way of life or when "visions" of an alternative order or a messianic leader appeared. In several instances these "caste wars" were, at least partially, religiously motivated. Not surprisingly, pre-Columbian religious beliefs and practices were part of these rebellions, but Christianity could also be important to the Indians in these struggles. Many Indian peoples, having been converted to Christianity were inspired by Christian symbols to rid themselves of those who had brought this religion to them.

In the eighteenth century such religiously inspired rebellions broke out in the Mayan areas of Chiapas and Yucatán in southern Mexico, where Indian traditions and ways had persisted in spite of European conquest. In 1712 the Tzeltal Maya of Chiapas rose up against Spanish society. The causes of the rebellion are uncertain, but Spanish authorities, especially the Dominicans, had been expanding their control and increasing their economic demands in spite of an epidemic that had lowered the population. The first signs of indigenous unrest involved new religious figures and visions. Indians began to worship and flock to the preaching of a mestizo hermit whom the Spaniards thought to be insane and soon after an Indian girl from the village of Cancuc claimed to have been visited by the Virgin Mary in her cornfield. Through her Indian "interpreters" the Virgin informed villagers that they should all come to Cancuc, because the Spanish God had died and an Indian redeemer had come.

The Indian who led the rebellion, Sebastián Gómez (he added "de la Gloria" to his name) called for the extermination of Spaniards, and ordained Indian priests into the new cult of the Virgin. The elders of Cancuc agreed that all European priests and Spaniards be killed, but they also wanted to kill all mestizos, blacks, and mulattoes "in order that only Indians remain in these lands." The rebellion was crushed after a couple of months, but at its height more than six thousand Indians were involved.

In 1761 a similar, but smaller, rebellion broke out in the Yucatán. Led by a prophet named Jacinto Canek, an estimated thousand to fifteen hundred Mayas rebelled against the Spaniards. Canek had called for an uprising, citing Spanish tyranny, floggings, and imprisonment of Indians and the venal behavior of Catholic priests. Emphasizing the religious character of the undertaking, Canek had himself proclaimed king in a church while exhorting his followers that they should not fear death because they would "find the doors of paradise open."[9] Canek found out shortly if this was true for he was executed in public by dismemberment. In both rebellions, Indians had turned to Christian faith and symbolism to help rid themselves of the Europeans.

For the Indian peoples of Peru the relationship between culture, race, exploitation, and resistance in eighteenth-century rebellions was even more complex. At times rebellious Indians in Peru, as in Mexico, used Christian symbolism and demonstrated Christian faith. On other occasions, however, symbols of Christianity were attacked while ancestor worship and other preconquest beliefs were extolled.

Millenarianism, a belief in the return of a Creator who would restore justice and harmony, combined with the legend of a supposed jungle kingdom of a surviving Inca monarchy and contributed to broad-based movements among Andean Indians. Two of the leading Indian rebels of the late colonial period, Juan Santos Atahualpa and Tupac Amarú II, benefited from these myths and enhanced the appeal they already enjoyed because of their claims of Inca lineage. Tupac Amarú also took on the attributes of Christian power, calling himself the Messiah and claiming the ability to raise the dead. Indigenous belief systems had been overlaid and intermingled with Christianity, but religion, both syncretic Catholicism and pre-Columbian, remained a potent cultural and political force among indigenous peoples.

Temporal factors were also important in opening the 1780 rupture between Indians and Spaniards that led to the Tupac Amarú rebellion. Population pressure eroded the Indians' resource base at the same time that, in an effort to increase revenues, tax collection was made more efficient. Moreover, the sales tax was increased from 4 to 6 percent and items produced by Indians, such as dried potatoes (*chuño*) and dried meat (*charqui*), were subjected to the tax. In 1754 the *reparto de mercancías* (forced distribution of goods) was legalized; abuse of the *reparto* by *corregidores* further heightened tensions. In the years just before the rebellion, the creation of the Viceroyalty of Río de la Plata disrupted trading patterns and economic life in the southern Andes. All these pressures called into question the relations and assumptions that underwrote the state's legitimacy, for compliance with new regulations was seen as threatening the survival of Indian communities.

The appeal of Tupac Amarú, a descendant of the executed sixteenth-century Inca of the same name, stemmed largely from his claim to the Inca throne, allowing him to attract a following that few others were able to acquire. The rebel leader was also a *kuraka* with influence over chiefs in other nearby communities in a region where the power of such traditional indigenous rulers remained strong. Nonetheless, most Indians were not ready to risk a rupture with the Spanish monarch. Recognizing this, Tupac Amarú rose in rebellion in the name of the king.

Despite deteriorating conditions and local leadership, only about half of the Indians in the Cuzco region participated in the 1780 rebellion. Furthermore because this was essentially a rural uprising, native peoples were tied to the agricultural cycle and forced to coordinate crop cultivation with warfare. Tupac Amarú also appealed to sympathetic non-Indians and incorporated them into the rebellion, but some of his followers, especially some of the Aymara rebels led by Tomás Katari and Julián Apasa (called Tupac Katari), wanted to rid themselves completely of Europeans. The divisions between rebels, however, went even deeper, reflecting regional and social divisions within Indian society. Tupac Amarú's elitist adherents from Cuzco espoused a neo-Inca nationalism whose goal was to unite all non-Spaniards, including creoles and mestizos while the nonelite followers of Tupac Katari preached a more radical, populist separatism. Thus even during a rebellion with strong organizational leadership, native peoples were not able to overcome their differences.

Racial identity did, however, provide a degree of solidarity in the eighteenth century, especially after the violence of Tupac Amarú's movement alienated his non-Indian supporters. Indians derisively referred to Spaniards as *puka kunka* or "rednecks." The practice of defining the opposition in negative terms served to unify Indians, allowing ethnic groups who otherwise might not have been able to cooperate to work together against a common enemy.

If racial hatred came to the fore in predominantly Indian areas, it exploded in Haiti in the 1790s, when a slave rebellion succeeded in overthrowing a European colonial power. In Haiti the French had established and maintained a slave regime that made liberal use of violence. Inspired in part by word of the French Revolution, in separate and antagonistic revolts, slaves and free blacks successfully rose up against the power structure and killed or drove out the Europeans. The example of Haiti struck fear in the hearts of Europeans and creoles. The possibility of a Haitian-style rebellion spilling over to the mainland was a serious concern during the 1790s, especially in areas such as Venezuela, where black revolts threatened to overturn Spanish order on more than one occasion during that decade. (See Fig. 54.)

In Mexico the colonial period drew to a close with large-scale, regional Indian participation in a creole-led rebellion against Spanish rule. By the early nineteenth century, many Indians in the Bajío, especially those living near mining centers such as Guanajuato, had developed a sense of identity as Indian peoples. Ironically, this identity was possible largely because many Indians had ceased living in Indian communities and opted instead for work in the cities or in Spanish enterprises as artisans, hacienda laborers, and miners. Loss of communal identity allowed these Indians to develop an identity based on race. Their resentment grew in part because even though they were now living as Europeans or mestizos, they were still subject to discriminatory laws, tribute, and Indian dress codes. When drought further aggravated conditions and a creole independence plot led by Hidalgo developed, the Bajío exploded. Fearing race warfare, creoles and Spaniards put aside their differences and crushed the rebellion.

In other regions of Mexico rural native peoples participated in the Hidalgo rebellion, but their actions stemmed from more traditional Indian concerns. Near Guadalajara in western Mexico, some Indian communities joined the rebellion for the same reasons they might have participated in village revolts: abusive treatment, a ruptured system of justice, a deteriorating relationship with colonial authorities, and a lack of resources to meet needs and demands. Indians near Lake Chapala, pressured by expanding haciendas, a growing population, and the replacement of the Franciscans by the secular clergy, rebelled. Harsh repression, including executions and destruction of property, prolonged the Chapala conflict. Other communities near Guadalajara, such as Zacoalco, joined the rebellion after losing lands in a series of court cases.

Not all Indians in the Guadalajara region joined the rebellion. Communities like Tlajomulco and the famous pottery- producing village of Tonalá remained neutral. The people of Tlajomulco had experienced less population growth than many of their neighbors, they had a strong communal sense of identity, the Spanish justice system functioned to protect their interests, they had a good relationship with their priest, and while resources were reduced, they still had sufficient lands. Likewise, in Tonalá people had a strong sense of community, and pottery production helped maintain economic well-being despite loss of land.

In communities such as Tonalá the system of relations that guided traditional behavior with the colonial state remained intact. As long as their social reproduction was not threatened nor their sense of justice outraged, Indian peoples resisted by nonviolent means. Only when they perceived that their interests were threatened did Indian peoples used violence as a means of maintaining themselves and their way of life.[10]

Conclusion

During more than two and a half centuries of Spanish colonial rule various forms of violence affected the rural peoples of Latin America. The Spanish conquest, European disease, and the imposition of colonial rule and Christian religion shook Indian society to its roots in the sixteenth century. For Indian peoples living in the Andes or Mesoamerica, the period between the conquest and the eighteenth century were years consumed recuperating from the cultural, physical, and demographic violence of conquest and its aftermath. Meeting colonial demands and confronting European values and culture while struggling to hold on to the essential elements of their own way of life was a full-time challenge. In the eighteenth century demographic growth and colonial policies and demands increased pressures on native peoples, eroded their way of life, and led to violent responses. In Mexico and Peru native peoples responded with revolts, tumults, and rebellion that sought to maintain the threatened order and sometimes to create a new, or restore a long lost, order. But as turbulent and violent as colonial life was, most Indian peoples who survived the trauma of conquest were able to function as Indians under Spanish colonial rule. Independence, instead of improving the lot of most native peoples, would only make their lives worse.

Mestizos, mulattoes, and other *castas,* or people of mixed descent, alienated from other segments of society, often were forced to struggle with their identity. While most of these people made their way as best they could, many individuals ended up on the margins of society, involved in crime and violence. Living under a regime of violence, slaves sometimes sought to alleviate their condition through flight and violence, or to resist their condition in more subtle ways such as sabotage. Because slaves almost always outnumbered those who depended upon and maintained the slave system, slave revolts were greatly feared.

Much of the daily violence that disrupted rural life had its roots not so much in politics or economics, but in racial, ethnic and gender tensions. Colonial rural society was, in many ways, a society divided against itself. In the eighteenth century, however, Bourbon officials and reforms created, and provided a focus for, discontent. Rural violence became more political and state authority, as well as the social order, came under attack from a cross-section of increasingly alienated colonial peoples.

Notes

1. *Hernando Cortes: Five Letters 1519-1526,* trans. John Bayard Morris (New York, 1929), 224.

2. John Hemming, *The Conquest of the Incas* (New York, 1970), 350.

3. Alfred W. Crosby, Jr., *The Colombian Exchange: Biological and Cultural Consequences of 1492* (Westport, Conn., 1972), 52–53.

4. Charles Gibson, *Spain in America* (New York, 1966), 141–42.

5. Felipe Guamán Poma de Ayala, *El primer nueva crónica y buen gobierno,* 3 vols. (Mexico City, 1980), 528–29, 542–43.

6. Nathan Wachtel, *The Vision of the Vanquished,* trans. Ben and Sian Reynolds (Sussex, 1977), 148, 258; Marcos Jiménez de Espada, *Relaciones Geográficas de Indias,* vol. 1 (Madrid, 1975), 379; R. C. Padden, *The Hummingbird and the Hawk: Conquest Sovereignty in the Valley of Mexico, 1503–1541* (New York, 1970), 232–33.

7. The material on the Maya is based on Inga Clendinnen, *Ambivalent Conquests: Maya and Spaniard in Yucatan, 1517–1570* (New York, 1987), 72–92, 161–207.

8. Father Pablo Joseph de Arriaga, *The Extirpation of Idolatry in Peru* (Lexington, 1968), 47, 55.

9. Robert Wasserstrom, "Ethnic Violence and Indigenous Protest: The Tzeltal (Maya) Rebellion of 1712," *Journal of Latin American Studies* 12, no. 1 (1980): 1–19.

10. For the situation in the Guadalajara region, see Eric Van Young, "Moving Towards Revolt: Agrarian Origins of the Hidalgo Rebellion in the Guadalajara Region," and William B. Taylor, "Banditry and Insurrection: Rural Unrest in Central Jalisco, 1790–1860." Both articles are in Katz, *Riot, Rebellion, and Revolution* (Princeton, 1988), 176–204; 205–46.

Interpretations of the Colonial Countryside

LOUISA SCHELL HOBERMAN

Rural history used to be the study of institutions: *encomienda*, mission, Indian village, and especially, the hacienda. In the past twenty years, however, this rather schematic vision of the countryside has been filled in and stretched out to include actors, processes, and viewpoints of which we had little knowledge before. Approaches and methodology from other disciplines—anthropology, linguistics, economics—have further enriched our understanding. Preparation for the quincentenary stimulated scholars to study the countryside, where cultural interaction and relationships of dominance and subordination occurred in a raw and dramatic fashion. Now, in the wake of the five hundredth anniversary of Columbus's voyage to the Americas, the history of rural Latin America has reached maturity in several areas. This volume is the result.

As a preface to the issues raised in this volume, we must remember that in the late eighteenth century Europeans and Americans engaged in a spirited debate over the biological and climatic endowment of the New World. This polemic pitted European critics against creole defenders. The former claimed the American climate was excessively cold and moist; its animals had always been smaller and fewer than in Europe, while noxious insects and lizards thrived. The latter pointed to bison and mammoths, and remarked on the variety of bedbugs found in Paris.[1] The recent revival of this controversy in a new form testifies to its importance. Now, defenders of Spain and Portugal's "record" in the New World remark on the plants, animals, and tools that Europeans brought to America. Sugarcane, fruit trees, barley, wheat; sheep, horses, cattle, chickens, and pigs increased the diversity of American flora and fauna, providing a better hedge against famine or, more optimistically, a hope for a higher standard of living. Tools, such as iron-tipped, animal-drawn plows, allowed fertile pampa soils to be utilized, and with harrows, grains could be sown using less labor.

Such claims of European benefits are contradicted by those who stress the environmental degradation that followed the conquest. The settlers depleted forests far more rapidly than had the Amerindians and their sheep destroyed the varied vegetation. The result was a cycle of soil erosion, less water infiltration, and the spread of mesquite and other semiarid grasses.[2] Operating on the assumption that nature was to be dominated, rather than to be accommodated, the European's deleterious effects on environment, in this view, greatly outweigh the benefits. Terms such as "environmental racism" or "ecological genocide," express this opinion in extreme fashion.

One contribution of the scholars here is to offer a more nuanced look at the encounter of the biospheres. They depict Indo-Euro reciprocity and considerable continuity of native physical culture, even within the terribly harsh constraints of colonialization: loss of land and water, disease, forced labor, and heavy taxation. In the sixteenth century Indians often selected items from the European repertoire useful to them. They learned how to profit from the chickens, sheep, and those unsung culinary heroes, the pigs, which were grazed on marginal land and whose ham, chitlins, and lard brought reliable income. In the Andes, Indians accepted the higher calorie, European wheat, partly because they were already familiar with another cereal, quinoa. Cattle preceded humans on the pampa, and their droppings greatly enriched the land by spreading hardier grasses, while the ash from fields that European settlers had burned also fertilized the soil. Moreover, erosion and loss of plant diversity occurred partly because of climate changes (variations in rainfall and the cooler temperatures of the Little Ice Age [1550–1700]), which the settlers could not control.

For their part, creole landowners learned to use the native bean in rotation with maize and wheat to fix nitrogen in the soil. Settlers in the Yucatán and southwest Brazil borrowed the native slash-and-burn technique of clearing the land. In the realm of diet, upper-class families adopted the maize tortilla and chocolate, manioc or potatoes. Meanwhile, in central Mexico the Indians preserved their traditional agave and irrigated chile cultivation. The Indian foot hoe and the intensively cultivated food plot (*chacra*) persisted along with the newly arrived oxen and plow.

By the late eighteenth century the "debate over the New World" had another component, which places the essays here in a different context. From the 1760s, it was the *colonial* material culture, not the pre-Columbian one, which was criticized as backward and inferior. The reforming ministers of state in Spain and Portugal sent engineers to the mines and architects to the cities to bring their realms up to date. However, they paid little attention to subsistence agriculture, the occupation of the majority. Although some landowners invested in dams and canals, most were not much interested in new methods to increase production. The sugar barons of coastal Brazil had adopted the metal-covered, three-roller vertical mill and other aspects of the advanced Dutch industry in the early seventeenth century, but by the late eighteenth they were still using hoes instead of plows for planting and declined to use any fertilizer besides wood ash. Even in the Valley of Mexico estate owners ignored manure fertilizer, higher yield seeds, or winnowing machines.

For the most part, the contributors to this volume agree that colonial technology was less advanced than that used, or at least, recommended in Europe. Nevertheless, they show that it could be complex and well-attuned to local needs, as in Garavaglia's description of the calendars of planting and harvesting cereals and of birthing, branding, and breaking in of livestock. If iron farm implements were rare in the Río de la Plata, so were they in colonial British North America. And if creole estate owners used aloe and agave natural fences, one can add that North American farmers relied on thorny hedgerows until barbed wire was invented in the late nineteenth century. Latin America had begun to fall behind, but the discrepancy in the late colony was not as marked as it became later in the nineteenth century.

The exchange of goods and techniques does not occur in a vacuum. It unfolds within an economic and political context. The countryside from 1492 to 1821 was embedded in a system that we can call *colonial* simply because Spanish and Portuguese America formed parts of the Iberian empires. The term colonial has a much broader meaning, however. Historians in this volume offer a new perspective on the economic, social, and cultural, as well as the political dimensions.

To introduce the discussion of how to define colonial, we should begin with the traditional view, expressed by the statesmen and entrepreneurs who themselves founded the empires, that colonies were regions that provided raw materials, tax revenues, and markets for goods produced in the metropolis. Since the 1960s, sociologists, such as André Gunder Frank, and historians, such as Fernando Novais, have concurred and added that the external, unequal metropolis-colony relationship stimulated an internal hierarchical relationship between two distinct types of economic enterprises within Latin America. There were those producing specialized goods for sale abroad and those producing subsistence goods for the household or for local and regional markets. The former were associated with a capitalist economy, in which workers, goods, and real estate were traded freely in an open market where payment was made in money. Mines were the best example. They provided coins and bullion for the world's monetary system (Europe, Asia, and Africa) and were themselves heavily capitalized, often used wage labor, and were technically efficient by the standards of the time. Plantations growing tropical products for export were another example, although their use of slave labor contradicted their status as "true" capitalist enterprises. (We shall look at the significance of slavery later.)

The contrasting type of locally oriented enterprise is more difficult to characterize. Historians such as Ruggiero Romano have spoken of an American feudalism, meaning that estates producing for local markets shared features with the manors of medieval Europe: use of barter rather than monetary exchange; lack of an internal market for which to produce tradable surpluses; and reliance on coerced laborers who worked for the right to cultivate land or use forests rather than for cash.[3] This was a "natural" rather than a "monetary" system. François Chevalier for New Spain and Murdo MacLeod for Central America viewed haciendas, especially during periods of economic decline, as an example; these estates, large by the standard of their region, produced foods and animal by-products mainly for themselves and nearby communities, required little investment, relied on workers coerced by debt, and only cultivated a portion of their fields. In Latin America (unlike in Europe) the two economies also had a racial component. Owners of both types of large enterprises were considered white, while small rural proprietors, it was thought, were more likely to be of mixed descent or Indians.

Many scholars of rural Latin America in recent years, however, have challenged the view that there were two distinct economies in the colonial countryside. The debate over the hacienda is a good point of departure. In this volume Schwartz draws on many works dealing with the actual operation of these large estates in the Valley of Mexico, Oaxaca, San Luis Potosí; coastal Venezuela; highland Colombia; the valleys of Ica and Ayacucho in Peru; and the Valley of Santiago in Chile, which reveal that the *hacendado* often exported the meat, wool, and wheat to inter-American and, in the case of hides, to European markets and actively sought profits. The view that labor was unfree because workers were indebted to owners has also changed. Martin notes that credit could be helpful to the hacienda worker and that he or she was not necessarily a servile, captive peon. In times of economic contraction, tenants, sharecroppers, or nearby villagers might produce more of the region's food than did the workers residing on the hacienda. (See Fig. 55.)

The importance of these smaller rural producers, who challenged the large estate's presumed monopoly of production, is one of the most significant findings of recent years. As Gudmundson shows, smallholders (and renters) were important in the sugar coast of Brazil and the Mexican Bajío alike. Indian villages persisted in the Andean and Mexican highlands, often sending their surplus to a local or regional market. Did they constitute a third type of economic system? We shall consider this interesting possibility later. In any case, they show that ownership of land was not necessarily the only basis of power or prosperity. In the "semitropical fringes" of southern Central America and southwestern Brazil, control of labor, ownership of livestock, and manipulation of kin networks were more important than access to land. Garavaglia demonstrates that in the outer circle of Buenos Aires' foodshed, livestock and labor were essential to economic success.

If the hacienda and its constellation of small farms, ranches, and village plots were more closely linked to a market economy than we used to think, the essays also show that the externally oriented enterprises, such as mines producing colonial Spanish America's chief export, or the ranches exporting hides and jerked beef, were not as capitalistic as some scholars have claimed. Again, we look at the labor force, whose character is crucial to defining the nature of the economy in the countryside. To what extent was there a mobile work force, which sold its skills for wages in the best market? We now know that legally free workers were often paid only partly in cash, and mainly in a combination of credit, food, land to cultivate, and tools. Sometimes they received religious "currency," as when the employer paid the fees workers owed for sacraments or became godparent to their child. Although cash payment was more common in the eighteenth century, still the wage rate did not reflect the demand for labor. When population had contracted in the seventeenth century, unskilled workers received only the customary rate of two reales a day and this rate continued in the late colony during a time of both inflation and population increase. Indians entered the wage work force to earn cash to pay their tribute, a tax based on their having been conquered in the 1530s, rather than on any economic rationale. Even at the mines, the pickmen and carriers were paid partly in ore. Moreover, as Bauer shows, what looked like a wage system in Potosí was actually subsidized by Indian villagers who paid forty to fifty pesos to buy substitutes to complete their turn of forced labor there.

Slave labor was, of course, legally unfree. Only enslaved workers would withstand the production requirements of the sugar or cacao plantation. Reflecting a new view of slavery, however, Klein stresses that skilled slaves could hire themselves out for wages, keeping the balance after they repaid their masters an agreed-upon rental, and that they could sell the produce from their provision grounds, which neither they nor their owners needed. But, our discovery of this degree of economic space in the life of enslaved workers does not alter the fact that slave labor was the most coerced of all forms studied here. Slavery made plantation production less a capitalist enterprise than it seems from other perspectives, such as its close links with the world market, the large amount of capital invested, the complex physical plant, and the industrial-style work organization in the mill.

The market-subsistence dualism that used to seem crucial to the colonial economy has also been blurred from another direction. Exports were not necessarily produced by large enterprises, as some have claimed. Gudmundson points out that the important exports of cochineal and indigo were cultivated partly by smallowners; by the 1780s one-third to one-half of indigo production came from smallholders in El Salvador and Guatemala. Throughout the colonial period, however, a tightly knit group of merchant-exporters based in Guatemala City or Mexico City paid for and shipped these crops abroad.[4] Production was diffuse, but circulation was not. The smallholders' production, therefore, was curtailed by elite control of marketing and credit.

One way scholars have tried to reconcile these apparent contradictions in the economy is to introduce the term *patrimonialism,* which social theorists have called an intermediate stage between capitalism and feudalism. Chronologically, the patrimonial society is associated with merchant capitalism in early modern Europe (sixteenth through eighteenth centuries); in Latin America, some analysts believe it still exists! The economic characteristic of a patrimonial society is that the ruler grants land and rights to labor to his leading subjects in exchange for their developing products for long-distance trade, whether by coerced or wage labor, which the ruler then taxes to maintain an increasingly centralized state.[5] This term both describes the relationship between the metropolis and the colony and accounts for the coexistence of elements from both feudal and capitalist economies. Unlike in Europe, though, precapitalist characteristics, such as state-imposed labor and tribute and restrictions on the consumption of luxury goods by commoners, derived partly from pre-Columbian societies. A patrimonial economy is also one that cannot develop into a dynamic capitalism because the elites prefer to limit production in order to monopolize wealth and maintain their power. Patrimonialism both fosters and restricts economic growth.

One key colonial institution, the Catholic church, beautifully illuminates the aptness of the term patrimonial. Nineteenth-century liberal historians criticized the church for its monopoly of an estimated one-third of the agricultural wealth of the colony and for the burden of the tithe tax and labor service. Clerical fees, which were collected from the seventeenth century on, gave rural priests a regular source of income, but by the same token, dramatically diminished the resources of their humble parishioners. The foundation of chaplaincies to support children's clerical careers weighed down elite properties with liens that were carried forward for decades and prevented owners from using that capital to increase production. The essays in this volume confirm these economic effects of the church.

But the contributors also emphasize that branches of the church, the *juzgado de capellanías* and the religious orders, financed a wide range of productive enterprises. The rural estates owned by the monastic orders grew *yerba mate,* tobacco, sugar, and cotton for export. The regular clergy also introduced European crafts and crops into the subsistence agriculture of the Indians. And, as Bauer puts it, "church income stayed in America, while royal revenues were shipped to Spain." But, one can ask: How was the income spent? Very often on ecclesiastical buildings, an elegant style of life for the higher clergy, and alliances with powerful lay groups. For the Indian villagers, nevertheless, a splendid church, built at great sacrifice, was a prized symbol of community identity and status.

The church was not simply an economic actor. Its primary purpose was to save souls. The church also validated the piety of the faithful, educated the elite, and maintained a chain of hospitals and charitable institutions for the needy. It stood for an religious ethos that downplayed worldly goods in favor of heavenly reward, at the same time that it relentlessly acquired more wealth. Its clerics extorted goods and labor from their parishioners, claiming that the honor of the cult and its continued appeal to wavering converts required these practices. Which behavior counted more? Since a patrimonial society was typically one of multifunctional institutions and conflicting goals, this term well describes the colonial church.

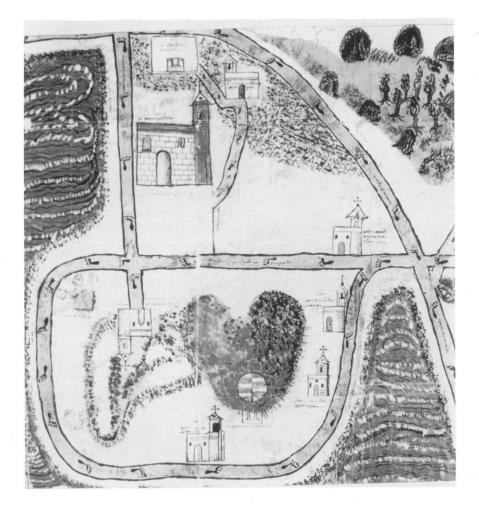

Fig. 55. Map of Chimalhuacan Toyac (México). (A.G.I., Mexico, Mapas y Planos).

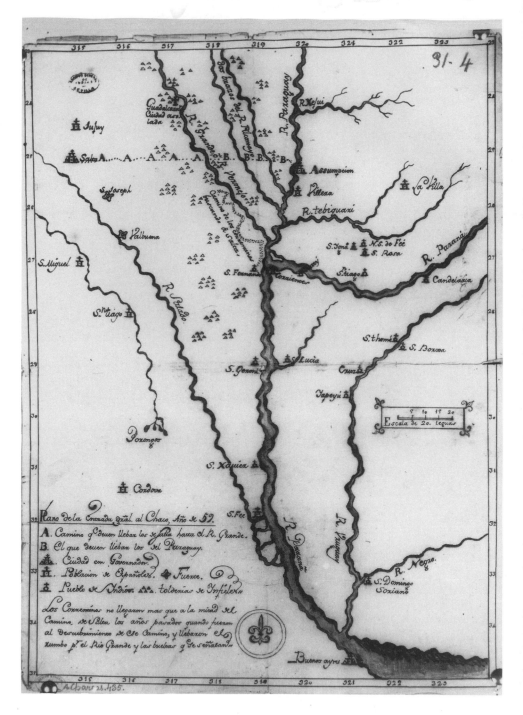

Fig. 56. Campaign against the Chaco Indians, 1759. (A.G.I. Mapas y Planos, Buenos Aires 62).

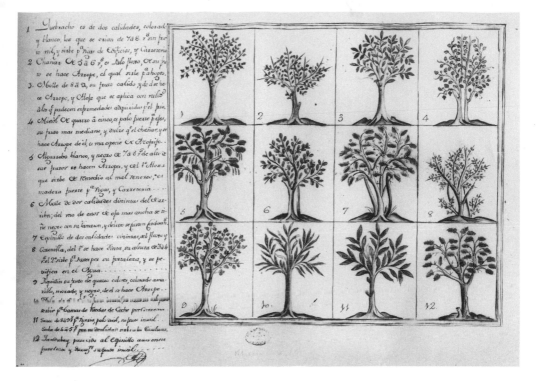

Fig. 57. Trees found in the region of Córdoba del Tucumán with information on their size, fruit, type of wood and uses. (A.G.I. Mapas y Planos, Buenos Aires 177).

243

Beside the diversity, symbiosis, and exchanges of the countryside stood severe inequality, starkly depicted here. Far more people suffered from the biosphere exchange than benefited from it. By the early seventeenth century, the size of the Indian population had diminished to 10 percent or less of its preconquest size. On the frontiers of Brazil or Mexico Indians were enslaved, despite prohibitions. Indians in villages were marched to mines instead of being allowed to harvest their crops. The average enslaved African only lived until his/her mid-twenties or early thirties. What could better demonstrate this inequality? Workdays of up to eighteen hours during harvest, scanty and monotonous diet of manioc, rice, bananas, and salt meat, inadequate clothing and shelter, the loss of immediate family members through sale, and the exhaustion of earnings to purchase freedom—all point to severe material deprivation, despite the ways slaves found to alleviate it. While the creole population was far better off, there was much inequality here as well. Within the clergy, the distribution of the income from tithe was quite uneven, with the archbishop and cathedral chapter obtaining the lion's share.

In addition, the contributors persuasively argue that the spread of commercially oriented production led to greater inequality rather than less. In Chile, after the Lima market for wheat expanded and made farmland more valuable, tenants on landed estates were forced to offer year-round labor service. Jesuit textile mill owners in Peru increased their labor demands for the same reason. In late colonial Brazil, the agricultural renaissance led to opportunities for free producers (and even some slaves) but also to a worsening of conditions for the majority of free people. In Guatemala, the indigo producers were more exploited by their merchant suppliers. Productivity grew quantitatively, but the distribution of greater wealth was more skewed in favor of elite groups. In the words of scholars known as dependency analysts, capitalist development initiated at the center of the global economy meant greater underdevelopment in the periphery: Latin America.

Yet, contributors also depict the ability of poor or struggling people from the early colony onward to extract some material benefit from this inequitable society. Martin points to the entrepreneurial *kurakas* of the Andes, with their sheep, coca farms, and textile workshops, while Gudmundson and Klein describe the ingenious independence of the muleteers. The mixture of crafts, farming, herding, and hunting-and-gathering activities of rural people throughout Latin America testifies to their skills, as does their use of the courts to retain their land and such less-formal techniques as withholding labor or working halfheartedly. And the demographic recovery that occurred throughout the continent by the mid-eighteenth century indicates the resilience of the descendants of the survivors of the epidemics of the sixteenth and seventeenth century. The sharp discrepancy in standard of living among different groups, therefore, was a structural characteristic that a part of the rural population succeeded in transcending.

To conclude this look at interpretations of the economy of the countryside, we can emphasize that the origins of inequality lay in the types of enterprises in colonial Latin America and the way they were linked to the world economy. Iberia and northern Europe benefited from limiting who could trade and when, from exchanging manufactured goods for raw materials, and from receiving tax revenues. Unequal terms of exchange between Ibero-America and Europe made it likely that the terms of exchange within the colony would be unequal also. But there is another approach, which stresses the importance of the social structure within Latin America. The composition of the different classes, how they interacted with one another, and their relationship to the state are crucial to the meaning of colonialism. Similar goods are made in many societies; what distinguished Latin America was the social structure that affected how sugar or wheat, for example, would be produced, sold, and its profits distributed.

Race, occupation, income, location, and possessions and manner of life were as critical to determining social position in the countryside as they were in the cities. But rural society was distinct in important ways. It was not the preferred place of residence for the landed elite, so that this class was more likely to be represented by an estate administrator or a younger sibling than by the head of the owner's family. The proportion of Indians and, in some locations, Africans and people of mixed ancestry was higher relative to the whites, because the latter clustered in urban centers. There were fewer public officials and elites were more likely to maintain their authority by informal methods of punishment and reward. Overall, the socio-racial hierarchy was simpler.

In the cities it was rare for nonwhites to become officials, priests, monks or nuns, lawyers and other professionals, or large storeowners. In the countryside mestizos, mulattoes, and occasionally Indians might fill some of these occupations, because whites were less likely to live there. The elites were still supposed to be white, and the friars and priests were mainly European, but the next level of landowners—the *rancheros, lavradores de cana,* and small-scale growers of indigo—as well as the transport specialists, craftspeople, peddlers, and low-level officials could be free coloreds or mestizos, New Christians, mulattoes, and also Indian or white.

Were the small proprietors a rural middle class? They should perhaps be seen as an intermediate, but not a middle class, because of their low income and an attachment to elite values. The smallholders might be wealthy, but typically were not, since they had to pay such a high percentage of their crop in charges to the landlord. Their hard-won gains were precarious. Also, the discrimination against the free colored shows that race was a serious obstacle to a career as a small cultivator or rural artisan. Middle groups were often divided rather than united by their mixed racial character. They might prefer to identify with the higher-ranking white group or they might simply find themselves in situations where they had to distance themselves from their Indian or African parent groups. Slave hunters were often the mixed-race descendants of Indian or African slaves and had a similar material culture and language. Petty officials (*corregidores* and *jueces de milpa*) had to enforce unwelcome laws on residents of the periphery who shared the same mestizo or mulatto racial background as they did. In rural Peru Indians readily traded ethnic insults with mestizos or mulattoes.

The Indian elite was a group more prominent in the countryside than the city. At first it was comprised of nobles, who demonstrated entrepreneurial talents and retained private landholdings in the Andes, Oaxaca, and highland New Granada. By the seventeenth century, though, they found themselves increasingly unable to deliver the tribute their villages owed; exploiting their subjects to make payments, the Indian elite eventually lost legitimacy. Over time the low-born holders of the post of *gobernador,* created by the Spaniards, became the community leaders. The merging of pre-Colombian village self-government with the Spanish-imposed city council nevertheless helped the Indians survive in the countryside. There was no formal African counterpart to this group, but the field hands clustered together generated their own spokespeople and social organizations. The maroon communities allowed mixed American-African government, but the *quilombos'* illegal status made self-rule ephemeral in most cases.

The countryside was the frontier of the Portuguese and Spanish empires. Was it also a place of greater freedom and opportunity? Not for the enslaved Apache or Araucanians, nor of course, the enslaved workers from Senegambia or Angola. However, the more acculturated groups flourished in the loose, peripheral societies in southern Brazil, Central America, and the plains of Venezuela and Argentina, where they combined military, administrative, and fiscal functions. In general, there was greater physical mobility and contact among different racial groups in the countryside then we used to think. Even in the settled, central regions, hacienda and sugar plantation work forces from the seventeenth century combined a variety of racial groups. By the late colony as Martin notes, residents of "Indian" villages were often mestizos, mulattoes, and a few Spaniards (all of whom the Laws of the Indies had excluded), as well as Indians born elsewhere. The widespread migration of laborers, peddlers, family members seeking kin, and tax collectors also illustrates a physical mobility that contributes to the nonfeudal character of rural society.

Another hallmark of rural society was the generous use of personal power by landlords, military commanders, or bureaucrats, however lowly. When all these functions were combined within one family, few dared to oppose its wishes. On the missions and in isolated parishes, the local *caudillo* could be a friar or priest, who intervened in all aspects of daily life. However, the state was not forgotten entirely. Elites felt the need to validate their informal power by obtaining, by merit or, more likely, by purchase, the titles of captain of the militia or district magistrate. Their new status could then be translated into more land and control over more workers, both of which reached legendary proportions in northeast Brazil, coastal Venezuela, and northern Mexico. Personal power was stronger in the seventeenth century, when weak Spanish and Portuguese crowns willingly delegated tax collection, coining, and policing to ambitious local elites. (See Fig. 56.)

Were there no checks on these American lords and their bureaucratic allies? One of the preoccupations of recent colonial research has been to reexamine relations of dominance and subordination in many spheres: the family, the Indian village, the plantation, the mission. New terms have come into use to challenge the presumed stark dichotomy between ruler and ruled. A new sub-field, subaltern studies, focuses on any group that is subordinated in terms of class, caste, age, gender, and office, and seeks to identify its range of responses in action, and even in thought, to the dominant groups.[6]

One new term is the word "negotiation", as when Indian peons bargained with the *hacendado* over the amount of credit extended. Slaves discussed with their masters the price at which they would rent themselves out or purchase their freedom. Creoles bargained with the crown about tax rates. Another strategy was "avoidance," as when poor rural people worked slowly or badly, or ran away.

"Contention" describes a more aggressive stance. Villagers took their claims for tribute reduction to court or sent a delegation to the *corregidor* to oppose a dam that diverted water from their fields. They might back their appeal up with selective violence, mainly against property. Measured contention was frequently an effective tactic, as confirmed for regions from southern Peru to northern Mexico. All these methods expressed "resistance" to aspects of colonial rule but not the expectation of ending it.

Historians now realize that the colonial relationship underwent constant readjustment at the hands of both rulers and ruled. This was sometimes interrupted by "outright rejection," when large numbers of Indians from different pueblos called for the overthrow of the king or church and killed or drove out their local representatives. These rebellions could be as short as a few months or three years or more; they might retain elements of Christianity, such as the priests in Tupac Amarú's revolt, or reject it entirely, but even the extremist Canek revolt in the Yucatán kept the Christian sacrament of extreme unction. These rebellions transcended loyalty to village and temporarily merged the different native ethnic groups into a movement against Spanish rule and mixed-race outsiders. As Stavig shows, the Taki Onkoy movement of six-teenth-century Peru temporarily united a wide variety of native groups, though it was not an Inca revival movement, since its originators worshiped pre-Inca gods. It proved impossible to sustain these alliances, however, until by the eighteenth century loyalty to particular villages were loosened enough to permit popular movements based on broad racial categories. The rebels adopted the European classification of Indian and turned it to their own advantage in the late eighteenth century in the Bajío when they recruited Indians from different ethnic groups to an insurgency that finally did destroy the colonial regime.

Increased exactions of state or church were a common cause of pragmatic village revolts and messianic rebellions alike. Another new approach of historians of rural revolt, such as William Taylor for New Spain or Scarlet O'Phelan

Godoy for Peru and Bolivia, is to show how such general causes as tax increases provoke violence when face-to-face relations between Indian governor, parish priest, or local Spanish official deteriorate. In Cusipata in rural Cuzco or Tonalá in the Guadalajara region, the relationship with the priest was crucial. Research on intra-Indian violence has also personalized the lives of the ruled.

Cultural history has shifted the historian's gaze from the influence of markets, classes, and the state to religious beliefs, sexual practices, and certain social norms, such as honor. These symbolize and structure the better-understood relations of economic and political power. Some scholars of culture also believe that documents in the archives should be read as literary texts, with the historian seeking the viewpoint of all the actors involved in the documents' creation, including his or her viewpoint as well; this approach asserts that documents cannot be read as accounts of a generally accepted historical reality. The novelty of this perspective may be judged by the fact that the most comprehensive review of research on colonial rural Mexico, written by Eric Van Young in 1983, barely needed to mention it.[7]

Cultural history has reinvigorated the older debate about the methods, efficacy, and for those who make value judgments, the legitimacy of the Spaniards' conversion of the Indians and Africans. Schwaller believes that the Indians were baptized and regularly received such sacraments as the Eucharist and confirmation, but other historians think the friars' methods of emphasizing dances and edifying plays underestimated Indian intellectual capacity. Certainly, the clergy prevented the Indians from becoming priests, heightening the existing Iberian division between official and folk Catholicism. Schwaller also raises the much-debated question of whether the Indians understood the sacraments as they were intended. For example, in central Mexico the Indians continued to view sin as impurity or filth that disrupted the corporate order of the universe rather than as an evil act that harmed one's chance for personal salvation. Perhaps there was simply no way to avoid these mutual conceptual misunderstandings, given the divergent cosmologies of each group.

Recent research has unearthed the continuation of so many pre-Christian practices as to exceed the friars' worst expectations. The village was the locus of some of these, such as the excessive (to Spanish eyes) consumption of pulque and animal sacrifices; others were carried out in the natural settings, caves and streams, with their even older associations to the divine. Rural isolation also favored the continuation of cults to African deities, and slaves with knowledge of these practices had higher prestige in their communities. But beliefs were modified too, as in the case of African gods associated with hunting and warfare giving way to deities related to family life and resistance. The outcome was not doctrinally correct by Christian standards, but it could show a degree of rapprochement with Christianity. Whether the result was disjunction and confusion or the creative resolution of contradictions, which the term syncretism implies, is a hotly debated issue.

Nothing could have been more different than the attitudes towards sexuality and gender roles held by the friars and some Indian groups. The Pueblo Indians' identification of intercourse with sanctity violently contradicted the clergy's view that chastity was the higher form of activity (or nonactivity). On a more mundane level, the Catholic view that sex must be limited to marriage for the purpose of procreation was challenged by the Andean practice, mentioned by Stavig, of premarital cohabitation to determine compatibility. Friars undermined traditional gender divisions of rural labor, forcing women out of the fields and into textile sweatshops or forcing men out of hunting and into house construction. Sometimes this was done intentionally as a way to humiliate the adult members of the village in front of their children, whom the clergy were trying to convert. In slave regions, overseers ignored African occupational distinctions too. On American plantations women were more likely to be found in great gang of fieldworkers, while in Africa their tasks were more varied.

One unfortunate theme in colonial family relations was the physical mistreatment of women who were forced into involuntary sexual relations with employers or other men, and enclosed in home or workplace. Did these abuses affect mainly lower-class women? Strict control of women was common to all ranks; wife beating was one method found in all classes. Among the late-eighteenth century Guaraní who fled the secularized missions of Paraguay, beating was common and sometimes ended in the woman's death.[8] But elite rural women had their dowries and their share of community property, as well as the prestige of their families, as "the moons among the stars." In marginal regions like São Paulo, matrilocal residence patterns prevailed, which gave women more power even in lower-class families. And when mothers survived the fathers, they could assume a patriarchal role, but of course, this position was beneficial only when the women had the means to fulfill her duties.

Cultural historians have joined geographers and archaeologists in calling our attention to the importance of the material surroundings in colonial Latin America. We now better appreciate how the fabrication and arrangement of objects can reflect social values. Country people lived in a simpler physical environment than urban dwellers. The typical dwelling for an Indian farmer was an adobe house, with dirt floor and a thatched roof, while the African hut was similar. Even the well-to-do, as Schwartz describes, were more inclined to spend their profits on land, livestock, and slaves than on furniture or jewelry; they saved their Chinese silks and good silver tableware for the city house where the people who mattered could see them. The main house of the large estate could provide security and a sense of place for the family without being an elaborate structure. Even elite diet was not that far removed from what the peons and slaves ate.

But, as Van Young highlights, a more austere private material culture co-existed with lavish churches and monumental public spaces, which poor as well as rich people felt were theirs. Why not? The poor had built the churches and paid for many of their adornments, and had leveled and maintained the plazas.

For the Iberians and the Indians both, the plaza bordered by the church with its open chapel was the center of society, spiritually as well as physically.

Now we know, however, that Indians invested the area around the church, as well as images within it, with an intense and literal sanctity. Although the Spaniards saw statues of the Virgins and Saints as representing their holy namesakes, the Indians believed holiness inhered within them. Pre-Columbian associations were continued in central Mexico, Schwaller points out, by the snake wall, the wall around the open chapel and its patio to the side of the church, which marked the whole complex off from the profane and disorderly space of the periphery. Similarly, the layout of the church-patio complex according to the four directions of the compass carried native practice into colonial urban design. As we might expect, more and more evidence is found of the use of Indian motifs in church architecture, such as native costume, flowers, and fruits, and of course, the guinea pig as a substitute for the Paschal Lamb. (See Fig. 57.)

While this volume reflects the growing maturity of the field of colonial rural history, many tantalizing questions remain. How should we characterize the rural economy? Although the old dichotomies of feudalism versus capitalism or subsistence versus market have been jettisoned, we have not yet devised general concepts to replace them. The contributors have shown in what circumstances they intersect, and we could suppose a dialectical unity on that basis. Still, a new term would be more satisfactory. *Patrimonialism* is one possibility, especially because it stresses how material and social or spiritual objectives are intertwined, but some criticize it for being linear. Patrimonialism implies a progressive development from one socioeconomic stage to another, based primarily on European experience.

Does the term *colonial* better describe rural economy and society? It accutely depicts trade and tax relations between Europe and the Americas, as well as the metropolitan assumptions of social and racial superiority that underlay them. But, colonial also homogenizes the diverse enterprises and social groups that constituted the countryside. It brings the old dichotomy "back in." More case studies about the contribution of different units to the overall value of regional production, about wages and prices and the organization of trade, could help us assess the value of colonial for the internal economy. Information about the Indian wage worker, the mulatto craftsman, the creole peddler, and especially, rural women of all types would be very useful. Recent research on Spanish captives on the Buenos Aires frontier offers an engaging glimpse of the lives of these women[9] but more is needed to place these groups in the social hierarchy.

Or, should we abandon characterizations of a general nature? Certainly, the realities of historical actors differed depending on their ethnicity, gender, age, occupation, and class. The postmodernist view is that the modern ideal of writing history with universal categories of analysis based on documentary sources that can be trusted to convey a knowable historical reality is irreparably flawed. Yet the postmodernist alternative has its limitations. Even diverse constructions of a particular event can share common ground, which constitutes a past that can be widely understood. Historians have the freedom to transcend their own social positions as well as the particularist perspectives of the people they study. In addition, by stressing the shifting, situational identities of historical actors, the postmodernist approach projects its own preoccupations; people in colonial Latin America might try to move from one socio-racial category to another, but their ultimate goal was a fixed status within the colonial hierarchy. The contingent persona was a means not an end. Despite its fruitful critique of other types of historical thinking, the postmodernist approach offers only a partial answer to the historian's eternal question: how do we present the past in its own terms yet make it comprehensible and compelling to us today?

Notes

1. D. A. Brading, *The First America: The Spanish Monarchy, Creole Patriots and the Liberal State, 1429–1867* (Cambridge, 1991), 429.

2. Elinor Melville, "Environmental and Social Change in the Valle de Mezquital, Mexico, 1521–1600," *Comparative Studies in Society and History* 32, no. 1 (January 1990): 35.

3. Ruggiero Romano, "American Feudalism," *Hispanic American Historical Review* 64, no. 1 (February 1984): 126–27, 132.

4. Louisa Hoberman, *Mexico's Merchant Elite, 1590–1660: Silver, State, and Society* (Durham, 1991), 125.

5. John R. Hall, "The Patrimonial Dynamic in Colonial Brazil," in Richard Graham, ed., *Brazil and the World System* (Austin, 1991), 65–66.

6. Florencia E. Mallon, "The Promise and Dilemma of Subaltern Studies: Perspectives from Latin American History," *American Historical Review* 99, no. 3 (December 1994): 1,493, 1,498.

7. Eric Van Young, "Mexican Rural History since Chevalier," *Latin American Research Review* 18, no. 3 (1983): 5–62.

8. Personal communication from Barbara Ganson, based on her dissertation, "Better Not Take My Manioc: Guaraní Religion, Society and Politics in the Jesuit Missions of Paraguay, 1500–1800," (Ph.D. diss., University of Texas, 1995).

9. Susan M. Socolow, "Spanish Captives in Indian Societies: Cultural Contact along the Argentine Frontier, 1600–1835," *Hispanic American Historical Review* 72, no. 1 (February 1992): 89.

Suggestions for Further Reading

General Sources

The history of the Latin American countryside is the subject of a rich and varied literature, some treating specifically rural subjects, some including rural life within a broader discussion of a region, such as northern Mexico, or of a topic, such as religion.

Recent introductions to the history of colonial Latin America include Mark Burkholder and Lyman Johnson, *Colonial Latin America* (Oxford, 1993) and Lewis Hanke and Jane M. Rausch, eds., *People and Issues in Latin American History: The Colonial Experience* (New York, 1993). Earlier but valuable works are Louisa Hoberman and Susan Socolow, eds., *Cities and Society in Colonial Latin America* (Albuquerque, 1986), Lyle N. McAlister's encyclopedic *Spain and Portugal in the New World* (Minneapolis, 1984) and Stuart Schwartz and James Lockhart, *Early Latin America* (Cambridge, 1983), especially for detail on rural economy and society.

An excellent overview with bibliographic essays is also to be found in the first two volumes of *The Cambridge History of Latin America* (7 vols. to date; Cambridge, 1984–). The chapters by Miguel León-Portilla, "Mesoamerica Before 1519," I, 3–36, and John Murra, "Andean Societies Before 1532," I, 59–90, depict pre-Columbian society in these key regions. The essays by Enrique Florescano ("The Formation and Economic Structure of the Hacienda in New Spain," II, 153–88) and Magnus Mörner ("The Rural Economy and Society of Colonial Spanish America," II, 189–218) provide a good description of the colonial countryside, as does Murdo MacLeod's "Aspects of the Internal

Economy of Colonial Spanish America: Labour, Taxation, Distribution, and Exchange," II, 219–64. For Brazil, A. J. R. Russell-Wood, "Colonial Brazil: The Gold Cycle, c.1690-1750," II, 547–600; Stuart B. Schwartz, "Colonial Brazil, c.1580–c.1750: Plantations and Peripheries," II, 423–99; and Dauril Alden, "Late Colonial Brazil, 1750–1808," II, 601–60 are very helpful overviews.

A few seminal articles offer a combination of bibliographic review and discussion of theoretical issues. Eric Wolf and Sidney Mintz, "Haciendas and Plantations in Middle America and the Antilles," *Social and Economic Studies*, 6:3 (1957), 452–71, is an important starting point. Eric van Young, "Mexican Rural History since Chevalier," *Latin American Research Review*, 18:3 (1983), 5–62; Magnus Mörner, "The Spanish American Hacienda: A Survey of Recent Research and Debate," *Hispanic American Historical Review* (hereafter referred to as *HAHR*), 53:1 (February 1973), 183–215; and Reinhard Liehr, "Orígenes, evolución y estructura socioeconómica de la hacienda hispanoamericana," *Anuario de Estudios Americanos*, 33 (1976), 527–77, are others. A good set of articles on large estates showing the use of quantitative techniques is found in Enrique Florescano, ed., *Haciendas, latifundios y plantaciones en América Latina* (Mexico City, 1975). Orlando Patterson, *Slavery and Social Death: A Comparative Study* (Cambridge, Mass., 1982), provides a crucial guide through the maze of issues in distinguishing slavery from all other forms of servile and forced labor.

The innovative work on colonial demography can be approached through two books of Sherburne F. Cook and Woodrow W. Borah, *The Aboriginal Population of Central Mexico on the Eve of Spanish Conquest* (Berkeley, 1963) and *Essays in Population History: Mexico and the Caribbean*, 3 vols. (Berkeley, 1971–79). William M. Denevan, ed., *The Native Population of the Americas in 1492* (Madison, 1976); Noble David Cook, *Demographic Collapse: Indian Peru, 1520–1620* (Cambridge, 1981); and David Henige, "On the Contact Population of Hispaniola: History as Higher Mathematics," *HAHR*, 58:2 (May 1978), 217–37, present additional perspectives on the controversy about the initial demographic impact of colonization. Noble David Cook, "Disease and the Depopulation of Hispaniola, 1492–1518," *Colonial Latin American Review*, 2:1–2 (1993) 213–45; and Noble David Cook and W. George Lovell, eds., *"Secret Judgements of God": Old World Disease in Colonial Spanish America* (Norman, Okla., 1992), are essential sources, as is Suzanne Austin Alchon, *Native Society and Disease in Colonial Ecuador* (New York, Cambridge, 1991). Nicolás Sánchez-Albornoz, *The Population of Latin America* (Berkeley, 1974) is a useful account of subsequent centuries as well; for the Portuguese American territories in the same period, see Maria Luiza Marcilio, "The Population of Colonial Brazil," *The Cambridge History of Latin America*, II, 37–63.

African forced migration to the Americas is the subject of Paul E. Lovejoy, "The Volume of the Atlantic Slave Trade: A Synthesis," *Journal of African History*, 22:4 (1982), 473–501, which supplements the original estimates given by Philip Curtin, *The Atlantic Slave Trade: A Census* (Madison, 1969). The important question of slave population growth is surveyed in two articles by Herbert S. Klein and Stanley L. Engerman, "Fertility Differentials between Slaves in the United States and the British West Indies: A Note on Lactation Practices and their Implications," *William and Mary Quarterly*, 35:2 (1978), 357–74; and "A demografia dos escravos americanos," in Maria Luiza Marcilio, ed., *Poplação e sociedade: Evolução das sociedades pré-industriais* (Petrópolis, 1984). Kenneth Kiple, *The Caribbean Slave: A Biological History* (Cambridge, 1984), is a classic study.

Well before the quincentenary commemorations of 1992, Alfred W. Crosby, Jr., popularized the term "Columbian exchange." For the transfer of plants and animals, as well as diseases, see his pioneering study, *The Columbian Exchange: Biological and Cultural Consequences of 1492* (Westport, Conn., 1972). See also George M. Foster, *Culture and Conquest: America's Spanish Heritage* (Chicago, 1960). James Axtell, "Columbian Encounters: Beyond 1992," *William and Mary Quarterly*, 49, 335–60, offers a good assessment of the controversies.

Precolonial Background

The pre-Columbian societies of Latin America are the subject of a sophisticated and rapidly expanding literature. For Mesoamerica the reader may wish to begin with such classic scholarly works as Eric Wolf, *Sons of the Shaking Earth: The People of Mexico and Guatemala—Their Land, History, and Culture* (Chicago, 1974); and Jacques Soustelle, *Daily Life of the Aztecs* (Stanford, 1970). *The Ancient American Civilizations* by Friedrich Katz (New York, 1974) is still one of the best guides to the subject. Inga Clendinnen, *Aztecs: An Interpretation* (New York, 1991), offers an elegant interpretation. Mary G. Hodge and Michael E. Smith, eds., *Economies and Polities in the Aztec Realm* (Austin, 1994), highlight the smaller-scale economic and political systems in central Mexico.

The collection of essays edited by George Collier et al., *The Inca and Aztec States, 1400–1800,* covers the fifteenth through the eighteenth centuries. Alonso de Zorita, *Life and Labor in Ancient Mexico: The Brief and Summary Relation of the Lords of New Spain* (New Brunswick, 1963); and Fr. Diego Durán, *The Aztecs: The History of the Indians of New Spain* (New York, 1964), are interesting accounts by sixteenth-century authors, as is Bernardino de Sahagán, *Historia general de las cosas de la Nueva España* (Mexico, 1975); and the Nahuatl-English version, *Florentine Codex*, 12 vols. (Salt Lake City, 1950–82).

For the Indian civilizations of South America, Alfred Metraux, *The History of the Incas* (New York, 1969); and Louis Baudin, *Daily Life in Peru at the Time of the Last Incas* (New York, 1962), are older valuable works; while

Frank Salamon, *Native Lords of Quito in the Age of the Incas: The Political Economy of North Andean Chiefdoms* (New York, 1986) employs the newer methodology of ethnohistory. Charles Stanish, *Ancient Andean Political Economy* (Austin, 1992), describes the zonal complementarity of the region.

For colonial views of the Inca empire, see Father Bernabé Cobo, *History of the Inca Empire* (Austin, 1979); Garcilaso de la Vega, El Inca, *Royal Commentaries of the Incas*, 2 vols. (Austin, 1966); and Father Joseph de Acosta, *The Natural and Moral History of the Incas* (London, 1880). Rolena Adorno, "The Genesis of Felipe Guamán Poma de Ayala's *Nueva crónica y buen gobierno*," *Colonial Latin American Review*, 2:1–2 (1993), 53–92, helps us understand how these views emerged.

For the European background Henry Kamen, *Spain, 1469–1714: A Society of Conflict* (London, 1983), is a good introduction to Spain on the eve of conquest, and Angus MacKay, *Spain in the Middle Ages: From Frontier to Empire, 1000–1500* (London, 1977), provides the medieval background to that era. John Lynch, *Spain, 1516–1598: From Nation State to World Empire* (Cambridge, 1991), is a revised classic. For a personal perspective, see Peggy Liss, *Isabel, the Queen: Life and Times* (Oxford, 1992). For Portugal, A. H. de Oliveira Marques, *History of Portugal*, 2 vols. (New York, 1972), is still valuable; and Charles Boxer, *The Portuguese Seaborne Empire, 1415–1825* (New York, 1969), is lively and informative.

Africa, especially its history of slavery, has been the subject of wide interest and controversy in recent years. An excellent attempt at classification and historical analysis is Paul E. Lovejoy, *Transformations in Slavery: A History of Slavery in Africa* (Cambridge, 1983). Patrick Manning, *Slavery and African Life: Occidental, Oriental and African Slave Trades* (New York, 1990), explains how the loss of population affected the structure of African societies. For specialized studies see Suzanne Miers and Igor Kopytoff, eds., *Slavery in Africa: Historical and Anthropological Perspectives* (Madison, 1977); and Claire C. Robertson and Martin A. Klein, eds., *Women and Slavery in Africa* (Madison, 1983). Gordon Murray, *Slavery in the Arab World* (1989), and James Watson, ed., *Asian and African Systems of Slavery* (Berkeley, 1980), provide comparative cases.

African slavery was well established in Iberia and the Atlantic islands before being brought to the Americas. A model study is A. C. de C. M. Saunders, *A Social History of Black Slaves and Freedman in Portugal, 1441–1555* (Cambridge, 1982). Alfonso Franco Silva, *La esclavitud en Sevilla y su tiempo a fines de la edad media* (Sevilla, 1979), is a good local study. Spanish slavery in the Atlantic islands is detailed in the recent work of Manuel Lobo Cabrera, *La esclavitud en las Canarias Orientales en el siglo XVI* (Tenerife, 1982), while the Portuguese Atlantic experience is analyzed in John L. Vogt, *Portuguese Rule on the Gold Coast, 1469–1682* (Athens, Ga., 1979); and the background chapters in Stuart B. Schwartz, *Sugar Plantations in the Formation of Brazilian Society: Bahia, 1550–1835* (Cambridge, 1985), provide the best available survey of the Madeira and Azorian experience.

The first contacts between Indians and Europeans, and the Africans who accompanied them, have long captured the imagination of writers on Latin America. Classics such as *The True History of the Conquest of New Spain, 1517–1521* by the conquistador Bernal Díaz de Castillo; Hernán Cortés's, *Letters from Mexico* (Oxford, 1972); and the contrasting perspective offered in *The Broken Spears: The Aztec Account of the Conquest of Mexico* (Boston, 1972), have been joined by newer studies, such as Inga Clendinnen, *Ambivalent Conquests: Maya and Spaniard in Yucatan, 1517–1570* (Cambridge, 1987). Nathan Wachtel, *The Vision of the Vanquished* (Sussex, 1977), provides primary accounts from Peru; while John Hemming, *The Conquest of the Incas* (New York, 1970), is a fine secondary study of this devastating confrontation. Kenneth Andrien and Rolena Adorno, eds., *Transatlantic Encounters: Europeans and Andeans in the Sixteenth Century* (Berkeley, 1991), is an interesting collection. The nineteenth-century works by William H. Prescott, *History of the Conquest of Peru*, and his companion work on Mexico (any edition) are also still good introductions to the conquest. The standard work on the Caribbean is Carl O. Sauer, *The Early Spanish Main* (Berkeley, 1966). For early contacts of Africans, see Gonzalo Aguirre Beltrán, *La población negra de México, 1492–1810* (2d ed.; Mexico, 1972); and Patrick J. Carroll, *Blacks in Colonial Veracruz: Race, Ethnicity, and Regional Development* (Austin, 1991). A model study of urban slavery in this period is Frederick P. Bowser, *The African Slave in Colonial Peru, 1524–1650* (Stanford, 1974).

Structures

Colonial Economy: Capital, Credit, Markets

Many of the essays in *Cambridge History of Latin America*, the introductory works cited in General Sources, and the books of Charles Gibson, *The Aztecs under Spanish Rule: A History of the Indians of the Valley of Mexico, 1519–1810* (Stanford, 1964); Murdo MacLeod, *Spanish Central America: A Socioeconomic History, 1520–1720* (Berkeley, 1973); Nancy Farriss, *Maya Society under Colonial Rule: The Collective Enterprise of Survival* (Princeton, 1984); as well as Collier (Precolonial Background) offer essential information about the colonial economy. Specifically on the mining sector, which greatly influenced the development of other branches of the economy, are Peter Bakewell, *Silver Mining and Society in Colonial Mexico, Zacatecas, 1546–1700* (Cambridge, 1971); Robert West, *The Mining Community in Northern New Spain: The Parral Mining District* (Berkeley, 1949); David Brading, *Miners and Merchants in Bourbon Mexico, 1763–1810* (Cambridge, 1971); and a perceptive article, D. A. Brading and Harry Cross, "Colonial Silver Mining: Mexico and Peru, *HAHR*, 52:4 (November 1972), 545–79.

Research on the rural economy should begin with the work of Florescano (see General Sources) and *Precios del maíz y crisis agrícola en México,*

1708–1810 (Mexico, 1969); James Lockhart, *Spanish Peru, 1532–1560: A Social History* (Madison, 1968), and *The Nahuas after the Conquest: A Social and Cultural History of the Indians of Central Mexico, Sixteenth Through Eighteenth Centuries* (Stanford, 1992); Mörner (General Sources) and "Economic Factors and Stratification in Colonial Spanish America," *HAHR*, 63:2 (May 1983), 335–70; William Taylor, *Landlord and Peasant in Colonial Oaxaca* (Stanford, 1972), and "Landed Society in New Spain: A View from the South," *HAHR*, 54:3 (August 1974), 387–413; and Eric Van Young, *Hacienda and Market in Eighteenth-Century Mexico* (Berkeley, 1981). A new collection of essays, Lyman Johnson and Enrique Tandeter, eds., *Essays on the Price History of Eighteenth-Century Latin America* (Albuquerque, 1990), demonstrates the importance of rare quantitative data to our understanding. Prices are also discussed in an interesting debate over "The Economic Cycle in Bourbon Central Mexico: A Critique of the Recaudación del diezmo líquído en pesos," *HAHR*, 69:3 (August 1989) by Arij Ouweneel and Catrien C. J. H. Bijleveld, complemented by the remarks of John Coatsworth, David Brading, and Hector Lindo, 531–58. Richard Garner's *Economic Growth and Change in Bourbon Mexico* (Gainesville, 1993), is an essential source on this debate.

John V. Murra, *Formaciones económicas y políticas del mundo andino* (Lima, 1975), but available in manuscript from the 1950s on, radically altered the approach to historical work on the Andes; as did Carlos Sempat Assadourian, *El sistema de la economía colonial: mercado interno, regiones y espacio económico* (Lima, 1982). John Hemming (see Precolonial Background) and *Red Gold: The Conquest of the Brazilian Indians* (Cambridge, Mass., 1978); Steve Stern, *Peru's Indian Peoples and the Challenge of Spanish Conquest: Huamanga to 1640* (Madison, 1982); Karen Spalding, *Huarochirí: An Andean Society under Inca and Spanish Rule* (Stanford, 1984); and Brooke Larson, *Colonialism and Agrarian Transformation in Bolivia: Cochabamba, 1550–1900* (Princeton, 1988), have greatly contributed to our knowledge of specific regions; as does Peter Bakewell, *Miners of the Red Mountain* (Albuquerque, 1984). Olivia Harris, Brooke Larson, and Enrique Tandeter, *Participación indígena en los mercados surandinos* (La Paz, 1987); and Luis Miguel Glave, *Trajinantes* (Cuzco, 1988), are examples of recent work on the Andes. Germán Colmenares, *Historia económica y social de Colombia, 1537–1719*, 2d ed. (Medellín, 1975); Robert J. Ferry, *The Colonial Elite of Early Caracas* (Berkeley, 1989); and Mario Góngora and Jean Borde, *Evolución de la propiedad rural en el valle de Puangue*, 2 vols. (Santiago, 1956), are also important sources. Alvaro Jara, *Guerra y sociedad en Chile: La transformación de la guerra de Arauco y la esclavitud de los indios* (Santiago, 1971); and Armando de Ramón and José Manuel Larraín, *Orígenes de la vida económica chilena* (Santiago, 1982), are fundamental for the Chilean economy.

Work on the economic and social role of the church is not abundant. Pablo Macera is the modern pioneer and the essays in his *Trabajos de historia*, 4 vols. (Lima, 1977), are generally excellent. Nicolas Cushner has studied the Jesuit holdings in *Lords of the Land: Sugar, Wine and Jesuit Estates of Coastal Peru, 1600–1676* (Albany, 1980); *Farm and Factory: The Jesuits and the Development of Agrarian Capitalism in Colonial Quito, 1600–1767* (Albany, 1982); and *Jesuit Ranches and the Agrarian Development of Colonial Argentina, 1650–1767* (Albany, 1983). Herman Konrad analyzed a key Jesuit hacienda in central Mexico in *A Jesuit Hacienda in Colonial Mexico: Santa Lucia, 1578–1767* (Stanford, 1980). Several recent works on the Jesuits in Peru and elsewhere in Spanish America are discussed in Arnold J. Bauer, "Jesuit Enterprise in Colonial Latin America," *Agricultural History*, 57:1 (1983), 90–104; and other works are assembled in Bauer, ed., *La iglesia en la economía de América Latina, siglos XVI al XIX* (Mexico City, 1986). Asunción Lavrin is a pioneer in work on the economic role of convents in "The Role of the Nunneries in the Economy of New Spain in the Eighteenth Century," *HAHR*, 56:4 (November 1966), 371–93; and Gisela von Wobeser, *San Carlos Borromeo* (Mexico, 1980), has original work on ecclesiastical credit.

Abundant information on the crucial credit provided by merchants in the seventeenth century may be found in Louisa Schell Hoberman, *Mexico's Merchant Elite, 1590–1660: Silver, State, and Society* (Durham, N.C., 1991); for the eighteenth century, consult Susan Migden Socolow, *The Merchants of Buenos Aires, 1778–1810; Family and Commerce* (Cambridge, 1978).

Material Life

Since material life is all around us, it should come as no surprise that historical writing on it is too, though it is sometimes just as slippery to deal with. Historians of early modern Europe have provided the model for much of what has been done on the history of material culture in the United States, and much of what will undoubtedly be done in the future on Latin America. Particularly admirable in this regard are relatively recent works by Simon Schama, *The Embarrassment of Riches: An Interpretation of Dutch Culture in the Golden Age* (New York, 1987); and the late Fernand Braudel, *The Structures of Everyday Life: The Limits of the Possible*, Vol. 1 of his *Civilization and Capitalism, 15th–18th Century* (New York, 1981). A very suggestive survey of the literature on North Atlantic consumer culture is Jean-Christophe Agnew, "Coming Up for Air: Consumer Culture in Historical Perspective," presented at the 82nd Meeting of the Organization of American Historians, 1989.

Among useful baseline studies for diet in pre-Columbian times are Jacques Soustelle, Alfred Metraux, and Louis Baudin (General Sources); and in a broader context, Ross Hassig, *Trade, Tribute, and Transportation: The Sixteenth-Century Political Economy of the Valley of Mexico* (Norman, Okla., 1985). An interesting new study is Sophie D. Coe, *America's First Cuisines* (Austin, 1994). For a large-scale treatment of dietary, technological, microbial, and other transfers between Old and New Worlds, see studies by Alfred W. Crosby, Jr., and George Foster (see General Sources). For the colonial period proper, food and colonization patterns are linked in John C. Super, *Food, Conquest and Colonization in Sixteenth-Century Spanish America* (Albuquerque, 1988), and some of the same concerns and approaches are carried forward usefully into the nineteenth century and beyond in John C. Super and Thomas C. Wright, eds., *Food, Politics and Society in Latin America* (Lincoln, Neb., 1985), especially in the chapters by Super and Vincent C. Peloso. The economic and social history of one of the great Latin American staple crops, and its influence on diet in both the Old World and the New is treated fascinatingly in Sidney Mintz, *Sweetness and Power: The Place of Sugar in Modern History* (New York, 1985). Arnold J. Bauer, "Millers and Grinders: Technology and Household Economy in Mesoamerica," *Agricultural History*, 64 (1990), 1–17, raises some interesting issues about food technologies and culture.

The specific dietary regimes in various parts of colonial Latin America tend to be embedded in other sorts of discussions. For Mexico see the essays in Sherburne F. Cook and Woodrow W. Borah, *Essays in Population History* (General Sources). On alcohol consumption amongst postconquest indigenous people see William B. Taylor, *Drinking, Homicide, and Rebellion in Colonial Mexican Villages* (Stanford, 1979); Jay Kinsbruner, *Petty Capitalism in Spanish America: The Pulperos of Puebla, Mexico City, Caracas, and Buenos Aires* (Boulder, 1987); and Jorge A. Bossio, *Historia de las pulperías* (Buenos Aires, 1972); and on diet and living standards in late colonial Mexico, Eric van Young, "Los ricos se vuelven más ricos y los pobres más pobres: Salarios reales y estandares populares de vida a fines de la colonial en México," in *La crisis del orden colonial: Estructura agraria y rebeliones populares de la Nueva España, 1751–1821* (Mexico: Alianza Editorial, 1992), 51–124. Lyman Johnson and Enrique Tandeter, *Essays* (see Colonial Economy), provide abundant information about diet and popular living standards, especially the chapters of Johnson on Buenos Aires, Kendall Brown on Arequipa (Peru), Brooke Larson on Cochabamba (Bolivia), Dauril Alden on Brazil, and Richard Garner on Mexico.

Invaluable information on diet, dress, architecture, and other aspects of material life is to be found in Jean Descola, *Daily Life in Colonial Peru, 1710–1820* (New York, 1968). Brazilian diet is analyzed in Warren R. Fish, "Changing Food Use Patterns in Brazil," *Luso-Brazilian Review*, 15 (1978), 69–89. The more specialized question of slave diet, dress, and housing is touched upon for Mexico in Ward J. Barrett, *The Sugar Hacienda of the Marqueses del Valle* (Minneapolis, 1970); and Herman Konrad, *Jesuit Hacienda* (Colonial Economy); and for Brazil, in Stuart B. Schwartz, *Sugar Plantations* (Precolonial Background). For Peru, consult Frederick P. Bowser, *African Slave* (Precolonial Background) and for the conditions of the Indian miners at the great pit at Potosí (Bolivia), there is Peter J. Bakewell, *Miners of the Red Mountains* (Colonial Economy).

There is a large literature on merchants and commercial circuits, and a growing one on property-holding and inheritance patterns, some of which is mentioned in the other essays in this volume. On country stores in seventeenth-century Mexico, see Peter Boyd-Bowman, "Two Country Stores in XVIIth-Century Mexico," *The*

Americas, 28 (1972), 237–51; on trade routes into the far north of Mexico, and to some degree, what was traded along them, Max L. Moorhead, *New Mexico's Royal Road: Trade and Travel on the Chihuahua Trail* (Norman, Okla., 1958); and on small storekeepers in city and country, Jay Kinsbruner, *Petty Capitalism* (above). The material possessions and testaments of more or less humble rural people are treated sensitively in Susan L. Cline and Miguel Leon-Portilla, eds., *The Testaments of Culhuacan* (Los Angeles, 1984); and those of Argentine *gauchos*, Mexican *vaqueros*, and other cattlemen of the New World in Richard Slatta, *Cowboys of the Americas* (New Haven, 1990).

Perhaps, the best single type of historical documentation on colonial material life consists of the accounts of travelers, whether missionizing churchmen, colonials themselves, or Europeans. The colonial travel literature is very large, but amongst the best accounts (interestingly, all but one from the 1820s) are, for Mexico, Joel R. Poinsett, *Notes on Mexico, made in the Autumn of 1822* (London, 1925); and Fanny Calderón de la Barca, *Life in Mexico: The Letters of Fanny Calderón de la Barca* (Garden City, N.Y., 1970)—a wonderful, richly illustrated and scholarly edition. For Chile and Brazil, no account surpasses that of Maria Graham, *Journal of a Residence in Chile, during the Year 1822. And a Voyage from Chile to Brazil in 1823* (London, 1824); for Brazil one of the best of the travel genre is Henry Koster, *Travels in Brazil* (Carbondale, Ill., 1966). Useful for the area of what would later become Argentina is E. E. Vidal, *Picturesque Illustrations of Buenos Ayres and Monte Video* (London, 1820, reprinted, Buenos Aires, 1943).

Ecology and Agrarian Technology

The question of the origins of the domestication of plants and animals is discussed in M. N. Cohen, *The Food Crisis in Prehistory: Overpopulation and the Origins of Agriculture* (New Haven, 1977); and P. J. Richerson, "Ecology and the Origins of Agriculture: A Review Essay," *Agricultural History*, 53:3 (1979), 637–43; as well as the articles in *Economic Botany* (1985, 1982, 1980).

For an ecological analysis, see P. Dansereau, *Biogeography: An Ecological Perspective* (New York, 1957); and for an historical perspective, E. LeRoy-Ladurie, *Histoire du climat depuis l'an mil* (Paris, 1967); and B. H. Slicher Van Bath, *The Agrarian History of Western Europe, A.D. (500–1850)* (London, 1963), are classics. Works on European agrarian history from an ecological standpoint include M. Bloch, *Les caractères originaux de l'histoire rurale française* (Paris, 1952); G. P. H. Chorley, "The Agricultural Revolution in Northern Europe," 1750–1880: Nitrogen, Legumes and Crop Productivity," *The Economic History Review*, 34:1, (1981), 71–93; and J. Meuvret, *La production des céréales et la société rurale* (Paris, 1987). For the timely topic of the impact of different societies on the environment, see Alfred Crosby, *Ecological Imperialism: The Biological Expansion of Europe, 900–1900* (Cambridge, 1986); and P. Blaikie and H. Brookfield, *Land Degradation and Society* (London, 1987).

Studies of specific environments in Latin America may focus on the unusual, such as T. Rojas Rabiela, *La agricultura chinampera: Compilación histórica* (Universidad Autónoma de Chapingo, Mexico, 1983); and the more typical, as in John V. Murra, *Formaciones* (Colonial Economy); and J. A. Licate, *Creation of a Mexican Landscape: Territorial Organization and Settlement in the Eastern Puebla Basin, 1520–1605* (Dept. of Geography, University of Chicago, Research Paper 201, 1981). Elinor Melville, *A Plague of Sheep: Environmental Consequences of the Conquest of Mexico* (New York, 1994), is a thoughtful, thorough work, essential for this subject. See also D. K. Abbass, "Herd Development in the New World Spanish Colonies: Conquistadores and Peasants," in Richard Herr, ed., *Themes in Rural History of the Western World* (Ames, 1993), 165–93.

Finally, there are other studies on the countryside that include information about the yield of seeds, crop rotation, availability of water, technology, and diet. For Mexico, we are fortunate to have L. B. Simpson, *Exploitation of Land in Central Mexico in the Sixteenth Century* (Ibero-Americana 36, Berkeley-Los Angeles, 1952); and Sherbourne Cook and Woodrow Borah, "Producción y consumo de alimentos en el México central antes y después de la conquista (1500–1650)," *Ensayos sobre historia de la población, Mexico y California*, III, (Mexico City, 1989), 124–64; as well as Claude Morin, *Michoacán en la Nueva España del siglo XVIII: Crecimiento y desigualdad en una economia colonial* (Mexico City, 1979); Sonya Lipsett, "Water and Social Conflict in Colonial Mexico: Puebla, 1680–1810," (Ph.D. dissertation, Tulane, 1988), and "Puebla's Eighteenth-Century Agrarian Decline: A New Perspective," *HAHR*, 70:3 (August 1990), 463–81. For sugar production technology, see Gloria Artés Espriu et al., *Trabajo y sociedad en la historia de México: siglos XVI–XVIII* (Tlalpan, 1992). For a preliminary study of drought see Robert H. Claxton, "The Record of Drought and Its Impact in Colonial Spanish America," in Herr, *Themes* (above), 194–226. An example of the kind of detailed study that forms the basis for conclusions about rural technology is A. Ouweneel, "Schedules in Hacienda Agriculture: The Cases of Santa Ana Aragón (1765–68) and San Nicolás de los Pilares (1793–95), Valley of Mexico," *Boletín de Estudios Latinoamericanos y del Caribe* (CEDLA, Amsterdam), 40, (1986). For Peru, similar studies are L. Huerta Vallejos, ed., *Ecología e historia: Probanzas de indios y españoles referentes a las catastróficas lluvias de 1578 en los corregimientos de Trujillo y Saña* (Chiclayo, 1987); and N. Sebill, *Ayllus y Haciendas: Dos estudios de caso sobre la agricultura colonial en los Andes* (La Paz, 1989).

Social Groups

The Landed Elite

The conquest was partly an economic enterprise; the victors and their descendants formed the core of a landowning elite, which was often the most powerful group in rural society. The classic formulation of the evolution of this group is François Chevalier, *Land and Society in Colonial Mexico* (Berkeley, 1963), which is a translation of the original French edition of 1952. Needed balance to Chevalier's work is found in William B. Taylor's works (Colonial Economy). Another classic is Mario Góngora and Jean Borde, *Evolución de la propiedad* (Colonial Economy) on estate formation in Chile, to which Marcello Carmagnani, "La tierra de los conquistadores," *Revista latinoamericana de historia economica y social* (hereafter referred to as *HISLA)*, 10 (1988), 3–14, adds quantitative information. Juan Friede, "Proceso de formación de la propiedad territorial en la America intertropical," *Jahrbuch für Geschichte von Staat, Wirtschaft und Gesellschaft Lateinamerikas*, 2 (1965), 75–87, discusses the creation of landed estates in New Granada and emphasizes the sixteenth century. On that area, Germán Colmenares, *Historia económica*, (Bogata, 1978), provides a good general introduction. For Peru there are a number of valuable studies. Robert G. Keith, *Conquest and Agrarian Change* (Cambridge, Mass., 1976), discusses the rise of Spanish agriculture on the coast. Keith A. Davies, *Landowners in Colonial Peru* (Austin, 1984), deals with Arequipa. Manuel Burga, *De la encomienda a la hacienda capitalista* (Lima, 1976), traces the commercial agricultural transition into the twentieth century.

In the process of estate formation, the question of the relationship between *encomienda* and *hacienda* has been discussed in James Lockhart, "Encomienda and Hacienda: The Evolution of the Great Estate in the Spanish Indies," *HAHR*, 49:3 (August 1969), 411–29; and Robert Keith, "Encomienda, Hacienda, and Corregimiento in Spanish America: A Structural Analysis," *HAHR*, 51:4 (November 1971), 431–46.

The regional approach has also yielded some of the best modern studies of large estates and landowners. Summary articles on various regions of Mexico are included in James Lockhart and Ida Altman, eds., *The Provinces of Early Mexico* (Los Angeles, 1976). Cheryl Martin, *Rural Society in Colonial Morelos* (Albuquerque, 1985), concentrates on hacienda-Indian community relations. Eric van Young, *Hacienda and Market* (Colonial Economy), on Guadalajara; and David A. Brading, *Haciendas and Ranchos in the Mexican Bajío* (Cambridge, 1978), on north-central Mexico, are among the best studies. Susan Deans-Smith, *Bureaucrats, Planters, and Workers: The Making of the Tobacco Monopoly in Bourbon Mexico* (Austin, 1992), includes a chapter on cultivation in Orizaba. See also John Frederick Schwaller, "Mexico City Market Structures and the Formation of the Hacienda," in Herr, *Themes* (Ecology), 249–62. Hermés Tovar Pinzón, *Hacienda colonial y formación social* (Barcelona, 1988), contains detailed quantitative analyses of eighteenth-century hacienda accounts in New Granada; while Germán Colmenares, *Cali: Terratenientes, mineros y comerciantes* (Cali, 1975), is a model regional study. Arnold J. Bauer, *Chilean Rural Society from the Spanish Conquest to 1930* (Cambridge, 1975), concentrates on the postcolonial era but includes a good summary chapter on the colonial period.

Most of these regional and theoretical studies, however, tend to emphasize the estates themselves or the land system in general rather than the landowners as a social category. We are fortunate to have the discussion by Mario Góngora, *Encomenderos y estancieros* (Santiago, 1970), of the social dimension of the transition from *encomendero* to *hacendado;* and more recently, Fred Bronner, "Peruvian Encomenderos in 1630: Elite Circulation and Consolidation," *HAHR,* 57:4 (November 1977), 633–60. Efraín Trelles, *Lucas Martínez Vegazo: Funcionamiento de una encomienda peruana inicial* (Lima, 1982), provides detailed information about the life and businesses of an early *encomendero.* Susan Ramírez, *Provincial Patriarchs: Land Tenure and the Economics of Power in Colonial Peru* (Albuquerque, 1987), offers several colorful portraits of elite landowner families on the Peruvian north coast.

Equally valuable works on the landowners as a social group are José F. de la Peña, *Oligarquía y propiedad en Nueva España, 1550–1624* (Mexico City, 1983); and on the aspirations of the landowners, Richard Konetzke, "La formación de la nobleza en Indias," *Estudios Americanos,* 3:10 (1951), 329–60, opens important issues. For the nobility, Doris Ladd, *The Mexican Nobility at Independence, 1780–1826* (Austin, 1976), offers a good start. Additional information with an emphasis on gender is provided by John Tutino, "Power, Class, and Family: Men and Women in the Mexican Elite," *The Americas,* 39:3 (1983), 359–81, and in his regional study "Hacienda Social Relations in Mexico: The Chalco Region in the Era of Independence," *HAHR,* 55:3 (August 1975), 496–528. More recently, Juan Carlos Garavaglia and Juan Carlos Grosso in "Mexican Elites of a Provincial Town: The Landowners of Tepeaca (1700–1870)," *HAHR,* 70:2 (May 1990), 255–93, have used a series of family histories to analyze a regional elite.

Perhaps the most complete study of a regional landed elite to date is Robert J. Ferry, *Colonial Elite* (Colonial Economy), which should be used in conjunction with P. Michael McKinley, *Pre-revolutionary Caracas* (Cambridge, 1985). Herbert Klein's "The Structure of the Hacendado Class in Late Eighteenth Century Alto Peru: The Intendencia de La Paz," *HAHR,* 60:2 (May 1980), 191–212, shows how quantitative techniques applied to census records can be used to reveal underlying aspects of a social class. Parallel materials are presented in Magnus Mörner, *Perfil de la sociedad rural del Cuzco a fines de la colonia* (Lima, 1978). Jacques A. Barbier, *Reform and Politics in Bourbon Chile, 1755–1796* (Ottawa, 1980), analyzes the structure of the landowning class as part of the Chilean elite.

Important theoretical observations on the structure of the landowning class may be found in D. A. Brading, "Government and Elite in Late Colonial Mexico," *HAHR,* 53:3 (August 1973), 389–413. Also valuable is Magnus Mörner, "Economic Factors" (Colonial Economy).

Also when a study concentrates on a particular property, the social aspects of the elite are sometimes evident. Two important examples of this technique are Wanderley Pinho, *Historia de um engenho do Recôncavo* (Rio de Janeiro, 1946); and Charles H. Harris, III, *A Mexican Family Empire: The Latifundio of the Sanchez Navarros Family, 1765–1867* (Austin, 1975). Studies of ecclesiastical estates or of highly atypical properties like those owned by Hernán Cortés are usually suggestive about the way in which common secular properties operated as well. In this regard Herman Konrad, *Jesuit Hacienda* (Colonial Economy); and Ward Barrett, *Sugar Hacienda* (Material Life), are models of single-estate studies.

On Brazil, conflict or collaboration of the landed oligarchy and the state was the focus of Raymundo Faoro, *Os donos de poder* (Pôrto Alegre, 1958), a book which influenced subsequent thinking about the landowners. There are few detailed monographic studies. Bahia has received the most attention. John Norman Kennedy, "Bahian Elites: 1750–1822," *HAHR*, 53:3 (August 1973), 415–39, is a starting point. David G. Smith and Rae Jean Flory, "Bahian Merchants and Planters in the Seventeenth and Eighteenth Centuries," *HAHR*, 58:4 (November 1978), 571–94; and Stuart B. Schwartz, *Sugar Plantations* (Precolonial Background), discuss the membership and attributes of the planter class. For other Brazilian regions the literature is less rich. An interesting demographic and structural analysis is Carlos de Almeida Prado Barcellar, "Os senhores da terra: Família e sistema sucessorio entre os senhores de engenho do oeste paulista, 1765–1855," (M.A. thesis, University of São Paulo, 1987). Muriel Nazzari, "Parents and Daughters: Change in the Practice of Dowry in São Paulo (1600–1770)," *HAHR*, 70:4 (November 1990), 639–66, and *Disappearance of the Dowry: Women, Families, and Social Change in São Paulo, Brazil, 1600–1900* (Stanford, 1991); and Alida C. Metcalf, "Fathers and Sons: The Politics of Inheritance in a Colonial Brazilian Township," *HAHR*, 66:3 (August 1986), 455–84, and *Family and Frontier in Colonial Brazil: Santana de Parnaíba, 1580–1822* (Berkeley, 1992), demonstrate how researchers may be able to reconstruct landowner family strategies. On the social and political ideology of the planter class, Evaldo Cabral de Mello, *Rubro veio* (Rio de Janeiro, 1986), and *O nome e o sangue* (São Paulo, 1989) discusses the Pernambucan sugar aristocracy.

The role of the *hacienda* and the landowners in late colonial society is discussed in Enrique Florescano, *Estructuras y problemas agrarios de Mexico, 1500–1821* (Mexico City, 1972). The growing politicization of the landowners in the late colonial era is noted in Jorge I. Domínguez, *Insurrection or Loyalty* (Cambridge, Mass., 1980), but the general topic still awaits its historian.

The Clergy

The clergy were first analyzed in detail by Robert Ricard, *The Spiritual Conquest of Mexico* (Berkeley, 1966), originally published in French in 1933. Although historians now question his depiction of evangelicization as a conquest, any study of this subject should begin with his book. There is no similar single-volume work available for Peru, although Antoine Tibesar, *Franciscan Beginnings in Colonial Peru* (Washington, 1953), is a good partial introduction. Rubén Vargas Ugarte has written the best work on the history of the church in Peru, *Historia de la iglesia en el Perú*, 5 vols. (Lima & Burgos, 1953–61). For Mexico the corresponding work is Mariano Cuevas, *Historia de la iglesia en Mexico*, 5 vols. (El Paso, 1928). Luis Nicolau D'Olwer, *Fray Bernardino de Sahagún* (Salt Lake City, 1987), is an account of one of the most important missionaries.

Intimate details of the administration of rural parishes in New Spain can be found in the 1569–70 questionnaires sent to the clergy. Collections of the replies to these can be found in Luis García Pimentel, ed., *Descripción del arzobispado de México lecha en 1570* (Mexico, 1897). Likewise the notes of Bishop Alonso de la Mota y Escobar, detailing his visitation to rural parishes, provides a wonderful insight into parochial administration, "Memoriales del obispo de Tlaxcala," *Anales del Instituto Nacional de Antropología e Historia*, 6a época, I (1945), 191–306. For a highly critical view of the clergy in Peru, one should consult Felipe Guamán Poma de Ayala, *El nueva crónica y buen gobierno*, 3 vols. (Mexico, 1980), which has been translated as *Letter to a King: A Peruvian Chief's Account of Life under the Incas and under Spanish Rule* (New York, 1978).

The importance of missions, especially in the frontier regions of the empire, is manifested by the wealth of works concerning them. Both the southwestern United States and Paraguay have received significant research interest. One of the ground-breaking works on the Jesuit missions of Paraguay was Magnus Mörner, *The Political and Economic Activities of the Jesuits in the La Plata Region* (Stockholm, 1953). For more detailed information about the missions one should consult Guillermo Furlong Cardiff, *Misiones y sus pueblos de Guaraníes* (Buenos Aires, 1962). See also David Block, *Mission Culture on the Upper Amazon: Native Tradition, Jesuit Enterprise, and Secular Policy in Moxos, 1660–1880* (Lincoln, 1994). For the sources of funds that supported the missions, see also Konrad (Landowners).

For the southwestern United States, John Kessel has written several important works, including *Mission of Sorrows* (Tucson, 1970). J. Manuel Espinosa, *The Pueblo Indian Revolt of 1696 and the Franciscan Missions in New Mexico: Letters of the Missionaries and Related Documents* (Norman, Okla., 1991); and Francisco Antonio Domínguez, *The Missions of New Mexico, 1776* (Albuquerque, 1956), are also valuable. A fascinating look into the biographies of some of the missionaries is provided by Maynard Geiger, *Franciscan Missionaries in Hispanic California, 1769–1848: A Biographical Dictionary* (San Marino, 1969).

Several new works focus on the difficulties involved in the early missionary activity, especially in translating Christian doctrine from a European-Spanish cultural and linguistic perspective into one that could be appreciated by the natives. For the difficulties encountered in this regard in New Spain, see Sarah Cline, "The Spiritual Conquest Reexamined: Baptism and Christian Marriage in Early Sixteenth-Century Mexico," *HAHR*, 73:3 (August 1993), 453–80; and Louise Burkhart, *The Slippery Earth: Nahua-Christian Moral Dialogue in*

Sixteenth-Century Mexico (Tucson, 1989). Though not as comprehensive as its sweeping subtitle implies, Serge Gruzinski's *Man-Gods in the Mexican Highlands: Indian Power and Colonial Society, 1520–1800* (Stanford, 1989), is an ambitious attempt to probe Indian consciousness through case studies of individuals who challenged Catholicism and Spanish rule at critical junctures of the colonial period. See also, Neomi Quezada, *Amor y magia amorosa entre los aztecas* (Mexico, 1975). Sabine MacCormack deftly examines the evangelization of Peru in "'The Heart Has Its Reasons': Predicaments of Missionary Christianity in Early Colonial Peru, *HAHR*, 65:3 (August 1985), 443–66, and *Religion in the Andes: Vision and Imagination in Early Colonial Peru* (Princeton, 1991). The legal perspective is offered by José A. Llaguno, *La personalidad jurídica del indio y el IIIer concilio provincial mexicano* (Mexico, 1963). Alonso de Molina, *Vocabulario en lengua castellana y mexicana* (Mexico, 1970), is a facsimile edition of this linguistic classic. John L. Phelan, *The Millenial Kingdom of the Franciscans in the New World* (Berkeley, 1970), presents the unusual way some Spaniards saw evangelicization. For a discussion of rural *cofradías* see Asunción Lavrin, "Diversity and Disparity: Rural and Urban Contraternities in Eighteenth-Century Mexico," in Albert Meyers and Diane Elizabeth Hopkins, eds., *Manipulating the Saints: Religious Brotherhoods and Social Integration in Postconquest Latin America* (Hamburg, 1988), 67–100.

Art and architecture also played critical roles in the life of the church in rural areas. Many important works have focused on Mexico, such as John McAndrew, *The Open-Air Churches of Sixteenth-Century Mexico* (New Haven, 1965). Nevertheless, the role of South America in the development of the baroque style is well described by Pal Kelemen, *Baroque and Rococo in Latin America*, 2 vols. (New York, 1967).

The role of the secular clergy in colonial Latin America has just begun to be analyzed. For some preliminary insights one can consult John Frederick Schwaller's works, especially *Church and Clergy in Sixteenth-Century Mexico* (Albuquerque, 1987) and *Origins of Church Wealth in Mexico* (Albuquerque, 1985). Also important is the study by Adriaan van Oss, which takes a look at the parish as the most important unit of ecclesiastical organization, *Catholic Colonialism: A Parish History of Guatemala, 1524–1821* (Cambridge, 1986). Paul B. Ganster, "A Social History of the Secular Clergy of Lima during the Middle Decades of the Eighteenth Century," (Ph.D. diss., UCLA, 1974), is a rare analysis of this group.

Middle People: Smallholders, Local Officials, and Rural Traders in Colonial Latin America

Valuable sources on the middling groups of rural society are often found in broader studies. For *lavradores* in the sugarcane areas of Brazil the essential work is Stuart Schwartz, *Sugar Plantations* (Precolonial Background), especially chapter 11, and "Free Labor in a Slave Economy: The Lavradores de

Cana of Colonial Brazil," in Dauril Alden, ed., *Colonial Roots of Modern Brazil* (Berkeley, 1973). Also useful is Emilio Willems, "Social Differentiation in Colonial Brazil," *Comparative Studies in Society and History*, 12:1 (1970), 31–49. Maria Thereza Schorer Petrone, *A lavoura canaveira em São Paulo* (São Paulo, 1968); and Maria Silvia de Carvalho Franco, *Homens livres na ordem escravocrata* (São Paulo, 1969), provide good descriptions of these smallholders in the sugar regions of São Paulo.

The *rancheros* of colonial Mexico are both social class and romantic symbol. The best works that include them are David Brading, *Haciendas and Ranchos* (Landowners); and Eric van Young, "Sectores medios rurales en el México de los Borbones: El interior de Guadalajara en el siglo XVIII," *HISLA*, 8 (1986), 99–117, and *Hacienda and Market* (Landowners). See also, Richard B. Lindley, *Haciendas and Economic Development: Guadalajara, Mexico at Independence* (Austin, 1983).

The classic works on cochineal growers in Oaxaca in southern Mexico are Brian R. Hamnett, *Politics and Trade in Southern Mexico, 1750–1821* (Cambridge, 1971); and William B. Taylor, *Landlord* (Colonial Economy). For the indigo producers of Guatemala and El Salvador, sources include Miles Wortman, *Government and Society in Central America, 1680–1840* (New York, 1982); Troy Floyd, "The Guatemalan Merchants, the Government, and the Provincianos, 1750–1800," *HAHR*, 41 (1961), 90–110, and "Salvadorean Indigo and the Guatemalan Merchants: A Study in Central American Socio-Economic History, 1750-1800," (Ph.D. diss., University of California at Berkeley, 1960); and Juan Carlos Solórzano, "Haciendas, ladinos, explotación colonial: Guatemala, El Salvador, Chiapas en el siglo XVIII," *Anuario de Estudios Centroamericanos* (Universidad de Costa Rica), 10 (1984), 95–124.

Works dealing with small farmers in southern Central America include David Radell, "A Historical Geography of Western Nicaragua: The Spheres of Influence of León, Granada, and Managua: 1519–1965." (Ph.D. diss., University of California at Berkeley, 1969); Linda Newson, *Indian Survival in Colonial Nicaragua* (Norman, Okla., 1988); Murdo MacLeod, *Spanish Central America* (Colonial Economy); Omar Jaén Suárez, *El istmo de Panamá del siglo XVI al XX* (Panamá, 1980); Lowell Gudmundson, *Costa Rica Before Coffee* (Baton Rouge, 1986); and Elizabeth Fonseca, *Costa Rica colonial: La tierra y el hombre* (San José, 1983).

For southwestern Brazil the studies by Elizabeth Anne Kuznesof are an important contribution: *Household Economy and Urban Development: São Paulo, 1765 to 1836* (Boulder, 1986); "Clans, The Militia and Territorial Government: The Articulation of Kinship with Polity in Eighteenth-Century São Paulo," in David J. Robinson, ed., *Social Fabric and Spatial Structures in Colonial Latin America* (Ann Arbor, 1979), 181–226; and "Household Composition and Headship as Related to Changes in Mode of Production: São Paulo, 1765 to 1836," *Comparative Studies in Society and History*, 22:1 (1980), 78–108. Insights can also be gained from the works by Warren Dean, *Rio Claro: A Brazilian Plantation System, 1820–1920* (Stanford, 1976); and John D. French, "Riqueza, poder e mano de obra numa economía de subsistencia:

São Paulo, 1596-1625," *Revista do Arquivo Municipal* (São Paulo), 45:195 (1982), 79–107.

The evolution of the smallholder class has also been debated recently in the cases of Chile, Colombia, and Argentina. See Arnold J. Bauer, *Chilean Rural Society* (Landed Elite); Ann Twinam, *Miners, Merchants, and Farmers in Colonial Colombia* (Austin, 1982); Juan Carlos Garavaglia, "Economic Growth and Regional Differentiation: The River Plate Region at the End of the Eighteenth Century" *HAHR*, 65:1 (February 1985), 51–89; Ricardo Salvatore and Jonathan Brown, "Trade and Proletarianization in late Colonial Banda Oriental: Evidence from the Estancia de las Vacas, 1791–1805," *HAHR*, 67:3 (August 1987), 431–59; and Jorge Gelman, "New Perspectives on an Old Problem and the Same Source: The Gaucho and the Rural History of the Colonial Río de la Plata," *HAHR*, 69:4 (November 1989), 715–45.

Corregidores and other local officials are touched on by William B. Taylor, *Drinking, Homicide* (Material Life); C. E. Castañeda, "The Corregidor in Spanish Colonial Administration," *HAHR*, 9 (1929), 446–70; Carlos Molina Argüello, "Gobernaciones, alcaldías mayores, corregimientos en el reino de Guatemala," *Anuario de Estudios Centroamericanos*, 17 (1960), 105–32; and Margaret A. Villanueva, "From Calpixqui to Corregidor: Appropriation of Women's Cotton Textile Production in Early Colonial Mexico," *Latin American Perspectives*, 12:1 (1985), 17–40.

The classic study of local administration was written by Guillermo Lohmann Villena, *El corregidor de indios en el Peru bajo las Austrias* (Madrid, 1957); but the most useful recent work is that edited by Woodrow Borah, *El gobierno provincial en la Nueva España, 1570–1787* (Mexico, 1985), especially its chapter on Oaxaca by Rodolfo Pastor, "El repartimiento de mercancías y los alcaldes mayores novohispanos: un sistema de explotación, de sus orígenes a la crisis de 1810," 201–37. Gudmundson describes the wayward *corregidores* of Nicoya in "Aspectos socioeconómicos del delito en Costa Rica, 1725–1850," *Revista de Historia* (Heredia, Costa Rica), 5 (1977), 101–48; while the *jueces de milpas* of Guatemala are discussed by Stephen Webre in "El trabajo forzoso de los indígenas en la política colonial guatemalteca (Siglo XVII)," *Anuario de Estudios Centroamericanos*, 13:2 (1987), 49–61. Richard Morse describes the early *bandeirantes* of São Paulo in *From Community to Metropolis: A Biography of São Paulo, Brazil* (Gainesville, 1958); as does Vianna Moog, *Bandeirantes and Pioneers* (New York, 1964).

Analyses of provincial commerce can be found in Van Young, "Rural Life in Eighteenth-Century Mexico: The Guadalajara Region, 1675–1820," (Ph.D. diss., University of California at Berkeley, 1978), which includes material not to be found in his book; Murdo MacLeod, *Spanish Central America* (Colonial Economy); Elizabeth Anne Kuznesof, "The Role of Merchants in the Economic Development of São Paulo: 1765–1850," *HAHR*, 60:4 (November 1980), 571–92; Linda L. Greenow, "Spatial Dimensions of the Credit Market in Eighteenth-Century Nueva Galicia," in David Robinson, ed., *Social Fabric*, 227–79; and Victor Hugo Acuña Ortega, "Capital comercial y comercio exterior en

América Central durante el siglo XVIII: una contribución," *Estudios Sociales Centroamericanos* (San José, Costa Rica), 26 (1980), 71–102. Gudmundson, "Nueva luz sobre la estratificación socioeconómica costarricense al iniciarse la expansión cafetalera," *Revista de Historia*, 4 (1976), 149–98; and José Antonio Fernández Molina, "Correspondencia comercial del siglo XVIII en el Reino de Guatemala," *Anuario de Estudios Centroamericanos*, 12:2 (1986), 147–57, discuss the indigo traders.

Important works on the better-known urban retail traders include John E. Kicza, *Colonial Entrepreneurs: Families and Business in Bourbon Mexico City* (Albuquerque, 1983); Jay Kinsbruner, *Petty Capitalism* (Material Life); and Jorge A. Bossio, *Historia* (Material Life). Perhaps the most illuminating work on rural petty trade is by Richard W. Slatta, "Pulperías and Contraband Capitalism in Nineteenth-Century Buenos Aires Province," *The Americas*, 38:3 (1982), 347–62.

Descriptions of transport workers, routes, and technologies can be found in the works on the indigo trade by Floyd, as well as in Stephen Webre, "The Social and Economic Bases of Cabildo Membership in Seventeenth-Century Santiago de Guatemala," (Ph.D. diss., Tulane University, 1980); Victor Hugo Acuña Ortega, "Historia económica del tabaco: Epoca colonial," *Anuario de Estudios Centroamericanos*, 4 (1979), 279–392; David R. Ringrose, "Carting in the Hispanic World: An Example of Divergent Development," *HAHR*, 50:1 (February 1970), 30–51; Richard Boyer, "Juan Vázquez, Muleteer of Seventeenth-Century Mexico," *The Americas*, 37:4 (1981), 421–44; Peter W. Rees, "Origins of Colonial Transportation in Mexico," *Geographical Review*, 65 (1975), 323–34, and *Transportes y comercio entre Mexico y Veracruz 1519–1910* (Mexico, 1976); and Richard P. Momsen, Jr., "Routes over the Serra do Mar: The Evolution of Transportation in the Highlands of Rio de Janeiro and São Paulo," *Revista Geografica*, (Rio de Janeiro), 32:58 (1963), 5–167.

Perhaps, the classic work on the mule trade and mule-breeding in all of colonial Latin America is by Nicolás Sánchez-Albornoz, *La saca de mulas de Salta al Peru, 1778–1808* (Rosario, Argentina, 1965). Two Brazilian works that document the impact of the muleteer tradition on both language and material culture are José Alipio Goulart, *Tropas e tropeiros na formação do Brasil* (Rio de Janeiro, 1961); and Tom Maia and Thereza Regina de Camargo Maia, *O folclore das tropas, tropeiros e cargueiros no vale do Paraíba* (Rio de Janeiro, 1981). The description of the Mico Mountain passage in Guatemala comes from the 1825 memoir of the Englishman George Alexander Thompson, as presented in Franklin D. Parker, *Travels in Central America, 1821–1840* (Gainesville, 1970).

Blacks

An understanding of Africans and Afro-Americans must begin with the Atlantic slave trade. For the early trade to Latin America, the fundamental work is Philip Curtin's *Atlantic Slave Trade* (General Sources), and Paul Lovejoy, ed., *Africans in Bondage: Studies in Slavery and the Slave Trade: Essays in*

Honor of Philip D. Curtin, 1986, recognizes his contribution. Herbert S. Klein, *The Middle Passage, Comparative Studies in the Atlantic Slave Trade* (Princeton, 1978); and Joseph Miller, *Way of Death: Merchant Capitalism and the Angolan Slave Trade, 1730–1830* (Madison, 1988) are valuable sources. Rolando Mellafe, *Negro Slavery in Latin America* (Berkeley, 1975) is still useful. Enriqueta Vila Vilar, *Hispano-América y el comercio de esclavos: Los asientos portugueses* (Seville, 1977), has substantially revised and added numbers to the earlier work of George Scelle, *La traite négrière aux Indes de Castille*, 2 vols. (Paris, 1906). Elizabeth Donnan, *Documents Illustrative of the History of the Slave Trade to America*, 4 vols. (Washington, D.C., 1930–35), is an excellent collection.

Barbara L. Solow, ed., *Slavery and the Rise of the Atlantic System* (Cambridge, [England], 1991), contains essays by many authorities and offers a comparative perspective. An example of a good local study of the trade is Jorge Palacios Preciado, *La trata de negros por Cartagena de Indias* (Tunja, Colombia, 1973). The health conditions of the slaves in the crossing have been analyzed by David L. Chandler, *Health and Slavery in Colonial Colombia* (New York, 1981); and Colin A. Palmer, *Human Cargoes, The British Slave Trade to Spanish America, 1700–1739* (Urbana, 1981); and for the French West Indies by Franz Tardo-Dino, *Le collier de servitude, la condition sanitaire des esclaves aux antilles françaises du xviie au xixe siècle* (Paris, 1985).

African slavery in the countryside of mainland Spanish American colonies was prevalent in mining, farming, and ranching. Peter J. Bakewell, *Silver Mining* and *Miners* (Colonial Economy) are two fundamental studies. The best general study of the plantation system is still Noel Deerr, *The History of Sugar*, 2 vols. (London, 1949–50). The Mexican and Peruvian sugar plantation regimes have been examined in Ward Barrett, *Sugar Hacienda* (Material Life); and Nicholas P. Cushner, *Lords of the Land* (Colonial Economy). Adriana Navela Chávez-Hita, *Esclavos negros en las haciendas azucareras de Cordoba, Veracruz, 1690–1830* (Xalapa, 1987), studies this neglected region; another interesting treatment of a peripheral area is Lolita Gutiérrez Brockington, *The Leverage of Labor: Managing the Cortés Haciendas in Tehuantepec, 1588–1688* (Durham, 1990).

For northern South America, and especially the local Choco mining industry, there is William F. Sharp, *Slavery in the Spanish Frontier: the Colombian Choco, 1680–1810* (Norman, Okla., 1976); and Adolfo Meisel Roca, "Esclavitud, mestizaje y haciendas en la Provincia de Cartagena, 1533–1851," *Desarrollo y sociedad*, 4 (1980), 229–77. Robert J. Ferry, "Encomienda, African Slavery and Agriculture in Seventeenth-Century Caracas," *HAHR*, 61:4 (November 1981), 609–35, analyzes the cacao plantations of Venezuela. For the Andes see Alberto Crespo, *Esclavos negros en Bolivia* (La Paz, 1977).

In the Spanish Caribbean, African slavery was present from the early sixteenth century but grew most rapidly in Cuba in the late colony. A classic on the history of slavery in the Caribbean as a whole is Eric Williams, *From Columbus to Castro, the History of the Caribbean 1492–1969* (London, 1970).

For early slavery on Hispaniola, see Carlos Esteban Deive, *La esclavitud del negro en Santo Domingo*, 2 vols. (Santo Domingo, 1980). For Puerto Rico, the chapters of José Curet and Ramos Mattei in Andrés A. Ramos Mattei, ed., *Azucar y esclavitud* (Río Piedras, 1982) are useful. The most important work to treat the unusual evolution of slavery and the plantation economy in Puerto Rico is Francisco A. Scarano, *Sugar and Slavery in Puerto Rico, The Plantation Economy of Ponce, 1800–1850* (Madison, 1984). Ward Barrett, "Caribbean Sugar-Production Standards in the Seventeenth and Eighteenth Centuries," in John Parker, ed., *Merchants and Scholars: Essays in the History of Exploration and Trade* (Minneapolis, 1965), is also valuable.

The early development of slavery and the plantation economy in Cuba is offered in Fernando Ortiz's classic *Hampa Afro-cubana: Los negros esclavos* (Havana, 1916). More modern studies include Herbert S. Klein, *Slavery in the Americas: A Comparative Study of Cuba and Virginia* (Chicago, 1967); and Roland T. Ely, *Cuando reinaba su magestad de azucar* (Buenos Aires, 1963). Important for all aspects of the development of the Cuban economy is Levi Marrero, *Cuba: Economía y sociedad. Azucar, ilustración y conciencia (1763–1868)*, 3 vols. (Madrid, 1983–84). Finally, the observations of the famous European scientist, Alexander von Humboldt, *The Island of Cuba*, trans. & notes by J. S. Thrasher (New York, 1856), are still pertinent; and Louis Pérez, Jr., ed., *Slaves, Sugar, and Colonial Society: Travel Accounts of Cuba, 1801-1899* (Wilmington, 1992), presents other first-person accounts.

Brazil was the longest-lived slavocracy in the Americas, and the historiography of enslaved and free Africans there is particularly rich. Two good introductions are Katia M. de Queirós Mattoso, *To Be a Slave in Brazil* (Rutgers, 1986); and Ciro Flamarion S. Cardoso, *Agricultura, escravidão e capitalismo* (Petrópolis, 1979). Gilberto Freyre, *The Masters and the Slaves* (New York, 1946), is a classic interpretation that many later works address. Slavery must be studied in relation to the colonial economy. Schwartz, *Sugar Plantations* (Precolonial Background) is complemented by F. Mauro, *Le Portugal et l'Atlantique au xviie siècle* (Paris, 1960); Charles R. Boxer, *The Golden Age of Brazil, 1695–1750* (Berkeley, 1966); and Jacob Gorender, *O escravismo colonial* (São Paulo, 1978).

For slaves in specific industries and localities, see A. J. R. Russell-Wood, *The Black Man in Slavery and Freedom in Colonial Brazil* (London, 1982); and Francisco Vidal Luna, *Minas Gerais; Escravos e senhores . . . (1718–1804)* (São Paulo, 1981), both concentrating on eighteenth-century Minas Gerais. Fernando Henrique Cardoso, *Capitalismo e escravidão no Brasil meridional* (São Paulo, 1962), focuses on São Paulo, while Mário José Maestri Filho, *O escravo no Rio Grande do Sul: A charquedada e a génese do escravismo gaucho* (Pôrto Alegre, 1984), discusses ranching in the southern regions. A traditional study that is still essential reading for regional developments is André João Antonil, *Cultura e opulência do Brasil* (1711; new ed., São Paulo, 1967).

Of Afro-American culture the most studied element has been that of its religious organization and expression. The major work in this respect has been done by anthropologists, psychologists, and sociologists. Among the most prominent names have been those of Meville Herskovitz, Alfred Metraux, and Roger Bastide. Bastide's *Les religions africaines aux Brésil* (Paris, 1960), is the definitive work on Candomble and other Afro-Brazilian cults. For Cuba the standard work still remains Fernando Ortiz, *Los negros brujos* (Havana, 1906). On the African and Afro-American experience within the Catholic church, the works of A. J. R. Russell-Wood, *Fidalgos & Philanthropists* (Berkeley, 1968); his article "Black & Mulatto Brotherhoods in Colonial Brazil," *HAHR*, 54:4 (November 1974), 567–602; and his recent book (1982) cited above are important. John Thornton, *Africa and the Africans in the Making of the Atlantic World, 1400–1680* (New York, 1992), describes labor, religion, and cultural adaptions of Africans in the Americas.

Runaway slave communities have awakened much interest, especially for scholars of Brazil. The standard survey of Palmares, the longest-lived settlement of runaway slaves, is Décio Freitas, *Palmares, a guerra dos escravos* (4th ed., Rio de Janeiro, 1982); along with Edison Carneiro, *O quilombo dos Palmares* (Rio de Janeiro, 1966). A good survey of the extensive literature on *quilombos* is Clóvis Moura, *Rebeliões de senzala: quilombos, insurreições, guerrilhas* (3rd ed., São Paulo, 1983). For the conspiracies and rebellions in early Spanish America the best single work to date is Carlos Fedérico Guillot, *Negros rebeldes y negros cimarones . . . siglo xvi* (Buenos Aires, 1961). Detailed studies on individual movements include María del Carmen Borrego Plá, *Palenques de negros en Cartagena de Indias a fines del siglo XVIII* (Seville, 1973); David M. Davidson, "Negro Slave Control and Resistance in Colonial Mexico, 1519–1650," *HAHR*, 46:3 (1966), 235–53; and Julio Pinto Vallejos, "Slave Control and Slave Resistance in Colonial Minas Gerais, 1700–1750," *Journal of Latin American Studies*, 17:1 (1985), 1–34.

The final chapter for a fortunate minority of slaves was freedom. The best single introduction to the free colored under slavery is the collection edited by David W. Cohen and Jack P. Greene, *Neither Slave Nor Free: The Freedmen of African Descent in the Slave Societies of the New World* (Baltimore, 1972). Studies of the origins of the freedmen began with the article by Katia M. de Queiros Mattoso, "A propósito de cartas de alforria: Bahia, 1779–1850," *Anais de História* (São Paulo), 4 (1972), who called attention to the formal certificates of freedom for liberated slaves as a vital source of information. The colonial period was analyzed in Stuart B. Schwartz, "The Manumission of Slaves in Colonial Brazil: Bahia, 1684–1745," *HAHR*, 54:4 (November 1974), 603–35. These Bahian studies were followed by a detailed analysis of the manumission process in the sugar producing and distilling center of Paraty, a *municipio* in the province of Rio de Janeiro, by James P. Kiernan, "The Manumission of Slaves in Colonial Brazil: Paraty, 1789–1822," (Ph.D. diss., New York University, 1976). Using these Brazilian studies as a model, Lyman

L. Johnson wrote the valuable "Manumission in Colonial Buenos Aires, 1776–1810," *HAHR*, 59:2 (May 1979), 258–279.

Indians

An extensive and ever-growing literature focuses on the history of indigenous rural society in colonial Spanish America. Readers might best begin with Charles Gibson's overview, "Indian Societies under Spanish Rule," in Leslie Bethell, ed., *Cambridge History* (General Sources), II, 381–419. In addition to the chapters by León-Portilla and John Murra, there is Jorge Hidalgo, "The Indians of Southern South America in the Middle of the Sixteenth Century," I, 91–117.

The large number of outstanding regional studies devoted to Indians in Mexico include Charles Gibson's influential classic, *The Aztecs* (Colonial Economy); John K. Chance, *Conquest of the Sierra: Spaniards and Indians in Colonial Oaxaca* (Norman, Okla., 1989); Nancy M. Farriss, *Maya Society* (Colonial Economy); William B. Taylor, *Landlord and Peasant* (Colonial Economy); Inga Clendinnen, *Ambivalent Conquests* (General Sources); and Bernardo García Martínez, *Los Pueblos de la Sierra: El poder y el espacio entre los indios del norte de Puebla hasta 1700* (Mexico City, 1987).

Some of the most perceptive studies in recent years have come from scholars using Nahuatl sources. James Lockhart has pioneered in the use of the documents. His *The Nahuas After the Conquest* (Colonial Economy) beautifully unites many years of research in these sources. Other useful works based on Nahuatl records include James Lockhart, Frances Berdan, and Arthur J. O. Anderson, *The Tlaxcalan Actas: A Compendium of the Records of the Cabildo of Tlaxcala (1545–1627)* (Salt Lake City, 1986), which provides a fascinating glimpse of village government as seen through the eyes of Indian scribes. Robert Haskett has effectively employed Nahuatl documents in his studies of colonial Cuernavaca, which explore the survival of indigenous governmental practices and the roles played by Indian women in local political life. See his "Indian Town Government in Colonial Cuernavaca: Persistence, Adaptation, and Change," *HAHR*, 67:2 (May 1987), 203–31, and *Indigenous Rulers: An Ethnohistory of Town Government in Colonial Cuernavaca* (Albuquerque, 1991). In *Colonial Culhuacan, 1580–1600: A Social History of an Aztec Town* (Albuquerque, 1986), Sue L. Cline uses a remarkable collection of Nahuatl wills to analyze changes in this central Mexican village.

Other works on Mexico include William B. Taylor, *Drinking, Homicide* (Material Life), which offers a stimulating comparison of life in the Indian villages of Oaxaca and their more strongly Hispanicized counterparts closer to Mexico City. Although based on sources from the Guadalajara region, Eric van Young's "Conflict and Solidarity in Indian Village Life: The Guadalajara Region in the Late Colonial Period," *HAHR*, 64:1 (February 1984), 55–79, draws conclusions about social differentiation within Indian villages that are substantially true for many parts of Mexico. For the relationship between villages and commercial agriculture in central Mexico, see Cheryl E. Martin, *Rural Society in Colonial Morelos* (Landowners), and "Haciendas and Villages in Late Colonial Morelos," *HAHR*, 62:3 (August 1982), 407–27. James D. Riley, "Crown Law and Rural Labor in New Spain: The Status of Gañanes during the Eighteenth-Century," *HAHR*, 64:2 (May 1984), 259–85, provides useful information about the status of Indians living on haciendas. For the effect of ranching on Indian communities see, Judith Francis Zeitlin, "Ranchers and Indians on the Southern Isthmus of Tehuantepec: Economic Change and Indigenous Survival in Colonial Mexico," *HAHR*, 69:1 (February 1989), 23–60. For Indian religious experience, see Gruzinski (Clergy), Burkhart (Clergy), and Kevin Gosner, *Soldiers of the Virgin: The Moral Economy of a Colonial Maya Rebellion* (Tucson, 1992).

Though not as abundant as the literature on Mexico, a number of excellent studies survey the effects of Spanish conquest on indigenous society in the Andes. Steve J. Stern, *Peru's Indian Peoples* (Colonial Economy), is an insightful and exceptionally well-written study of one region's adaptation to the new colonial order. In *Moon, Sun, and Witches: Gender Ideologies and Class in Inca and Colonial Peru* (Princeton, 1987), anthropologist Irene Silverblatt offers a stimulating analysis of the way in which the Inca and Spanish conquests altered traditional notions of gender in the Andes. Also important are three works by Karen Spalding: "*Kurakas* and Commerce: A Chapter in the Evolution of Andean Society," *HAHR*, 53:4 (November 1973), 581–99; "Social Climbers: Changing Patterns of Mobility Among the Indians of Colonial Peru," *HAHR*, 50:4 (November 1970), 645–64; and *Huarochirí* (Colonial Economy). Ann Wightman, *Indigenous Migration and Social Change: The Forasteros of Cuzco* (Durham, 1990), ably analyzes this neglected and important group in postconquest society.

In *Colonialism and Agrarian Transformation* (Colonial Economy), Brooke Larson traces the impact of commercial estates on indigenous society in eastern Bolivia. The most comprehensive study of forced labor in the viceroyalty of Peru is Jeffrey Cole, *The Potosí Mita* (Stanford, 1985).

Studies of native society on the frontiers offer essential perspectives on the varied responses of the Amerindians. For northern Mexico they include Edward H. Spicer, *Cycles of Conquest: The Impact of Spain, Mexico, and the United States on the Indians of the Southwest, 1533–1960* (Tucson, 1962); and William B. Griffen, *Indian Assimilation in the Franciscan Area of Nueva Vizcaya* (Tucson, 1979). For information on Indian labor in the north, consult Susan M. Deeds, "Rural Work in Nueva Vizcaya: Forms of Labor Coercion on the Periphery," *HAHR*, 69:3 (August 1989), 425–49; and José Cuello, "The Persistence of Indian Slavery and Encomienda in the Northeast of Colonial Mexico, 1577–1723," *Journal of Social History*, 21:4 (1988), 683–700. Though written largely from a Spanish military point of view, Philip Wayne Powell, *Soldiers, Indians and Silver: The Northward Advance of New Spain, 1550–1600* (Berkeley, 1952); and Max L. Moorhead, *The Apache Frontier: Jacobo Ugarte and Spanish-Indian Relations in Northern New Spain* (Norman, Okla., 1968), provide insight into the ways in which the Chichimecas and Apaches impeded the northward expansion of the colony. Ramón Gutiérrez's book, *When Jesus Came, the Corn Mothers Went Away: Marriage, Sexuality and Power in New Mexico, 1500–1846* (Stanford, 1991), is a major source for those interested in the social and cultural impact of European colonization on the Pueblo peoples. For a concise introduction to New Mexico's Pueblo Rebellion of 1680, see Angélico Chávez, "Pohe-Yemo's Representative and the Pueblo Revolt of 1680," *New Mexico Historical Review*, 42 (1967), 85–115. Indians along a South American frontier are discussed in Barbara Ganson, "The Evuevi of Paraguay: Adaptive Strategies and Responses to Colonials, 1528–1811," *The Americas*, 45:3 (1989), 461–88.

There are few studies available in English on colonial Chile. Della Flusche and Eugene H. Korth, *Spanish Policy in Colonial Chile: The Struggle for Social Justice, 1535–1700* (Detroit, 1983), details the conquest of Chile from a Jesuit point of view. Alvaro Jara's *Guerra y sociedad* (Colonial Economy) surveys Spanish-Indian relations in Chile through 1612, while Mario Góngora's *Encomenderos* (Landowners) gives substantial information on the development of the Chilean *encomienda* into the latter half of the seventeenth century. A perspective on Indian women in colonial Chile can be found in Della M. Flusche and Eugene H. Korth, *Forgotten Females: Women of African and Indian Descent in Colonial Chile, 1535–1800* (Detroit, 1983).

Conflict, Violence and Resistance

Overviews of violent resistance to colonial rule include the comprehensive study edited by Friedrich Katz, *Riot, Rebellion, and Revolution: Rural Social Conflict in Mexico* (Princeton, 1988); and Steve J. Stern, ed., *Resistance, Rebellion, and Consciousness in the Andean Peasant World, 18th to 20th Centuries* (Madison, 1987). Richard Price edited a survey for African Latin America in his *Maroon Societies: Rebel Slave Communities in the Americas* (Baltimore, 1979); while Ann M. Pescatello, ed., *The African in Latin America* (Washington, 1975), introduces several themes in the history of slavery. Magnus Mörner, *Race Mixture in the History of Latin America* (Boston, 1967), illustrates a range of nonviolent contacts and discusses concepts of race.

For the degree of violent conflicts in pre-Columbian society, consult Robert C. Padden, *The Hummingbird and the Hawk: Conquest and Sovereignty in the Valley of Mexico, 1503–1541* (New York, 1970), and the works noted in General Sources. Woodrow Borah takes up the issue of colonial justice in *Justice by Insurance: The General Indian Court of Colonial Mexico and the Legal Aides of the Half-Real* (Berkeley, 1983); as does William B. Taylor, *Landlord* (Colonial Economy) and *Drinking, Homicide* (Material Life). The role of village government as mediator between the two races is described by Charles Gibson, *Tlaxcala in the Sixteenth Century* (New Haven, 1952), and in his

Aztecs. For South America, the works of Karen Spalding (Colonial Economy) and Steve Stern (Indians) treat the variety of Indian responses; as does *Domination and Cultural Resistance: Authority and Power among an Andean People* by Roger Neal Rasnake (Durham, N.C., 1988). *Rethinking History and Myth: Indigenous South America Perspectives on the Past*, Jonathan Hill, ed. (Champaign, Ill., 1988), also seeks to understand the Indian perspective.

Religion and conflict over values are fascinating topics that have recently received long overdue attention, especially for the Andes. Father Pablo José de Arriaga, *The Extirpation of Idolatry in Peru* (Lexington, Ky., 1968); Irene Silverblatt, "'The Universe has turned inside out . . . There is no justice for us here': Andean Women under Spanish Rule," in *Women and Colonization: Anthropological Perspectives*, eds. Mona Etienne and Eleanor Leacock (New York, 1980); Sabine MacCormack, "Pachacuti: Miracles, Punishments, and Last Judgment: Visionary Past and Prophetic Future in Early Colonial Peru," *American Historical Review*, 93:4 (1988), 960–1006 and her book (Clergy); and David Cahill, "Curas and Social Conflict in the Doctrinas of Cuzco, 1780–1814," *Journal of Latin American Studies*, 16:2 (1984), 241–76, are examples of this new literature. For sexual values see Richard Price, "Trial Marriage in the Andes," *Ethnology*, 4:3 (July 1965), 310–22; and W. E. Carter, "Trial Marriage in the Andes?," in *Andean Kinship and Marriage*, eds. Ralph Bolton and Enrique Mayer (Washington, D.C., 1977). For Mexico, see Sarah Cline, "The Spiritual Conquest" (Clergy).

For the position of black slave laborers in the Andes, see Nicholas P. Cushner, *Lords of the Land* (Colonial Economy); Frederick Bowser, *African Slave* (Precolonial Background); and Robert Brent Toplin, ed., *Slavery and Race Relations in Latin America* (Westport, 1974).

For changes in government, village revolts, and rebellions, there is a growing body of scholarship. Those wishing a good introduction to the vast literature on the rebellion of Tupac Amarú and other rural unrest in the Andes should begin with the essays and bibliographies in Stern, *Resistance* (above), especially Leon G. Campbell, "Ideology and Factionalism during the Great Rebellion, 1780–1782"; and Jan Szeminski, "Why Kill the Spaniard? New Perspectives on Andean Insurrectionary Ideology in the Eighteenth Century." Ward Stavig, "Ethnic Conflict, Moral Economy, and Population in Rural Cuzco on the Eve of the Thupa Amaro II Rebellion," *HAHR*, 68:4 (November 1988), 737–70, offers a fresh perspective on this key upheaval. See also John Fisher, *Government and Society in Colonial Peru: The Intendant System, 1784–1814* (London, 1970); and Scarlett O'Phelan Godoy, *Rebellions and Revolts in Eighteenth-Century Peru and Upper Peru* (Cologne, 1985). Adalberto López, *The Revolt of the Comuneros, 1721–1735* (Cambridge, Mass., 1976), analyzes a multirace uprising, as does *Reform and Insurrection in Bourbon New Granada and Peru*, John Fisher, Allan Kuethe, and Anthony McFarlane, eds. (Baton Rouge, 1990). Brooke Larson, "Rural Rhythms of Class Conflict in Eighteenth-Century Cochabamba," *HAHR*, 60:3 (August 1980),

407–30, focuses on this neglected region. See also Ward Stavig, "The Indian Peoples of Rural Cuzco in the Era of Thupa Amaro," (Ph.D. diss., University of California, Davis, 1991); and Ana Sánchez, *Amancebados, hechiceros, y rebeldes: Chancay, siglo XVII* (Cuzco, 1991). The closest Mexico came to it is described by Robert Wasserstrom, "Ethnic Violence in Indigenous Protest: The Tzeltal (Maya) Rebellion of 1712," *Journal of Latin American Studies*, 12:1 (1980), 1–19. See also Roberto Mario Salmón, "The Marginal Man: Luis of Saric and the Pima Revolt of 1751," *The Americas*, 45:1 (1988), 61–77.

Glossary

abusos y excesos	abuses and excesses; misuse and mistreatment
agregado	a free (nonslave) dependent, often living in the master's household or on his land
alcabala	excise or sales tax
alcalde	town magistrate
alcalde mayor	governor and magistrate of a district; justice of the peace
alférez	military rank equivalent to ensign or second lieutenant
arancel	price list of priestly services
atole	maize gruel (Mexico)
audiencia	royal high court
ayllu	Andean kin group with right to land
bachiller	recipient of the first university degree
bandeirantes	members of quasi-military slave-hunting and prospecting expeditions
bargueño	a wooden chest with several small drawers, highly decorated with wood carvings which are gilded and/or painted
batab	local ruler in Yucatán
bayeta	baize; a flannellike cloth
bozal	African-born slave
brancos da terra	dark-skinned whites in Brazil
caballería	a unit of agricultural land equivalent to approximately 105 acres

cabecera	chief provincial Indian town
cabildo	city council
cacique	hereditary Indian chieftain
caja de comunidad	Indian town council's chest
calpulli	Indian clan (Mesoamerica) with right to land
canna, cana	sugarcane brandy
capellanía	chaplaincy established by a lien on real property to say prayers for the dead
capitán major	captain major (Spanish America)
capitão-mor	captain major; civil and military officer (Brazil)
casa grande	main house of a plantation or hacienda
casco	main house of an estancia
casta	person of mixed racial ancestry
censo	lien on real property
chacra	farm; usually a small agricultural holding
chalchihuitles	semiprecious decorative stones
charqui	jerked beef; beef cut into strips and dried in the sun
chicha	alcoholic beverage made of fermented maize or corn
chinampa	food plot planted on earth-covered reed raft in lake around Mexico City
chuño	concentrated potato starch
chupa	soup (Andes)
coatepantli	snake wall
cobrador	tax collector
cofradía	religious lay brotherhood
compadre	godparent
composición	payment to the crown to regularize a land or water deed or an illegal act
comuneros	supporters of a popular revolt
concierto	work contract
congregación	resettlement of Indians from hamlets into larger and fewer towns
corregidor	district governor and magistrate
criollo	American-born white
cuadrilla	gang, crew, team of four of more persons
doctrina	Indian congregation served by regular clergy; also catechism classes
donatário	recipient of an extremely large land grant along with judicial and fiscal power in sixteenth-century Brazil
encomienda	royal grant giving the recipient permission to use Indian labor of specified villages
engenho	sugar plantation and mill in Brazil (equivalent to the Spanish term ingenio)

entrada	military campaign against the Indians
estancia	cattle ranch
estanciero	owner of an estancia
fanega	grain measurement of approximately 1.5 bushels
fanegada	land measurement unit of about 7.16 acres
fazenda	large estate in Brazil (same as Spanish-American hacienda)
fazendeiro	owner of a fazenda (same as Spanish-American hacendado)
finca	small farm
fiscal	legal officer of a secular or clerical institution; also church steward
forastero	Indian residing in a town or district other than where s/he was born
frazada	man's blanketlike cloak
frijoles	kidney beans (Mexico)
fuero	set of legal privileges granted to a certain group
fundo	rural property
gañan	day laborer; farm hand
gobernador	town governor, executive; supposed to be an Indian
guarapo	sugarcane brandy
guardián	local superior of a convent of the order of Saint Francis
habilitaciones	advances of cash and goods to producers
hacendado	owner of an hacienda
hacienda	large landed estate usually used for agricultural activities and raising livestock
hato	cattle ranch (Venezuela; Cuba)
hidalgo	gentleman; member of the petty nobility
ingenio	sugar plantation and mill in Spanish America (equivalent to the Portuguese term engenho)
inquilino	tenant farmer who owed labor service to the landowner
jacal	hut or meager dwelling
kuraka	local hereditary Indian ruler in the Andes
labor	cultivated field
ladino	Central American term for a person of Spanish and Indian ancestry or mixed culture; also an enslaved person of African descent born in Europe
latifundio	any large landholding
lavrador	Brazilian term for a sugar producer who did not own a mill
legua	measure of distance equal to 3 1/2 miles; league

liberto	ex-slave who had personally experienced manumission
llano	grass-covered plains (Venezuela)
lugarteniente	deputy, lieutenant
manga	Mexican cloak or poncho
mantilla	woman's lace shawl, which usually covers head and shoulders
manto	woman's cloak
masa	dough
mayorazgo	entailed estate
mayordomo	foreman, manager
mayorquino	a native of Mayorca, one of the Spanish Balearic Islands
mercader viandante	peddlar; traveling salesman
merced	royal grant or gift
mescal	liquor made of the juice of the maguey cactus (Mexico)
mestizo	person of mixed Spanish and Indian ancestry
mestre de campo	leader of a slaving expedition (Brazil)
metate	curved stone on which maize is ground (Mexico)
mindala	Indian merchants in the Andes
mita	state system of forced Indian labor
moneda sonante	hard coin
morador	inhabitant
nopal	prickly pear cactus (Mexico)
numeración	general general head-count; census
obraje	primitive textile workshops found primarily in Mexico, Ecuador, and Peru
palenque	Spanish American term for a fortified runaway slave community
panocha	semirefined sugar (Mexico)
patronato real	crown authority over many aspects of church administration
paulista	inhabitant of São Paulo
peón	rural worker; laborer
peso de minas	Spanish-American monetary unit
petate	straw or reed mat (Mexico)
pisco	clear grape brandy (Peru; Andes)
pochteca	Indian merchants in Mesoamerica
poncho	man's cloak (Argentina)
porteño	inhabitant of Buenos Aires
pozole	Mexican barley stew
presidio	frontier military garrison
principales	Indian village leaders

puchero	stew of meat and vegetables
puka kunka	"red neck"
pulpería	general store or dry goods shop which usually also sold alcoholic beverages
pulque	fermented juice of the agave cactus (Mexico)
quilombo	runaway slave community in Brazil
quinta	small rural property so called because each plot was originally one-fifth of a league
ración	commodity tax
ranchero	owner of a rancho
rancho	small farm (Mexico)
rastra	harrow
rayador	farm overseer (Mexico)
rebozo	woman's shawl (Mexico)
reducción	settlement of Indians who have been converted to Christianity
regidor	town alderman
regula (Latin)	fundamental rules governing a religious order
repartimiento	system of Indian draft labor
reparto de mercancias	forced distribution and sale of goods to Indian communities
rollo	round pillar; column of stone
ruana	man's cloak, open in the front, used in the northern Andes, especially Nueva Granada
sala	living room
sarape	man's cloak (Mexico)
sargento	major Spanish America military rank; sergeant major
sargento-mor	Brazilian military rank; sargeant major
saya	long straight skirt (Peru)
senhor de engenho	owner of a large sugar plantation (Brazil)
senzala	slave quarters (Portuguese)
sertão	arid backland of northeastern Brazil
servicio	personal service
sesmaria	land grant made to sixteenth-century colonists by the Portuguese crown
sujeto	Indian town subordinate to a cabecera
takionqo	follower of the Taki Onqoy movement
tala	large urticaceous tree that grows in the Río de la Plata region
tambo	rural inn in Andean South America
tamenes	human carriers in Mesoamerica
terciado	long dagger, cutlass, or broad sword
tianguis	marketplaces in Mesoamerica

tienda de raya	company store
tlatoani	hereditary local Indian rulers in Mesoamerica
troxero; trojero	storekeeper
vara	linear unit of measure equivalent to approximately thirty-three inches
vecino	inhabitant of a particular town, usually a propertied person of Spanish descent
vicario	vicar or curate; local ecclesiastic judge
visitador	royal inspector
yanacona	landless Indian laborer, tied to a large estate
yerba mate	plant or the bitter tea that is made from its leaves; Paraguayan herb tea
zambo	person of African-American and Indian ancestry

Index

Notes on Contributors

A.J. Bauer, Professor of History at the University of California, Davis, received his Ph.D. from the University of California, Berkeley. He has written *Chilean Rural Society from the Spanish Conquest to 1930* (Cambridge: Cambridge University Press, 1975) and *La iglesia en la economía de Latinoamérica* (Mexico City, 1985). He is currently engaged in a project on the material culture of Latin America.

Juan Carlos Garavaglia, Directeur d'Etudes en la Ecole des Hautes Etudes en Sciences Sociales en Paris, received his Ph.D. from the Ecole des Hautes Etudes. He is author or coauthor of *Puebla desde una perspectiva micohistórica. La villa de Tepeaca y su entorno agrario: población, prodducción e intercambio (1740–1870)*, en colaboración con Juan Carlos Grosso (Mexico City: Claves Latinoamericanas, 1994); *Población, sociedad, familia y migraciones en el espacio rioplatense, Siglos XVIII y XIX*, en colaboración con José Luis Moreno (Buenos Aires: Ediciones Cántaro, 1993); *Spagna e Portogallo in America. Conquista e colonizzazione* (Florence: Giunti, 1993); *Hombres y mujeres de la colonia*, en coloboración con Raúl Fradkin (Buenos Aires, Editorial Sudamericana, 1992); *Las alcabalas novohispanas (1776–1821)*, en coloboración con Juan Carlos Grosso (Mexico City: Archivo General de Nación, 1988); *Economia, sociedad y regiones* (Buenos Aires: Ediciones de la Flor, 1987); *and Mercada interno y economía colonial* (Mexico City: Editorial Grijalbo, 1983).

Lowell Gudmundson, who received his Ph.D. from the University of Minnesota, is Professor and Chair of Latin American Studies at Mount Holyoke College. He is the author of *Costa Rica Before Coffee* (Baton Rouge: Louisiana State University

Press, 1986; San José Editorial Costa Rica, 1990, 1993); co-author (with Héctor Lindo-Fuentes) of *Central America, 1821–1871: Liberalism before Liberal Reform* (Tuscaloosa: University of Alabama Press, 1995) and co-editor (with William Roseberry and Mario Samper) of *Coffee, Society, and Power in Latin America* (Baltimore: Johns Hopkins University Press, 1995). He is currently researching the social history of *ladino* Guatemala during the nineteenth century.

Louisa Schell Hoberman, Lecturer at the University of Texas, Austin, received her Ph.D. from Columbia University. She is the author of *Mexico's Merchant Elite: Silver, State, and Society, 1590–1660* (Durham: Duke University Press, 1991) and editor (with Susan Socolow) of *Cities and Society in Colonial Latin America* (Albuquerque: University of New Mexico Press, 1986). She is now working on a comparative analysis of Aztec and Spanish political economy and on an interdisciplinary collection of essays on seventeenth century Latin America.

Herbert S. Klein is Professor of History at Columbia University and obtained his doctorate at the University of Chicago. He is author of three comparative studies of slavery— *Slavery in the Americas, A Comparative Study of Cuba and Virginia* (1967); *The Middle Passage: Comparative Studies of the Atlantic Slave Trade* (1978); and *African Slavery in Latin America and the Caribbean* (1987)—as well as six volumes on Bolivian history and co-author of a six volume collection of Colonial Royal Treasury records and a contemporary survey of Brazilian

social history. Currently he is writing a general history of the Atlantic slave trade.

Cheryl English Martin, a specialist on the social history of colonial Mexico, received her Ph.D. from Tulane University in 1976. Her publications include *Rural Society in Colonial Mexico* (Albuquerque: University of New Mexico Press, 1985) and *Governance and Society in Colonial Mexico: Chihuahua in the Eighteenth Century* (Stanford: Stanford University Press, 1996), and she co-edited (with William Beezley and William E. French) *Rituals of Rule, Rituals of Resistance: Public Celebrations and Popular Culture in Mexico* (Wilmington, Delaware, Scholarly Resources, 1994). She is currently a Professor of History at the University of Texas at El Paso.

John Frederick Schwaller is Associate Provost at the University of Montana. He received his Ph.D. from Indiana University. His works include *The Origins of Church Wealth in Mexico* (Albuquerque: University of New Mexico Press, 1985) and *Church and Clergy in Sixteenth-Century Mexico* (Albuquerque: University of New Mexico Press, 1987). He continues to study the Church in early colonial Mexico and is working on a biography of don Luis de Velasco, the Younger, Viceroy of Mexico and Peru and President of the Council of the Indies.

Stuart B. Schwartz, Professor of History at the University of Minnesota, received his Ph.D. from Columbia University. His research has concentrated on colonial Brazil. He is the author of *Sugar Plantations in the Formation of Brazilian Society*

(Cambridge: Cambridge University Press, 1985) and *Slaves, Peasants and Rebels* (Urbana, University of Illinois Press, 1992). In addition, he has published in Spanish America and is the co-author (with James Lockhart) of *Early Latin America* (Cambridge: Cambridge University Press, 1983. He is also co-editor of the South America volume of *Cambridge History of Native American Peoples*. He is currently working on two different projects: a general study of the rebellion of Portugal and the crisis of the Iberian Atlantic in the seventeenth century; and a social history of Caribbean hurricanes from Columbus to the present.

Susan Socolow, the Dobbs Professor of Latin American History at Emory University, received her Ph.D. from Columbia University. The author of *The Merchants of Viceregal Buenos Aires: Family and Commerce, 1778–1810* (New York: Cambridge University Press, 1978) and *The Bureaucrats of Buenos Aires, 1769–1810: Amor al Real Servicio* (Durham: Duke University Press, 1987), she has studied the frontier in colonial Buenos Aires and is currently working on a history of rural women. With Louisa S. Hoberman, Susan Socolow edited *Cities and Society in Colonial Latin America* (Albuquerque: University of New Mexico Press, 1986).

Ward Stavig, Assistant Professor of History at the University of South Florida, received his Ph.D. from the University of California, Davis. His research is on indigenous peoples in the Andes during the late colonial period, with special focus on questions of ethnicity, gender, and mentalities in indigenous society. He is finishing a "ground up" history of the peoples who were at the center of the Thupa Amara rebellion and has begun work on another project related to native peoples who lived in the orbit of Potosí. He has published in the *Hispanic American Historical Review*, *Latin American Research Review*, and other journals and has edited works in the United States and Peru.

Eric Van Young, Professor of History at the University of California, San Diego, received his Ph.D. from the University of California, Berkeley. His publications include *Hacienda and Market in Eighteenth-Century Mexico* (Berkeley: University of California Press, 1981); *La crisis del orden colonial* (Mexico City, 1992); and the edited anthology *Mexican Regions: Comparative History and Development* (San Diego: University of California Press, 1992). He is currently completing a book on the popular sectors during the Mexican wars for independence, *The Other Rebellion: Popular Violence and Ideology in Mexico, 1810–1816,* and hopes to turn his future efforts to a comparative study of peasant disturbances in Mexico and the Andes, 1500–1900, and to a social and cultural history of Mexican psychiatry, 1750–1930.